THE GAME

Neil Strauss is a regular contributor to the *New York Times* and *Rolling Stone*. He is also the co-author of three *New York Times* bestsellers—Jenna Jameson's *How to Make Love Like a Porn Star*, Mötley Crüe's *The Dirt* and Marilyn Manson's *The Long Hard Road Out of Hell*—and a *Los Angeles Times* bestseller, Dave Navarro's *Don't Try This at Home*. He lives in Los Angeles.

THE GAME

PENETRATING THE SECRET SOCIETY
OF PICK-UP ARTISTS

NEIL STRAUSS

TEXT PUBLISHING MELBOURNE AUSTRALIA

The paper used in this book is manufactured only from wood grown in sustainable regrowth forests.

The Text Publishing Company
Swann House
22 William St
Melbourne Victoria 3000 Australia
www.textpublishing.com.au

First published in the USA by Regan Books, an imprint of HarperCollins Publishers
First published by Text Publishing in association with Canongate Books Ltd 2005
Reprinted 2005, 2006 (twice), 2007, 2008 (twice), 2009

Typeset by Palimpsest Book Production Ltd, Polmont, Stirlingshire
Printed and bound by Griffin Press

ISBN 978 1 920885 98 4

In order to protect the identity of some women and members of the community, the nicknames and identifying characteristics of a small number of incidental characters in this book have been changed, and two minor characters are composites.

Dedicated to the thousands of people I talked to in
bars, clubs, malls, airports, grocery stores, subways,
and elevators over the last two years.

If you are reading this, I want you to know that I
wasn't running game on you. I was being sincere.
Really. You were different.

"I COULD NOT BECOME ANYTHING: NEITHER BAD NOR GOOD, NEITHER A SCOUNDREL NOR AN HONEST MAN, NEITHER A HERO NOR AN INSECT. AND NOW I AM EKING OUT MY DAYS IN MY CORNER, TAUNTING MYSELF WITH THE BITTER AND ENTIRELY USELESS CONSOLATION THAT AN INTELLIGENT MAN CANNOT SERIOUSLY BECOME ANYTHING; THAT ONLY A FOOL CAN BECOME SOMETHING."

FYODOR DOSTOEVSKY,
Notes from Underground

Those who have read early drafts of this book
have all asked the same questions:

....

IS THIS TRUE?

DID IT REALLY HAPPEN?

ARE THESE GUYS
FOR REAL?

....

Thus, I find it necessary to employ
an old literary device . . .

THE FOLLOWING IS A TRUE STORY.

....

IT REALLY HAPPENED.

....

Men will deny it,
Women will doubt it.
But I present it to you here,
Naked, vulnerable, and
disturbingly real.
I beg you for your forgiveness in advance.

DON'T HATE THE PLAYER ...
HATE THE GAME.

CONT

ENTS

SELECT A TARGET

MEN WEREN'T REALLY THE ENEMY—
THEY WERE FELLOW VICTIMS
SUFFERING FROM AN OUTMODED
MASCULINE MYSTIQUE THAT MADE
THEM FEEL UNNECESSARILY
INADEQUATE WHEN THERE WERE
NO BEARS TO KILL.

—Betty Friedan
The Feminine Mystique

MEET MYSTERY

The house was a disaster.

Doors were split and smashed off their hinges; walls were dented in the shape of fists, phones, and flowerpots; Herbal was hiding in a hotel room scared for his life; and Mystery was collapsed on the living room carpet crying. He'd been crying for two days straight.

This wasn't a normal kind of crying. Ordinary tears are understandable. But Mystery was beyond understanding. He was out of control. For a week, he'd been vacillating between periods of extreme anger and violence, and jags of fitful, cathartic sobbing. And now he was threatening to kill himself.

There were five of us living in the house: Herbal, Mystery, Papa, Playboy, and me. Boys and men came from every corner of the globe to shake our hands, take photos with us, learn from us, be us. They called me Style. It was a name I had earned.

We never used our real names—only our aliases. Even our mansion, like the others we had spawned everywhere from San Francisco to Sydney, had a nickname. It was Project Hollywood. And Project Hollywood was in shambles.

The sofas and dozens of throw pillows lining the floor of the sunken living room were fetid and discolored with the sweat of men and the juices of women. The white carpet had gone gray from the constant traffic of young, perfumed humanity herded in off Sunset Boulevard every night. Cigarette butts and used condoms floated grimly in the Jacuzzi. And Mystery's rampage during the last few days had left the rest of the place totaled and the residents petrified. He was six foot five and hysterical.

"I can't tell you what this feels like," he choked out between sobs. His whole body spasmed. "I don't know what I'm going to do, but it will not be rational."

He reached up from the floor and punched the stained red upholstery of the sofa as the siren-wail of his despondency grew louder, filling the room with the sound of a grown male who has lost every characteristic that separates man from infant from animal.

He wore a gold silk robe that was several sizes too small, exposing his scabbed knees. The ends of the sash just barely met to form a knot and the curtains of the robe hung half a foot apart, revealing a pale, hairless chest and, below it, saggy gray Calvin Klein boxer shorts. The only other item of clothing on his trembling body was a winter cap pulled tight over his skull.

It was June in Los Angeles.

"This living thing." He was speaking again. "It's so pointless."

He turned and looked at me through wet, red eyes. "It's Tic Tac Toe. There's no way you can win. So the best thing to do is not to play it."

There was no one else in the house. I would have to deal with this. He needed to be sedated before he snapped out of tears and back into anger. Each cycle of emotions grew worse, and this time I was afraid he'd do something that couldn't be undone.

I couldn't let Mystery die on my watch. He was more than just a friend; he was a mentor. He'd changed my life, as he had the lives of thousands of others just like me. I needed to get him Valium, Xanax, Vicodin, anything. I grabbed my phone book and scanned the pages for people most likely to have pills—people like guys in rock bands, women who'd just had plastic surgery, former child actors. But everyone I called wasn't home, didn't have any drugs, or claimed not to have any drugs because they didn't want to share.

There was only one person left to call: the woman who had triggered Mystery's downward spiral. She was a party girl; she must have something.

Katya, a petite Russian blonde with a Smurfette voice and the energy of a Pomeranian puppy, was at the front door in ten minutes with a Xanax and a worried look on her face.

"Do not come in," I warned her. "He'll probably kill you." Not that she didn't entirely deserve it, of course. Or so I thought at the time.

I gave Mystery the pill and a glass of water, and waited until the sobs slowed to a sniffle. Then I helped him into a pair of black boots, jeans, and a gray T-shirt. He was docile now, like a big baby.

"I'm taking you to get some help," I told him.

I walked him outside to my old rusty Corvette and stuffed him into the tiny front seat. Every now and then, I'd see a tremor of anger flash across his face or tears roll out of his eyes. I hoped he'd remain calm long enough for me to help him.

"I want to learn martial arts," he said docilely, "so when I want to kill someone, I can do something about it."

I stepped on the accelerator.

Our destination was the Hollywood Mental Health Center on Vine Street. It was an ugly slab of concrete surrounded day and night by homeless men who screamed at lampposts, transvestites who lived out of shopping carts, and other remaindered human beings who set up camp where free social services could be found.

Mystery, I realized, was one of them. He just happened to have charisma and talent, which drew others to him and prevented him from ever being left alone in the world. He possessed two traits I'd noticed in nearly every rock star I'd ever interviewed: a crazy, driven gleam in his eyes and an absolute inability to do anything for himself.

I brought him into the lobby, signed him in, and together we waited for a turn with one of the counselors. He sat in a cheap black plastic chair, staring catatonically at the institutional blue walls.

An hour passed. He began to fidget.

Two hours passed. His brow furrowed; his face clouded.

Three hours passed. The tears started.

Four hours passed. He bolted out of his chair and ran out of the waiting room and through the front door of the building.

He walked briskly, like a man who knew where he was going, although Project Hollywood was three miles away. I chased him across the street and caught up to him outside a mini-mall. I took his arm and turned him around, baby talking him back into the waiting room.

Five minutes. Ten minutes. Twenty minutes. Thirty. He was up and out again.

I ran after him. Two social workers stood uselessly in the lobby.

"Stop him!" I yelled.

"We can't," one of them said. "He's left the premises."

"So you're just going to let a suicidal man walk out of here?" I couldn't waste time arguing. "Just have a therapist ready to see him if I get him back here."

I ran out the door and looked to my right. He wasn't there. I looked left. Nothing. I ran north to Fountain Avenue, spotted him around the corner, and dragged him back again.

When we arrived, the social workers led him down a long, dark hallway and into a claustrophobic cubicle with a sheet-vinyl floor. The therapist sat behind a desk, running a finger through a black tangle in her hair. She was a slim Asian woman in her late twenties, with high cheekbones, dark red lipstick, and a pinstriped pantsuit.

Mystery slumped in a chair across from her.

"So how are you feeling today?" she asked, forcing a smile.

"I'm feeling," Mystery said, "like there's no point to anything." He burst into tears.

"I'm listening," she said, scrawling a note on her pad. The case was probably already closed for her.

"So I'm removing myself from the gene pool," he sobbed.

She looked at him with feigned sympathy as he continued. To her, he was just one of a dozen nutjobs she saw a day. All she needed to figure out was whether he required medication or institutionalization.

"I can't go on," Mystery went on. "It's futile."

With a rote gesture, she reached into a drawer, pulled out a small package of tissues, and handed it to him. As Mystery reached for the package, he looked up and met her eyes for the first time. He froze and stared at her silently. She was surprisingly cute for a clinic like this.

A flicker of animation flashed across Mystery's face, then died. "If I had met you in another time and another place," he said, crumpling a tissue in his hands, "things would have been different."

His body, normally proud and erect, curved like soggy macaroni in his chair. He stared glumly at the floor as he spoke. "I know exactly what to say and what to do to make you attracted to me," he continued. "It's all in my head. Every rule. Every step. Every word. I just can't . . . do it right now."

She nodded mechanically.

"You should see me when I'm not like this," he continued slowly, sniffling. "I've dated some of the most beautiful women in the world. Another place, another time, and I would have made you mine."

"Yes," she said, patronizing him. "I'm sure you would have."

She didn't know. How could she? But this sobbing giant with the crumpled tissue in his hands was the greatest pickup artist in the world. That was not a matter of opinion, but fact. I'd met scores of the self-proclaimed best in the previous two years, and Mystery could out-game them all. It was his hobby, his passion, his calling.

There was only one person alive who could possibly compete with him. And that man was sitting in front of her also. From a formless lump of nerd, Mystery had molded me into a superstar. Together, we had ruled the world of seduction. We had pulled off spectacular pickups before the disbelieving eyes of our students and disciples in Los Angeles, New York, Montreal, London, Melbourne, Belgrade, Odessa, and beyond.

And now we were in a madhouse.

MEET STYLE

I am far from attractive. My nose is too large for my face and, while not hooked, has a bump in the ridge. Though I am not bald, to say that my hair is thinning would be an understatement. There are just wispy Rogaine-enhanced growths covering the top of my head like tumbleweeds. In my opinion, my eyes are small and beady, though they do have a lively glimmer, which is doomed to remain my secret because no one can see it behind my glasses. I have indentations on either side of my forehead, which I like and believe add character to my face, though I've never actually been complimented on them.

I am shorter than I'd like to be and so skinny that I look malnourished to most people, no matter how much I eat. When I look down at my pale, slouched body, I wonder why any woman would want to sleep next to it, let alone embrace it. So, for me, meeting girls takes work. I'm not the kind of guy women giggle over at a bar or want to take home when they're feeling drunk and crazy. I can't offer them a piece of my fame and bragging rights like a rock star or cocaine and a mansion like so many other men in Los Angeles. All I have is my mind, and nobody can see that.

You may notice that I haven't mentioned my personality. This is because my personality has completely changed. Or, to put it more accurately, I completely changed my personality. I invented Style, my alter ego. And in the course of two years, Style became more popular than I ever was—especially with women.

It was never my intention to change my personality or walk through the world under an assumed identity. In fact, I was happy with myself and my life. That is, until an innocent phone call (it always starts with an innocent phone call) led me on a journey into one of the oddest and most exciting underground communities that, in more than a dozen years of journalism, I have ever come across. The call was from Jeremie Ruby-Strauss (no relation), a book editor who had stumbled across a document on the Internet called the layguide, short for *The How-to-Lay-Girls Guide*. Compressed into 150 sizzling pages, he said, was the collected wisdom of dozens of pickup artists who have been exchanging their knowledge in newsgroups for nearly a decade, secretly working to turn the art of seduction into an exact science. The information needed to be rewritten and organized into a coherent how-to book, and he thought I was the man to do it.

I wasn't so sure. I want to write literature, not give advice to horny adolescents. But, of course, I told him it wouldn't hurt to take a look at it.

The moment I started reading, my life changed. More than any other book or document—be it the Bible, *Crime and Punishment*, or *The Joy of Cooking*—the layguide opened my eyes. And not necessarily because of the information in it, but because of the path it sent me hurtling down.

When I look back on my teenage years, I have one major regret, and it has nothing to do with not studying hard enough, not being nice to my mother, or crashing my father's car into a public bus. It is simply that I didn't fool around with enough girls. I am a deep man—I reread James Joyce's *Ulysses* every three years for fun. I consider myself reasonably intuitive. I am at the core a good person, and I try to avoid hurting others. But I can't seem to evolve to the next state of being because I spend far too much time thinking about women.

And I know I'm not alone. When I first met Hugh Hefner, he was seventy-three. He had slept with over a thousand of the most beautiful women in the world, by his own account, but all he wanted to talk about were his three girlfriends—Mandy, Brandy, and Sandy. And how, thanks to Viagra, he could keep them all satisfied (though his money probably satisfied them enough). If he ever wanted to sleep with somebody else, he said, the rule was that they'd all do it together. So what I gathered from the conversation was that here was a guy who's had all the sex he wanted his whole life and, at seventy-three, he's still chasing tail. When does it stop? If Hugh Hefner isn't over it yet, when am I going to be?

If the layguide had never crossed my path, I, like most men, would never have evolved in my thinking about the opposite sex. In fact, I probably started off worse than most men. In my preteen years, there were no games of doctor, no girls who charged a dollar to look up their skirts, no tickling classmates in places I wasn't supposed to touch. I spent most of teenage life grounded, so when my sole adolescent sexual opportunity arose—a drunken freshman girl called and offered me a blow job—I was forced to decline, or else suffer my mother's wrath. In college I began to find myself: the things I was interested in, the personality I'd always been too shy to express, the group of friends who would expand my mind with drugs and conversation (in that order). But I never became comfortable around women: They intimidated me. In four years of college, I did not sleep with a single woman on campus.

After school I took a job at the *New York Times* as a cultural reporter, where I began to build confidence in myself and my opinions. Eventually, I gained access to a privileged world where no rules applied: I went on the road with Marilyn Manson and Motley Crue to write books with them. In all that time, with all those backstage passes, I didn't get so much as a single kiss from anyone except Tommy Lee. After that, I pretty much gave up hope. Some guys had it; other guys didn't. I clearly didn't.

The problem wasn't that I'd never been laid. It was that the few times I did get lucky, I'd turn a one-night stand into a two-year stand because I didn't know when it was going to happen again. The layguide had an acronym for people like me: AFC—average frustrated chump. I was an AFC. Not like Dustin.

I met Dustin the year I graduated from college. He was friends with a classmate of mine named Marko, a faux-aristocratic Serbian who had been my companion in girllessness since nursery school, thanks largely to his head, which was shaped like a watermelon. Dustin wasn't any taller, richer, more famous, or better looking than either of us. But he did possess one quality we didn't: He attracted women.

When Marko first introduced me to him, I was unimpressed. He was short and swarthy with long curly brown hair and a cheesy button-down gigolo shirt with too many buttons undone. That night, we went to a Chicago club called Drink. As we checked our coats, Dustin asked, "Do you know if there are any dark corners in here?"

I asked him what he needed dark corners for, and he replied that they were good places to take girls. I raised my eyebrows skeptically. Minutes after entering the bar, however, he made eye contact with a shy-looking girl who was talking with a friend. Without a word, Dustin walked away. The girl followed him—straight to a dark corner. When they finished kissing and groping, they parted wordlessly, without an obligatory exchange of phone numbers or even a sheepish see-you-later.

Dustin repeated this seemingly miraculous feat four times that night. A new world opened up before my eyes.

I grilled him for hours, trying to determine what sort of magical powers he possessed. Dustin was what they call a natural. He had lost his virginity at age eleven, when the fifteen-year-old daughter of a neighbor used him as a sexual experiment, and he had been fucking nonstop since. One night, I took him to a party on a boat anchored in New York's Hudson River. When a sultry brown-haired, doe-eyed girl walked by, he turned to me and said, "She's just your type."

I denied it and stared at the floor, as usual. I was afraid he'd try to make me talk to her, which he soon did.

When she walked past again, he asked her, "Do you know Neil?"

It was a stupid icebreaker, but it didn't matter now that the ice was broken. I stammered out a few words, until Dustin took over and rescued me. We met her and her boyfriend at a bar afterward. They had just moved in together. Her boyfriend was taking their dog for a walk. After a few drinks, he took the dog home, leaving the girl, Paula, with us.

Dustin suggested going back to my place to cook a late-night snack, so we walked to my tiny East Village apartment and, instead, collapsed on the bed, with Dustin on one side of Paula and me on the other. When Dustin started kissing her left cheek, he signaled me to do the same on her right cheek. Then, in synchronicity, we moved down her body to her neck and her breasts. Though I was surprised by Paula's quiet compliance, for Dustin this seemed to be business as usual. He turned to me and asked if I had a condom. I found one for him. He pulled off her pants and moved into her while I continued lapping uselessly at her right breast.

That was Dustin's gift, his power: giving women the fantasy they never thought they'd experience. Afterward, Paula called me constantly. She wanted to talk about the experience all the time, to rationalize it, because she couldn't believe what she had done. That's how it always worked with Dustin: He got the girl; I got the guilt.

I chalked this up to a simple difference of personality. Dustin had a natural charm and animal instinct that I just didn't. Or at least that's what I thought, until I read the layguide and explored the newsgroups and websites it recommended. What I discovered was an entire community filled with Dustins—men who claimed to have found the combination to unlock a woman's heart and legs—along with thousands of others like myself, trying to learn their secrets. The difference was that these men had broken down their methods to a specific set of rules that anybody could apply. And each self-proclaimed pickup artist had his own set of rules.

There was Mystery, a magician; Ross Jeffries, a hypnotist; Rick H., a millionaire entrepreneur; David DeAngelo, a real estate agent; Juggler, a stand-up comedian; David X, a construction worker; and Steve P., a seductionist so powerful that women actually pay to learn how to give him better head. Put them on South Beach in Miami and any number of better-looking, muscle-bound bullies will be kicking sand in their pale, emaciated faces. But put them in a Starbucks or Whiskey Bar, and they'll be taking turns making out with that bully's girlfriend as soon as his back is turned.

Once I discovered their world, the first thing that changed was my vocabulary. Terms like AFC, PUA (pickup artist), sarging (picking up women), and HB (hot babe)[1] entered my permanent lexicon. Then my daily rituals changed as I became addicted to the online locker room these pickup artists had created. Whenever I returned home from meeting or going out with a woman, I sat down at my computer and posted my questions of the night on the newsgroups. "What do I do if she says she has a boyfriend?"; "If she eats garlic during dinner, does it mean she isn't planning on kissing me?"; "Is it a good or a bad sign when a girl puts on lipstick in front of me?"

And online characters like Candor, Gunwitch, and Formhandle began replying to my questions. (The answers, in order: use a boyfriend-destroyer pattern; you're overanalyzing this; neither.) Soon I realized this was not just an Internet phenomenon but a way of life. There were cults of wanna-be seductionists in dozens of cities—from Los Angeles to London to Zagreb to Bombay—who met weekly in what they called lairs to discuss tactics and strategies before going out en masse to meet women.

In the guise of Jeremie Ruby-Strauss and the Internet, God had given me a second chance. It wasn't too late to be Dustin, to become what every woman wants—not what she says she wants, but what she really wants, deep inside, beyond her social programming, where her fantasies and daydreams lie.

But I couldn't do it on my own. Talking to guys online was not going to be enough to change a lifetime of failure. I had to meet the faces behind the screen names, watch them in the field, find out who they were and what made them tick. I made it my mission—my full-time job and obsession—to hunt down the greatest pickup artists in the world and beg for shelter under their wings.

And so began the strangest two years of my life.

---

[1] A glossary has been provided on page 439 with detailed explanations of these and other terms used by the seduction community.

APPROACH
AND OPEN

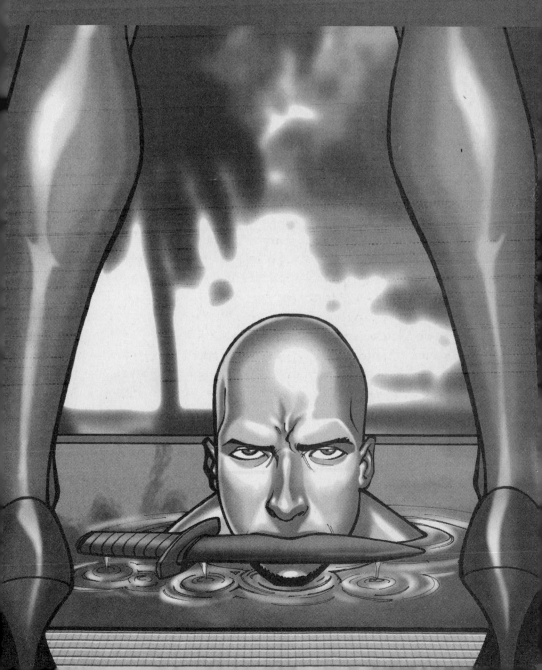

THE FIRST PROBLEM FOR ALL OF US,

MEN AND WOMEN, IS NOT TO LEARN,

BUT TO UNLEARN.

....

—GLORIA STEINEM,
commencement speech, Vassar College

I withdrew five hundred dollars from the bank, stuffed it into a white envelope, and wrote Mystery on the front. It was not the proudest moment of my life.

But I had dedicated the last four days to getting ready for it anyway—buying two hundred dollars worth of clothing at Fred Segal, spending an afternoon shopping for the perfect cologne, and dropping seventy-five bucks on a Hollywood haircut. I wanted to look my best; this would be my first time hanging out with a real pickup artist.

His name, or at least the name he used online, was Mystery. He was the most worshipped pickup artist in the community, a powerhouse who spit out long, detailed posts that read like algorithms of how to manipulate social situations to meet and attract women. His nights out seducing models and strippers in his hometown of Toronto were chronicled in intimate detail online, the writing filled with jargon of his own invention: sniper negs, shotgun negs, group theory, indicators of interest, pawning—all of which had become an integral part of the pickup artist lexicon. For four years, he had been offering free advice in seduction newsgroups. Then, in October, he decided to put a price on himself and posted the following:

> *Mystery is now producing Basic Training workshops in several cities around the world, due to numerous requests. The first workshop will be in Los Angeles from Wednesday evening, October 10, through Saturday night. The fee is $500 (U.S.). This includes club entry, limo for four evenings (sweet huh?), an hour lecture in the limo each evening with a thirty-minute debriefing at the end of the night, and finally three-and-a-half hours per night in the field (broken up into two clubs per night) with Mystery. By the end of Basic Training, you will have approached close to fifty women.*

It is no easy feat to sign up for a workshop dedicated to picking up women. To do so is to acknowledge defeat, inferiority, and inadequacy. It is to finally admit to yourself that after all these years of being sexually active (or at least sexually cognizant), you have not grown up and figured it out. Those who ask for help are often those who have failed to do something for themselves. So if drug addicts go to rehab and the violent go to anger management class, then social retards go to pickup school.

Clicking send on my e-mail to Mystery was one of the hardest things I'd ever done. If anyone—friends, family, colleagues, and especially my lone ex-girlfriend in Los Angeles—found out I was paying for live in-field lessons on picking up women, the mockery and recrimination would be instant and merciless. So I kept my intentions secret, dodging social plans by telling people that I was going to be showing an old friend around town all weekend.

I would have to keep these two worlds separate.

In my e-mail to Mystery, I didn't tell him my last name or my occupation. If pressed, I planned to just say I was a writer and leave it at that. I wanted to move through this subculture anonymously, without either an advantage or extra pressure because of my credentials.

However, I still had my own conscience to deal with. This was, far and away, the most pathetic thing I'd ever done in my life. And unfortunately—as opposed to, say, masturbating in the shower—it wasn't something I could do alone. Mystery and the other students would be there to bear witness to my shame, my secret, my inadequacy.

A man has two primary drives in early adulthood: one toward power, success, and accomplishment; the other toward love, companionship, and sex. Half of life then was out of order. To go before them was to stand up as a man and admit that I was only half a man.

A week after sending the e-mail, I walked into the lobby of the Hollywood Roosevelt Hotel. I wore a blue wool sweater that was so soft and thin it looked like cotton, black pants with laces running up the sides, and shoes that gave me a couple extra inches in height. My pockets bulged with the supplies Mystery had instructed every student to bring: a pen, a notepad, a pack of gum, and condoms.

I spotted Mystery instantly. He was seated regally in a Victorian arm-chair, with a smug, I-just-bench-pressed-the-world smile on his face. He wore a casual, loose-fitting blue-black suit; a small, pointed labret piercing wagged from his chin; and his nails were painted jet black. He wasn't nec-essarily attractive, but he was charismatic—tall and thin, with long chest-nut hair, high cheekbones, and a bloodless pallor. He looked like a computer geek who'd been bitten by a vampire and was midway through his transformation.

Next to him was a shorter, intense-looking character who introduced himself as Mystery's wing, Sin. He wore a form-fitting black crew neck shirt, and his hair was pitch black and gelled straight back. He had the complex-ion, however, of a man whose natural hair color is red.

I was the first student to arrive.

"What's your top score?" Sin leaned in and asked as I sat down. They were already assessing me, trying to figure out if I was in possession of a thing called *game*.

"My top score?"

"Yeah, how many girls have you been with?"

"Um, somewhere around seven," I told them.

"Somewhere *around* seven?" Sin pressed.

"Six," I confessed.

Sin ranked in the sixties, Mystery in the hundreds. I looked at them in wonder: These were the pickup artists whose exploits I'd been following so avidly online for months. They were another class of being: They had the magic pill, the solution to the inertia and frustration that has plagued the great literary protagonists I'd related to all my life—be it Leopold Bloom, Alex Portnoy, or Piglet from *Winnie the Pooh*.

As we waited for the other students, Mystery threw a manila envelope full of photographs in my lap.

"These are some of the women I've dated," he said.

In the folder was a spectacular array of beautiful women: a headshot of a sultry Japanese actress; an autographed publicity still of a brunette who bore an uncanny resemblance to Liv Tyler; a glossy picture of a *Penthouse* Pet of the Year; a snapshot of a tan, curvy stripper in a negligee who Mystery said was his girlfriend, Patricia; and a photo of a brunette with large silicone breasts, which were being suckled by Mystery in the middle of a nightclub. These were his credentials.

"I was able to do that by not paying attention to her breasts all night," he explained when I asked about the last shot. "A pickup artist must be the exception to the rule. You must not do what everyone else does. Ever."

I listened carefully. I wanted to make sure every word etched itself on my cerebral cortex. I was attending a significant event; the only other credible pickup artist teaching courses was Ross Jeffries, who had basically founded the community in the late 1980s. But today marked the first time seduction students would be removed from the safe environs of the seminar room and let loose in clubs to be critiqued as they ran game on unsuspecting women.

A second student arrived, introducing himself as Extramask. He was a tall, gangly, impish twenty-six-year-old with a bowl cut, overly baggy clothing, and a handsomely chiseled face. With the right haircut and outfit, he would easily have been a good-looking guy.

When Sin asked him what his count was, Extramask scratched his head uncomfortably. "I have virtually zero experience with girls," he explained. "I've never kissed a girl before."

"You're kidding," Sin said.

"I've never even held a girl's hand. I grew up pretty sheltered. My parents were really strict Catholics, so I always had a lot of guilt about girls. But I've had three girlfriends."

He looked at the floor and rubbed his knees in nervous circles as he listed his girlfriends, though no one had asked for the particulars. There was Mitzelle, who broke up with him after seven days. There was Claire, who told him after two days that she'd made a mistake when she agreed to go out with him.

"And then there was Carolina, my sweet Carolina," he said, a dreamy smile spreading across his face. "We were a couple for one day. I remember her walking over to my house the next afternoon with her friend. I saw her across the street, and I was excited to see her. When I got closer, she yelled, 'I'm dumping you.'"

All of these relationships apparently took place in sixth grade. Extramask shook his head sadly. It was hard to tell whether he was consciously being funny or not.

The next arrival was a tanned, balding man in his forties who'd flown in from Australia just to attend the workshop. He had a ten-thousand-dollar Rolex, a charming accent, and one of the ugliest sweaters I'd ever seen—a thick cable-knit monstrosity with multi-colored zigzags that looked like the aftermath of a finger-painting mishap. He reeked of money and confidence. Yet the moment he opened his mouth to give Sin his score (five), he betrayed himself. His voice trembled; he couldn't look anyone in the eye; and there was something pathetic and childlike about him. His appearance, like his sweater, was just an accident that spoke nothing of his nature.

He was new to the community and reluctant to share even his first name, so Mystery christened him Sweater.

The three of us were the only students in the workshop.

"Okay, we've got a lot to talk about," Mystery said, clapping his hands together. He leaned in close, so the other guests in the hotel couldn't hear.

"My job here is to get you into the game," he continued, making piercing eye contact with each of us. "I need to get what's in my head into yours. Think of tonight as a video game. It is not real. Every time you do an approach, you are playing this game."

My heart began pounding violently. The thought of trying to start a conversation with a woman I didn't know petrified me, especially with these guys watching and judging me. Bungee jumping and parachuting were a cakewalk compared to this.

"All your emotions are going to try to fuck you up," Mystery continued. "They are there to try to confuse you, so know right now that they cannot be trusted at all. You will feel shy sometimes, and self-conscious, and you must deal with it like you deal with a pebble in your shoe. It's uncomfortable, but you ignore it. It's not part of the equation."

I looked around; Extramask and Sweater seemed just as nervous as I was. "I need to teach you, in four days, the whole equation—the sequence of moves you need to win," Mystery went on. "And you will have to play the game over and over to learn how to win. So get ready to fail."

Mystery paused to order a Sprite with five slices of lemon on the side, then told us his story. He spoke in a loud, clear voice—modeled, he said, on the motivational speaker Anthony Robbins. Everything about him seemed to be a conscious, rehearsed invention.

Since the age of eleven, when he beat the secret to a card trick out of a classmate, Mystery's goal in life was to become a celebrity magician, like David Copperfield. He spent years studying and practicing, and managed to parlay his talents into birthday parties, corporate gigs, and even a couple of talk shows. In the process, however, his social life suffered. At the age of twenty-one, when he was still a virgin, he decided to do something about it.

"One of the world's greatest mysteries is the mind of a woman," he told us grandiosely. "So I set out to solve it."

He took a half hour bus ride into Toronto every day, going to bars, clothing stores, restaurants, and coffee shops. He wasn't aware of the online community or any other pickup artists, so he was forced to work alone, relying on the one skill he did know: magic. It took him dozens of trips to the city before he even worked up the guts to talk to a stranger. From there, he tolerated failure, rejection, and embarrassment day and night until, piece by piece, he put together the puzzle that is social dynamics and discovered what he believed to be the patterns underlying all male-female relationships.

"It took me ten years to discover this," he said. "The basic format is FMAC—find, meet, attract, close. Believe it or not, the game is linear. A lot of people don't know that."

For the next half hour, Mystery told us about what he called group theory. "I have done this specific set of events a bazillion times," he said. "You do not walk up to a girl who's all by herself. That is not the perfect seduction. Women of beauty are rarely found alone."

After approaching the group, he continued, the key is to ignore the woman you desire while winning over her friends—especially the men and anyone else likely to cockblock. If the target is attractive and used to men fawning all over her, the pickup artist must intrigue her by pretending to be unaffected by her charm. This is accomplished through the use of what he called a neg.

Neither compliment nor insult, a neg is something in between—an accidental insult or backhanded compliment. The purpose of a neg is to lower a woman's self esteem while actively displaying a lack of interest in her—by telling her she has lipstick on her teeth, for example, or offering her a piece of gum after she speaks.

"I don't alienate ugly girls; I don't alienate guys. I only alienate the girls I want to fuck," Mystery lectured, eyes blazing with the conviction of his aphorisms. "If you don't believe me, you will see it tonight. Tonight is the night of experiments. First, I am going to prove myself. You are going to watch me and then we are going to push you to try a few sets. Tomorrow, if you do what I say, you will be able to make out with a girl within fifteen minutes."

He looked at Extramask. "Name the five characteristics of an alpha male."

"Confidence?"

"Right. What else?"

"Strength?"

"No."

"Body odor?"

He turned to Sweater and me. We were also clueless.

"The number one characteristic of an alpha male is the smile," he said, beaming an artificial beam. "Smile when you enter a room. As soon as you walk in a club, the game is on. And by smiling, you look like you're together, you're fun, and you're somebody."

He gestured to Sweater. "When you came in, you didn't smile when you talked to us."

"That's just not me," Sweater said. "I look silly when I smile."

"If you keep doing what you've always done, you'll keep getting what you've always gotten. It's called the Mystery Method because I'm Mystery and it's my method. So what I'm going to ask is that you indulge in some of my suggestions and try new things over the next four days. You are going to see a difference."

Besides confidence and a smile, we learned, the other characteristics of an alpha male were being well-groomed, possessing a sense of humor, connecting with people, and being seen as the social center of a room. No one bothered to tell Mystery that those were actually six characteristics.

As Mystery dissected the alpha male further, I realized something: The reason I was here—the reason Sweater and Extramask were also here—was that our parents and our friends had failed us. They had never given us the tools we needed to become fully effective social beings. Now, decades later, it was time to acquire them.

Mystery went around the table and looked at each of us. "What kind of girls do you want?" he asked Sweater.

Sweater pulled a piece of neatly folded notebook paper out of his pocket. "Last night I wrote down a list of goals for myself," he said, unfolding the page, which was filled with four columns of numbered items. "And one of the things I'm looking for is a wife. She needs to be smart enough to hold up her end of any conversation and have enough style and beauty to turn heads when she walks into a room."

"Well, look at you," Mystery said. "You look average. People think if they look generic, then they can seduce a wide array of women. Not true. You have to specialize. If you look average, you're going to get average girls. Your khaki pants are for the office. They're not for clubs. And your sweater—burn it. You need to be bigger than life. I'm talking over the top. If you want to get the 10s, you need to learn peacock theory."

Mystery loved theories. Peacock theory is the idea that in order to attract the most desirable female of the species, it's necessary to stand out in a flashy and colorful way. For humans, he told us, the equivalent of the fanned peacock tail is a shiny shirt, a garish hat, and jewelry that lights up in the dark—basically, everything I'd dismissed my whole life as cheesy.

When it came time for my personal critique, Mystery had a laundry list of fixes: get rid of the glasses, shape the overgrown goatee, shave the expensively trimmed tumbleweeds on my head, dress more outrageously, wear a conversation piece, get some jewelry, get a life.

I wrote down every word of advice. This was a guy who thought about seduction nonstop, like a mad scientist working on a formula to turn peanuts into gasoline. The archive of his Internet messages was 3,000 posts long—more than 2,500 pages—all dedicated to cracking the code that is woman.

"I have an opener for you to use," he said to me. An opener is a prepared script used to start a conversation with a group of strangers; it's the first thing anyone who wants to meet women must be armed with. "Say this when you see a group with a girl you like. 'Hey, it looks like the party's over here.' Then turn to the girl you want and add, 'If I wasn't gay, you'd be *so* mine.'"

A flash of crimson burned up my face. "Really?" I asked. "How is that going to help?"

We were witnessing group theory in action. The more Mystery performed for the guys, the more the blonde clamored for attention. And every time, he pushed her away and continued talking with his two new friends.

"I don't usually go out," Baio was telling Mystery. "I'm over it, and I'm too old."

After a few more minutes, Mystery finally acknowledged the blonde. He held his arms out. She placed her hands in his, and he began giving her a psychic reading. He was employing a technique I'd heard about called cold reading: the art of telling people truisms about themselves without any prior knowledge of their personality or background. In the field, all knowledge—however esoteric—is power.

With each accurate sentence Mystery spoke, the blonde's jaw dropped further open, until she started asking him about his job and his psychic abilities. Every response Mystery gave was intended to accentuate his youth and enthusiasm for the good life Baio said he had outgrown.

"I feel so old," Mystery said, baiting her.

"How old are you?" she asked.

"Twenty-seven."

"That's not old. That's perfect."

He was in.

Mystery called me over and whispered in my ear. He wanted me to talk to Baio and his friend, to keep them occupied while he hit on the girl. This was my first experience as a wing—a term Mystery had taken from *Top Gun*, along with words like target and obstacle.

I struggled to make small talk with them. But Baio, looking nervously at Mystery and his date, cut me off. "Tell me this is all an illusion," he said, "and he's not actually stealing my girlfriend."

Ten long minutes later, Mystery stood up, put his arm around me, and we left the club. Outside, he pulled a cocktail napkin from his jacket pocket. It contained her phone number. "Did you get a good look at her?" Mystery asked. "That is what I'm in the game for. Everything I've learned I used tonight. It's all led up to this moment. And it worked." He beamed with self-satisfaction. "How's that for a demonstration?"

That was all it took. Stealing a girl right from under a celebrity's nose—has-been or not—was a feat even Dustin couldn't have accomplished. Mystery was the real deal.

As we took the limo to the Key Club, Mystery told us the first commandment of pickup: the three-second rule. A man has three seconds after spotting a woman to speak to her, he said. If he takes any longer, then not only is the girl likely to think he's a creep who's been staring at her for too long, but he will start overthinking the approach, get nervous, and probably blow it.

The moment we walked into the Key Club, Mystery put the three-second rule into action. Striding up to a group of women, he held out his hands and asked, "What's your first impression of these? Not the big hands, the black nails."

As the girls gathered around him, Sin pulled me aside and suggested wandering the club and attempting my first approach. A group of women walked by and I tried to say something. But the word "hi" just barely squeaked out of my throat, not even loud enough for them to hear. As they continued past, I followed and grabbed one of the girls on the shoulder from behind. She turned around, startled, and gave me the withering what-a-creep look that was the whole reason I was too scared to talk to women in the first place.

"Never," Sin admonished me in his adenoidal voice, "approach a woman from behind. Always come in from the front, but at a slight angle so it's not too direct and confrontational. You should speak to her over your shoulder, so it looks like you might walk away at any minute. Ever see Robert Redford in *The Horse Whisperer*? It's kind of like that."

A few minutes later, I spotted a young, tipsy-looking woman with long, tangled blonde curls and a puffy pink vest standing alone. I decided that approaching her would be an easy way to redeem myself. I circled around until I was in the ten o'clock position in front of her and walked in, imagining myself approaching a horse I didn't want to frighten.

"Oh my God," I said to her. "Did you see those two girls fighting outside?"

"No," she said. "What happened?"

She was interested. She was talking to me. It was working.

"Um, two girls were fighting over this little guy who was half their size. It was pretty brutal. He was just standing there laughing as the police came and arrested the girls."

She giggled. We started talking about the club and the band playing there. She was very friendly and actually seemed grateful for the conversation. I had no idea that approaching a woman could be this easy.

Sin sidled up to me and whispered in my ear, "Go kino."

"What's kino?" I asked.

"Kino?" the girl replied.

Sin reached behind me, picked up my arm, and placed it on her shoulder. "Kino is when you touch a girl," he whispered. I felt the heat of her body and was reminded of how much I love human contact. Pets like to be petted. It isn't sexual when a dog or a cat begs for physical affection. People are the same way: We need touch. But we're so sexually screwed up and obsessed that we get nervous and uncomfortable whenever another person touches us. And, unfortunately, I am no exception. As I spoke to her, my hand felt wrong on her shoulder. It was just resting there like some disembodied limb, and I imagined her wondering what exactly it was doing there and how she could gracefully extricate herself from under it. So I did her the favor of removing it myself.

"Isolate her," Sin said.

I suggested sitting down, and we walked to a bench. Sin followed and sat behind us. As I'd been taught, I asked her to tell me the qualities she finds attractive in guys. She said humor and ass.

Fortunately, I have one of those qualities.

Suddenly, I felt Sin's breath on my ear. "Sniff her hair," he was instructing.

I smelled her hair, although I wasn't exactly sure what the point was. I figured Sin wanted me to neg her. So I said, "It smells like smoke."

"Nooooo!" Sin hissed in my ear. I guess I wasn't supposed to neg.

She seemed offended. So, to recover, I took another whiff. "But underneath that, there's a very intoxicating smell."

She cocked her head to one side, furrowed her brow ever so slightly, scanned me up and down, and said, "You're weird." I was blowing it.

Fortunately, Mystery soon arrived.

"This place is dead," he said. "We're going somewhere more target-rich." To Mystery and Sin, these clubs didn't seem to be reality. They had no problem whispering in students' ears while they were talking to women, dropping pickup terminology in front of strangers, and even interrupting a student during a set and explaining, in front of his group, what he was doing wrong. They were so confident and their talk was so full of incomprehensible jargon that the women rarely even raised an eyebrow, let alone suspected they were being used to train wanna-be ladies' men.

I bid my new friend good-bye as Sin had taught me, pointing to my cheek and saying, "Kiss good-bye." She actually pecked me. I felt very alpha.

On the way out, as I stopped to use the bathroom, I found Extramask standing there, twirling an unwashed lock of hair in his fingers. "Are you waiting for the toilet?" I asked.

"Sort of," he replied nervously. "Go ahead."

I gave him a quizzical look. "Can I tell you something?" he asked.

"Sure."

"I have a lot of trouble peeing beside guys in urinals. When there's another guy standing there, I can't fucking pee. Even if I'm peeing already and a guy walks up, I stop. And then I just stand there all nervous and shit."

"No one's judging you."

"Yeah," he said. "I remember about a year ago, a guy and I were trying to piss in these urinals that were right next to each other, but we both just ended up standing there. We stood there for around two minutes, recognizing each other's pee-shyness, until I zipped up and went to another bathroom."

He paused. "The guy never thanked me for changing bathrooms that day."

I nodded, walked to the urinal, and discharged my duties with a distinct lack of self-consciousness. Compared to Extramask, I was going to be an easy student.

As I left the bathroom, he was still standing there. "I always liked urinal dividers," he said. "But you only seem to find them at the classy places."

I was in high spirits in the limo to the next bar. "Do you think I could have kissed her?" I asked Mystery.

"If you think you could have, then you could have," he said. "As soon as you ask yourself whether you should or shouldn't, that means you should. And what you do is, you phase-shift. Imagine a giant gear thudding down in your head, and then go for it. Start hitting on her. Tell her you just noticed she has beautiful skin, and start massaging her shoulders."

"But how do you know it's okay?"

"What I do is, I look for IOIs. An IOI is an indicator of interest. If she asks you what your name is, that's an IOI. If she asks you if you're single, that's an IOI. If you take her hands and squeeze them, and she squeezes back, that's an IOI. And as soon as I get three IOIs, I phase-shift. I don't even think about it. It's like a computer program."

"But how do you kiss her?" Sweater asked.

"I just say, 'Would you like to kiss me?'"

"And then what happens?"

"One of three things," Mystery said. "If she says, 'Yes,' which is very rare, you kiss her. If she says, 'Maybe,' or hesitates, then you say, 'Let's find out,' and kiss her. And if she says, 'No,' you say, 'I didn't say you could. It just looked like you had something on your mind.'"

"You see," he grinned triumphantly. "You have nothing to lose. Every contingency is planned for. It's foolproof. That is the Mystery kiss-close."

I furiously scribbled every word of the kiss-close in my notebook. No one had ever told me how to kiss a girl before. It was just one of those things men were supposed to know on their own, like shaving and car repair.

Sitting in the limo with a notebook on my lap, listening to Mystery talk, I asked myself why I was really there. Taking a course in picking up women wasn't the kind of thing normal people did. Even more disturbing, I wondered why it was so important to me, why I'd become so quickly obsessed with the online community and its leading pseudonyms.

Perhaps it was because attracting the opposite sex was the only area of my life in which I felt like a complete failure. Every time I walked down the street or into a bar, I saw my own failure staring me back in the face with red lipstick and black mascara. The combination of desire and paralysis was deadly.

After the workshop that night, I opened my file cabinet and dug through my papers. There was something I wanted to find, something I hadn't looked at in years. After a half hour, I found it: a folder labeled "High School Writing." I pulled out a piece of lined notebook paper covered from top to bottom with my chicken scratching. It was the only poem I've ever attempted in my life. It was written in eleventh grade, and I never showed it to anyone. However, it was the answer to my question.

SEXUAL FRUSTRATION
BY NEIL STRAUSS

The only reason you go out,
The only objective in mind,
A glimpse of a familiar pair
Of legs on a busy street or
A squeeze from a female who
You can only call your friend.

A scoreless night fosters hostility.
A scoreless weekend breeds animosity.
Through red eyes all the world is seen,
Angry at friends and family for no
Reason that they can perceive.
Only you know why you are so mad.

There is the 'just friends' one who you've
Known for so long, who respects you
So much that you can't do what you want.
And she no longer bothers to put on her
False personality and flirt because she thinks
You like her for who she is when what you
Liked about her was her flirtatiousness.

When your own hand becomes your best lover,
When your life-giving fertilizer is wasted
In a Kleenex and flushed down the toilet
You wonder when you are going to stop
Thinking about what could have happened
That night when you almost got somewhere.

There is the coy one who smiles
And looks like she wants to meet you,
But you can't work up the nerve to talk.
So instead she will become one of your nighttime
Fantasies, where you could have but didn't.
Your hand will be substituted for hers.

When you neglect work and meaningful activities,
When you neglect the ones who really love you,
For a shot at a target that you rarely hit.
Does everyone get lucky with women but you,
Or do females just not want it as bad as you do?

In the decade since I'd written that poem, nothing had changed. I still couldn't write poetry. And, more important, I still felt the same way. Perhaps signing up for Mystery's workshop had been an intelligent decision. After all, I was doing something proactive about my lameness.

Even the wise man dwells in the fool's paradise.

Chapter

On the last night of the workshop, Mystery and Sin took us to a bar called the Saddle Ranch, a country-themed meat market on the Sunset Strip. I'd been there before—not to pick up women, but to ride the mechanical bull. One of my goals in Los Angeles was to master the machine at its fastest setting. But not today. After three consecutive nights of going out until 2:00 A.M. and then breaking down approaches with Mystery and the other students far beyond the allotted half-hour, I was wiped out.

Within minutes, however, our tireless professor of pickup was at the bar, making out with a loud, tipsy girl who kept trying to steal his scarf. Watching Mystery work, I noticed that he used the exact same openers, routines, and lines—and got a phone number or a tonguedown nearly every time, even if the woman was with a boyfriend. I'd never seen anything like it. Sometimes a woman he was talking to was even moved to tears.

As I walked toward the mechanical bull ring, feeling foolish in a red cowboy hat Mystery had insisted I wear, I saw a girl with long black hair, a formfitting sweater, and tan legs sticking out of a ruffled skirt. She was talking animatedly to two guys, bouncing around them like a cartoon character.

One second. Two seconds. Three.

"Hey, looks like the party's over here." I spoke to the guys, then turned to face the girl. I stuttered for a moment. I knew the next line—Mystery had been pushing it on me all weekend—but I'd been dreading using it.

"If . . . if I wasn't gay, you'd be so mine."

A huge smile spread across her face. "I like your hat," she screeched, grabbing the brim.

I guess peacocking did work. "Hey, now," I told her, repeating a line I had heard Mystery use earlier. "Hands off the merchandise."

She responded by throwing her arms around me and telling me I was fun. Every ounce of fear evaporated with her acceptance. The secret to meeting women, I realized, is simply knowing what to say, and when and how to say it.

"How do you all know each other?" I asked.

"I just met them," she said. "My name is Elonova." She curtseyed clumsily.

I took that as an IOI.

I showed Elonova an ESP trick Mystery had taught me earlier that evening, in which I guessed a number she was thinking between one and ten (hint: it's almost always seven), and she clapped her hands together gleefully. The guys, in the presence of my superior game, wandered off.

When the bar closed, Elonova and I moved outside. Every AFC we walked past gave me the thumbs up and said, "She's hot" or "You lucky bastard." What idiots. They were fucking up my game—that is, if I could figure out a way to tell Elonova I was straight. Hopefully, she'd figured it out on her own by now.

I remembered Sin telling me to kino, so I put my arm around her. This time, however, she backed away. That was definitely not an IOI. As I took a step toward her to try again, one of the guys she'd been with in the bar arrived. She flirted with him as I stood there stupidly. When she turned back to me a few minutes later, I told her we should hang out sometime. She agreed, and we exchanged numbers.

Mystery, Sin, and the boys were all in the limo, watching the whole exchange go down. I climbed inside, thinking I was hot shit for number-closing in front of them all. But Mystery wasn't impressed.

"You got that number-close," he said, "because you forced yourself on her. You let her play with you."

"What do you mean?" I asked.

"Have I ever told you about cat string theory?"

"No."

"Listen. Have you ever seen a cat play with a string? Well, when the string is dangling above its head, just out of reach, the cat goes crazy trying to get it. It leaps in the air, dances around, and chases it all over the room. But as soon as you let go of the string and it drops right between the cat's paws, it just looks at the string for a second and then walks away. It's bored. It doesn't want it anymore."

"So . . ."

"So that girl moved away from you when you put your arm around her. And you ran right back to her like a puppy dog. You should have punished her—turned away and talked to someone else. Let her work to get your attention back. After that, she made you wait while she talked to that dork."

"What should I have done?"

"You should have said, 'I'll let you two be alone,' and started to walk away, as if you were giving her to him—even though you knew she liked you more. You have to act like you are the prize."

I smiled. I think I really understood.

"Yeah," he said. "Be the dancing string."

I grew silent and thought about it, kicking my legs up against the bar counter of the limousine and slouching into the seat. Mystery turned to Sin, and they talked amongst themselves for several minutes. It felt like they were discussing me.

I tried not to make eye contact with them. I wondered if they were going to tell me that I'd held the workshop up, that I wasn't yet ready for it, that I should study for another six months and then take it again.

Suddenly, Mystery and Sin ended their huddle. Mystery broke into a wide smile and looked straight at me.

"You're one of us," he said. "You're going to be a superstar."

Chapter

MSN GROUP: Mystery's Lounge
SUBJECT: Sex Magic
AUTHOR: Mystery

My Mystery Method workshop in Los Angeles kicked ass. I've decided to teach several impressive ways to demonstrate mind power through magic at my next workshop. After all, some of you need *something* with which to convey your charming personalities. If you are going in without an edge—like if you say, "Hi, I'm an accountant"—you will not capture your target's attention and curiosity.

So, since the workshop, I've retired the FMAC model and broken down the approach to thirteen detailed steps. Here is the basic format to all approaches:

1. Smile when you walk into a room. See the group with the target and follow the three-second rule. Do not hesitate—approach instantly.

2. Recite a memorized opener, if not two or three in a row.

3. The opener should open the group, not just the target. When talking, ignore the target for the most part. If there are men in the group, focus your attention on the men.

4. Neg the target with one of the slew of negs we've come up with. Tell her, "It's so cute. Your nose wiggles when you laugh." Then get her friends to notice and laugh about it.

5. Convey personality to the entire group. Do this by using stories, magic, anecdotes, and humor. Pay particular attention to the men and the less attractive women. During this time, the target will notice that you are the center of attention. You may perform various memorized pieces like the photo routine,[2] but only for the obstacles.

6. Neg the target again if appropriate. If she wants to look at the pictures, for example, say, "Oh my god, she's so grabby. How do you roll with her?"

7. Ask the group, "So, how does everyone know each other?" If the target is with one of the guys, find out how long they've been together. If it's a serious relationship, eject politely by saying, "Pleasure meeting you."

8. If she is not spoken for, say to the group, "I've sort of been alienating your friend. Is it all right if I speak to her for a couple of minutes?" They always say, "Uh, sure. If it's okay with her." If you've executed the preceding steps correctly, she will agree.

9. Isolate her from the group by telling her you want to show her something cool. Take her to sit with you nearby. As you lead her through the crowd, do a kino test by holding her hand. If she squeezes back, it's on. Start looking for other IOIs.

10. Sit with her and perform a rune reading, an ESP test, or any other demonstration that will fascinate and intrigue her.

11. Tell her, "Beauty is common but what's rare is a great energy and outlook on life. Tell me, what do you have inside that would make me want to know you as more than a mere face in the crowd?" If she begins to list qualities, this is a positive IOI.

12. Stop talking. Does she reinitiate the chat with a question that begins with the word "So?" If she does, you've now seen three IOIs and can . . .

---

[2] The photo routine involves carrying an envelope of photos in a jacket pocket, as if they've just been developed. Each photo, however, is pre-selected to convey a different aspect of the PUA's personality, such as images of the PUA with beautiful women, with children, with pets, with celebrities, goofing off with friends, and doing something active like roller-blading or skydiving. The PUA should also have a short, witty story to accompany each photo.

13. Kiss close. Say, out of the blue, "Would you like to kiss me?" If the setting or circumstances aren't conducive to physical intimacy, then give yourself a time constraint by saying, "I have to go, but we should continue this." Then get her number and leave.

—Mystery

The Mystery Method course handout

Sure, there is Ovid, the Roman poet who wrote *The Art of Love;* Don Juan, the mythical womanizer based on the exploits of various Spanish noblemen; the Duke de Lauzun, the legendary French rake who died on the guillotine; and Casanova, who detailed his hundred-plus conquests in four thousand pages of memoirs. But the undisputed father of modern seduction is Ross Jeffries, a tall, skinny, porous-faced self-proclaimed nerd from Marina Del Rey, California. Guru, cult leader, and social gadfly, he commands an army sixty thousand horny men strong, including top government officials, intelligence officers, and cryptographers.

His weapon is his voice. After years of studying everyone from master hypnotists to Hawaiian Kahunas, he claims to have found the technology—and make no mistake about it, that's what it is—that will turn any responsive woman into a libidinous puddle. Jeffries, who claims to be the inspiration for Tom Cruise's character in *Magnolia,* calls it Speed Seduction.

Jeffries developed Speed Seduction in 1988, after ending a five-year streak of sexlessness with the help of neuro-linguistic programming (NLP), a controversial fusion of hypnosis and psychology that emerged from the personal development boom of the 1970s and led to the rise of self-help gurus like Anthony Robbins. The fundamental precept of NLP is that one's thoughts, feelings, and behavior—and the thoughts, feelings, and behavior of others—can be manipulated through words, suggestions, and physical gestures designed to influence the subconscious. The potential of NLP to revolutionize the art of seduction was obvious to Jeffries.

Over the years, Jeffries has either outlasted, sued, or crushed any competitor in the field of pickup to make his school, Speed Seduction, the dominant model for getting a woman's lips to touch a man's—that is, until Mystery came along and started teaching workshops.

Thus, the clamor online for an eyewitness account of Mystery's first workshop was overwhelming. Mystery's admirers wanted to know if the class was worthwhile; his enemies, particularly Jeffries and his disciples, wanted to tear him apart. So I obliged, posting a detailed description of my experiences.

At the end of my review, I issued a call for wings in Los Angeles, asking only that they be somewhat confident, intelligent, and socially comfortable. I knew that in order to become a pickup artist myself, I would somehow have to internalize everything I had seen Mystery do. This would happen only through practice—through hitting the bars and clubs every night until I became a natural like Dustin, or even an unnatural like Mystery.

The day my report on the workshop hit the Internet, I received an e-mail from someone in Encino nicknamed Grimble, who identified himself as a Ross Jeffries student. He wanted to "sarge" with me, as he put it. Sarging is pickup artist jargon for going out to meet women; the term evidently has its origin in the name of one of Ross Jeffries's cats, Sargy.

An hour after I sent him my phone number, Grimble called. More than Mystery, it was Grimble who would initiate me into what could only be described as a secret society.

"Hey, man," he said, in a conspiratorial hiss. "So what do you think of Mystery's game?"

I gave him my assessment.

"Wow, I like it," he said. "But you have to hang out with Twotimer and me some time. We've been sarging with Ross Jeffries a lot."

"Really? I'd love to meet him."

"Listen. Can you keep a secret?"

"Sure."

"How much technology do you use in your sarges?"

"Technology?"

"You know, how much is technique and how much is just talking?"

"I guess fifty-fifty," I said.

"I'm up to 90 percent."

"What?"

"Yeah, I use a canned opener, then I elicit her values and find out her trance words. And then I go into one of the secret patterns. Do you know the October Man sequence?"

"Never heard of it, unless Arnold Schwarzenegger was in it."

"Oh, man. I had a girl over here last week, and I gave her a whole new identity. I did a sexual value elicitation, and then changed her whole timeline and internal reality. Then I brushed my finger along her face, telling her to notice"—and here he switched to a slow, hypnotic voice—"how wherever I touch . . . it leaves a trail of energy moving through you . . . and wherever you can feel this energy spreading ... the deeper you want to allow your-self ... to feel these sensations ... becoming even more ... intense."

"And then what?"

"I brushed my finger along her lips, and she started sucking it," he exclaimed triumphantly. "Full-close!"

"Wow," I said.

I had no idea what he was talking about. But I wanted this technology. I thought back to all the times I'd taken women to my house, sat on the bed next to them, leaned in for the kiss, and been deflected with the "let's just be friends" speech. In fact, this rejection is such a universal experience that Ross Jeffries invented not just an acronym for it, LJBF, but a litany of responses as well.[3]

I talked to Grimble for two hours. He seemed to know everybody—from legends like Steve P., who supposedly had a cult of women paying cash for the privilege of sexually servicing him, to guys like Rick H., Ross's most famous student, thanks to an incident that involved him, a hot tub, and five women.

Grimble would make a perfect wing.

---

[3] One such response from Jeffries is, "I don't promise any such thing. Friends don't put each other into boxes like that. The only thing I'll promise is never to do anything unless you and I both feel totally comfortable, willing, and ready."

I drove to Grimble's house in Encino the following night to go sarging. This would be my first time in the field since Mystery's workshop. It would also be my first time hanging out one-on-one with a stranger I'd met online. All I really knew about him was that he was a college student and he liked girls.

When I pulled up, Grimble strode outside and flashed a big smile that I didn't quite trust. He didn't seem dangerous or mean. He just seemed slippery, like a politician or a salesman or, I suppose, a seducer. He had the complexion of barley tea, though he was actually German. In fact, he claimed to be a descendent of Otto von Bismarck. He wore a brown leather jacket over a silver floral-print shirt, which was unbuttoned to reveal an eerily hairless chest thrust out further than his nose. In his hands was a plastic bag full of videotapes, which he dumped into the back of my car. He reminded me of a mongoose.

"These are some of Ross's seminars," he said. "You'll really like the DC seminar, because he gets into synesthesia there. The other tapes are from Kim and Tom"—Ross's ex-girlfriend and her new boyfriend. "It's their New York seminar, 'Advanced Anchoring and Other Sneaky Stuff.'"

"What's anchoring?" I asked.

"My wing Twotimer will show you when you meet him. Ever experienced condiment anchoring before?"

I had so much to learn. Men generally don't communicate to one another with the same level of emotional depth and intimate detail as most women. Women discuss everything. When a man sees his friends after getting laid, they ask, "How'd it go?" And in return, he gives them either a thumbs up or a thumbs down. That's how it's done. To discuss the experience in detail would mean giving your friends mental images they don't really want to have. It is a taboo among men to picture their best friends naked or having sex, because then they might find themselves aroused—and we all know what that means.

So, ever since I'd first started harboring lustful thoughts in sixth grade, I'd assumed that sex was something that just happened to guys if they went out a lot and exposed themselves to chance—after all, that's why they called it getting lucky. The only tool they had in their belt was persistence. Of course, there were some men who were sexually comfortable around women, who would tease them mercilessly until they had them eating out of their hands. But that wasn't me. It took all of my courage to simply ask a woman for the time or where Melrose Avenue was. I didn't know anything about anchoring, eliciting values, finding trance words, or these other things Grimble kept talking about.

How did I ever get laid without all this technology?

It was a quiet Tuesday night in the Valley, and the only place Grimble knew to go was the local T.G.I. Friday's. In the car, we warmed up—listening to cassette tapes of sarges by Rick H., practicing openers, faking smiles, and dancing in our seats to get energetic. It was one of the most ridiculous things I'd ever done, but I was entering a new world now, with its own rules of behavior.

We walked in the door of the restaurant—confident, smiling, alpha. Unfortunately, no one noticed. There were two guys at the bar watching a baseball game on television, a group of businesspeople at a corner table, and a mostly male bar staff. We strutted to the balcony. As we pushed the door open, a woman appeared. Time to put what I'd learned to the test.

"Hey," I said to her. "Let me get your opinion on something."

She stopped and listened. She was about four foot ten, with short, frizzy hair and a marshmallow body, but she had a nice smile; she would be good practice. I decided to use the Maury Povich opener.

"My friend Grimble there just got a call today from the Maury Povich show," I began. "And it seems they're doing a segment on secret admirers. Evidently, someone has a little crush on him. Do you think he should go on the show or not?"

"Sure," she answered. "Why not?"

"But what if his secret admirer is a man?" I asked. "Talk shows always need to put an unexpected twist on everything. Or what if it's a relative?"

It's not lying; it's flirting.

She laughed. Perfect. "Would you do the show?" I asked.

"Probably not," she answered.

Suddenly, Grimble stepped in. "So you would make me go on the show, but you wouldn't do it yourself," he teased her. "You're not adventurous at all, are you?" It was great to watch him work. Where I would have let the conversation wane into small talk, he was already leading her somewhere sexual.

"I am," she protested.

"Then prove it to me," he said, smiling. "Let's try a little exercise. It's called synesthesia." He took a step closer to her. "Have you ever heard of synesthesia? It will enable you to find all kinds of resources to accomplish and feel the things you want in life."

Synesthesia is the nerve gas in the arsenal of the speed seducer. Literally, it is an overlapping of the senses. In the context of seduction, however, synesthesia refers to a type of waking hypnosis in which a woman is put into a heightened state of awareness and told to imagine pleasurable images and sensations growing in intensity. The goal: to make her uncontrollably aroused.

She agreed and closed her eyes. I was finally going to get to hear one of Ross's secret patterns. But as soon as Grimble began, a stocky, red-faced jock wearing a pocket undershirt marched up to him.

"What are you doing?" he asked Grimble.

"I was showing her a self-improvement exercise called synesthesia."

"Well, that's my wife."

I had forgotten to check for a wedding ring, though I doubted minor inconveniences like marriage mattered to Grimble.

"Go disarm the guy," Grimble turned to me and hissed, "while I work on the girl."

I had no idea how to disarm him. He didn't seem quite as laid-back as Scott Baio. "He can show you the exercise, too," I said wanly. "It's really cool."

"I don't know what the fuck you're talking about," the guy said. "What is this thing supposed to do to me?" He took a step closer and leaned his face into mine. He smelled like whiskey and onion rings.

"It tells you whether . . . whether . . ." I stammered. "Never mind."

The guy lifted his hands and pushed me backward. Though I tell girls I'm five feet and eight inches, I'm actually five foot six. The top of my head just reached his shoulders.

"Stop it," his wife, our former sarge, said. She turned to us. "He's drunk. He gets like this."

"Like what?" I asked. "Violent?"

She smiled sadly.

"You seem like a great couple," I said. My attempt to disarm him had clearly failed, because he was about to disarm me. His red drunken face was two inches from mine and yelling about ripping something.

"Pleasure meeting you both," I squeaked, slowly backing away.

"Remind me," Grimble said as we retreated to the car, "to teach you how to handle the AMOG."

"The AMOG?"

"Yes, the alpha male of the group."

Oh, I see.

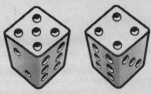

Chapter

Four days later, as I sat at home alone on a Saturday afternoon watching the videos Grimble had given me, he called with good news. He and his wing, Twotimer, were going to meet Ross Jeffries at California Pizza Kitchen for an expedition to the Getty Museum, and I was invited.

I arrived fifteen minutes early, selected a booth, and read through printouts of seduction board posts until Ross, Grimble, and Twotimer arrived. Twotimer had black hair gelled to the texture of a licorice vine, a matching leather jacket, and a snake-like quality. With his round, babyish face, he looked like a Grimble clone who'd been inflated by a bicycle pump.

As I stood up to introduce myself, Ross cut me off. He was not the most polite person I'd ever met. He wore a long wool overcoat, which flowed loosely around his legs when he walked. He was thin and gawky with gray stubble and greasy skin. His hairline was a receding mop of short, unkempt, ash-colored curls, and the hook in his nose was so pronounced he could have hung his overcoat on it.

"So what did you learn from Mystery?" Ross asked with a sneer.

"A lot," I told him.

"Like what?"

"Well, one of my sticking points was knowing when a girl was attracted to me. Now I know."

"And how do you know?" he asked.

"When I get three indicators of interest."

"Name them."

"Let's see. When she asks you what your name is."

"That's one."

"When you take her hands in yours and squeeze them, and she squeezes back."

"That's two."

"And, uh, I can't remember the rest right now."

"Aha." He leapt to his feet. "Then he's not a very good teacher, is he?"

"No, he was a great teacher," I protested.

"Then name the third indicator of interest."

"I can't think of it right now." I felt like an animal backed into a corner.

"Case closed," he said. He was good.

A short waitress with blue nails, a touch of baby fat, and sandy brown hair arrived to take our order. Ross looked at her, and then winked at me. "These are my students," he told her. "I'm their guru."

"Really?" she asked, feigning interest.

"What would you say if I told you that I teach people how to use mind control to attract any person they desire?"

"Get out of here."

"Yes, it's true. I could make you fall in love with any person at this table."

"And how's that? With mind control?" She was skeptical, but bordering on curious.

"Let me ask you something. When you're really attracted to somebody, how do you know? In other words, what signals do you get from yourself, inside, that allow you to realize"—and here he lowered his voice, slowly pronouncing each word—"you're . . . really . . . attracted . . . to . . . this guy?"

The purpose of the question, I would find out later, was to make the waitress feel the emotion of attraction in his presence, and thus associate those feelings with his face.

She thought about it for a moment. "Well, I guess I get a funny feeling in my stomach, like butterflies."

Ross put his hand, palm up, in front of his stomach. "Yes, and I bet that the more attracted you become, the more those butterflies rise up from your stomach"—he began slowly raising his hand to the level of his heart—"until your face begins to flush . . . like it is right now."

Twotimer leaned over and whispered: "That's anchoring. It's when you associate a feeling—like attraction—with a touch or a gesture. Now, every time Ross raises his hand like that, she gets attracted to him."

After a few more minutes of Ross's flirtatious hypnospeak, the waitress's eyes began to glaze over. Ross seized the opportunity to toy with her mercilessly. He raised his hands like an elevator from his stomach to his face every few seconds, smiling as it made her blush every time. The dishes she was carrying were forgotten, balancing precariously on her weakening arm.

"With your boyfriend," Ross continued, "were you attracted right away?" He snapped, freeing her from her trance. "Or did it take time?"

"Well, we broke up," she said. "But it took a while. We were friends first."

"Isn't it so much better, though, when you just feel that sense of attraction"—he moved his hand up like an elevator and her eyes began to glaze again—"right away for someone." He pointed to himself, which I assumed was another NLP trick to make her think he was that someone. "It's incredible, isn't it?"

"Yes," she agreed, completely oblivious to her other tables.

"What was wrong with your boyfriend?"

"He was too immature."

Ross seized the opportunity. "Well, you should date more mature men."

"I was just thinking that, about you, as we were talking." She giggled.

"I bet that when you first came to the table, I was the last person you thought you'd be attracted to."

"It's strange," she said, "because you're not my usual type."

Ross suggested they get together for coffee when she wasn't working, and she jumped at the opportunity to give him her phone number. His technique was so different than Mystery's, but he seemed to be the real deal too.

Ross let out a loud, victorious laugh. "Well, your other customers are probably getting angry. But before you go, I'll tell you what. Why don't we take all those good feelings you're having right now"—raising his hands again—"and put them into this pack of sugar"—he picked up a sugar pack and rubbed his raised hand on it—"so that you can carry them around with you all day."

He handed her the sugar pack. She put it in her apron and walked away, still beet red.

"That," Twotimer hissed, "is condiment anchoring. After he's gone, the sugar pack will remind her of the positive emotions she felt with him."

As we left the restaurant, Ross ran the exact same routine on the hostess and collected her number. Both women were in their twenties; Ross was in his forties. I was floored.

We pressed into Ross's Saab and headed to the Getty. "Anything you want from a woman—attraction, lust, fascination—is just an internal process that she runs through her body and her brain," he explained as he drove. "And all you need to evoke that process are questions that make her go into her body and brain and actually experience it in order to answer you. Then she will link those feelings of attraction to you."

Sitting in the back seat with me, Twotimer scanned my face for a reaction. "What do you think?" he asked.

"Amazing," I said.

"Evil," he corrected, letting a thin smile creep over his lips.

When we arrived at the Getty, Twotimer turned his attention to Ross. "I wanted to ask you about the October Man sequence," he prodded. "I've been switching around a few of the steps."

Ross turned to him. "You understand that these things are very bad?" As he spoke, Ross wagged a finger at Twotimer's chest, over his heart. He was anchoring again, trying to associate the notion of badness with the forbidden pattern. "There's a reason I don't teach them at my seminars."

"Why is that?" Twotimer asked.

"Because," Ross answered, "it's like giving dynamite to children."

Twotimer smiled again. I could tell exactly what he was thinking—because, in my mind, the word *evil* was anchored to that smile.

"Darwin talked about survival of the fittest," Twotimer explained to me as we walked through the museum's collection of pre-twentieth century art. "In earlier times, this meant that the strong survived. But strength doesn't help one get ahead in society today. Women breed with seducers, who understand how to trigger, through words and touch, the fantasy parts of the female brain." There was something artificial and rehearsed about the way he spoke, the way he moved, the way he looked at me. It felt as if he were sucking my soul into his eyes. "So the whole idea of survival of the fittest is an anachronism. As players, we stand at the gate of a new era: the survival of the smoothest."

I liked the idea, though unfortunately I was no smoother than I was strong. My voice was fast and choppy, my movements effete, my body language awkward. For me, survival was going to take work.

"Casanova was one of us," Twotimer went on. "But we live a better lifestyle."

"Well, it probably took a lot more work to seduce a woman back then because of the morals of the day," I said, trying to contribute something useful.

"And we have the technology."

"You mean NLP?"

"Not just that. He had to work alone." He grinned as his gaze bore deeper into my eyes. "We have each other."

We lurked through the galleries, gazing at the people gazing at paintings. I watched as Grimble and Twotimer talked to various women. But I was far too scared to approach in front of Ross: It felt like trying to play the cello in front of Yo-Yo Ma. I was afraid he'd criticize everything I did or get upset that I wasn't using enough of his technology. On the other hand, this was a guy who advised students to get over their fear of approaching by walking up to random women and saying, "Hi, I'm Manny the Martian. What's your favorite flavor of bowling ball?" So I really didn't have to worry about looking foolish in front of him. He created fools.

At the end of the day, Ross had three numbers. Twotimer and Grimble had two each. And I had nothing.

As we took the train downhill to the museum parking lot, Ross slid into the seat next to me. "Listen," he said. "I have a seminar coming up in a few months. And I will let you sit in and take it for free."

"Thanks," I said.

"I am going to be your guru. Not Mystery. You'll see that what I am teaching is a hundred times more powerful."

I wasn't sure how to respond. They were competing over me—an AFC.

"And one more thing," Ross said. "In exchange, I want you to take me to five—no, six—Hollywood parties, with super-hot babes. I need to widen my horizons."

He smiled and asked, "Do we have a deal?" as he rubbed his thumb on his chin. I was sure he was anchoring me.

STEP 3
DEMONSTRATE VALUE

MY MAN IS SMOOTH LIKE BARRY,
AND HIS VOICE GOT BASS.
A BODY LIKE ARNOLD WITH A
DENZEL FACE . . .
HE ALWAYS HAS HEAVY
CONVERSATION FOR THE MIND,
WHICH MEANS A LOT TO ME, 'CAUSE
GOOD MEN ARE HARD TO FIND.

—SALT-N-PEPA,
"Whatta Man"

Chapter

The best predators don't lie on the jungle floor with their teeth bared and claws out. The prey is going to avoid them. They approach the prey slowly and harmlessly, win its trust, and then attack.

At least, that's what Sin told me. He facetiously called it Sin Method.

Though Mystery had flown back to Toronto after the workshop, I stayed in touch with Sin. I'd watch as a woman came over to his house for the first time and he'd throw her against the wall by her neck, then release her just before he kissed her, shooting her adrenaline level through the roof with equal parts fear and arousal. Then he'd cook her dinner and never speak a word about it until dessert, when he'd stare at her like a tiger eying its prey and say, in a tone of restrained lust, "You don't even want to know the things I'm thinking of doing to you right now." That was generally the point when I'd excuse myself to go home.

Along with the sneakier Grimble, the more predatory Sin became a faithful wing. But our friendship didn't last long. One afternoon, after a sarging session at the Beverly Center mall, Sin informed me that he'd enrolled in the Air Force as an officer.

"The military is a steady paycheck," he explained as we sat in a mall café. "And I can live wherever I want. I've been an unemployed computer programmer for too long."

I tried to talk him out of it. Sin was into astral projection, goth rock, S and M, and pickup. He would have to hide all that if he joined the military. But his mind was made up. "I was talking to Mystery about you," he said, leaning low over the metal latticework of the table. His tone, as always, was deadly serious. "He wants to schedule his next workshop in December. Since I'm not going to be around to wing him, he wants you to do it."

As I thought of another weekend with Mystery and all his secrets, like the triple-stacked patterns he used to move girls to tears, I tried to control the excitement in my voice. "I think I'll be free," I said.

Out of all the potential pickup artists in the world, I couldn't believe that Mystery was choosing me. He must not know that many people.

There was just one small problem: I wasn't going to be free in December. I'd booked a flight to Belgrade to visit Marko, the schoolmate who had introduced me to Dustin and his natural ways. It was too late to cancel on Marko, but there was no way I was going to miss the opportunity to wing Mystery either.

There had to be a solution.

That night, I called Mystery in Toronto, where he was living with his parents, his two nieces, his sister, and her husband.

"Hey, buddy," Mystery said when he answered. "I'm bored out of my mind here."

"I find that hard to believe."

"Well, it's raining and I want to go out. But I have no one to go out with and no clue where to go." He paused to tell his nieces to shut up. "I'll probably just get some sushi alone."

I'd assumed that the great Mystery would have girls lined up every night of the week and a wait-list of sargers eager to take him out clubbing. Instead, he was stagnating at home. His father was sick. His mother was overburdened. And his sister was separating from her husband.

"Can't you go out with Patricia?" I asked. Patricia was Mystery's girl-friend, the one pictured in her negligee in his pickup resume.

"She's mad at me," he said. Mystery had met Patricia four years ago, when she was fresh off the boat from Romania. He tried to mold her into his ideal girl—he talked her into getting a boob job, giving him blow jobs (which she'd never done before), and taking a job as a stripper—but she drew the line at bisexuality. For Mystery, this was a dealbreaker.

Everyone has their own reason for getting into the game. Some, like Extramask, are virgins who want to experience what it's like to be with a woman. Others, like Grimble and Twotimer, desire new girls every night. And a few, like Sweater, are searching for the perfect wife. Mystery had his own specific goal.

"I want to be loved by two women," he said. "I want a blonde 10 and an Asian 10, who will love each other as much as they love me. And Patricia's heterosexuality is affecting my sex life with her, because unless I imagine another girl there, I can't always keep my boner." He moved the phone to another room because his sister and her husband were arguing, and continued, "I'd just break up with Patricia, but there aren't any 10s in Toronto. No outrageous glitter girls. It's all 7s, at best."

"Move to L.A.," I urged. "This is where all the peacocky girls you like live."

"Yeah, I really need to get out of here," he sighed. "So I want to schedule a bunch of workshops. I've got people interested in Miami, Chicago, and New York."

"How about Belgrade?"

"What? Isn't there a war going on there?"

"No, the war's over. And I have to visit an old friend. He said it's safe. We can stay with him for free, and Slavic women are supposed to be the most beautiful in the world."

He hesitated.

"And I have a free companion ticket."

Silence. He was considering it.

I pushed further. "What the hell. It's an adventure. At the very worst, you'll have a new picture for your photo routine."

Mystery thought like a flowchart. And if he agreed to something, his assent was given instantly and always with the same word, which he spoke next: "Done."

"Great," I said. "I'll e-mail you the flight times." I couldn't wait for the six hour plane ride. I wanted to vacuum every piece of knowledge—every magic trick, every pickup line, every story—out of his head. I wanted to mimic exactly what I'd seen him do, word for word, trick for trick, simply because it worked.

"But wait," he said. "There's something else."

"What?"

"If you're going to be my wing, you can't be Neil Strauss," he said with the same air of finality with which he had spoken the word *done*. "It's time for you to change, to just snap and become someone else. Think about it: Neil Strauss, writer. That isn't cool. Nobody wants to sleep with a writer. They're at the bottom of the social ladder. You must be a superstar. And not just with women. You are an artist in need of an art. And I think your art is actually the social skills you're learning. I watched you in the field; you adapted quickly. That's why Sin and I picked you. Hold on a minute."

I heard him rustling through some papers. "Listen," he said. "These are my personal development goals. I want to raise the money for a touring illusion show. I want to live in posh hotels. I want a limo to and from shows. I want specials on TV with big illusions. I want to levitate over Niagara

Falls. I want to travel to England and Australia. I want jewelry, games, a model airplane, a personal assistant, a stylist. And I want to act in *Jesus Christ Superstar*—as Jesus."

At least he knew what he wanted in life. "What I'm really after," he finally said, "is for people to be envious of me, for women to want me and men to want to be me."

"You never got much love as a child, did you?"

"No," he replied sheepishly.

At the end of the conversation, he said he was going to e-mail me the password to a secret online community called Mystery's Lounge. He had created Mystery's Lounge two years before, after an enterprising bartender he'd slept with in Los Angeles found an Internet post he'd written about her on a public seduction newsgroup. After spending a weekend poring through the rest of his online archive, she e-mailed Mystery's girlfriend, Patricia, and told her about her boyfriend's extracurricular activities. The fallout nearly destroyed his relationship, and in the process taught him that there was a downside to being a pickup artist: getting caught.

Unlike the other seduction boards I had been reading, where hundreds of newbies were constantly begging for advice from just a few experts, Mystery had cherry-picked the best pickup artists in the community for his private forum. Here they not only shared their secrets, stories, and techniques, but also posted pictures of themselves and their women—even, on occasion, video and audio recordings of their exploits in the field.

"But remember," Mystery said sternly. "You are no longer Neil Strauss. When I see you in there, I want you to be someone else. You need a seduction name." He paused and reflected: "Styles?"

"How about Style?" That was one thing I prided myself on: I may never have been socially comfortable, but at least I knew how to dress better than those who were.

"Style it is. Mystery and Style."

Yes, it was Mystery and Style giving a workshop. It had a nice ring to it. Style the pickup artist—teaching lovable losers how to meet the women of their dreams.

But as soon as I hung up, I realized something: First, Style needed to teach himself. After all, it had only been a month since my workshop with Mystery. I still had a long way to go.

It was time for a motherfucking change.

Chapter

One of my teenage heroes was Harry Crosby. He was a poet from the 1920s, and, frankly, his poetry sucked. But his lifestyle was legendary. The nephew and godson of J. P. Morgan, he hobnobbed with Ernest Hemingway and D. H. Lawrence, was the first person to publish parts of Joyce's *Ulysses*, and became a decadent symbol of the lost generation. He lived a fast, opium-enhanced life, and swore he would be dead by the age of thirty. When he was twenty-two, he married Polly Peabody, the inventor of the strapless bra, and persuaded her to change her name to Caresse. For their honeymoon, they locked themselves in a bedroom in Paris with stacks of books and just read. At the age of thirty-one, when he realized that his lifestyle hadn't killed him yet, Crosby shot himself.

I didn't have a Caresse to lock up with me, but I shut myself in the house for a week Harry Crosby-style, reading books, listening to tapes, watching videos, and studying the posts in Mystery's Lounge. I immersed myself in seduction theory. I needed to shed Neil Strauss and rewire myself to become Style. I wanted to live up to Mystery and Sin's faith in me.

To do so, I'd have to change not just the things I said to women, but the way I acted around them. I needed to become confident, to become interesting, to become decisive, to become graceful, to become the alpha male I was never raised to be. I had a lot of lost time to make up for—and six weeks to do it in.

I bought books on body language, flirting, and sexual technique. I read anthologies of women's sexual fantasies, like Nancy Friday's *My Secret Garden*, in order to internalize the idea that women actually want sex as much as—if not more than—men; they just don't want to be pressured, lied to, or made to feel like a slut.

I ordered books on marketing, like Robert Cialdini's seminal *Influence*, from which I learned several key principles that guide the majority of people's decisions. The most important of these is social proof, which is the notion that if everyone else is doing something, then it must be good. So if you are in a bar with a beautiful female friend on your arm (a pivot, as they call it in the community), it's much easier to meet women than if you're hanging out alone.

I watched the videos Grimble had given me and took notes on each, memorizing affirmations ("if a woman enters my world, it will be the best thing that can ever happen to her") and patterns. There is a difference between a line and a pattern. A line is basically any prepared comment made to a woman. A pattern is a more elaborate script, specifically designed to arouse her.

Men and women think and respond differently. Show a man the cover of *Playboy*, and he's ready to go. In fact, show him a pitted avocado and he's ready to go. Women, according to the speed seducers, aren't persuaded as easily by direct images and talk. They respond better to metaphor and suggestion.

One of Ross Jeffries's most famous patterns uses a Discovery Channel show about roller coaster design as a metaphor for the attraction, trust, and excitement that are often necessary preconditions for sex. The pattern describes the "perfect attraction," which provides a feeling of excitement as the roller coaster rises to a summit and then whooshes down in a rush; then it offers a feeling of safety, because it was designed to allow you to have this experience in a comfortable, safe environment; finally, as soon as the ride is over, you want to climb back on and ride it again and again. Even if it seems unlikely that a pattern like this will turn a girl on, at least it's better than talking about work.

It wasn't enough, though, for me just to study Ross Jeffries. A lot of his ideas are simply applications of neuro-linguistic programming. So I went to the source and bought books by Richard Bandler and John Grinder, the University of California professors who developed and popularized this fringe school of hypnopsychology in the 1970s.

After NLP, it was time to learn some of Mystery's tricks. I spent one hundred and fifty dollars at magic stores, buying videos and books on levitation, metal bending, and mind reading. I'd learned from Mystery that one of the most important things to do with an attractive woman was to demonstrate value. In other words, what makes me any different from the last twenty guys who approached her? Well, if I can bend her fork by looking at it or guess her name before even speaking to her, that's a little different.

To further demonstrate value, I bought books on handwriting analysis, rune reading, and tarot cards. After all, everyone's favorite subject is themselves.

I took notes on everything I studied, developing routines and stories to test in the field. I neglected my work, my friends, and my family. I was on an eighteen-hour-a-day mission.

When I finally crammed as much information in my brain as it could hold, I started working on body language. I signed up for lessons in swing and salsa dancing. I rented *Rebel Without A Cause* and *A Streetcar Named Desire* to practice the looks and poses of James Dean and Marlon Brando. I studied Pierce Brosnan in the remake of *The Thomas Crown Affair*, Brad Pitt in *Meet Joe Black*, Mickey Rourke in *Wild Orchid*, Jack Nicholson in *The Witches of Eastwick*, and Tom Cruise in *Top Gun*.

I looked at every aspect of my physical behavior. Were my arms swinging when I walked? Did they bow out a little, as if trying to get around massive pectorals? Did I walk with a confident swagger? Could I stick my chest out further? Hold my head up higher? Swing my legs out further, as if trying to get around massive genitalia?

After correcting what I could on my own, I signed up for a course on Alexander Technique to improve my posture and rid myself of the round-shouldered curse I'd inherited from my father's side of the family. And because no one ever understands a word I say—my voice is too fast, quiet, and mumbly—I started taking weekly private lessons in speech and singing.

I wore stylish jackets with bright shirts and accessorized as much as I could. I bought rings, a necklace, and fake piercings. I experimented with cowboy hats, feather boas, light-up necklaces, and even sunglasses at night to see which received the most attention from women. In my heart, I knew most of these gaudy accouterments were tacky, but Mystery's peacock theory worked. When I wore at least one item that stood out, women who were interested in meeting me had an easy way to start a conversation.

I went out with Grimble, Twotimer, and Ross Jeffries nearly every night and, chunk by chunk, learned a new way to interact. Women are sick of generic guys asking the same generic questions: "So where are you from? . . . What do you do for work?" With our patterns, gimmicks, and routines, we were barroom heroes, saving the female of the species from certain ennui.

Not all women appreciated our efforts, of course. Though I was never hit, yelled at, or doused with a drink, stories of spectacular failures circled constantly in the back of my mind. There was the story of Jonah, a twenty-three-year-old virgin in the seduction community who was hit in the back of the head—twice—by a drunk girl who took his negs the wrong way. And there was Little Big Dick, a sarger from Alaska, who was sitting at a table talking to a girl when her boyfriend came up from behind, yanked him out of his seat, threw him to the ground, and kicked him in the head for two minutes straight, fracturing his left eye socket and leaving boot marks on his face.

But they were the exceptions, I hoped.

These beat-downs were foremost in my mind as I drove my car to Westwood, home to UCLA, for my first attempt at sarging during the daytime. Despite the cheat sheet of my favorite openers and routines in the back pocket of my jeans, I was petrified as I roamed the streets, trying to select someone for my first approach.

As I walked past an Office Depot, I saw a woman with brown glasses and short blonde hair that danced on her shoulders. She was thin, with smooth, gentle curves, jeans that were just tight enough, and a beautiful complexion, like burned butter. She looked like the undiscovered treasure of the campus.

She walked into the store, and I decided to move on. But then I saw her again through the window. She looked like a cool intellectual whose inner bombshell hadn't blossomed yet, someone I could talk with about Tarkovsky movies and then take to a monster truck rally. Maybe this would be my Caresse. I knew that if I didn't approach her, I'd chastise myself afterward and feel like a failure. So I decided to attempt my first daytime pickup. Besides, I told myself, she probably wasn't that good-looking up close anyway.

I walked into the store and found her in an aisle looking at mailing envelopes.

"Hey, maybe you can help me settle a debate I'm having," I told her. As I recited the Maury Povich opener, I noticed that she was even more beautiful at close range. I had stumbled across a genuine 10. And I had to follow protocol and neg her.

"I know this is wrong to say," I blurted, "but I grew up on Bugs Bunny cartoons as a child, and you have the most adorable Bugs Bunny overbite."

I was worried I'd gone too far. I'd made the neg up on the spot and was probably about to get slapped. But she actually grinned. "After all those years of braces, my mom's going to be mad," she replied. She was flirting back with me.

I performed the ESP routine, and fortunately she picked seven. She was amazed. I asked her what she did for work, and she said she was a model and hosted a show on TNN. The longer we talked, the more she seemed to enjoy the conversation. But as I noticed the material working, I became nervous. I couldn't believe that a woman who looked like this was into me. Everyone in Office Depot was staring at us. I couldn't go on.

"I'm late for an appointment," I told her. My hands were shaking from nerves. "But what steps can we take to continue this conversation?"

This was Mystery's number-close routine. A pickup artist never gives a girl his phone number, because she might not call. A PUA must make a woman comfortable enough to give him her number. He must also avoid asking for it directly, because she could always say no, and instead lead her to suggest the idea herself.

"I could give you my number," she offered.

She wrote down her name, followed by her number and e-mail address. I couldn't believe it.

"I don't go out much, though," she warned, as an afterthought. Maybe she was already having regrets.

When I returned home, I pulled the scrap of paper out of my pocket and placed it in front of the computer. Since she was supposedly a model, I wanted to look for a picture of her online. She had only given me her first name, Dalene, but fortunately her e-mail address contained her last name, Kurtis. I typed the words into Google, and nearly a hundred thousand results came up.

I had just number-closed the reigning Playmate of the Year.

I sat in front of my phone and stared at Dalene Kurtis's number every evening. But I couldn't bring myself to call. I wasn't confident and good-looking enough for this perfect specimen of femininity. I mean, what was I going to do on a date with her?

I remember meeting a girl named Elisa for lunch at a summer job when I was seventeen. I was so nervous, I couldn't stop my hands from shaking or my voice from quavering. And the more awkward I became, the more uncomfortable she grew. By the time the food arrived, I was too self-conscious even to chew in front of her. It was a disaster—and it wasn't even a date. So what hope did I have with the Playmate of the Year?

There's a word for this: unworthiness. I felt unworthy.

So I waited three days to call, then put it off to the next day, and then decided that calling on the weekend would sound like I had no social life, so I figured I'd call her Monday. And by then a week had passed. She'd probably forgotten about me. We'd talked for ten minutes at most, and it had been, admittedly, a soft close. I was just some weird, interesting guy she had met in an office-supply store. There was no reason this woman, who could have her choice of any man in the hemisphere, would want to see me again. So I never called.

I was my own worst enemy.

My first legitimate success didn't come until a week later. Extramask, from Mystery's workshop, dropped by my apartment in Santa Monica unannounced one Monday night. He was very excited because he'd just made a fascinating discovery.

"I always used to think jerking off and pain came hand in hand," he announced the moment I opened the door.

Extramask looked different. He had dyed and spiked his hair, pierced his ears, and bought rings, a necklace, and punk-looking clothes. He actually appeared cool. In his hands, he had an Anthony Robbins book, *Unlimited Power*. We were clearly on the same path.

"What are you talking about?" I asked.

"Okay. I beat off, clean up, and then pull up my underwear, right?" He walked inside and flopped onto my couch.

"I guess I follow."

"But what I didn't realize until yesterday was that I still had cum in my penis hole. So I'd go to sleep, and the cum would harden in my cockhole. Then I'd wake up in the morning and take a pee, but the pee wouldn't come out." He put a hand on his crotch and wiggled it to illustrate the point. "So I'd push harder and a chunk of jizz would fly out of my penis and smash into the wall or some shit."

"You're out of your mind." I'd never experienced or even heard of this phenomenon before. Extramask was the strange result of a repressive Catholic education and an expansive stand-up comedy ambition. I could never tell if he was experiencing serious angst or just trying to entertain me.

"It hurt like a fucker," he continued. "It was so bad I even stopped jerking off for a week because I didn't want the pain. But last night I squeezed that shit right out of the cock as soon as I blew a load."

"And now you can masturbate to your heart's delight?"

"Exactly," he said. "And I haven't even told you the good news yet."

"I thought that was the good news."

He raised his voice excitedly. "I can pee beside people now! It's all about confidence. So the stuff I learned in Mystery's workshop isn't just for chicks after all."

"That's true."

"It's used for pissing too."

We drove to La Salsa for burritos. At a table nearby, there was an attractive but slightly unkempt woman stuffing receipts into a bulging Filofax. She had long, curly brown hair; tiny ferret-like features; and immense breasts that refused to be concealed by her sweatshirt. I broke the three-second rule by about two hundred and fifty seconds but finally worked up the confidence to approach. I didn't want to look like an AFC in front of Extramask.

"I've been taking a course in handwriting analysis," I told her. "While we're waiting for our food, do you mind if I practice on you?" She looked at me skeptically but then decided I was harmless and consented. I handed her my notebook and told her to write a sentence in it.

"Interesting," I said. "Your handwriting has no slant. It's straight up and down, which means you're a self-sufficient person and don't always need to be around others to feel good about yourself."

I made sure she was nodding in agreement, and then continued. This was a technique I had learned from a book on cold-reading that exposed the truisms and body-language-reading techniques that sham psychics use. "You don't have a great organizational system to your writing, which means that in general you're not good at keeping yourself organized and sticking to a schedule."

With each tidbit I told her, she leaned in closer and nodded her head more vigorously. She had a wonderful smile and was easy to talk to. She'd just finished a comedy class nearby, she said, and offered to read me some jokes from her notebook.

"I open my shows with this one," she said after my analysis. "I just got back from the gym, and boy are my arms tired." This was her opener. She had it on a cheat sheet that she kept in her back pocket. Picking up women, I realized, was a lot like stand-up comedy or any other performing art. They each require openers, routines, and a memorable close, plus the ability to make it all seem new every time.

She said she was spending the night at a hotel in town, so I offered to drive her there. As I dropped her off, I pointed to my cheek and said, "Kiss goodbye." She kissed my cheek. Extramask kicked the back of my seat excitedly. Then I told her I had work to do, but that I'd call her for a drink when I was finished.

"Do you want to go out clubbing with Vision and me tonight?" Extramask asked after she left.

"No, I should see this girl."

"Well, I'm going out anyway," he said. "But when I get home afterward, I'm going to pound out the biggest batch thinking about that girl who just kissed you."

Before leaving to pick her up that night, I printed one of the forbidden Ross Jeffries patterns Grimble had e-mailed me. I was determined to make up for my recent mistake.

We went to a dive bar and had a drink. She had changed into a frayed blue sweater and saggy jeans, which made her look somewhat dumpy. Nonetheless, I was happy to be on an actual date with a woman I'd picked up. Finally, I had an opportunity to experiment with more advanced material.

"There's a way," I told her, "that you can bring better focus to your goals and your life." I felt like Grimble in T.G.I. Friday's.

"What is that?" she asked.

"It's a visualization exercise. A friend taught it to me. I don't know it by heart, but I can read it to you."

She wanted to hear it.

"Good." I said, as I unfolded the paper with the pattern on it and began reading. "Maybe you can try to remember the last time you felt happiness or pleasure. As you feel it now, where in your body are those feelings?"

She pointed to the center of her chest.

"And how good does it feel on a scale of one to ten?"

"Seven."

"Okay, now, as you focus in on this feeling right here, notice that you can begin now to see a color flowing from this feeling. What is the color?"

"Purple," she said, as she closed her eyes.

"Good, now what would it be like if you were to allow all of the purple flowing from that spot to fill with warmth and intensity? With each breath that you take, I want you to let the purple grow just a little bit brighter."

Her body began to relax; I could see her chest rise and fall through her sweater. I was doing it now—evoking a response like the one I had seen Ross Jeffries get at California Pizza Kitchen. I continued with the pattern more confidently, making the color expand and grow in intensity inside her as she fell deeper into trance. I imagined Twotimer mouthing the word *evil* in the background.

"How do you feel now, on a scale of one to ten?" I asked.

"Ten," she said. I guess it was working.

Then I had her shrink the color to a tiny purple pea that contained all the power and intensity of the pleasure she was feeling. I had her place the imaginary pea in my hand. Then I traced my hand all along her body, first at a distance and then lightly touching it.

"Notice how my touch can become like a paintbrush, transferring those colors and that sensation up your wrist, through your arm, and to the surface of the face."

To be honest, I had no idea whether this was turning her on or not. She was listening, and she seemed to be enjoying it, but she didn't start sucking my fingers like the girl in Grimble's story. In fact, I felt not only a little stupid but also lecherous using the pretext of hypnosis to touch her. I didn't like these forbidden patterns. I got into the game to learn confidence, not mind control.

I stopped and asked her what she thought. "It felt good," she said, and smiled her ferret smile. I couldn't tell whether she was humoring me or not, but I suppose most people are willing to try something new if it seems safe.

I folded the piece of paper, put it in my pocket, and drove her back to her hotel. But instead of dropping her off, I pulled into the garage. We climbed out of the car, and I followed her to her room. I was too scared to say a word, afraid she might suddenly turn on me and ask, "Why are you following me?" But she seemed to have mentally consented: It looked like we were going to have sex tonight. I couldn't believe my luck. After all that practice, I was finally getting results.

According to Mystery, it takes roughly seven hours for a woman to be comfortably led from meet to sex. These seven hours can take place all in one night, or over several days: approaching and talking for an hour; speaking on the phone for an hour; meeting for drinks for two hours; talking on the phone for another hour; and then, on the next meeting, hanging out for two more hours before going to bed together.

Waiting seven hours or more is what Mystery calls solid game. But occasionally a woman either goes out with the specific intention of taking someone home, or can be easily led to sex in a shorter amount of time. Mystery calls this fool's mate. I had spent an hour with this girl at La Salsa and two hours at the bar. I was about to experience my first fool's mate.

She put the card key in the lock of her room and the green light appeared—an omen, I felt, of the night of passion to come. She opened the door, and I followed her inside. She sat on the foot of the bed—just like in the movies—and pulled her shoes off. First the left, then the right. She was wearing white socks, which I found rather endearing. She flexed the toes of both feet upward, then curled them downward as she collapsed backward on the bed.

I took a step toward her, prepared to fall on her in an embrace. But suddenly the foulest smell I have ever encountered assailed my nostrils. It literally pushed me backward. It was the exact rancid-cheese smell that homeless alcoholics on New York subways have. The kind that clears the whole subway car. No matter how many steps back I took, the intensity of the smell did not diminish. It filled the entire room, every available space.

I looked at her, lying back on the bed, wanton, oblivious. It was her feet. Her feet were stinking up the room.

I had to get out of there.

Chapter

Every night after outings and dates, seduction students and masters post online breakdowns of their experiences, called field reports. The goals in chronicling their adventures vary: Some want help with mistakes, others want to share new techniques, and a few just want to brag.

The day after my misadventure with the stinky-footed comedian, Extramask posted a field report online. Evidently, he had experienced his own odd adventure that same night. His time in the seduction community had already paid off. He could pee in toilet stalls next to other men; he could masturbate without hurting himself; and, now, at the age of twenty-six, he had finally lost his virginity— though not in the way he expected.

MSN GROUP: Mystery's Lounge
SUBJECT: Field Report—I F-closed a Girl!
AUTHOR: Extramask

I, Extramask, have f-closed a girl for the first time—eliminating my virgin status (even though I didn't blow my load). I'll start from the beginning.

On Monday, I went sarging with Vision. We went to this three-story club that had about fifteen rooms, each with its own individual bar. We pretty much sarged the whole place.

Overall for the night, I was feeling out of state, and it was reflecting in my sarges. I wasn't doing as well as I normally do. I went to the second floor and found Vision. Some girl was wearing his scarf and he couldn't find her. So I was talking to him about this, and then this girl, WideFace, walked by and gave me serious eye contact. She said, "Hi."

Chicks rarely open me, so I said to her, "Hey, have you seen this guy's scarf?"

I just talked bullshit. I knew it didn't matter what I said by the look on her wide face.

After scarf chat:

WIDEFACE: You are very beautiful (*spoken with a quarter Chinese/quarter English/quarter rich Chinese/quarter Zsa Zsa Gabor accent*).

EXTRAMASK: Is that right? Thank you.

WIDEFACE: So, when did you get here?

As you can see, the conversation was lame, but I knew it was on. I knew if I ran my routines on her, then I'd be going backward in the sarge.

We talked about standard shit: work, what we did tonight, brief history of ourselves, etc. We moved to a location that wasn't as crowded. (She requested the move.) As we stood around chatting, Vision gave me social proof by occasionally walking by and patting me on the shoulder and shit like that. It all helps.

WIDEFACE: What are you looking for tonight?

EXTRAMASK: *(Thinking:* Holy Shit—I think I'm gonna get laid.)

EXTRAMASK: I don't know. What are you looking for?

WIDEFACE: I am looking for excitement.

EXTRAMASK: Yeah, I'm looking for excitement too *(spoken casually)*.

WIDEFACE: Would you like to come with my friend and me?

EXTRAMASK: Sure, just let me tell my friend that I'm leaving.

WIDEFACE: Okay, I'll be right over there.

I went looking for Vision.

EXTRAMASK: Dude, it's on. I think I'm gonna get laid.

VISION: Go, go. Get out of here.

Okay, so I found WideFace and her Serbian girlfriend. We held hands and walked to her car, which was about fifteen minutes away. I was pretty nervous about the whole thing. Then I calmed the fuck down.

What did we talk about on the way to her car? Nothing much, just lame talk about how cold it was, what I do, and other general chitchat. It was so implied that this was a one-night stand. We got to her car and her friend said she wanted pizza. Here's what Exttamask was thinking:

EXTRAMASK: FUCK PIZZA, YOU STUPID BITCH. I'M A VIRGIN AND I WANT TO GET LAID FUCKING NOW. GO TAKE YOUR OWN CAR AND GET YOUR OWN FUCKING PIZZA.

Conveniently, WideFace forgot about the pizza and accidentally passed by the store. We dropped her friend off, and I moved to the front seat. I was looking at her mediocre body thinking, "This is cool. I'm gonna get to touch all of that shit."

Again, the conversation in the car wasn't about sex. It was lame chitchat. When I previously asked her what course she was taking in school, she said, "I'll tell you later." I asked her this about three times, and each time she got more frustrated with me. I didn't care. It fucking bugged me that this was the only thing she wouldn't tell me.

She ended up telling me when we were alone in her car. It was some lamo general college course. It was a nonissue. Then she told me her "dream job." I asked her about it, even though I didn't give a shit.

WIDEFACE: I want to be a police officer.
EXTRAMASK: (*Thinking*: You'd be the worst police officer on the planet.
   You'll never be a police officer.)
EXTRAMASK: Why don't you pursue your dream?
WIDEFACE: Blah blah blah, drivel drivel drivel, jibber jabber jibber jabber.

We got to her place. She lives in the penthouse of this big fucking condo with a roommate. Her room was fucking huge. She had this big Trinitron TV in it. She told me to choose some music, because she was going to the bathroom for a bit. I put on some hip-hop channel since she said she liked that kind of stuff earlier.

She came out in her pajamas. I pinned her to the ground and bukkaked her! No, seriously . . . she came out in her pajamas and told me I could go use the bathroom. I didn't need to, but I figured this was part of the whole sex thing, so I went. Remember, brothers, I was virgin at this point—I had no clue. So I went to the bathroom and just kinda stood there. I didn't wash my cock or anything. The only thing I thought of doing was calling Vision to tell him that I was about to fuck her, but I thought that would be lame.

So, I was thinking, should I walk out totally nude? Hmm. I decided to walk out the same way I went in, which was wearing everything except for my dress shirt. Imagine if I walked out totally nude with a throbbing boner just pulsating in the air?

The lights were off. She was lying on the bed. I walked over and started making out with her. I kissed her neck and her earlobes. Then she took my hand and put it on her right boobie! So I started rubbing that while kissing her. Then somehow I started rubbing her vagina (over her pajamas). She was moaning and shit. So I took my pants off, but I left my underwear on.

I bet you fuckers didn't think I'd be writing this much detail, did you?

So I was kissing her and rubbing her poon down. This was pretty hard. I couldn't concentrate on kissing her and rubbing her at the same time. I was doing my best though.

She started rubbing my cock, and it felt pretty cool. LOL.

> **WIDEFACE:** Fuck me Extramask.
> **EXTRAMASK:** Okay.

So I tore off my fucking underwear. I kneeled there on her bed with my rock-hard boner pulsating, throbbing—you know it.

> **WIDEFACE:** Put on a condom. I have one.
> **EXTRAMASK:** I have one of my own.

I didn't want to use hers. I was freaked out about it for some reason, like she would sabotage it or some shit.

> **WIDEFACE:** What brand?
> **EXTRAMASK:** Sheik.

Again, I was a virgin at this point and I didn't know how to properly put a condom on.

> **EXTRAMASK:** Put the condom on, it turns me on.
> **WIDEFACE:** Okay.

She couldn't get the condom on, so she went to get hers. As she went and got hers, I ended up getting my own on. Then I fucked her!

I fucked her and fucked her and fucked her and fucked her and fucked her and fucked her.

About fifteen minutes into the whole thing, I was thinking, "This fucking sucks. This is fucking sex? I hate this. I want to leave." I legitimately wanted to leave. I was thinking, "I busted my fucking balls for months for this?"

I was sitting there pumping this girl missionary style for fifteen minutes getting no feeling.

She was all moaning and shit, and I'm just pumping away like a tool. So I decided to move her around and try some positions—just like in the porno movies!

I had her on top. I had always fantasized about this. So she was on top of me and I was thinking, "Holy shit, this fucking hurts. My cock is gonna fucking snap off."

After about two minutes, I changed positions because it hurt so much. I got her into doggy-style position. I thought this would be interesting. So I had her from behind and I was trying to find the slot, but I couldn't. I was sitting there fishing around her ass and upper legs looking for the entry. It was horrible, just like the sex. I couldn't find the hole. She started to whine because of the long delay. I was thinking, "You're whining? Calm it down, China—seriously." I wasn't getting any arousal out of this deal.

I got it in for two strokes, then it popped out. Then she started whining again. So I switched positions and, for some reason, I went to the her-on-top position again. Dumb move, Extramask. I feared my cock would break right the fuck off. After about four minutes of that, we went back to missionary, and I slammed her hard.

Hey, she said she wanted it.

I was saying shit like:

"You like that?"

"Say my name!"

"You like it hard?"

Keep in mind, I was bored out of my mind during this whole experience. I was pretty disappointed. LOL.

After thirty minutes:

WIDEFACE: Change your condom.

EXTRAMASK: *(Thinking:* I guess this is something you do after a half hour of sex. But overall I was pissed that the sex wasn't over.)

So I took my condom off and opened a new one.

WIDEFACE: What are you doing?

EXTRAMASK: I'm putting on another condom.

WIDEFACE: Why?

EXTRAMASK: I thought you said you wanted me to?

WIDEFACE: No.

I didn't care. I was happy with that.

So then we just lay naked together and kissed a bit. She wanted to cuddle. I didn't really want to, but I did.

This was a mistake on my part. After sex I should have ripped my condom off, sat on her bed, and jerked off until completion. I should have wacked my load all over the place, her face, and her Trinitron TV set.

WIDEFACE: Lie down and rest for five minutes. Then I will call a cab.

EXTRAMASK: What? Five minutes? Why are you trying to rush me out of here?

WIDEFACE: No, I didn't mean it like that. It's just good to rest after sex for five minutes.

EXTRAMASK: What's with the five minutes thing?

WIDEFACE: No. Just relax.

EXTRAMASK: But why five minutes?

Five minutes later she called a cab. She was on hold with the cab company, and she started getting all frustrated because she had to wait, which was annoying. So I got ready to leave.

I chatted with her a bit more. She said she noticed in the club that I had lots of energy. She liked it.

WIDEFACE: What are you going to do now? (*It was 3:30* A.M.)

EXTRAMASK: I'm going to another club to hook up with my friends. (*I got even more energetic. I jumped around.*)

She totally didn't like that I said I was going out again. And I really wasn't. I just lied to her. I did it because I was pissed that she was trying to get rid of me so quickly. Overall, I wanted to leave her place immediately—I just wanted to leave on my terms.

So the cab arrived and I left her place. We kissed about three times before my exit.

I didn't get her number because:

1. I didn't want to fuck her again.

2. It was obvious this was a one-night stand.

Just to be on the safe side, I made sure I wrote down her exact address when I left—just in case I forgot shit there. I would rather have it than not have it.

So that's it. I stuck my junk in a chick. I lost my virginity. The sex was horrible. I felt a bit dirty and used after the act.

Overall, I don't feel any different compared to when I was a virgin. However, I believe this will help me subconsciously in my sarges. I mean, I've had sex now. I know this. So from here on in, any girl I chat with, I'll be even more like, "Who gives a fuck? I don't *need* what you got."

—Extramask

How do you kiss a girl?

The distance between you and her is just three inches. It's not a long stretch, by any standard. You barely even have to move your body to bridge the gap. Yet it is the most difficult three inches a man has to move in his life. It is the moment when the male must concede all the privileges that are his birthright; put his pride, ego, esteem, and hard work aside; and just hope—hope that she doesn't deflect it with her cheek or, even worse, the let's-just-be-friends speech.

As I went out every night training to wing Mystery's workshop, I soon developed a routine that worked—at least to a point. Rejection wasn't an option. I knew how to open a group, respond to most contingencies, and leave with a phone number and a plan to meet again.

Every time I went home, I reviewed the events of the night, looking for parts of a sarge that I could have done better. If the approach didn't work, I thought of ways to improve it—angles of advance, backturns, takeaways, time constraints. If I didn't get the phone number, I didn't blame it on the girl for being cold or bitchy, as so many other sargers did. I blamed myself and analyzed every word, gesture, and reaction until I pinpointed a tactical error.

I had read in a book called *Introducing NLP* that there is no such thing as failure, only learning lessons. I wanted the learning lessons to take place in my head, so that in the field I was flawless. I would have to prove myself to Mystery's students, just as Sin had proven himself to me. And one public failure would discredit everything. The students would post reviews saying that Style was an imposter, a joke.

But there was still one problem I couldn't work through. Though an opener, a neg, and a demonstration of higher value were enough to get anyone's phone number, I had no idea what to do next. No one had taught me.

I mean, I technically knew the words of the Mystery kiss-close: "Would you like to kiss me?" But I was too petrified to actually speak them. After spending so much time bonding with a girl (whether for a half hour in a club or several hours at our next meeting), I was too scared to break the rapport and trust I had built. Unless she gave me a clear indication that she was sexually interested in me, I felt like trying to kiss her would disappoint her and she'd think I was just like all the other guys.

It was such stupid AFC thinking. There was still a nice guy lurking in my head that I had to get rid of. But, unfortunately, there wasn't going to be time to do so before Belgrade.

I'd learned several sleights of hand, a principle of magic called equivoque, the fundamentals of rune reading, and a way to make lit cigarettes disappear. It had been the most productive plane trip of my life. And now Mystery and I were in Belgrade at probably the worst time of the year. Ice and slush lay heavy on the street as Marko drove us to his apartment in a silver 1987 Mercedes that had a habit of stalling every time he put it into second gear.

Mystery, hair unwashed and held back in a greasy ponytail, fumbled through his backpack in the front seat, producing a long black overcoat. He had cut away the bottom third of the coat and sewn in its place black fabric covered with stars. It looked like something one would wear to a Renaissance fair. Mystery had made his ring himself, too, painting an eyeball on the plastic surface. He was clearly more of a geek than I had ever been. His greatest illusion was transforming himself into a good-looking player every night he went out.

"You're going to have to shave your head," he said as he looked at me.

"No thanks. What if I have a strange-shaped skull, or weird marks on my head like my dad?"

"Look at you. You're wearing glasses because your vision sucks. You have a hat on to cover a huge bald spot. You're ghostly white. And you look like you haven't seen the inside of a gym since grade school. You're doing well because you're smart and you're a fast learner. But looks count too. You're Style, so start being Style. Just snap: shave your head, get Lasik, join a gym."

He was a very persuasive geek.

He turned to Marko: "Is there a barbershop around here?"

Unfortunately, there was. Marko pulled in front of a small building, and we walked inside to find an elderly Serbian man presiding over an empty shop. Mystery sat me in a chair, told Marko to instruct the barber to remove my tumbleweeds, and then supervised the procedure to make sure the barber shaved down to the skull.

"Balding is not a choice, but bald *is* a choice," he said. "If anyone asks you why your head is shaved, tell them, 'I used to have it down past my ass, but then I realized I was covering up my best feature.'" He laughed. "Or you could say, 'Well, most Greco-Roman wrestlers shave their heads." I made a mental note to add both replies to my cheat sheet.

When the barber finished, I looked in the mirror and saw a chemo patient staring back at me.

"It looks good," Mystery said. "Let's see if there's a tanning salon around here. We'll have you looking like a thug in no time."

"Okay. But I'm not getting Lasik in Serbia."

My first thought once I was shaven-headed and tan was: What took me so long? I looked much better. I had transformed from a 5 to a 6.5 on the attractiveness scale. This trip was turning out to be a good idea.

Marko looked as if he could use a makeover himself. A big-boned six foot three, he was much stockier than most Serbians, with an olive complexion and the out-of-proportion head of a Peanuts character. He wore an overcoat that was one size too big, a thick gray Brooks Brothers sweater with flecks of white, and a cream-colored turtleneck that actually made him look like a turtle.

Marko had been unable to live his dream of being a high-society socialite after graduating from college in America, so he'd moved to a smaller pond, Serbia, where his father was a well-known artist.

He drove us to his one-bedroom apartment, which contained only a cot and a twin bed. Because there was no sleeping bag or even a couch, we agreed to take turns sharing the larger bed.

While Mystery showered, Marko pulled me aside.

"What are you doing with this guy?"

"What do you mean?"

"I mean, he's totally superficial. We went to the Latin School of Chicago. We went to Vassar College. This is not the kind of guy who can fit in at these places. He's not one of us."

"I know. I know. You're right. But trust me, this guy will change your life."

"Well," Marko said. "We'll see. I met a girl last month who's different than all the rest, and I want to do it right. So make sure Mystery doesn't ruin it with all his pickup tricks and embarrass me."

Marko hadn't dated a single woman since he'd moved to Belgrade. But a few months ago, through friend of his, he'd met a girl named Goca, and he was sure she was the one. He took her out on dates, bought her flowers, treated her to dinner, and dropped her off at home afterward, like a perfect gentleman.

"Have you slept with her yet?" I asked him.

"No. I haven't even kissed her."

"Dude, you're behaving like a total AFC. One day a guy is going to walk up to her in a club, say, 'Do you think magic spells work?' and take her home. She wants an adventure. She wants to have sex. All girls do."

"Well," Marko said, "she's different from all those girls. People have more class here than they do in L.A."

The PUAs have a name for this: They call it one-itis. It's a disease AFCs get: They become obsessed with a girl they're neither dating nor sleeping with, and then start acting so needy and nervous around her that they end up driving her away. The cure for one-itis, PUAs like to say, is to go out and have sex with a dozen other girls—and then see if this flower is still so special.

Chapter

The prop bag I wore to the Belgrade workshop was black, Armani, and the size of a hardcover novel, with a single shoulder strap so that it could be slung artfully across my torso. With so many magic tricks, gimmicks, and other tools of the trade necessary to use in the field, it was impossible to fit everything into just four pants pockets. So nearly every PUA in the game had a prop bag. The contents of mine were as follows:

1 PACK OF GUM, WRIGLEY'S BIG RED

No matter how good your game is, you're not going to get a kiss-close if your breath reeks.

1 PACK OF CONDOMS, TROJAN, LUBRICATED

Necessary not only in case you have sex but also for the psychological boost of knowing you're prepared to.

1 PENCIL, 1 PEN

For writing down phone numbers, taking notes, performing magic tricks, and analyzing handwriting.

1 PIECE OF DRYER LINT

For the lint opener: Walk up to a woman, stop, wordlessly remove lint (hidden in the palm of your hand) from her clothing, ask, "How long has that been there?," then hand her the piece of lint.

1 ENVELOPE OF PRESELECTED PHOTOS

For Mystery's photo routine.

1 DIGITAL CAMERA

For Mystery's digital photo routine: First take a photo of yourself and a girl smiling, then another one striking a serious pose, and, finally, one kissing (on the cheek or lips). Afterward, look through the photos with her. At the final photo, say, "We make a good couple, don't we?" If she agrees, you're in.

1 BOX OF TIC TACS

For the Tic Tac routine: Put two Tic Tacs in your hand. Eat one very slowly. Then feed the second one to her. If she accepts it, say, "There's something I forgot to tell you. I'm an Indian giver. I want my Tic Tac back." Then kiss her.

LIP BALM, COVERUP, EYELINER, BLOTTING PAPER

Optional male makeup.

CHEAT SHEET, THREE PAGES

One page of favorite routines for quick reference. Two pages of new routines and lines to practice.

1 SET OF WOODEN RUNES IN CLOTH BAG

For rune readings.

1 NOTEBOOK

For phone numbers, notes, magic tricks, and Ross Jeffries's crappy sketch artist opener, in which you very seriously draw a portrait of a girl, tell her "your beauty has inspired me to high art," and then show her a stick figure with a title like, "Semipretty Girl in Coffee Shop, 2005."

1 KRYPTOLIGHT NECKLACE

Glow in the dark necklace, for peacocking.

2 SETS OF FAKE EAR AND LIP PIERCINGS

Optional body adornment.

1 SMALL DIGITAL RECORDER

For surreptitiously recording sarges to play back and critique afterward.

2 SPARE CHEAP NECKLACES, 2 SPARE THUMB RINGS

To give to girls as gifts after a number-close. Ask, "You're not a thief, are you?" Then slowly remove your necklace or thumb ring, put it on her, kiss her, and say, "This is still mine. It's something to remember me by. I want it back next time I see you." After she leaves, replace your jewelry with a spare from the bag.

1 SMALL BLACKLIGHT

For pointing out lint and dandruff on girls' clothing—a neg.

4 SAMPLE BOTTLES OF DIFFERENT COLOGNES

For smelling good. And for the cologne opener: Spritz a different cologne on each wrist. Then have a girl smell your wrists and choose a favorite. Afterward, mark her choice on the appropriate wrist with a pen. Tally the results at the end of the night to find the best scent for yourself.

VARIOUS MAGIC TRICKS

For bending forks, making cigarettes vanish, and levitating beer bottles.

Yes, I was bringing out the big guns. It was an important night—my first workshop as a wing—and I needed to prove myself.

I had neglected to tell Mystery that his standard workshop fee was half the annual salary of the average Serbian, so most of our students were from out of the country. They met us at Ben Akiba, a lounge just off the central square in Belgrade. Exoticoption was an American who had taken a train from Florence, Italy, where he was going to school; Jerry was a ski instructor from Munich, Germany; and Sasha was a local who had been studying in Austria.

Strangers size each other up in seconds: a hundred tiny details, from dress to body language, combine to create a first impression. Mystery's task—and now mine—was to fine-tune the details and make PUAs out of these three.

Exoticoption was cool; in fact, he was trying so hard to be cool that it was going to work against him. Jerry had a great sense of humor but came off on first impression as boring. And Sasha—well, he was badly in need of repair. Just socializing was going to be a challenge for him: He looked like a big baby goose with acne.

This time, it was my turn to go around the table and ask, "What's your score?" and "What are your sticking points?" and "How many girls would you like to sleep with?"

Exoticoption, who was twenty, had been with two women. "I have the balls to approach, and I did pull some hons in the past," he began, draping his left arm casually over a neighboring seat. "But my sticking point is the at-tract phase. Even when I get vibes that I attract them, I still don't close."

Jerry, who was thirty-three, had been with three women. "I can work coffee shops and most other low-noise environments, but I'm uncomfort-able in clubs."

And Sasha, who was twenty-two, said he had been with one woman, though we suspected he was exaggerating by one. "I'm into the game be-cause it's like Dungeons and Dragons. When I learn a neg or a routine, it's like getting a new spell or a staff that I can't wait to use."

One by one, they placed their fears, and their voice recorders, on the table. My job was to get them into the game. I needed to get what was in my head into theirs.

The teaching portion of the workshop was easy. All I had to do was keep Mystery on track—he loved the sound of his own voice—and give them material. The challenge was going to be the demonstration part.

As we spoke, we sent the boys on missions to various tables. We had them open sets,[4] watched their body language and the responses of the women, then gave them feedback:

"You were leaning into the set, which showed neediness. Stand up straight and rock on your back foot as if you might walk away at any moment."

"You were making them uncomfortable by hovering over them for so long. You should have sat down and given yourself a time constraint. Say, 'I can only stay for a couple minutes because I have to rejoin my friends soon.' This way they won't worry that you're going to sit there all night."

---

[4] A set is a group of people in a public place. A two-set is a group of two people; a three-set is three people, and so on.

Sasha did the worst. He fumbled through his openers, stared at his shoes, and lacked even a modicum of confidence. Girls listened to him only out of politeness.

At the bar, I noticed a delicate black-haired girl and a tall blonde with a perfect fake tan, deep dimples, and hair in Bo Derek braids. They radiated energy and confidence. This was not going to be an easy set. So I gave it to Sasha.

"Go into the two-set over there," I instructed him. It didn't take any game to send guys into sets. "Tell them you're showing some friends from America around and want suggestions for good clubs to take them to."

It was a crash-and-burn mission. Sasha meekly approached them from behind and tried several times to get them to notice him. Once he had their attention, it was a struggle for him to keep it. Like many guys, he didn't communicate with energy. All those years of insecurity and social ostracism had chased his spirit and joy of life deep within his body. Whenever he opened his mouth, there was no need for anyone to strain to make out his faint mumblings. The message was clear: "I was built to be ignored."

"Go in," Mystery said to me as he watched Sasha flounder with the Bo Derek blonde.

"What?"

"Go in. Help him out. Show the boys how it's done."

Fear seizes hold in your chest first. It clamps gently to the top of the heart, like a vice made of rubber. Then you really feel it. Your stomach churns. Your throat closes. And you swallow, desperately trying to avoid the dryness and hoping that when you open your mouth, a confident, clear voice will emerge. Even after all my training, I was terrified.

Women, by and large, are much more perceptive than men. They can instantly spot insincerity and bullshit. So a great pickup artist must either be congruent with his material—and really believe it—or be a great actor. Anyone talking to a woman while simultaneously worrying about what she thinks of him is going to fail. Anyone caught thinking about getting into a woman's pants before she starts thinking about what's in his pants is going to fail. And most men fall into this category. Sasha does. I do. We can't help it: It's our nature.

Mystery calls it dynamic social homeostasis. We are constantly buffeted about by, on one hand, our overwhelming desire to have sex with a girl and, on the other, the need to protect ourselves when approaching. The reason this fear exists, he says, is because we are wired evolutionarily for a tribal existence, where everyone in the community knows when a man is rejected by a woman. He is then ostracized and his genes, as Mystery puts it, are unapologetically weeded out of existence.

As I approached, I tried to push the fear out of my chest and rationally assess the situation. Sasha's problem was his body position. Both women were facing the bar, and he had approached from behind. So they had to turn around to respond.

But if they wanted to get rid of him, all they had to do was to turn back toward the bar, and he'd be shut out.

I looked back. Mystery and the other two students were watching me as I approached. I had to work the angles right. So I came in from the left side of the bar, next to the black-haired girl—the obstacle, as Mystery would say.

"Hi," I rasped. I cleared my throat. "I'm the friend Sasha was telling you about. So what clubs did you recommend?"

I could sense a silent sigh of relief from all parties that someone had come in to make things less awkward.

"Well, Reka is a fun place for dinner," the black-haired girl said. "And along the waterfront there are some great boats, like Lukas, Kruz, and Exil. Underground and Ra are fun too, though they're not the kinds of places I go to."

"Hey, as long as we're talking, I want to get your opinion on something." I was on familiar ground now. "Do you think spells work?"

By now, I was getting used to telling the spells opener—a story about a friend who fell in love with a woman after she surreptitiously cast an attraction spell on him. So while my mouth moved, my brain thought strategy. I needed to reposition myself next to the Bo Derek blonde. Yes, I was going to steal my student's girl. It's not like he had a chance with her anyway.

When I finished, I said, "I'm asking because I never believed in that stuff before, but I had an amazing experience recently. Here"—I addressed the blonde—"let me show you something."

I maneuvered myself around to the other side of their stools, so that I was next to my target.

Now that I was one-on-one with her, I still needed to sit down; otherwise she'd eventually get uncomfortable with me lurking over her. However, there weren't any open stools, so I'd have to improvise.

"Give me your hands," I told her, "and stand up for a moment."

As soon as she stood, I wheeled around behind her and slid into her seat. Now I was finally in the set, and she was lurking awkwardly on the outside. This was the science of approaching perfectly executed, like a good game of chess.

"I just stole your chair," I laughed.

She smiled and punched me teasingly in the arm. The game had begun.

"I'm just kidding," I continued. "Stay close. We'll try an ESP experiment. But I can only stay for a moment. Then you can have your chair back."

Even though I guessed her number wrong (it was ten), she still enjoyed the process. As we talked afterward, Mystery walked up to Sasha and told him to keep the black-haired woman occupied so she wouldn't pull my target away.

Marko was right: The girls were gorgeous here. They were also extremely bright and, much to my relief, spoke better English than I did. I truly enjoyed listening to this girl; she was captivating, well-read, and had an MBA.

When it came time to leave, I told her it would be great to see her again before I left. She pulled a pen from her purse and gave me her phone number. I could feel Mystery's approval—and the students' acceptance. Style was the real deal.

Sasha was still talking to the black-haired girl, so I whispered in his ear, "Tell her we have to go, and ask for her e-mail." He did and, lo and behold, she gave it to him.

We rejoined the group and left the café. Sasha was a new man. Flushed with excitement, he skipped down the street like a little boy, singing in Serbian. He was being, in his own awkward way, himself. He'd never gotten a girl's e-mail address before.

"I'm so happy," Sasha raved. "This is probably the best day of my life."

As anyone who regularly reads newspapers or true-crime books knows, a significant percentage of violent crime, from kidnappings to shooting sprees, is the result of the frustrated sexual impulses and desires of males. By socializing guys like Sasha, Mystery and I were making the world a safer place.

Mystery threw his arm around my neck and pulled my face into his wizard's overcoat. "You've done me proud," he said. "It's not just about getting the girl. It's about the students seeing it happen and believing it can be done."

It was then that I realized the downside to this whole venture. A gulf was opening between men and women in my mind. I was beginning to see women solely as measuring instruments to give me feedback on how I was progressing as a pickup artist. They were my crash-test dummies, identifiable only by hair colors and numbers—a blonde 7, a brunette 10. Even when I was having a deep conversation, learning about a woman's dreams and point of view, in my mind I was just ticking off a box in my routine marked rapport. In bonding with men, I was developing an unhealthy attitude toward the opposite sex. And the most troubling thing about this new mindset was that it seemed to be making me more successful with women.

Marko drove us to Ra, an Egyptian-themed nightclub guarded by two concrete statues of Anubis. Inside, it was nearly empty. There were just security guards, bartenders, and a group of nine noisy Serbians clustered on barstools around a small circular table.

We were about to leave when Mystery spied, among the group of Serbians, a lone girl. She was young and slender with long black hair and a red dress that showed off a set of perfectly tapered legs. It was an impossible set: She was surrounded by stocky guys with crewcuts. These were men who had clearly been in the military during the war, men who had probably killed before, maybe even with their bare hands. And Mystery was going in.

The pickup artist is the exception to the rule.

"Here," he told me. "Clasp your hands together. And when I say so, act as if you can't open them."

He pretended, through the art of illusion, to seal my hands together. I pretended to be amazed.

The commotion attracted the attention of the bouncers in the club, who asked him to try the feat with their hammy fists. Instead, Mystery performed his watch-stopping illusion for them. Soon, the club manager was giving him free drinks and the table of Serbians had halted their conversation and were gawking at him, including his target.

"If you can make a girl envy you," Mystery told the students, "you can make a girl sleep with you."

Two principles were at work. First, he was generating social proof by earning the attention and approval of the club staff. And, second, he was pawning—in other words, he was using one group to work his way into another, less approachable group nearby.

For his coup de grace, Mystery told the club manager he would levitate a beer bottle. He approached the table of Serbians, asked to borrow an empty bottle, and made it float in the air in front of him for a few seconds. Now he was in his target's group. He performed a few illusions for the guys and ignored the girl for the requisite five minutes. Then he relented, started talking to her, and isolated her to a couch nearby. He had pawned the entire club just to meet her.

Since the girl spoke only a little English, Mystery used Marko as a translator. It was a longer set than usual, because Mystery needed to convince her that he wasn't practicing any form of witchcraft or black magic. "Everything you've seen tonight is fake," Mystery finally told her, via Marko. "I created all this to meet you. It's a social illusion."

The two finally exchanged numbers—"I can't promise you anything other than good conversation," Mystery instructed Marko to tell her—and we collected the students to leave the club. However, on our way out, an AMOG from the table blocked Mystery's path. He wore a tight black T-shirt, exposing a physique that made Mystery's doughy body look feminine in comparison.

"So you like Natalija, magic man?" he asked.

"Natalija? We're going to be seeing each other. Is that okay with you?"

"She's my girlfriend," the AMOG said. "I want you to stay away from her."

"That's up to her," Mystery replied, taking a step closer to the AMOG. Mystery wasn't backing down. He was an idiot.

I looked at the AMOG's hands and wondered how many Croatian necks he had snapped in his day.

The AMOG lifted his waistband, exposing the black handle of a pistol. "So, magic man, can you bend this?" This was no invitation; it was a threat.

Marko turned to me, panicked. "He's going to get us killed," he said. "Most of the guys at these clubs are ex-soldiers and mobsters. Killing someone over a girl is nothing for them."

Mystery waved his hand over the AMOG's forehead. "You saw me move that beer bottle without touching it," he said. "It weighs eight hundred grams. Now imagine what I could do to one tiny brain cell in your head." He snapped his fingers to indicate the pop of a brain cell.

The AMOG looked Mystery in the eyes to see if he was bluffing. Mystery held his eye contact. One second passed. Two seconds. Three. Four. Five. It was killing me. Eight. Nine. Ten. The AMOG lowered his shirt back over the gun.

Mystery had the advantage here: No one in Belgrade had ever seen a magician perform live before. They'd only been exposed to magic on television. So when Mystery disproved in an instant the belief that magic was just camera tricks, an older belief replaced it: the superstition that just maybe magic is real.

The AMOG stood there, silent, as Mystery walked out unscathed.

Some girls are different.

That's what Marko thought. After everything he'd seen during Mystery's workshop, he was in no way a convert. Goca wasn't like those other girls, he insisted. She came from a good family, she was well-educated, and she had morals, unlike that materialistic club trash.

I'd heard it all before from dozens of guys. And I'd heard just as many intelligent women say, "That wouldn't work on me," when I told them about the community. Yet minutes or hours later, I'd see them exchanging phone numbers—or saliva—with one of the boys. The smarter a girl is, the better it works. Party girls with attention deficit disorder generally don't stick around to hear the routines. A more perceptive, worldly, or educated girl will listen and think, and soon find herself ensnared.

And so it was that Mystery and I found ourselves out on New Year's Eve with Marko and his one-itis, Goca. Marko put on a gray suit, picked her up at 8:00 P.M., ran around and opened the car door for her, and handed her a dozen roses. She seemed like a bright, successful, well-bred girl. She was short with long chestnut hair, gentle eyes, and a smile that arced just a little wider on one side. Marko was right: She did look like the marrying kind.

The restaurant was traditional Serbian fare, heavy on the red peppers and red meat. And the music was pure anarchy: Four brass bands wandered the rooms, blaring a cacophony of overlapping parade marches. I watched Marko and Goca carefully all night, curious to see if this whole dating thing worked.

They sat next to each other awkwardly. Their interaction consisted only of the necessary formalities of the evening: the menu, the service, the atmosphere. "Ha ha, wasn't that funny when the waiter gave you my steak?" The tension was killing me.

It wasn't as if Marko was a natural. In grade school he'd never been that popular, largely on account of being foreign, having the nickname Pumpkinhead, and joining the Young Republican Club. By the time he had graduated, he was probably worse off than I was: At least I'd kissed a girl.

In college, he began taking steps toward relations with the opposite sex. He purchased a leather jacket, invented an aristocratic background for himself, put Terence Trent D'Arby braids in his hair, and bought his first Mercedes-Benz. The effort earned him some attention, even a few female friends. But it wasn't until junior year that he was finally comfortable enough around women to start removing clothes with them, thanks largely to a younger student he befriended: Dustin. The taste of those first small victories was so sweet that Marko stayed in college for three more years, basking in his hard-won popularity.

One of Marko's more peculiar habits is that he takes hour-long showers every night. No one has ever come up with a plausible explanation of what he does in there, because nothing makes sense—masturbating, for example, doesn't take *that* long. If you have any theories, please send them to: ManOfStyle@gmail.com.

After watching Marko sit uselessly next to Goca for an hour, I cracked. I grabbed my camera and ran Mystery's digital photo routine on the pair. I asked them to take a picture smiling, then one looking serious, and finally a passionate picture—kissing, for example. Marko stuck his neck out toward her, chicken-like, and pecked.

"No, a real kiss," I insisted, concluding the routine as the two would-be betrothed's lips bumped in what was the clumsiest first kiss I had ever witnessed.

After dinner, Mystery and I terrorized the two-room restaurant, dancing with the old men, performing magic tricks for the waiters, and flirting indiscriminately with the married women. When we returned to the table glowing, Goca's eyes met mine; for a moment they seemed to sparkle, as if searching for something in my gaze. I could swear it was an IOI.

That night, I was awoken by a warm body climbing under the covers. It was my turn to share the bed with Marko, but this wasn't Marko. It was a woman's body. I felt a pair of warm hands caress my newly shaven skull.

"Goca?!"

"Shh," she said, and sucked my upper lip into her mouth.

I pulled loose. "But what about Marko?"

"He's in the shower," she said.

"Did you and he . . . ?"

"No," she said with a contempt that surprised me.

Goca and I had hit it off that night; so had Goca and Mystery. She had made a pass at Mystery earlier, and he'd pretended not to notice. But it was harder not to notice her when she was in my bed, in my nostrils, in my mouth. Sure, she'd had a few drinks, but alcohol has never caused anyone to do something they didn't want to. It only enables them to do what they've always wanted but repressed. And right now it looked like Goca wanted to be with a man who possessed all six of the five characteristics of an alpha male.

Logically, it's easy to say that it's wrong to sleep with a girl your friend is pursuing. But when her body is pressed against yours so submissively, and you can smell the conditioner in her hair (strawberry), and that storm cloud of passion created by her desire has begun gathering around the two of you, try saying no. It's just too . . . right there.

I ran my hands beneath her hair and slowly dragged my fingernails upward along her scalp. A shiver of pleasure ran through her body. Our lips met, our tongues met, our chests met.

I couldn't do this. "I can't do this."

"Why?"

"Because of Marko."

"Marko?" she asked, as if she'd never heard the name before. "He's sweet, but he's just a friend."

"Listen," I said. "You should go. Marko will probably be out of the shower soon."

Fifty minutes later, Marko was out of the shower. I heard him and Goca arguing in Serbian in the hallway. A door slammed.

Marko walked wearily into the room and collapsed onto his half of the bed.

"Well?" I asked. He was never one to show much emotion.

"Well, I want to take Mystery's next workshop."

I couldn't bridge the fucking gap. There she was, my Bo Derek blonde with an MBA, sitting next to me on a couch at a café. Her thigh was grazing mine. She was playing with her hair. And I was wussing out.

The great Style, the apprentice PUA whose magnetism was so strong that it made Marko look like an AFC to his own true love, was still too scared to kiss a girl.

I had great opening game, but no follow through. I should have taken care of the problem before Belgrade. But it was too late. I was blowing it. I was scared of rejection, and of feeling uncomfortable afterward.

Mystery, in the meantime, was getting along just fine with Natalija, who was thirteen years his junior. They had nothing in common, not even a language. But there they were, sitting together. His legs were crossed and he was leaning back, letting her work to get his attention. She was leaning into him, with her hand on his knee.

I walked my date back to her house after coffee. Her parents weren't even home. All I had to say was, "Can I use the bathroom?," and I could have been upstairs. But my mouth wouldn't speak the words. Countless successful approaches had helped reduce my fear of social rejection and made me seem like a promising pickup artist to others, but inside I knew I was just an approach artist. To become a PUA, there was a far-more-devastating mental obstacle I still needed to overcome: my fear of sexual rejection.

In the course of my seduction research, I'd read *Madame Bovary* by Gustave Flaubert. And I remembered how much work and persistence it had taken the aristocratic dandy Rodolphe Boulanger de la Huchette to get just a kiss from the unhappily married Madame Bovary. But once he persuaded her to submit the first time, it was all over. She was obsessed.

One of the tragedies of modern life is that women as a whole do not hold a lot of power in society, despite all the advances made in the last century. Sexual choice, however, is one of the only areas where women are indisputably in control. It's not until they've made a choice, and submitted to it, that the relationship is inverted—and the man is generally back in a position of power over her. Perhaps that is why women, to the frustration of men everywhere, are so cautious about saying yes.

In order to excel at anything, there are always hurdles, obstacles, or challenges one must get past. It's what bodybuilders call the pain period. Those who push themselves, and are willing to face pain, exhaustion, humiliation, rejection, or worse, are the ones who become champions. The rest are left on the sidelines. To seduce a woman successfully, to inspire her to take the risk of saying yes, I would have to grow some balls and be willing to leave my comfort zone. And it was by watching Mystery win over Natalija that I learned this lesson.

"I just got a haircut," he told her as they left the cafe. "I have itchy hairs on my neck. I want to take a bath. Come wash me."

Natalija, predictably, said that seemed like a bad idea. "Oh, okay," he told her. "I gotta get going, because I need to take a bath. Bye."

As he walked away, her face fell. The thought that she might never see him again seemed to flash through her mind. This is what Mystery calls a false takeaway. He wasn't really leaving; he was just letting her think he was.

Mystery took five steps—counting as he went—then turned around and said, "I've been living in a shitty apartment for the past week. I'm going to get a hotel room right there and take a bath." He pointed to the Hotel Moskva down the street. "You can come with me or just get an e-mail from me in two weeks when I return to Canada."

Natalija hesitated for a moment, then followed him.

And that's when I realized the mistake I'd been making my whole life: to get a woman, you have to be willing to risk losing her.

When I returned to the house, Marko was packing.

"I'm in shock," Marko said. "I tried to do everything right. Goca was my last hope for all women."

"So what are you doing? Moving to a monastery?"

"No, I'm driving to Moldova."

"Moldova?"

"Yeah, all the most beautiful girls in Eastern Europe come from Moldova."

"Where's that?"

"It's a tiny country that used to be part of Russia. Everything there is dirt-cheap. Just being American is enough to get you laid."

My philosophy is, if someone wants to go to a country I've never heard of and there's not a bloody revolution in progress there, I'm game. Life is short and the world is large.

Between us, we didn't know a single person who'd ever been to Moldova or could even pronounce the name of its capital, Chisinau. So I couldn't think of a better reason to drive there. I like the idea of filling in a colored shape on a map with real fact, feeling, and experience. And traveling with Mystery would be a perk. We would have adventures everywhere, the kind I'd always dreamed about.

Chapter

There are few moments in life as shot through with potential as that of having a car, a full tank of gas, a map of an entire continent spread out in front of you, and the best pickup artist in the world in your back seat. You feel like you can go anywhere you want. What are borders, after all, but checkpoints letting you know that you've reached a new stage in your adventure?

Well, all this may be true most of the time, but let's say you're working at Rand McNally, finishing the latest edition of your map of Eastern Europe. And let's say there's a tiny country bordering Moldova—perhaps a renegade Communist state—but no other government recognizes this country diplomatically, or in pretty much any other way. What do you do? Do you include the country on your map or not?

A magician, a faux aristocrat, and I were driving across Eastern Europe when we quite accidentally discovered the answer to this question. It had been a fruitless drive so far. Mystery was slumped in the back seat underneath a blanket, unable to conjure his way out of a fever. Oblivious to the dramatic snowy Romanian landscape that passed by each day, he covered his eyes with his hat and complained. Every so often, he'd leap to alertness and disgorge the contents of his mind. And every time the contents of his mind were another map of sorts.

"My plan is to tour North America and promote my shows in strip clubs," he said. "I just need to come up with a good illusion for strippers. You can be my assistant, Style. Imagine that: You and I touring strip clubs and taking all the girls to the show the next day."

After a couple of uneventful days in Chisinau—where the only beautiful women we saw were on magazine covers and billboards—we figured, "Why stop there?" Odessa was so close. Maybe the adventure we were seeking lay further ahead.

So we left Chisinau on a cold, snowy Friday and drove northeast to the Ukrainian border. The snow-blanketed roads out of the city were recognizable only by icy tire tracks stretching into the horizon. The vista looked like a scene from an epic Russian romance, with tree branches coated with crystallized ice and frozen wine groves running along the hilly landscape. The car reeked of Marlboro smoke and McDonald's grease; every time it stalled, it became trickier to restart.

But soon, all of that was the least of our problems. What looked on the map like a forty-five-minute trip to Odessa ended up taking nearly ten hours.

The first sign that something unusual was afoot came when we reached a bridge over the Dniester River and found a military checkpoint complete with several army and police vehicles, camouflaged bunkers on either side of the road, and an immense tank with its barrel pointing in the direction of oncoming traffic. We stopped in a line of ten cars, but a military officer directed us around the queue and waved us through the checkpoint. Why? We will never know.

Mystery wrapped himself tighter in his blanket in the back seat. "I have a version of the knife-through-body illusion I want to do. Style, do you think you can dress up as a clown and heckle me from the audience? Then I'm going to bring you onstage and push you into a chair. I'll play 'Stuck In the Middle With You' from *Reservoir Dogs* while I put my fist straight through your stomach. I'll wiggle my fingers when they reach the other side. Then I'm going to lift you straight up, out of the chair, impaled on my arm. I need you to do that with me."

The second sign that something was not quite right came when we stopped by a gas station to stock up on snack food. When we offered them Moldovan lei, they told us they didn't accept that currency. We paid in American dollars, and they gave us change in what they said were rubles. When we examined the coins, we noticed that each had a large hammer-and-sickle on the back. Even stranger, they had been minted in 2000: nine years after the Soviet Union had supposedly collapsed.

Mystery pulled his hat down to just above his mouth, which was moving with the grandiosity of a carnival barker. "Ladies and gentlemen," he announced from the back seat as Marko worked to start the car, "he levitated over the Niagara Falls, he jumped off the Space Needle and survived . . . presenting superstar daredevil illusionist, Mystery!"

I guess his fever was breaking.

As we drove on, Marko and I began to see Lenin statues and communist posters through the car window. One billboard depicted a tiny sliver of land with a Russian flag on its left and, on its right, a red and green flag with a slogan beneath. Marko, who spoke some Russian, translated it as a call for a Soviet Re-union. Where were we?

"Imagine this: Mystery the superhero." Mystery wiped his nose with a shredded tissue. "There could be a Saturday morning cartoon, a comic book, an action figure, and a feature film."

Suddenly, a police officer (or at least someone dressed as one) stepped into the road in front of the car with a radar detector in his hand. We'd been driving ninety kilometers an hour, he told us—ten over the speed limit. After twenty minutes and a two-dollar bribe, he let us go. We slowed down to seventy-five, but a few minutes later we were pulled over again. This officer also told us we were speeding. Though there were no signs, he claimed that the speed limit had changed half a kilometer back.

Ten minutes and two dollars later, we were on our way again, crawling at fifty-five just to be safe. In short order, we were pulled over and told we were driving *below* the minimum speed. Wherever we were, it was the most corrupt country on earth.

"I need to figure out my ninety-minute show. It will begin with a raven flying into the audience and landing on the stage. Then—boom—it will turn into me."

When we finally reached the border, two armed soldiers asked for our papers. We showed our Moldovan visas, and that was when we were told that we were no longer in Moldova. They showed us the local passport—an old Soviet document—and yelled something in Russian. Marko translated: They wanted us to drive back to the military checkpoint on the bridge we had crossed three police bribes ago and obtain the proper documents.

"I will dress as Mystery, with platform boots and the works. I won't wear suits anymore. I will be goth and club cool. I will tell the audience how as a child I'd play with my brother in the attic and dream about being a magician. Then I'll go back in time and turn into a child."

When Marko told a border guard there was no way we were going back to the bridge, he pulled out his gun and pointed it at Marko. Then he asked for cigarettes.

"Where are we?" Marko asked.

With pride, the guard answered back, "Pridnestrovskaia."

If you've never have heard of Pridnestrovskaia (or Trans-Dniester, in English), don't worry: neither had we. Trans-Dniester is neither recognized diplomatically nor mentioned in any of the guide books or maps we carried.

But when there's a border guard pressing a pistol into your waist, well, suddenly Pridnestrovskaia seems very real.

"I'll do a science experiment where I transport a lab technician over the Internet. Then the finale will be a bank heist and cage vanish. So I need a male kid, a raven, you, someone to play the lab technician, and a couple people to be bank guards."

Marko gave the guard his entire pack of Marlboros and started arguing with him. The guard didn't lower his gun once. After a long exchange, Marko yelled something and thrust out his hands as if asking to be handcuffed. Instead, the guard turned and disappeared into an office. When Marko returned to the car, I asked him what he had said.

"I said, 'Listen, just arrest me. I'm not going back.'"

This was getting ugly.

Mystery thrust his head over the seat partition. "Imagine this. A poster of just my hands, with black nails, and the word *Mystery* at the bottom. How amazing would that be?"

For the first time, I lost it with him. "Dude, this is not the fucking time. Open your eyes."

"Don't tell me what to do," he snapped.

"We're about to get thrown in jail. No one wants to hear your shit right now. Does nothing exist except for you and your fucking magic show?"

"Listen, if you want to go at it, I'll go at it," he thundered. "I'll take you down right now. Just step out of the fucking car, and I'll deal with you."

The guy was a foot taller than me, and the border crossing was full of armed soldiers. There was no way I was going to tangle with him. But I was angry enough to consider it. Mystery had been dead weight this entire trip. Maybe Marko was right: Mystery wasn't one of us. He hadn't gone to the Latin School of Chicago.

I took a deep breath and stared straight ahead, trying to contain my rage. The guy was a narcissist. He was a flower that bloomed with attention—be it positive or negative—and wilted when ignored. Peacock theory wasn't just to attract girls. It existed first and foremost to attract attention. Even picking a fight with me was just another plea for attention, because I'd been ignoring him for the past hundred miles.

When I glanced at the rearview mirror and saw him pouting in the back seat with his hat pulled over his eyes, however, I actually began to feel bad for him. "I didn't mean to snap at you," I told him.

"I don't like it when someone tells me what to do. My dad used to tell me what to do. And I hate him."

"Well, I'm not your dad," I said.

"Thank God for that. He ruined my life and my mom's life." He pulled his hat up. Tears lay over his eyes like contact lenses, unable to escape on their own. "I used to lie in bed at night, thinking of ways to kill my dad. When I got really depressed, I'd imagine going to his bedroom with a shovel, smashing his head in, and then killing myself."

He paused and wiped his eyes with the back of his gloved hand. "When I think of my father, I think of violence," he continued. "I remember seeing him punch people in the face when I was really young. When we had to kill our dog, he took a gun out and blew its head off right in front of me."

The border guard emerged from an office and motioned for Marko to step out of the car. They spoke for several minutes; then Marko handed him several bills. While we waited to see if our bribe of forty dollars—the equivalent of one month's salary in Trans-Dniester—was effective, Mystery opened up to me.

His father, he said, was an alcoholic German immigrant who verbally and physically abused him. His brother, who was fourteen years older than him, was gay. And his mother blamed herself for smothering his brother with love to make up for her husband's abuse. So, to compensate, she was emotionally distant from Mystery. When he was still a virgin at age twenty-one, he began to worry that maybe he was gay. So, in a bout of depression, he began formulating what would become the Mystery Method, dedicating his life to pursuing the love he never received from his parents.

It took two more bribes of equivalent sum, spread between two other officials, to grease our way across the border. It was never enough for them just to accept the money. Each separate bribe took an hour and a half of discussion. Maybe they were just trying to give Mystery and I more time to get to know each other.

When we finally reached Odessa, we asked our hotel clerk about Trans-Dniester. She explained that the country was the result of a civil war in Moldova, triggered largely by former communist apparatchiks, military elite, and black berets who wanted to return to the glory days of the Soviet Union. It was a place with no rules—the Wild West of the Eastern bloc and a country few foreigners dared to visit.

When Marko told her about our experience at the border, she said, "You shouldn't have asked them to arrest you."

"Why?" he asked.

"Because they don't have jails there."

"Then what would they have done with us?"

She shaped her fingers into a gun, pointed them at Marko, and said, "Pow."

When we returned to Belgrade, driving some five hundred miles out of our way to avoid Trans-Dniester, Marko's voice mail was full. Mystery's seventeen-year-old, Natalija, had left a dozen messages. Mystery phoned her back, but the call was intercepted by her mother, who cussed him out for hijacking her daughter's mind.

Natalija continued to call Marko after Mystery and I flew home, asking when he was going to come back for her. Finally, Marko put her out of her misery. "He was a wizard," he told her. "He put a spell on you. Get some help and stop calling me."

Marko e-mailed me constantly in the months that followed, asking for a password to Mystery's Lounge. He had tasted the forbidden fruit and wanted more. But I never let him in. At the time, I thought it was because I wanted to keep my new identity separate from my past. But the truth was that, despite all my rationalizations, I still felt embarrassed by what I was doing and the degree to which I was letting it consume my life.

MSN GROUP: Mystery's Lounge
SUBJECT: Sticking Point
AUTHOR: Style

I'm hitting a sticking point, which I hope you all can help me get past.

Mystery and I just returned from Belgrade, where I met a beautiful, intelligent girl who probably would have been my Serbian girlfriend if it weren't for my sticking point: I'm having huge trouble kiss-closing.

For some reason, transitioning to the kiss is a big hurdle for me. I'll feel the window open, and then instantly I start thinking all the "what-ifs"—"what if she rejects me," "what if I ruin the rapport we have," "what about that thing she said about her ex-boyfriend." Then either I build up too much anxiety and go for it tentatively (and fuck up), or the window closes and I miss it and get pissed at myself.

So what's my problem? I'm so damn close to that golden ring of PUA-dom, but this little sticking point is holding me back.

—Style

MSN GROUP: Mystery's Lounge
SUBJECT: Re: Sticking Point
AUTHOR: Nightlight9

What if she rejects me? Yeah, and what if a meteor hits your house.

You asked how to tell if she's ready. The way to tell is the other three-second rule. It works 100 percent of the time. While sitting close, just let the conversation trail off. Look her in the eye while you pause the conversation. If she looks back for a count of three seconds, she wants to kiss. The uncomfortableness you may experience is my favorite thing in the whole world—sexual tension.

—Nightlight9

MSN GROUP: Mystery's Lounge
SUBJECT: Re: Sticking Point
AUTHOR: Maddash

I've never had a woman over to my place in a one-on-one situation who I didn't at least kiss-close. Here is my routine:

1. I have her come over to pick me up and only let her stay a couple minutes. This is because it's a lot easier to get a woman back to your house at the end of the night if you've already had her over and nothing has happened.

2. At the end of the date, I invite her back to my place and pour drinks.

3. If she notices my guitar (it is prominently placed), I pick it up and play her a song.

4. We play with my puppy.

5. I show her the rooftop.

6. I bring her back to the apartment and show her the Winamp music program on my computer while I sit her down on my lap. While she's playing with the visualizations in Winamp, I kiss her on the cheek.

7. She either turns and kisses me on the lips, or she continues playing with Winamp. If she hesitates, I just show her more things on the computer and then kiss her on the cheek again. She wants to be directed and ordered about. That is what almost all women want.

8. You can figure out the rest.

—Maddash

MSN GROUP: Mystery's Lounge
SUBJECT: Re: Sticking Point
AUTHOR: Grimble

One of my favorite closing routines is massage. When we're back at my place, I tell her I'm sore from playing basketball and need a back massage. But during the massage, I constantly tell her she's doing it all wrong. Finally, I pretend to be exasperated and insist on showing her how it's done. While massaging her back, I tell her she carries a lot of tension in her legs and that I give amazing leg massages to my friends. I start to massage her through her pants, but then tell her to remove them because they're getting in the way. If you act as if you are the authority, she will not question you.

At first, I stick to the legs. But, slowly, I work my way up to her buttocks. When she begins to get turned on, I begin rubbing her through her panties until she's dripping wet. At this point, I usually just unbutton my pants, put on a condom, and start fucking her without kissing or actual foreplay.

This technique is not for the timid.

—Grimble

MSN GROUP: Mystery's Lounge
SUBJECT: Re: Sticking Point
AUTHOR: Mystery

Want to know how I solve this problem? I don't just say, "I don't care what she thinks." I actually don't care what she thinks. When I was younger, this was such a big deal for me. But now, whether I get it or not, I am still the guy who goes for it.

It helps to just think of the girl as practice. If the fear is still there inside, just say, "Phase-shift! I'm now a caveman! I'm no longer Style. Let's see if she hates me. If so, fuck it. I don't give a shit."

Look back to girls you didn't caveman, and they aren't in your life. So fucking what? Do you care that she has a fond memory of some guy she met six months ago while a caveman is now fucking her? You gotta actually hit on her sometime. Say, "Stick your tongue out." Then suck on it. If she slaps you, good! That story would rock.

Maddash talked about how using well-chosen props are a great way to focus a girl's attention on something else so she doesn't resist overt sexual moves. I agree. Say, "Look at the puppet show over there," while you play with her tits. If she hesitates about the tit-play, simply point to the puppets and laugh, "Look at the puppets. Look, they are funny puppets." Then play with the tits again.

—Mystery

MSN GROUP: Mystery's Lounge
SUBJECT: Sticking Point Solved
AUTHOR: Style

Thanks for all your help. I think I finally figured out a solution. The answer came to me out of the blue a week ago, and I've field-tested it successfully nearly every night since.

It struck me when I was sitting at the Standard with an Irish girl who told me she married young, recently divorced, and now craves adventure. When I started to get IOIs, I thought about your posts. I realized that if I lunged for her, she'd be startled and reject me. So I decided to take baby steps in the direction of kissing while doing something like Mystery's puppet show and talking logically the whole time. Lo and behold, it worked, as it has ever since. Problem solved.

Here's what I did—the evolution phase-shift routine:

1. I leaned in and told her she smelled good. I asked her what perfume she was wearing, and then discussed how animals always sniff each other before they mate and how we're evolutionarily wired to feel aroused when someone smells us.

2. Then I discussed how lions bite each other's mane during sex, and how pulling the back of the hair is another evolutionary trigger. As I spoke, I ran my hand up the back of her neck, grabbed a fistful of hair at the roots, and pulled it firmly downward.

3. She didn't seem upset, so I pushed further. I told her how the most sensitive parts of the body are usually hidden from contact with the air—for example, where the arm bends on the other side of the elbow. Then I took her arm, bent it a little, and erotically bit the crease on the opposite side of the elbow. She said it gave her the chills.

4. Afterward, I said, "But do you know what the best thing in the world is? A bite . . . right . . . here." I pointed to the side of my neck. Then I said, "Bite my neck," as if I expected her to do it. She refused to at first, so I turned away calmly to punish her. I waited a few seconds, then turned back and repeated, "Bite me right here." This time, she did. It was cat-string theory in action.

5. However, her bite was lame. So I told her, "That's not how you bite. Come here." Then I swept her hair aside, gave her a good bite on the neck, and instructed her to try again. This time, she did a great job.

6. I smiled approvingly and said, very slowly, "Not bad." Then we finally kissed.

We had a few more drinks, then I took her to my place. After a brief tour, I did a Maddash move and had her sit on my lap while showing her a video on the computer. I massaged and kissed the back of her neck until she turned around and started making out with me. Then she asked if she could lie on the floor for a second. I laid down next to her and—guess what happened—she passed out. Cold!

I took off her shoes, threw a blanket over her, put a pillow under her head, and climbed into my own warm bed.

So the joke was on me, but at least I get it now. All it took was one night, really, to get to the other side of this.

I am ready, finally, for the next step.

—Style

DISARM
THE OBSTACLES

A MAN HAS ONLY ONE ESCAPE FROM HIS OLD SELF: TO SEE A DIFFERENT SELF IN THE MIRROR OF SOME WOMAN'S EYES.

—CLARE BOOTHE LUCE

The Women

Choose a dojo.

There's Ross Jeffries and the school of Speed Seduction, where sublim-inal language patterns are used to get a girl aroused.

Or Mystery and the Mystery Method, in which social dynamics are ma-nipulated to snag the most desirable woman in a club.

Or David DeAngelo and Double Your Dating, in which he advocates keeping the upper hand over a woman through a combination of humor and arrogance that he calls cocky funny.

Or Gunwitch and Gunwitch Method, in which the only thing students have to do is project animalistic sexuality and escalate physical contact un-til the woman stops them. His crude motto: "Make the ho say no."

Or there's David X, David Shade, Rick H., Major Mark, and Juggler—the newest guru on the scene, who appeared online one day claiming he could pick up women better and faster than any other PUA simply by read-ing his grocery list. Then there are the inner-circle teachers, like Steve P. and Rasputin, who reveal their techniques only to those they deem worthy.

Yes, there are plenty of mentors to choose from, each with his own methods and disciples, each operating under the belief that his way is *the* way. And the giants do battle constantly—threatening, name-calling, de-bunking, competing.

My goal was to feed from all of them. I've never been a true believer in anything. I've preferred to combine teaching and wisdom from various sources, find what applies to me, and discard what doesn't. The problem is that when you drink from the source of knowledge, there is a price. And that price is faith. Every single teacher wanted to know that he was the best, that his students were the most loyal, that the competition wasn't getting laid. Yet every single student wanted to absorb as much information from as many different experts as possible. It is a crisis that's specific not to the com-munity but to humanity: Power is retained by attracting loyalty, and subju-gation is guaranteed by giving it.

Though I had enjoyed teaching in Belgrade, I didn't want followers. I wanted more teachers. I still had a lot to learn. I found that out when Extramask took me to a party at the Argyle hotel on Sunset Boulevard.

I was dressed rakishly, in a black sport coat with long tails and a thin, shaped goatee. Extramask, meanwhile, looked better and more outrageous every time I saw him. He now had his hair cut and spiked into a four-inch Mohawk.

At the party, I noticed a pair of heavily peacocked twins sitting on a couch like alabaster statues. Though their well-coiffed hair and matching vintage dresses earned them admiring looks; the girls didn't say a word to anyone all night.

"Who are they?" I asked Extramask, who was talking to a petite moon-faced woman who seemed very interested in him.

"They're the Porcelain TwinZ," he said. "They do a goth burlesque show together. They're also well-known groupies. They double-team band members. I've masturbated with my penis about them and blown spectacular loads."

"Introduce me."

"But I don't know them."

"That's okay. Introduce me anyway."

Extramask walked over to the girls and said, "This is Style."

I shook their hands. They were surprisingly warm hands for girls who looked half-dead. "We were just having a discussion about magic spells," I told them. "Do you think spells work?"

I knew this was the perfect opener, because it was clear they believed in spells—for some reason, most girls who strip or exploit their sexuality for a living do. Then I transitioned into the ESP number-guessing routine.

"Entertain us more," they cooed.

I'd gone too far. "I'm not a dancing monkey," I replied. "Besides, I'm a guy. I need a few minutes to recharge."

It was a line of Mystery's. They laughed on cue.

"I'll tell you what," I continued. "I've shown you a couple of cool things. Why don't you teach me something?"

They had nothing to show me. "I'm going to talk to some friends," I said. "I'll give you five minutes to think of something."

I wandered away and struck up a conversation with a cherubic little punk named Sandy. Ten minutes later, the twins approached.

"We have something to teach you," they said proudly.

I actually hadn't planned on speaking to them again. I didn't think they'd come up with anything. But they stood there and taught me sign language for five minutes. IOI.

We sat down together and made small talk, which the PUAs refer to somewhat disparagingly as fluffing. The girls were easy to tell apart, because one had chicken pox scars and the other had punctures in her face from removed piercings. They were visiting from Portland and planned to fly home the next day. They told me about their striptease show, in which they dance on stage and simulate lovemaking together.

As we talked, I realized they were just ordinary, insecure girls. That's why they'd been so quiet. Most men make the mistake of believing that an attractive woman who doesn't talk to or acknowledge him is a bitch. Most of the time, however, she's just as shy or insecure as the less attractive women he's ignoring—if not more so. What made the Porcelain TwinZ different is that they tried to compensate for their inner plainness with outer ostentatiousness. They were just sweet girls looking for a friend. And now they had found one. As we exchanged numbers, I felt the window open. But I didn't know whether to go for one twin, the other, or both. I couldn't figure out how to separate them, but I didn't know what to do to seduce them simultaneously either. I was stuck. So I excused myself and went to find to Sandy.

As I talked to Sandy, she sidled up next to me. She seemed like she wanted something. So I did the evolution phase-shift routine, then pulled her into the bathroom to make out. I wasn't really attracted to her: I was just excited about being able to kiss women so easily now. I was already abusing my newfound power.

When we emerged ten minutes later, the twins had left the party. I'd blown it once again by taking the easy road rather than pushing myself.

I returned to my apartment in Santa Monica empty-handed. Mystery was sleeping on my couch, and I told him about my failure with the twins. Fortunately, the next day, I received a message from the girls. Their plane had been canceled, and they were stuck at a Holiday Inn near the airport. I still had a chance to redeem myself.

"What should I do?" I asked Mystery.

"Invite yourself over. Just say, 'I'm coming over.' Don't give them any option."

"Then what happens when I'm in this weird hotel room with them? How do I get things started?"

"Do what I always do. As soon as you walk in, run yourself a bath. Then take off your clothes, get in, call the girls in to scrub your back, and take it from there."

"Wow. That's pretty ballsy."

"Trust me," he said.

So I called the twins back that evening and told them I was coming over.

"We're just lying around in our sweats watching TV," they warned.

"No problem. I haven't showered or shaved in a month."

"Are you serious?"

"No."

So far, everything was going according to plan.

I drove to the hotel, rehearsing every move in my head. When I walked in the room, they were lying on adjacent twin beds watching *The Simpsons*.

"I need to take a bath," I told them. "My hot water at home isn't working."

It's not lying; it's flirting.

I made small talk while the water ran. Then I turned the corner into the bathroom, left the door open, removed my clothes, and sat in the tub.

I didn't want to use soap yet because it would make the water dirty. So I sat naked in the bathwater, trying to work up the courage to call the girls in. I felt so vulnerable sitting there pale, skinny, and naked. I needed to take Mystery's advice and start working out.

A minute passed. Five minutes. Ten minutes. I could still hear *The Simpsons* coming from the television set. The girls probably thought I'd drowned by now.

I had to make my move. I'd hate myself if I didn't. I sat there for five more minutes until I finally mustered the courage to stutter: "Hey, can you help me sort of wash my back?"

One of the girls yelled something. There was silence, then whispering. I sat in the bathtub panicking, worried they wouldn't even come in. What a dumb thing to say. The only thing more embarrassing would be if they actually came in, and saw me sitting here naked with my dick floating in the water like a lily pad. I thought of my favorite line from *Ulysses,* when sexually frustrated Leopold Bloom imagines his impotent manhood in the bathwater and calls it the limp father of thousands. And then I thought, if I was smart enough to quote James Joyce in the bathtub, why did I feel so stupid in front of these girls?

Finally, one of the twins walked in. I'd been hoping for both, but beggars can't be choosers. With my back to her, I reached over the side of the tub and handed her the soap. I was too embarrassed to look her in the eye.

I straightened my spine so it didn't look too much like the dinosaur scales of Mr. Burns. She rubbed the soap in circles on my back. It wasn't erotic; it was workmanlike. I knew she wasn't turned on, and I hoped she wasn't grossed out. Then she wet the washcloth in the tub and wiped the soap off. My back was clean.

Now what?

I thought sex was supposed to automatically happen afterward. But she was just kneeling there, doing nothing. Mystery hadn't told me what I was supposed to do after asking them to wash my back. He'd just said take it from there, so I assumed the whole sex thing would unfold organically. He hadn't told me how to transition from a back scrub to a hand job. And I had no idea. The last woman to wash my back was my mother, and that was when I was small enough to fit in the sink.

But now was the moment. Something had to be done.

"Um, thanks," I told her.

She walked out of the bathroom.

Fuck. I'd blown it.

I finished washing myself, climbed out of the bath, toweled off, and put my dirty clothes back on. I sat on the edge of the bed of the girl who had washed me, and we talked. I decided to try to adapt the evolution phase-shift pattern to a party of two. I told the other sister to sit on the bed with us.

"Mmm, you both smell so good," I began. Then I pulled their hair simultaneously and bit each of their necks. But it still didn't get anything going. They were both so passive.

I had them each massage one of my hands as we talked about their stage show. I wasn't going to leave the room a failure.

"You know what's funny," one of them said. "We get all our physicality out on stage. We never even touch or hug each other in real life. We're probably more distant than most sisters."

I left their hotel room, a failure. On the way home, I stopped by Extramask's house, where he lived with his parents.

"I'm confused," I told him. "I thought you said they did guys together."

"Yeah, but I was just joking around. I thought you knew."

Extramask had a date the following week with the moon-faced woman he'd been talking to at the party. Women with wide faces seemed to find him attractive.

We lay on the floor for two hours talking about the game and our progress. Since adolescence, whenever I'd had the opportunity to make a wish (on an eyelash, a digital clock at 11:11, an ever-increasing number of birthday candles), thrown in with the usual pleas for world peace and personal happiness, I'd ask for the ability to attract any woman I wanted. I had fantasized about an incredible seductive energy entering my body like a lightning bolt, suddenly making me irresistible. But instead it was coming in a slow drizzle and I was running around underneath it with a bucket, working to catch each drop.

In life, people tend to wait for good things to come to them. And by waiting, they miss out. Usually, what you wish for doesn't fall in your lap; it falls somewhere nearby, and you have to recognize it, stand up, and put in the time and work it takes to get to it. This isn't because the universe is cruel. It's because the universe is smart. It has its own cat-string theory and knows we don't appreciate things that fall into our laps.

I would have to pick up my bucket and work.

So I took Mystery's advice. I got Lasik surgery, shedding my nerdy glasses once and for all. I paid to get my teeth laser-whitened. And I joined a gym and took up surfing, which was not only a cardiovascular workout but also a way to get tan. In some respects, surfing reminded me of sarging. Some days you go out and catch every wave and think you're a champ; other days you don't get one good wave and you think you suck. But no matter what, every day you go out and you learn and you improve. And that's what keeps you coming back.

However, I hadn't joined the community just to get a makeover. I needed to complete my mental transformation, which I knew would be much more difficult. Before Belgrade, I had taught myself the words, skills, and body language of a man of charisma and quality. Now I needed to develop the confidence, self-worth, and inner game to back it up. Otherwise, I'd just be a fake, and women would sense it instantly.

I had two months off until my next workshop with Mystery in Miami, and I wanted to really blow away the students there. I aimed to outdo Mystery's sarge at Club Ra in Belgrade. So I gave myself an assignment: to meet, in the next few months, every top PUA there was. I planned to make myself a seducing machine, designed from pieces of all the best PUAs. And now that I had some status in the community as Mystery's new wing, it would be easy to meet them.

Chapter

The first person I wanted to learn from was Juggler. His posts intrigued me. He advised AFCs to overcome their shyness by trying to talk a homeless person into giving them a quarter or by calling people randomly out of the phone book to ask for movie recommendations. He told others to challenge themselves and intentionally make pickups more difficult by saying they worked as trash collectors and drove '86 Impalas. He was an original. And he had just announced his first workshop. The cost: free.

One of the reasons Juggler rose so quickly in the community, besides his competitive pricing, was his writing: His posts had flair. They weren't the disorganized scrawlings of a high school senior in perpetual conflict with his testosterone. So when I called Juggler to discuss using a field report of his in the book, he asked if he could write something new instead: the story of the day he sarged me at his first workshop in San Francisco.

FIELD REPORT—THE SEDUCTION OF STYLE
BY JUGGLER

I clicked off the cell phone. "Style talks really fast," I said to my housemate's cat, who understands these things and was my longstanding partner in crime when it came to getting girls to the house. (The offer of, "Want to come back to my place and watch the cat do back flips?" hardly ever failed.)

That was my first impression of Style's real life persona. Two weeks later I sat in a restaurant in San Francisco's Fisherman's Wharf waiting for Style to arrive, mentally tallying a list of crazy things that could be wrong with him. I ignored the waiter who was trying to upgrade my beer and made a prayer to myself. "Please, goddess of seduction and patron saint of pickup artists and guys trying to get nookie everywhere, please do not let Style be weird."

Talking too fast is usually a sign of a deep lack of confidence. People who feel that others aren't interested in what they think talk fast for fear of losing the attention of their audience. Others are so in love with perfection that they have a difficult time editing it all down and continuously speed up in hopes of getting it all in. Such people usually become writers. That was it: weirdo or writer. I hoped it was the latter. I needed a friend and equal in this world of seduction, not another student.

I'd first heard of Style on the Internet. We had come to admire each other's postings on a website dedicated to the art of seduction. He wrote with grace and eloquence. He seemed to be a positive guy who was focused on sharing. What he saw in my posts I can only guess.

Style entered the room with a galloping lope. Were those platform shoes he was wearing? He made easy eye contact, beamed with a beautiful smile, and was a touch nervous in just the right amount to make him endearing—an effect I'm sure was deliberate. With his relatively short stature, baby-like shaved head, and soft-spoken voice, no one would ever suspect him of being a pickup artist. I perked up. This guy could be good.

I liked Style right away. He was obviously very practiced at making people like him. He made me feel important. He had a way of summing up many of my more clunkily expressed ideas into simple, beautiful statements—all the while attributing the eloquence back to me. He was the perfect accomplice for an up-and-coming guru.

And yet I wasn't sure what his weakness was. We all do that as we get to know someone. Like a tabloid editor, we search for both greatness and weakness, jotting notes in our heads for future exploitation. We are never comfortable with those who have no visible flaw. Style's softness was not real weakness. My only guess as to Style's flaw was a pride in his ability to get others to open up and reveal themselves. Pretty lame as far as a weakness goes but that was all I had to go on.

He was a cool guy. But he had a lack of confidence that made no sense, as if he felt there was something missing about himself—a piece that would make him complete. I was pretty sure he was searching for it outside when he would eventually find it inside.

After lunch, we did exactly what all hot pickup artists on the make do in San Francisco. We went to the Museum of Modern Art.

We walked downstairs and spread out—commandoes of seduction. I turned a corner in the dimly lit new media section and noticed a cute twenty-year-old. She was small. I love petite women. There is something about their inherent weakness that turns me on. I joined her at a video projection on the floor. The scene looped every minute or so—white petals falling delicately off seasoned branches.

Height can be intimidating. I am the scarecrow in *The Wizard of Oz*—tall and thin with bits of prickly straw sticking out of my sleeves. I sat down on the bench there. She relaxed. Our eyes touched—hers almond green, mine blood-shot from jet lag. The best seductions happen when the woman seduces you. You have to lead to be a good seducer but you also have to follow. In that moment I realized I wanted her to take me by the hand to her secret camp in the woods. I wanted her to show me her goofy magic trick. I wanted her to read me the naughty poems she writes on coffee shop napkins.

CLICKITY CLOMP, CLICKITY CLOMP, CLICKITY CLOMP.

Style and his shoes were moving along the backside of the divider that bisected the long room. I didn't want him to join us. It is not that I didn't appreciate Style. He had me at a humble, "Greetings, I am the one called Style." It was just that the vibe between her and me and the never-ending white petals was so . . . mesmerizing. And also because I am a wolf and this little doe separated from her herd was mine. If Style shows up, I might have to bite his face.

The first thing you say to a woman matters very little. Some guys tell me they can't think of anything or they need a really good line. I tell them they are thinking too much. You are not that important. I am not that important. We have never thought a thought so great that it needs to be wrapped with so much care. Give up your need for perfection. As far as opening lines go, a grunt or a fart is sufficient.

"How are you?" I asked.

That is one of my usual openers. Just something you hear every day from the grocery store clerk. Ninety-five percent respond with a one-word, noncommittal answer: "fine" or "okay." Three percent respond with enthusiasm: "great" or "super." Those are the ones you learn to stay away from—they're nuts. And two percent respond with an honest, "Terrible. My husband just left me for his yoga teacher's receptionist. How fucking Zen." Those are the ones you love.

She tells me she is "fine." Her voice is rough for such a small package. She must have been up late screaming at the Courtney Love concert. I am not really into the loud rock scene. I like elevator music. But I forgive her. I don't screen women. That would only limit my adventures. I only screen on how well I get treated.

I look at her expectedly. She takes the hint. "How are you?" she asks.

I ponder a moment. "I'm an 8."

I'm always an 8, sometimes an 8.5.

There are two paths to move a conversation. You can either ask questions:

"Where are you from?"; "How many ways can you curl your tongue?"; "Do you believe in reincarnation?"

Or you can make statements: "I live in Ann Arbor, Michigan—home to hundreds and hundreds of ice cream shops"; "I had a girlfriend who could curl her tongue into a poodle"; "My housemate's cat is the reincarnation of Richard Nixon."

I spent my early twenties trying to get to know girls by asking tons of questions—open-ended questions, smart questions, strange questions, the most heartfelt questions wrapped in beautiful boxes. I thought they would appreciate my interest. All I got was name, rank, serial number, and sometimes the finger. Interrogation is not seduction. Seduction is the art of setting the stage for two people to choose to reveal themselves to each other.

Talking in statement form is the way old friends speak to each other. Statements are the mode of the intimate, the confident, and the giving. They invite others to share and make perfect metaphysical sense. Trust me on that—you do not have to spend nights lying in the grass, staring up into our spread-eagled Milky Way galaxy figuring it all out. I have done it for you.

"This video makes me feel peaceful," I said. "Like raking leaves into a big pile and falling into them. But if they had some actual leaves here that we could play in—now that would be art."

She smiled. "I got thrown in the leaves a lot by my older brothers when I was growing up."

I chuckled. The thought of this tiny girl being tossed gleefully into a huge pile of leaves was funny.

"You know," I said, "I have a friend who swears he can figure out a person's personality based on the age and sex of their siblings."

"Like having older brothers makes me butch?" She adjusted her Harley-Davidson belt buckle. "That is so much bullshit."

You can't lead without being able to follow. "Crazy bullshit," I agreed. "The guy is completely wigged out. Of course, he did read me exactly."

"Really?"

"Yeah, he knew I had one older sister. Just like that."

"How did he know?"

"He said I was needy."

"Are you?"

"Yes, of course. All my girlfriends have to write me love notes and give me backrubs. I'm high maintenance."

She laughed musically. It was like the soundtrack to falling leaves.

CLICKITY CLOMP, CLICKITY CLOMP, CLICKITY CLOMP.

Focus is passé. In the modern world we want to feel everything all the time. There is no point in just taking a walk in the park when we can also listen to headphones, munch on a hot dog, crank up our vibrating soles to the maximum, and check out the passing carnival of humanity. Our choices shout the creed of a new world order: stimulation! Thought and creativity have become subservient to the singular goal of saturating our senses. But I'm old school. If you are not prepared to focus on me when you are with me— conversation, touch, our momentary entwining of souls—then get out of my face and go back to your 500 channels of surround-sound life.

"Look, I can't talk to you anymore."

"Why not?"

"I am enjoying this but you either have to commit to talking with me or go look at art. And, besides, with you standing there I'm going to get a crick in my neck."

She smiled and joined me on the bench. Ah.

CLICKITY CLOMP, CLICKITY CLOMP, CLICKITY CLOMP.

"I'm Juggler."

"I'm Anastasia."

"Hi Anastasia."

Her tiny hand felt calloused. Her nails were trimmed short. They were the hands of a worker bee. I needed to investigate fully. I pulled her closer. She came willingly.

CLICKITY CLOMP, CLICKITY CLOMP, CLICKITY CLOMP CLOMP CLOMP.

Style entered the scene. His perfume wisped and his Italian fabric rustled. Did he flourish? It felt like he flourished. What was wrong with him? Couldn't he see I was enjoying an intimate moment with this girl? Was he so focused on some sort of entertainment phase of seduction that he couldn't see we were beyond that? My moment with this girl evaporated. A growl built deep in my chest.

"Do I know you?" I asked him.

"Does anyone truly know anyone?" Style retorted.

He made me laugh. Damn him to hell—in that moment I hated Style for his mischievous timing but loved him for his way with words. I decided not to bite his face—this day.

I could tell Style was eager to demonstrate himself in action. I introduced the two of them. Then something freaky happened. Style's eyes rolled back in his head, and he became someone else. My best guess as to whom he was channeling was Harry Houdini—a fast-talking Harry Houdini. He performed tricks. He had her punch him in the stomach. He mentioned sleeping on a bed of nails. She was enjoying herself. Her phone number appeared out of thin air. That was good enough for Harry. We left her where I found her.

There is pride involved in being a pickup artist. It is a challenge. I have performer friends who can explode on stage like samurai and kill five hundred people, but they are afraid to approach a girl in a bar. I don't blame them. Most audiences are horny to be fucked. They want it hard and deep. But the girl sitting on the barstool is more difficult. She is scarier. She is the five hundred pound gorilla in a little black dress. And she can bust you up, if you let her. But she is also horny to be fucked. We are all horny to be fucked.

San Francisco was my first group workshop. I had booked six guys. We met up with them at a restaurant near Union Street. Style helped me quickly check their credentials. They were six members in good standing of the community.

We spent dinner making up conversation starters, such as the pretend-someone-is-a-movie-star opener. On the way back from the restroom, I approached a good-looking middle-aged couple at a nearby table.

"I hope I am not interrupting," I said to the woman, "but I just had to tell you that I loved you in that one with the boy and the lighthouse. It made me cry for three days. I stayed up late watching it with my housemate's cat. He used to be the president."

They nodded and smiled amicably. "You . . . thank . . . very much," the woman responded in broken English. "It is great."

"Where are you from?" I asked.

"Czechoslovakia."

I gave her a hug and shook the man's hand. "Welcome to America."

Pickup artists are the only real diplomats left in the world.

I didn't start out as a pickup artist. I began as a small boy obsessed with taking things apart. I carried a screwdriver everywhere. I had a burning desire to know firsthand how things worked. Toys, bicycles, coffee makers—everything comes apart if you know where the screws are. My dad would go to cut the grass, but the lawnmower would be in pieces. My sister would switch on the television . . . and nothing. All the vacuum tubes were under my bed. I was much better at taking things apart than putting them back together. My family was reduced to living in the Stone Age.

Later my research shifted toward understanding people and myself. I became a variety act—juggler, street performer, comedian. It's the backwater of entertainment, but a great place to learn about human interaction. As a side effect, I became good with women. By my twenty-third birthday, I had slept with only one woman. By my twenty-eighth, I could sleep with as many as I wanted. My approach became subtle and efficient, my game graceful and compact.

Then I found the community. Although my interest was much broader than just seduction, their dedication to understanding human interaction was like coming home.

Then I met Style and felt a kinship on an entirely new level. Style listened. Most people don't listen because they are afraid of what they might hear. Style had no preconceived notions. He was cool with however anyone wanted to be. He didn't find bitchy girls who had to be broken. He found feisty girls who were fun to play with. He didn't see a path of random obstacles. He saw an opportunity to explore new territory. Together we were the Lewis and Clark of seduction.

When the workshop ended at 3:00 A.M., Style and I decided to share a hotel room with some of his family who were in town. We talked in hushed voices so as not to wake them. I teased Style's fashion sense. He made fun of my midwestern sensibilities. We shared stories from our experiences with the community and counted up the loot—a couple of kisses for Style, a couple of telephone numbers for me.

The mood was giddy. We felt on the edge of something.

"It's really amazing, man," Style said. "I can't wait to see where all this leads."

He was so full of wide-eyed optimism in the power of pickup, in the benefits of self-improvement, in the belief that we—the community—had the answer to the problems that had plagued him his whole life. I wanted to tell him that the answer he was seeking lay elsewhere. But I never got around to it. We were having too much fun.

When I returned home from San Francisco, where the only person I spent the night with was Juggler, I received a phone call from Ross Jeffries.

"I'm having a workshop this weekend," he said. "If you want, you can come sit in for free. It's at the Marina Beach Marriott hotel on Saturday and Sunday."

"Sure," I told him. "I'd love to go."

"There's just one thing: You owe me parties. Good Hollywood parties with hot chicks. You promised me."

"Got it."

"And, before we hang up, you can wish me a happy birthday."

"It's your birthday?"

"Yes, your guru of gash is forty-four. And my youngest this year was twenty-one."

I had no idea he was inviting me to his seminar not as a student, but as a conquest.

I arrived on Saturday afternoon to find a standard hotel conference room, the kind that's so brightly lit and mustard yellow it seems designed as a habitat more for salamanders than for human beings. Rows of men sat behind white rectangular tables, facing the front of the room. Some were greasy-haired students, others were greasy-haired adults, and a few were greasy-haired dignitaries—top-ranking officials at Fortune 500 companies and even the Justice Department. In the front was our porous, bony guru of gash, talking into a headset.

He was telling the students about the hypnotic technique of using quotes in a conversation. An idea is more palatable, he explained as he paced the room, if it comes from someone else. "The unconscious thinks in terms of content and structure. If you introduce a pattern with the words, 'My friend was telling me,' the critical part of her mind shuts off. Do you follow me?"

He looked around the room for a response. And that was when he noticed me, sitting in the back row between Grimble and Twotimer. He stopped speaking. I felt the heat of his glare on me. "Brothers, this is Style."

I smiled wanly. "He has seen what Mystery has to offer and decided to become my disciple. Isn't that right, Style?"

Every greasy head in the room turned to look at me. The reviews of Mystery's Belgrade workshop had hit the Internet, and my skills in the field had been soundly praised. People were curious to meet Mystery's new wing—or, in Ross's case, to own him.

I stared at the thin black headset coiling around his face like a spider. "Something like that," I said.

That was not enough for him. "Who is your guru?" he asked.

It was his room. But it was my mind. I didn't know what to say. Since the best way to deflect pressure is with humor, I tried to think of a joke response. I couldn't come up with one.

"I'll get back to you on that," I answered.

I could see that he wasn't happy with my response. After all, this wasn't just a seminar he was running. It was a cult.

When the meeting broke for lunch, Ross pulled me aside. "Why don't you join me for some Italian?" he asked, twirling his ring, a replica of the one worn by the superhero Green Lantern.

"I wasn't aware that you were still a big supporter of Mystery," he said over lunch. "I thought you had come over to the good side of the force."

"I don't think your two methods have to be mutually exclusive. I told Mystery what you did with the waitress at California Pizza Kitchen, and he flipped out. I think for the first time, he saw how Speed Seduction could really be effective."

Ross's face turned purple. "Stop!" he said. It was a hypnosis word, a pattern interrupt. "Do not share anything with him. I don't want that guy taking my best work, stealing it, and making money off it. This is disturbing." He stabbed a fork into his chicken. "I knew something was wrong. If you're going to be this deeply involved with Mystery, then I'm going to have a problem. If you're going to learn privately with me, I forbid you from telling him the details."

"Listen," I tried to appease the angry guru. "I haven't told him anything in detail. I just let him know that you were the real deal."

"Fine, then. Just tell him you saw me get a chick hot as hell and wetting her panties just by asking a couple of questions and making some gestures. Let the arrogant fuck figure it out for himself!"

I watched his nostrils flare and the veins in his forehead bulge as he spoke. He was clearly a guy who'd been beaten down early in life. Not by the brutality of his father like Mystery; Ross's parents were a smart, good-humored Jewish couple. I knew because they'd arrived at the seminar a few minutes after me and instantly started teasing him. Rather, Ross had been beaten down socially, which probably took a great toll on his psyche when combined with the constant teasing and high expectations of his parents. His siblings must have been overwhelmed as well. His two brothers had turned to God and became Jews for Jesus. As for Ross, he had turned to to a religion of his own making.

"You are being led into the inner sanctum of power, my young apprentice," he warned, wiping the gray stubble on his chin with the back of his hand, "and the price for betrayal is dark beyond measure of your mortal mind. Keep quiet and keep your promises, and I will keep opening the door."

Ross's severity and anger, though unconscionable, were understandable. The fact was that Ross had built the seduction community almost single-handedly. Sure, there'd always been a stable of men giving pickup advice, like Eric Weber, whose book *How to Pick Up Girls* helped start the trend that culminated in the movie *The Pick-Up Artist* with Molly Ringwald and Robert Downey Jr. But there had never been a community of guys before Ross. The reason was fortuitous timing. As Speed Seduction was developing, so was the Internet.

In his twenties, by all accounts, Jeffries was an angry man. His ambition was stand-up comedy and screenwriting. One of his scripts, *They Still Call Me Bruce*, was even produced, but it flopped. So Jeffries drifted between paralegal jobs, lonely and girlfriendless. That all changed when he was in the self-help section of a bookstore and his hand, he claims, involuntarily reached out and grabbed a book. That tome was *Frogs Into Princes*, the classic book on NLP by John Grinder and Richard Bandler. Ross went on to devour every book on the subject he could find.

One of his heroes had always been the Green Lantern, who was endowed with a magic ring able to bring the desires of his will and imagination to life. After using NLP to end a long streak of involuntary chastity by seducing a woman who'd applied for a job in the law office where he worked, Ross Jeffries believed he had found that ring. The power and control that had eluded him his whole life was finally his.

His professional pickup career began with a seventy-page self-published book. The title pretty much summed up where he was coming from emotionally at the time—*How to Get the Women You Desire Into Bed: A Down and Dirty Guide to Dating and Seduction for the Man Who's Fed Up With Being Mr. Nice Guy.* He sold the book through small classified ads in the back of *Playboy* and *Gallery.* When he added seminars to his repertoire, he began marketing on the Internet as well. One of his students, a legendary computer hacker named Louis DePayne, soon created the newsgroup alt.seduction.fast. Out of that forum, an international cabal of PUAs gradually came into being.

"When I first came out with this stuff, I was savagely ridiculed," Ross said. "I was called every name in the book and accused of the worst things. I was really angry for a while. Very pissed off. But gradually the argument went from 'Is this real?' to 'Should they be doing it?'"

And that is why every guru owes at least a pledge of allegiance to Ross Jeffries. He laid the groundwork. It's also why every time new teachers pop up, Ross tries to shoot them down; in a few cases, he has even threatened to reveal a young competitor's online seduction activities to his parents or school administration.

Worse than Mystery, in his mind, was a former Speed Seduction student named David DeAngelo. Originally, DeAngelo called himself Sisonpyh—hypnosis spelled backward—and worked his way into the Speed Seduction hierarchy. But the two of them had a falling out when Ross supposedly hypnotized a girlfriend of DeAngelo's into fooling around with him.

According to Ross, DeAngelo had brought the girl to him to seduce. It wasn't uncommon, he said, for students to bring him women as a sacrifice of sorts. According to DeAngelo, Ross was in no way given permission to touch the girl. Whatever the case, the result was that the two stopped speaking and DeAngelo set up a rival business called Double Your Dating. It was based not on NLP or any other form of hypnosis, but rather on evolutionary psychology and DeAngelo's principle of cocky funny.

"You know, my cheapjack imitator David DeAnushole is having his first seminar in L.A.," Ross said. "The guy is so fucking good-looking and well-connected in the nightclub scene it just astounds me that people think he could ever understand their situation and the difficulties they encounter in dealing with women."

I made a mental note to sign up for the seminar.

"There's a certain view of women that David DeAnushole, Gun Bitch, and Misery have," Ross continued, working himself into a rage. "These guys are focusing on the worst tendencies of some of the worst women out there and spreading it like a cloud of fertilizer on all women."

Ross reminded me of an old rhythm-and-blues artist who has been ripped off so much that he trusts no one. But at least there are publishing companies and copyrights in place to protect songwriters. There is no way to copyright a woman's arousal, to declare certain authorship over her choice of a partner. His paranoia, sadly, made sense—especially when it came to Mystery, the only seducer with the ideas and skills to supplant him.

The waiter cleared our pasta. "I am so passionate about this because I care about these kids," Ross was saying. "I think that 20 percent of my students have been abused. They have been severely impacted. Not just with women but with all people, male and female. And a lot of problems in society come from the fact that we all have such strong drives, but live in a culture that discourages us from exploring them freely."

He turned around and noticed three businesswomen eating dessert a few tables away. He was about to freely explore his sex drive.

"How's that berry cobbler?" Ross yelled at them.

"Oh, it's good," one of the woman replied.

"You know," Ross said to them, "people have signal systems for dessert." He was off and running. "The signals say: This is sugar-free; this melts in my mouth. And the signal system fires up your body's responsiveness to get ready for what comes next. It's tracing an energy flow through your body."

He had the women's attention now. "Really?" they asked.

"I teach courses in energy flow," Ross told them. The women *ooohed* in unison. The word energy is the equivalent of the smell of chocolate to most women in Southern California. "We were just talking about whether men really understand women. And we think we've figured it out."

In a flash, he was at their table. As he spoke, the women forgot completely about their dessert and stared at him rapt. I couldn't tell sometimes if his patterns really worked on the sophisticated subconscious level he claimed, or if most conversations were so boring that simply saying something different and intriguing was enough to trigger attraction.

"Oh my God," one of the women said when he finished running a pattern about the qualities women look for in a man. "I've never heard it said like that before. Where do you teach? I'd love to know more."

Ross collected her phone number and returned to the table. He turned to me, smiled, and said, "Now do you see who's teaching the true way?"

Then he rubbed his thumb on his chin.

In Sin's eyes, I was a pawn.

"Ross is a seductionist and a plotter," he said when I called him in Montgomery, Alabama, where he'd been stationed. He was living with a girl he'd met who liked being taken out on the end of a leash and collar. Unfortunately, the military frowned on such perversions, so Sin had to drive all the way to Atlanta to walk her on the downlow.

"You have a special place in Ross's plans," he warned. "You are the marketing tool he's using to attack Mystery. You are Mystery's first and best student, the only guy who's sarging regularly with him. So every time Ross asks you a question like, 'Are you lying to your guru?,' and you answer, the presupposition that he's your guru is affirmed. Every little thing he does is to prove you are a convert and you've disavowed your old religion to embrace the true one that actually works. That is his message. So be careful."

There was a catch to learning NLP, manipulation, and self-improvement. No action—whether yours or another's—was devoid of intent. Every word had a hidden meaning, and every hidden meaning had weight, and every weight had its own special place on the scale of self-interest. However, as much as Ross may have been nurturing a friendship with me in order to crush Mystery, he also had a reputation for befriending younger students just so they'd take him to parties.

I invited Ross to his first event the following week. Monica, a struggling but well-connected actress I'd sarged, had invited me to her birthday party at Belly, a tapas bar on Santa Monica Boulevard. I thought it would be a good scene full of beautiful people for Ross to dazzle with his skills. I was wrong.

I met Ross at his parents' place, a middle-class red brick house on the west side of L.A. His father, a retired chiropractor, school principal, and self-published novelist, sat on a couch near his mother, who clearly wore the pants in the family. On the wall were a purple heart and a bronze star that Ross's father had won during World War II in Europe.

"Style's very successful," Ross told them. "He gets a lot of chicks using my material." Even pickup artists in their forties still seek the approval of their parents.

I talked to his mother for a while about her son's line of work. "Some people think if he talks about sex and women, it's terrible," his mom said. "But he's not crude and vulgar. He's a very bright boy." She stood up and ambled to a wall of shelving. "I have a book of poetry he wrote when he was nine years old. Do you want to read some of it? One of them says he's a king and he's on a throne."

"No, you don't want to read that," Ross interrupted. "Jesus Christ, this was a mistake. Let's get going."

The party was a disaster. Ross couldn't handle himself around classy people. He spent most of the night thinking he was flirting by acting as if he were my gay lover and crawling on all fours behind Carmen Electra, pretending to be a dog sniffing her ass. When I was talking to another girl, he interrupted to brag about a pickup he had just done. At 10:00 P.M., he said he was tired and demanded that I drive him home.

"Next time, we should stay later," I said.

"No, next time we have to arrive at the right time," he scolded me. "I can stay out late, provided I get about twelve hours notice so I can take it easy and nap in the afternoon."

"You're not that old."

I made a mental note never again to take Ross anywhere cool. It was an embarrassment. Since I'd started spending so much time with PUAs, I'd lowered my standards for people I hung out with. All my old friends had fallen by the wayside. Now my social life was monopolized by a caliber of nerd I'd never associated with before. I was in the game to have more women in my life, not men. And though the community was all about women, it was also completely devoid of them. Hopefully, this was just part of the process, the way cleaning a house often makes it messier first.

For the rest of the drive back to his apartment in Marina del Rey, Ross harangued me about his rivals. Of course, Ross's detractors weren't any kinder to him. They had recently nicknamed him Mine '99, claiming that whenever Ross took someone else's tactic and made it his own, he liked to insist it was something he had developed at his 1999 Los Angeles seminar.

"That traitorous creep David DeAnushole," Ross seethed as I dropped him off. "His seminar is tomorrow, and I just found out some of my students are scheduled to speak. They didn't even have the courtesy to let me know."

I didn't have the heart to tell Ross that I'd be going also.

Attraction is not a choice.

Those were the words David DeAngelo had projected on the wall. The seminar was packed. There were more than a hundred and fifty people in the room. Many of them I recognized from other seminars, including Extramask.

It was getting to be an all-too-familiar sight: a person onstage with a headset instructing a group of needy men on how to save themselves from nightly onanism. But there was a difference. DeAngelo was a good-looking guy, like Ross Jeffries had said. He reminded me of Robert DeNiro, if DeNiro had been a mama's boy who'd never been in a fight in his life.

DeAngelo stood out from the other gurus precisely because he didn't stand out. He wasn't charismatic or interesting. He didn't have the crazy gleam of a wanna-be cult leader or some gaping hole in his soul that he was trying to fill with women. He didn't even claim to be good at the game. He was very ordinary. But he was dangerous because he was organized.

He had clearly spent months working on his seminar. It was not only entirely scripted but cleaned up for mass consumption. It was a school of pickup instruction that could be presented to the mainstream without shocking anyone with its crudeness, its attitude toward women, or the deviousness of its techniques—except, that is, for his recommendation of reading the book *Dog Training* by Lew Burke for tips on handling girls.

DeAngelo was a bright guy—and a threat to Ross. Many of the speakers at his seminar were, like himself, Ross's former students: among them Rick H., Vision, and Orion, an uber-nerd who was famous as the first PUA to sell videotapes of himself approaching girls on the street. This video series, *Magical Connections,* was considered hard evidence that nerds with hypnosis skills could get laid.

"Seduction," DeAngelo read from his notes, "is defined in the dictionary as an 'enticement to wrongdoing, specifically the offense of inducing a woman to consent to unlawful sexual intercourse by enticements which overcome her scruples.'"

"In other words," he continued, "seduction implies tricking, being dishonest, and hiding your motives. That is not what I am teaching. I'm teaching something called attraction. Attraction is working on yourself and improving yourself to the point where women are magnetically attracted to you and want to be around you."

Not once did DeAngelo mention the names of his competitors and rivals. He was too smart for that. He was going to try to take this whole underground world up for air, and he was going to do it by not acknowledging the underground world at all. He had stopped posting online and, instead, let his employees stick up for him when he was flamed. He wasn't a genius or an innovator like Mystery and Ross. But he was a great marketer.

"How do you make someone want something?" he asked, after making his students practice giving each other James Dean underlooks. "You give it value. You show that others like it. You make it scarce. And you make them work for it. I want you to think about other ways during lunch."

I joined DeAngelo and some of his other students for a burger and found out a little more about him. A struggling real estate agent from Eugene, Oregon, he moved to San Diego for a fresh start. Lonely, he yearned to cross that invisible barrier separating two strangers at a club. So he began searching the Web for tips and cultivating friends who were good with women. One of those friends was Riker, a Ross Jeffries protégé who turned him onto using America Online to meet women. Sending instant messages was a way for DeAngelo to practice flirting the way his new player friends did, but without risking public embarrassment.

"That was the *chi*," he said as students milled about awkwardly, trying to overhear. "I was learning new ideas, implementing them, and then noticing how women responded on AOL. That's when I learned that busting women's balls and really slamming them immediately didn't have the effect that the intuitive mind would guess it would. So I became cocky and funny. I stole their lines, teased them, accused them of hitting on me, and never gave them a break."

Flushed with his new findings, DeAngelo delivered a fifteen-page screed to Cliff's List, one of the most established online seduction newsletters. The then-nascent seduction community ate it up: A new guru had arrived. Cliff, the middle-aged Canadian businessman who ran the list by day and hunted for new master PUAs to bring into the community by night, helped convince DeAngelo to spend three weeks turning his manifesto into an e-book, *Double Your Dating*.

While we were talking, Rick H. joined us. He was one of the friends DeAngelo had cultivated and was now his roommate in the Hollywood Hills. I'd heard a lot about Rick H. He was supposed to be the best, a master PUA who specialized in bisexual women. His garish style of dress, like that of a Vegas lounge lizard, was one of the inspirations for Mystery's peacock theory.

Rick H. was short, slightly stocky, and dressed in a large-collared shirt and a red blazer. Trailing behind him were six attraction adepts eager to soak up his wisdom. I recognized two of them: Extramask, whose eyes were swollen nearly shut, and Grimble, who was beginning to have doubts about his application of Speed Seduction. Hypnotizing women into being groped in clubs wasn't getting him any girlfriends. So after spending time with Rick H., Grimble had turned cocky funny. His new approach was to stick his elbow out whenever a woman walked past, bump her, and then yell "owwww" loudly, as if she'd hurt him. When she stopped, he'd accuse her of grabbing his ass. It was much more rewarding, he realized, to be funny in a bar than creepy.

Rick took a seat at the table and spread himself out comfortably. While students crammed around him, he began holding court.

He had two rules for women, he said.

The first: No good deed goes unpunished. (A phrase, ironically, that was coined by a woman, Clare Boothe Luce.)

The second: Always have a better answer.

One of the corollaries of Rick's second rule was to never give a woman a straight answer to a question. So if a woman asks what you do for a living, keep her guessing: Tell her you're a cigarette lighter repairman or a white slave trader or a professional hopscotch player. The first time I tried this, it didn't go so well. In a five-set in a hotel lobby one night, a woman asked what my job was. I told her the response I had written on my cheat sheet for the night: white slave trader. As soon as the words left my mouth, I realized I probably wasn't going to get a number-close. Everyone in the set was African-American.

One thing I noticed as Rick talked was that people who liked the sound of their own voice tended to do better with women—except for soft-spoken Dustin. Cliff, of Cliff's List, called it big mouth theory.

"Why is this shit so fun to talk about?" Rick H. asked DeAngelo.

"Because we're guys," DeAngelo said, as if it were the most obvious thing in the world.

"Oh, yeah," Rick said. "That's what we do."

When the gurus left, I sat with Extramask. He was sipping apple juice from a small can. He had a barbell-shaped piercing in the back of his neck now and if it weren't for his swollen eyes, he would have been the coolest looking guy at the seminar.

"What happened to you?" I asked.

"I went out with that moon-faced girl and got my second lay ever," he said. "But even though we fucked three times, I didn't blow my load again. Either condoms fucking suck or I have mental anxiety and need to calm down—or Mystery's right and I'm a homo."

"But what does that have to do with your eyes? Did she punch you?"

"No, she had a feather pillow or some shit, and I got an eye infection because of my allergies."

He said he met her for coffee. They sat together and he ran the ESP test, a psychological game called the cube, and other demonstrations of value. When she started laughing at all his jokes—even the ones that weren't funny—he knew she liked him. They rented the movie *Insomnia,* went back to her house, and cuddled together on the couch.

"I had a pretty legit boner going on," he said, matter-of-factly. "You know, that kind of rock-hardness where you get the pre-cum dabbing your Underoos."

"I know. Do go on."

"And it was cool because one of her legs was pressed up against my juicy, rock-hard cock. She definitely felt the hardness. I took off my shirt, and she started kissing me and feeling my chest. It was cool." He paused and took a sip of apple juice through a narrow straw. "Then I took her shirt off, so she was wearing just a bra. I felt her boobies. But when we went to the bedroom, I had a problem."

"An erection problem?"

"No. She still had her bra on."

"So what's the problem? Just take it off."

"I have no clue how to take off bras. So I just left it on."

"I guess unhooking a bra is something you learn from experience."

"I have a plan, though. Want to hear it?"

"Um, sure."

"What I'm going to do is take one of my mom's bras and tie it around a pole or something. Then I'm gonna walk toward the pole blindfolded like in pin the tail on the donkey, reach the bra, and try to undo it."

I gave him a funny look. I couldn't tell if he was joking or not.

"I'm dead serious," he said. "It's a legit way to learn, and you know it'll work too."

"How was the sex this time?"

"It was like last time. I fucked her beyond belief, for probably a half hour straight. I was very hard and luscious. But I couldn't spunk a load. I hate this shit. Seriously, I really want to blow it during sex."

"You're probably thinking about it too much. Or maybe you're just not into the girls, emotionally."

"Or maybe I just adore the tight grip I use for masturbating," he said, rubbing his eyes. "I think I got my first blow job, too. Like, I saw her head near my penis, and I couldn't tell whether she was sucking or not. But it was cool when my balls were licked."

Grimble walked by and clapped a hand on my shoulder. "The seminar's starting again," he told me. "Steve P. and Rasputin are speaking, and you definitely don't want to miss them."

I stood up and left Extramask at the table, alone with his apple juice.

"You know what else I did?" he yelled after me as I left. "I fingered her!"

I turned back to look at him. He made me laugh. He pretended to be so confused and helpless, but maybe he was smarter than all of us.

"The inside of a vagina isn't at all what I thought it would feel like," he shouted excitedly. "It feels very organized."

Maybe not.

Though David DeAngelo taught the seminars on cocky funny, the undisputed heavy-weight of the genre was a forty-year-old Canadian writer known as Zan. Where PUAs like Mystery advocated going under the radar, Zan flaunted the fact that he was a ladies' man. He considered himself a seducer in the tradition of Casanova and Zorro, and enjoyed dressing up as them for costume parties. In four years on the seduction boards, he never once asked for advice; he only gave it.

MSN GROUP: Mystery's Lounge
SUBJECT: Zan's Cocky Funny Waitress Technique
AUTHOR: Zan

One thing I have going for me is that I am fearless around women. My method is very simple. Every single thing a girl says or does to me is an IOI. Period. She wants me. It doesn't matter who she is. And when you believe that, they start to believe it too.

I am a slave to my love of women. They can sense it. The weakness of women is language and words. Fortunately, that is one of my strong points. If they try to repel my advances, I act like they are from Mars and what they are saying doesn't make any sense.

I never try to defend myself or apologize for being a womanizer. Why? Because a reputation is attractive to women. It's true. I am the other man who guys worry about when they marry a girl.

So with that in mind, I'd like to share with you today my patented cocky funny waitress technique:

Usually when a group of guys is confronted with a new and devastatingly pretty waitress, they stare at her ass when she walks by, then talk about her be-hind her back. But when she comes to their table, they become downright cour-teous and nice and act like they are not interested in her.

Instead, I go cocky funny immediately. I am going to be very detailed in my description of what I do because I think some guys don't really understand cocky funny role-playing.

When I see her coming toward us, I immediately engage a buddy across the table in seemingly deep conversation. I make sure to face my body away from her.

When she comes up and asks us what we would like to drink, I ignore her for a few seconds or so. Then I glance in her direction and pretend I am just now seeing her for the very first time. Immediately, I show great interest in her—as if she were a new discovery. I glance quickly at her body, just long enough for her to notice, then turn myself fully around to face her. A big smile and a wink, and the game begins.

> **HER:** What can I get for you?
> **ZAN:** (*Ignoring the question*) Hello, I haven't seen you around before. What's your name?
> **HER:** My name is Stephanie. What's yours?
> **ZAN:** I'm Zan. And I will have a gin and tonic. (*Big smile*)

So far I've broken the ice a bit and, by exchanging names, she has given me the implicit right to be more familiar with her. So the next time she comes around, I smile and wink again.

> **ZAN:** You again? Wow, you sure like to hang around us, don't you?
> **HER:** (*Laughs*) (some stuff)
> **ZAN:** (Some other stuff)
> **HER:** (Some other stuff)
> **ZAN:** (*As she is leaving*) I bet you'll come back again real soon. I can see it in your eyes.
> **HER:** (*Smiling*) Yeah, I can't resist.

Now I have established a cocky funny theme—her wanting to hang around us and that is why she keeps coming back to our table. Of course, she has to come back to our table: She's the waitress. And when she does, I smile at her and give the other guys a knowing look in front of her as if to say, "See, I was right." All along, I strive to make the interaction come off like I have known her for a long time. This establishes a level of familiarity that usually takes several meetings to build.

So now, after a while, I will say something like:

> **HER:** Can I get you another drink?

> **ZAN:** (*Smile, wink*) You know what? You're kinda cute. I think I'm going to call you.
>
> **HER:** You think so, huh? You don't have my number.
>
> **ZAN:** Why, you're right! Okay, tell me and I will write it down.
>
> **HER:** (*Smiling*) Not a good idea. I have a boyfriend.
>
> **ZAN:** (*Pretending to write*) Whoa, slow down. I didn't quite catch your number there. You better repeat it for me. Let's see . . . 555 . . .
>
> **HER:** (*Laughs and rolls her eyes*)

The absurdity of this exchange is that there is no way she is going to give me her phone number in front of a bunch of my friends. No girl would. But her digits are not the goal just yet.

Now she and I have a rapport, in a manner of speaking. And I've made myself memorable enough that the next night we go there, she'll recognize me. This way, I can walk up, put my arm around her, and continue with my usual "You would make a good girlfriend for me" talk. And since everything is said in a half-joking manner, she doesn't know if I'm really hitting on her or if I'm just fooling around. So when I return:

> **HER:** (*Laughing*) Oh no! Not you again!
>
> **ZAN:** Stephanie, my sweet! Hey, listen, sorry I didn't return your call last night. You know how it is. I'm just a busy guy.
>
> **HER:** (*Playing along*) Yeah, I'm really mad about that.

This gets the whole table laughing, including her. And it's back on again for the evening.

Later:

> **ZAN:** You know what, Stephanie. You're a terrible girlfriend. In fact, I can't even remember the last time we had sex. That's it. We're through.
>
> **ZAN:** (*Pointing to another waitress*) She's going to be my new girlfriend.
>
> **HER:** (*Laughing*)
>
> **ZAN:** (*Playing with my phone*) You are now downgraded from Booty Call #1 to Booty Call #10.
>
> **HER:** (*Laughing*) No, please, I'll do anything to make it up to you.

And later still:

ZAN: (*Motioning for her to come over and pointing at my knee*) Stephanie, come and sit down. I'll tell you a bedtime story. (*Smile, wink*)

I have used that last line for years. It is gold.

Some of you guys are probably thinking, "Okay, now what? How do you transition from funny ball-busting to more serious, romantic, sexual talk?"

It's simple, actually. At some point, I just talk to her quietly alone. Remember to turn on the bedroom eyes.

ZAN: (*No longer cocky funny*) Stephanie, do you want me to call you?
HER: You know I have a boyfriend.
ZAN: That's not what I asked. Do you want me to call you?
HER: Tempting, but I can't.
ZAN: Sneak away with me, girl. I'll take you higher up the slopes of Parnassus than you have ever been. Etc.

Everything you just read actually happened last Thursday and Friday evening with me and a waitress named Stephanie. She was easily the hottest thing around in a long time. The jury is still out on this one, but she has no illusions about my intentions. My friends she views as nice guys, but not me. She knows that any interaction with me is going to be passionate from the start. And now she can choose to accept it or reject it.

The truth is, she may very well reject my overtures. But it doesn't matter. She won't soon forget me. And you can bet that the other waitresses know all about the things I said to her. And that is very good, especially since I have said almost the exact same things in the exact same way to all the other waitresses there. And I will continue to do so—right in front of Stephanie.

The net effect is social proof. When you go in, you own the place. You wave the waitresses over, point to your cheek, and say, "Hey, girl, where's my sugar?" No one is intimidated because you treat them all the same way. In this particular restaurant, there are four waitresses who have come home with me, three less attractive waitresses who want to come home with me, and several more who are works-in-progress (including Stephanie). And you can bet they all know about each other. But, again, that is very good.

—Zan

Chapter

The highlight of the seminar was an appearance by two people who would give me my much-coveted inner game and more: Steve P. and Rasputin. These were guys I'd heard whispered about in the seduction community since I'd joined—the true masters; leaders of women, not men.

The first thing they did when they walked onstage was hypnotize everybody in the room. They both talked at the same time, telling different stories—one to occupy the conscious mind and the other to penetrate to the subconscious. When they woke us up, we had no idea what they had installed in our heads. All we knew was that these were two of the most confident speakers we'd ever seen. Every ounce of fire and charisma that DeAngelo lacked, they possessed in bulk.

Wearing a leather vest and an Indiana Jones hat, Steve P. was equal parts Hell's Angel and Native American shaman. Rasputin was a strip club bouncer with mutton-chop sideburns who looked like a steroid-jacked Wolverine. The two had met in a bookstore while both reaching for the same NLP book. Now they worked as a team and were among the most powerful hypnotists in the world. Their advice on seducing women was simply: "Become an expert in how to feel good."

Toward that end, Steve P. had figured out a way to get women to pay to have sex with him. For anywhere from several hundred to a thousand dollars, he trained women to have orgasms from a single vocal command; he taught them five different stages of deep throat he had devised; and, most fantastically, he claimed to give hypnotic breast enlargements, which he said could make a woman jump as much as two cup sizes.

Rasputin's forte was what he called hypnotic sexual engineering. Sex, he explained, must be viewed as a privilege for the woman, not a favor to you. "If a woman wants to give me a blow job," he elaborated, "I tell her, 'You only get three sucks. And you may only go down as far as you receive pleasure.'" His chest stuck out like the top of a Volkswagen. "Afterward, I tell her, 'Didn't that feel nice? Next time, you get five sucks.'"

"What if you're scared of getting caught trying to manipulate her?"

asked a businessman in the front row who looked like a miniature Clark Kent.

"There is no such thing as fear," Rasputin replied. "Emotions are just energy and motion that you trap inside your body because of a thought."

Mini-Clark Kent stared at him stupidly.

"Do you know how you get over it?" Rasputin looked at his interlocutor like a wrestler about to break a folding chair in half. "You don't shower or shave for a month, until you smell like a sewer. Then you walk around for two weeks wearing a dress and a goalie mask with a dildo strapped to the front. That's what I did. And I will never be afraid of public humiliation again."

"You have to live in your own reality," Steve cut in. "I had a girl once tell me I was kind of pudgy. I said, 'Well, if that's what you think, you don't get to pat the Buddha belly or ride the jade stalk.'"

He paused, then added as an afterthought, "But I said it in a gentle fucking way, on the spiritual fucking path."

Afterward, DeAngelo introduced me to the pair. The top of my head came up to Rasputin's Volkswagen.

"I'd love to learn more about what you do," I said.

"You're nervous," Rasputin said.

"Well, you two are a little intimidating."

"Let me get rid of that anxiety," Steve offered. "Tell me your phone number backward."

I started saying, "Five . . . four . . . nine . . . six." As I did, Steve snapped his fingers.

"Okay, take a deep breath and now blow out hard," he commanded.

As I did, Steve traced his fingers up from my navel and made a whooshing sound. "Be gone!" he commanded. "Now watch that feeling just blow away like a smoke ring on a windy day. Notice how it's gone; it's no more. Take a tour of your body and try and find where it was. Notice how there's a different vibration there. Okay. Open your eyes. Try really hard to bring any piece of it back. See? You can't."

I couldn't tell whether it had worked or not, but I was reeling. He'd definitely taken my mind and body on some kind of one-minute trip.

He took a step back and scanned my face, as if reading a diary. "A guy named Phoenix offered to pay me two thousand dollars to follow me around for three days," Steve P. said. "And I told him no, because he wants to make women his slaves. You seem like you may care about women: You don't just want to stuff your meat bat in some hole. You're willing to explore shit."

Suddenly, we heard a commotion behind us. Two sisters and their mother had made the mistake of walking down a hotel hallway full of pickup artists, and the vultures were descending on the carrion. Orion the uber-nerd was reading one of the girls' palms; Rick H. was telling the mother that he was Orion's manager; Grimble was moving in on the remaining girl; and a crowd of wanna-be PUAs had gathered around, trying to see the masters at work.

"Listen," Steve P. said, in a rush. "Here's my card. Call me if you ever want to learn some inner-circle shit."

"I'd love to."

"But this is classified," he warned. "If we let you in, you cannot share these techniques with anybody. They're very powerful, and in the wrong hands they could really screw a girl up."

"Got it," I said.

He twisted a piece of white paper into the shape of a rose, then bounded off in the direction of the carrion. He approached the girl Grimble was sarging, told her to smell the flower, and within thirty seconds she was passed out in Steve's arms. This *was* inner-circle shit. And I was about to learn it.

And so began the weirdest phase of my education.

Every weekend, I'd drive two hours south to San Diego and stay at Steve P.'s small, squalid apartment, where he raised two sons the same way he talked to his students—with compassionate obscenity. His thirteen-year-old was already a better hypnotist than I would ever be.

In the afternoons, Steve and I drove to see Rasputin. They'd sit me in a chair and ask what I wanted to learn. I had a list: to believe that I was attractive to women; to live in my own reality; to stop worrying about what other people thought of me; to move and speak with an air of strength, confidence, mystery, and depth; to get over my fear of sexual rejection; and, of course, to attain a sense of worthiness, which Rasputin defined as the belief that one deserves the best the world has to offer.

It was easy to memorize routines, but mastering inner game after a lifetime of bad habits and thought patterns was not easy. These guys, however, had the tools to fix me in time for Mystery's next workshop in Miami.

"We're going to reframe you to where you're not glad to have some boopsy sucking your dick," Steve explained. "It will be a privilege for her to get to drink from the nectar of the master."

At each session, they'd put me under, and Rasputin would tell complex metaphorical stories into one of my ears as Steve P. issued commands to my subconscious in the other ear. They'd leave open loops (or unfinished metaphors and stories) in my mind that they'd close a week later. They'd play music designed to elicit specific psychological reactions. They'd put me into trances so deep that hours went by in the blink of an eye.

Afterward, I'd go back to Steve's house and read his NLP books while he screamed lovingly at his kids.

I have a theory that most naturals, like Dustin, lose their virginity at a young age and consequently never feel a sense of urgency, curiosity, and intimidation around women during their critical pubescent years. Those who must learn to meet women methodically, on the other hand—like myself and most students in the community—generally suffer through high school without girlfriends or even dates. Thus, we're forced to spend years feeling intimidated by and alienated from women, who hold in their sole possession the key to releasing us from the stigma blighting our young adult lives: our virginity.

Steve fit in with my theory on naturals. He was initiated into sex when he was in first grade. An older girl wanted to give him a blow job; he responded by trying to hit her with a rock. But she eventually convinced him, and the experience set off a lifelong obsession with oral sex. When he was seventeen, he said, a cousin hired him to work in the kitchen of a Catholic girls' school. After he gave oral sex to one of the girls, word spread and he soon became the sexual go-to guy on campus. In addition to giving the girls pleasure, however, he also gave them guilt. And after a few too many confessions that involved the boy in the kitchen, Steve was fired.

He ran with a bike gang for a while but left soon after accidentally shooting a guy in the nuts. He now devoted his life to a self-styled mix of sexuality and spirituality. And for all his crude talk, he was at heart a good person. Unlike many of the other gurus I'd met, I trusted him.

After Steve's kids went to sleep each night, he taught me inner-circle magic he'd learned from shamans whose names he'd sworn never to pronounce. The first weekend I stayed over, he gave me a lesson in soul-gazing, which is when you look deep into a woman's right eye with your own right eye as you breathe together.

"Once you do this with her, she's going to bond real strong with you," he warned. His cautionary speeches were often longer than the actual teaching process. "When you do this, you become anamchara, which in Gaelic means friend of the soul. A soul friend."

The following weekend I learned about ménage-à-trois management, and how to train a woman to eat another woman's pussy by having her put a dried nectarine in her mouth and chew erotically on it during sex. The next weekend he showed me how to throw *chi* through my hands into a woman's abdomen. And the next weekend he taught me to contain and cycle orgasmic energy, so that a woman can stack one withheld orgasm on top of another—until, as Steve P. put it, she's "shaking like a dog shitting peach seeds." Finally, he shared what he considered to be his greatest skill: guiding any woman, through words and touch, to a powerful orgasm that "gushes like Niagara Falls."

This was a whole new level of game. He was giving me super powers.

I was in a whirlwind of learning. I didn't call my friends. I barely talked to my family. I turned down every writing assignment that came my way. I was living in an alternate reality.

"I told Rasputin," Steve said one night, "that more than all the other seduction boys out there, I'd like you to become one of our trainers."

It was an offer I'd have to turn down. The seduction world was a palace of open doors. Walking through one, no matter how tempting the treasures inside, would mean having to shut the rest.

I returned home one Sunday night from San Diego to find a message on my machine from Cliff, of Cliff's List. He was in town, and he wanted to take me to meet his latest PUA discovery—a biker turned construction worker who called himself David X.

Cliff had been in the community since its inception. He was in his forties and was as nice as he was uptight. Though he was conventionally handsome, he was also the living embodiment of the word square. He looked like he'd stepped out of a 1950s family sitcom. He had a closet in his home, he claimed, with more than a thousand pickup books. There were issues of the *Pick-Up Times,* a short-lived magazine from the seventies; an original edition of Eric Weber's classic *How to Pick Up Girls;* and misogynist obscurities with titles like *Seduction Begins When the Woman Says No.*

David X was one of half a dozen PUAs Cliff had discovered over the years and promoted on his list, which he'd started in 1999 after Ross criticized him on the Speed Seduction mailing list for discussing a pickup technique that wasn't related to NLP. Every PUA had a specialty, and David X's was harem management—juggling relationships with multiple women without lying to them.

When we walked into the dim sum restaurant, I was shocked by what I saw waiting for me. David X was quite possibly the ugliest PUA I'd ever met. He made Ross Jeffries look like a Calvin Klein underwear model. He was immense, balding, and toadlike, with warts covering his face and the voice of a hundred thousand cigarette packs.

My meal with him was like so many I'd had before. Except the rules were always different. His were:

  I. Who cares what she thinks?
  II. You are the most important person in this relationship.

His philosophy was to never lie to a female. He prided himself on bedding women by trapping them with their own words. For example, on meeting a girl at a bar, he'd get her to say that she was spontaneous and didn't have any rules; then, if she was reluctant to leave the bar with him, he'd say, "I thought you were spontaneous. I thought you did what you wanted."

He spread out in his chair like a melting shard of Swiss cheese and informed us: "The only lies I'll ever tell are: 'I won't come in your mouth' and 'I'll just rub it around your ass.'" It wasn't a pretty visual.

His philosophy was in direct contrast to what I had learned from Mystery, and he let me know it—all through dinner. He was evidence of Cliff's big mouth theory, a natural alpha male.

"The best thing is," he boasted, "there are guys like me and guys like you and Mystery out there. While you're still in the bar doing magic tricks, I'm coming back for seconds."

It was an interesting dinner, and I learned a lot of little pieces of game I would go on to use scores of times. But by the time brunch was over, I'd realized something: I didn't need to meet any more gurus.

I had every piece of information I needed to become the greatest pickup artist in the world.

I had hundreds of openers, routines, cocky funny comments, ways to demonstrate value, and powerful sexual techniques. And I'd been hypnotized to Valhalla and back. It wasn't necessary to learn anything else, unless it was for my own fun and interest. I just needed to be in the field constantly—approaching, calibrating, fine-tuning, and working through sticking points. I was ready for Miami, and all the workshops to follow.

As Cliff drove me home, I made a promise to myself: If I ever met a guru again, it would be not as a student but as an equal.

ISOLATE
THE TARGET

IT IS UNFAIR TO TEAR SOMEBODY
APART WHEN HER HEALTH AND
EXUBERANCE THREATEN YOU.

—JENNY HOLZER,
Benches

Chapter

As Mystery and I traveled the world doing workshops, meeting all the players in the game, the seduction community became more than just a bunch of anonymous screen names. It became a flesh-and-blood family. Maddash was no longer seven letters of type but a funny, Jeremy Piven-like entrepreneur from Chicago; Stripped was an uptight book editor from Amsterdam with male-model looks; Nightlight9 was a lovable nerd who worked for Microsoft.

Over time, the posers and keyboard jockeys were outed, and the superstars were given their due. And Mystery and I were the superstars because we delivered: Miami, Los Angeles, New York, Toronto, Montreal, San Francisco, and Chicago. Every workshop made us better, stronger, more driven. All the other gurus I had met clung to the safety of the seminar room. They had never been forced to prove their teachings in the field city after city, night after night, woman after woman.

Every time we left a city, a lair sprung up if one didn't exist already, bringing together students eager to practice their new skills. Through word of mouth, the lairs soon doubled, tripled, and quadrupled in size. And all these guys worshipped Mystery and Style: We were living the life they wanted, or so they thought.

Each workshop generated more online reviews praising my newly acquired game. Each field report I posted triggered a flood of e-mails from students wanting to be my wing. The list of sargers in my phone book was actually starting to surpass the number of girls I'd met.

Most of the time when my phone rang, it was a guy asking for Style. And, dispensing with introductions, he'd ask, "When you call a girl, should you block your number or not?" or "I was in a three-set, and the obstacle ended up liking me and giving me her phone number. Do I still have a chance with the target?"

The game was consuming my old life. But it was worth it, because it was part of the process of becoming that guy in the club—the one I'd always envied, the one in the corner making out with a girl he'd just met. The Dustin.

Before I discovered the community, the only time I'd ever made out with a girl I met in a club was when I first arrived in Los Angeles. But in the middle of kissing, she pulled away and said, "Everyone must think you're a producer or something." The subtext was that she was otherwise too hot to be making out with a slob like me. It shattered me for months. I was too insecure to handle what was, in retrospect, her own form of neg.

But now, when I walked into a club, I felt a rush of power, wondering which woman would have her tongue down my throat within a half hour. For all the self-improvement books I had read, I still wasn't above shallow validation-seeking. None of us were. That's why we were in the game. Sex wasn't about getting our rocks off; it was about being accepted.

Mystery, in the meantime, had gone through his own metamorphosis during our travels. He had developed a radical new form of peacocking. It was no longer enough to wear just one item to catch the attention of the opposite sex. Now, all his items were larger-than-life, turning Mystery into a mobile sideshow. He wore six-inch platform boots and a bright red tiger-striped cowboy hat, which combined to make him seven feet tall. He added skintight black PVC pants, futuristic goggles, a plastic-spiked backpack, a mesh see-through shirt, black eyeliner, white eye shadow, and as many as seven watches on his wrists. Every head turned as he walked down the street.

He didn't need openers. The women opened him. Girls followed him for blocks. Some grabbed his ass; one older woman even bit his crotch. And all he had to do if he was interested was perform a few magic tricks, which seemed to justify his outlandishness.

His new look also served as a great litmus test for women. It repelled the type of girl he wasn't interested in and attracted the type he was. "I'm dressing for the outrageous club girls, the hot slutty girls, the ones I could never get," he explained one night when I accused him of looking like a clown. "They're playing groupie, so I gotta play rock star."

Mystery constantly encouraged me to dress as outlandishly as he did. Though I buckled one afternoon and bought a purple fur vest in a Montreal lingerie shop, I didn't get off on the constant gawking and attention. Besides, I was doing well enough without it.

My reputation stemmed largely from the Miami workshop, where in a period of thirty minutes I put my previous six weeks of hypnosis, training, and guru-chasing into action. It was a night that would go down in the annals of community history. It was seduction not as wrestling but as ballet: a perfect example of form. It was the night of my official graduation from AFC to PUA.

It was the perfect sarge.

When they walked into the VIP area of Miami's Crobar, everyone noticed. They were both platinum blondes with well-tanned fake breasts and identical outfits—tight white tank tops and tight white pants. How could anyone not notice? They were what the PUAs would call perfect 10's, and they were dressed to turn men into beasts. This was South Beach, where testosterone levels run high, and the pair had been whistled and hollered at all night. The girls seemed to enjoy the attention almost as much as they savored shooting down the men who gave it to them.

I knew what to do—and that was to do what everyone else wasn't doing. A pickup artist must be the exception to the rule. I had to suppress every evolutionary instinct inside me and pay them no attention whatsoever.

With me were Mystery and two of our students, Outbreak and the Matador of Love. The rest of our pupils were sarging on the perimeter of the dancefloor downstairs.

Outbreak went in first, complimenting the platinum twins on their outfits. They brushed him off like a gnat. Next, the Matador of Love moved in with the Maury Povich opener. He too crashed and burned.

Now it was my turn. This was going to take every bit of confidence and self-esteem that Steve P. and Rasputin had hypnotized into me. If I showed even a flicker of weakness or doubt, they'd eat me alive.

"That tall one isn't a 10," Mystery leaned in and whispered to me. "She's an 11. This is going to take some hardcore negging."

The girls strolled to the bar, where they began talking to a transvestite in a black tutu. I moved in, not even glancing at them, and greeted the transvestite as if I knew him. I asked if he worked at the club, and he said no. It didn't really matter what I said to him: I was just maneuvering into position, pawning him for the two-set.

Now that I was in range, it was time to neg. "That girl over there is biting your style," I said to the 10, the shorter of the two. "Look at her." I pointed to another platinum blonde in a white outfit.

"She's just got the same hair," the 10 replied, dismissively.

"No, look at her outfit," I persisted. "It's almost the exact same."

They looked over, and here was the make-or-break moment. If I didn't come up with something good to follow, I'd lose their interest and be branded just another weirdo. So I continued with the negging. "You know what?" I told them. "You both look like strange little snowflakes."

It was a bizarre, cryptic comment, but now I had their attention. I could sense it, and my heart began to pump faster. I continued with what I knew all along would be my true opener: "I have to ask you something. Is your hair real?"

The 10 looked shocked, then recovered her composure. "Yes," she said. "Feel it."

I pulled it gently. "Hey, it moved. It's not real."

"Pull harder."

I complied, and yanked it so hard that her neck jerked back. "Okay," I said. "I believe you. But how about your friend there?"

The 11's face reddened. She leaned over the bar and looked me hard in the eye. "That is really rude. What if I'm bald underneath here? That could really hurt someone's feelings. It's disrespectful. How would you feel if someone said that to you?"

The pickup is a high stakes game, and to win you have to play hard. All I had done so far was commandeer their attention and provoke an emotional reaction. Sure, it was a negative one, but now we had a relationship. If I could turn her anger around, I'd be in.

Fortunately, I happened to be trying to make a point to the students and was wearing a black mod wig and a fake lip piercing—just to show that looks don't matter. It's all game.

I leaned over the bar and stared the 11 down. "Well," I told her. "I actually *am* wearing a wig, and I *am* bald underneath here."

I paused, and she looked at me with her mouth open. She didn't know how to respond. Now it was time to reel her in. "And I'll tell you something else. Whether I go out totally bald, in this wig, or in some crazy longhaired wig, it doesn't change the way I'm treated by other people. It's all your attitude. Don't you agree?"

Everything I say in a pickup has an ulterior motive. I needed to let her know that unlike every other guy in the bar, I am not and will not be intimidated by her looks. Beauty to me was now a shit test: It weeded out the losers who got dumbstruck by it.

"I live in Los Angeles," I continued. "It's where the most beautiful women in the country come to try and make it. You look around a club there, and everyone's good-looking. It makes this VIP room look like a dive bar." They were words I'd learned, almost verbatim, from Ross Jeffries. And they were working.

I let her look around, then continued: "And do you know what I've learned? Beauty is common. It's something you're born with or you pay for. What counts is what you make of yourself. What counts is a great outlook and a great personality."

Now I was in. It was the girls who were dumbstruck now, not me. I had entered their world, as Jeffries once put it to me, and demonstrated authority over it. And, to ensure my position there, I threw in one more neg, but softened with a slight compliment, as if they were winning me over: "And you know what? You have a great smile. I can tell that underneath all that, you're probably a good person."

The 10 sidled up to me and said, "We're sisters."

A lesser pickup artist would have thought that his work was done, that he had won them over. But no, this was just one more shit test. I looked very slowly at both of them, and then took a chance. "Bullshit," I said, smiling. "I bet a lot of guys believe you, but I'm a very intuitive person. When I look at you both, I can tell you're very different. Too different."

The 10 broke into a guilty smile. "We never tell anyone this," she said, "but you're right. We're just friends."

Now I'd broken through her programming, moved her away from the auto-pilot responses she gives to men, and demonstrated that I was not just another guy. I took another chance: "And I'd be willing to bet that you haven't even been friends for that long. Usually, best friends start to have the same mannerisms, and you two don't really."

"We've only known each other a year," the 10 admitted.

Now it was time to back off my game and fluff a little. However, I made sure never to ask questions; instead, as Juggler had taught me, I made open-ended statements that led them to ask me the questions.

The 10 told me they were from San Diego, so we fluffed for a while about the West Coast and Miami. As we talked, I kept my back to the 11, as if I were less interested in her. This was classic Mystery Method: I wanted her thinking more about me, wondering why I wasn't giving her the attention she was so used to. Nothing in the game is an accident.

I think of a woman's interest in me as a fire, and when it starts to die out, it's time to turn around and stoke it. So, just when the 11 was about to walk away to find someone to talk to, I turned around and delivered a beautiful line: "You know what? When I look at you, I can see exactly what you looked like in middle school. And I'm willing to bet you weren't so outgoing or popular then."

Sure, it was a truism. But she stared at me flabbergasted, wondering how I could possibly know that. To seal the victory, I laid out one last beauty-neutralizing cold-reading routine. "I bet a lot of people think you're a bitch. But you're not. You're actually shy in a lot of ways."

She began to give me the doggy dinner-bowl look, as the PUAs call it. It is the look that is the goal of any approach. Her eyes glazed over, her pupils dilated, and she just watched my lips move, entranced and attracted. I noticed, however, that the more interested the 11 became, the more kino the 10 gave me.

"You're interesting," the 10 gushed, pressing her breasts against me. I could see Mystery, Outbreak, and the Matador of Love rooting me on in the background. "We have to hang out with you in L.A."

She leaned in and gave me a tight hug. "Hey, that'll be thirty dollars," I told her, disentangling myself. "This shit ain't free."

The more you push them away, the more they run toward you. "I love him," she told her friend. Then she asked if she and her friend could stay with me next time they were in L.A.

"Sure," I said. But as the words left my mouth, I realized, too late, that I should have made my hospitality more of a challenge. There's so much to remember and juggle during a pickup that it is hard to get everything perfect. But no matter. She gave me her phone number, and I gave her mine.

You may have noticed that I haven't been referring to these girls by their names. That's because I never introduce myself during a pickup. As Mystery had taught me at that first workshop, I wait for the woman to introduce herself or ask for my name. That way, I know she's interested. So, as we exchanged numbers, I received my first real IOIs and learned that the 10 was Rebekah and the 11 was Heather. Now it was time to separate the two of them and see if I could get enough IOIs to kiss-close Heather.

A guy they knew suddenly showed up and bought three shots—for Heather, Rebekah, and himself. I held out my empty hand and looked around, pretending to be hurt. Heather, who I was slowly realizing was actually a sweet girl beneath that laboriously wrought exterior, took the bait. "Don't mind him," she said, pointing to their guy friend. "He's just rude."

As she called the bartender over and ordered me a shot, Rebekah threw her a dirty look. "Remember our rule?" she whined.

I knew what their rule was: Girls like this love it when guys buy them drinks. But David X had taught me better: Girls don't respect guys who buy them drinks. A true pickup artist knows never to buy meals, drinks, or gifts for a girl he hasn't slept with. Dating is for tools.

"We promised not to buy any drinks on this trip," Rebekah whined.

"But you're not buying a drink for yourself," I told them. "You're buying one for me. And I'm different from all the other guys."

I'm not really that arrogant, but in the game there are rules. And the rules must be obeyed, because they work.

Suddenly, Mystery walked toward me and whispered in my ear, "Isolate!"

"I want to show you something," I said to Heather, as I took her by the hand. I led her to a nearby booth, sat her down, and performed the ESP experiment. Behind me, I saw Mystery punching his fist into his open hand in slow motion. It was a code: the signal to phase shift, to slow down and move in for the kill.

I told her about soul-gazing and, with house music and dozens of conversations blaring around us, we stared into each other's eyes and shared a moment together. In my head, I imagined her as the pudgy middle school student she used to be. If I'd been thinking about how beautiful she really was, I would have been too nervous to sully her with my lips, as I was about to attempt to do.

I slowly moved my head toward hers.

"No lips," she said, quietly.

I held up my index finger, placed it against her lips, and said, "Shhhh." Then I kissed her—on the lips.

It would have been the most beautiful kiss of my life. But I was so lost in the seduction that I forgot I was wearing a fake lip ring. Worried that it would fall out (or, even worse, end up on her lip), I pulled back, looked at her again, and then nibbled on her lower lip.

Her tongue darted out of her mouth. "Hey, not so fast," I told her, as if she were the one hitting on me. The key to physical escalation, David DeAngelo had said in his seminar, is always two steps forward, one step back.

We made out carefully, and then I returned her to Rebekah at the bar. I had a workshop to wing, so I told them both that it was a pleasure meeting them and I should rejoin my friends. We confirmed our plans to spend a weekend together, and I left with my heart singing.

The Matador of Love was the first person to run up to me. He took my hand in his and kissed it. "In India, we put ourselves prostrate before people like you," he said, flapping his arms excitedly. "You've given me a new meaning on life. It was like watching John Elway do the two-minute drive. You knew he had game before, but in that moment he really proved it. You got the Super Bowl ring."

For the rest of the night, I was on fire. Women who hadn't even seen me with the platinum non-sisters were opening me. They could smell it.

When I ran into Heather again, I asked her, "You're not a thief, are you?"

"No," she said.

I removed my necklace and very slowly put it around her neck. "This is still mine," I whispered, kissing her lightly. "It's something to remember tonight by. But I want it back next time I see you. It's very special to me."

As I walked away, I knew I'd just made her night.

It didn't even matter whether I got laid or not, because this was the game artfully played. It was exactly what I'd been working so hard for. I just didn't realize that I'd ever be able to pull it off so smoothly or that, in the process, I was creating a hunger that could never be satiated.

After another two months of workshops, I flew back to Los Angeles for a break. But I grew restless sitting at home alone. There were clubs and bars full of sets to be opened, each one a potential new adventure. The compulsion to sarge consumed my body like a fever.

Fortunately, I received a call from Grimble. He was at the Whiskey Bar and had started talking to Heidi Fleiss, the former Hollywood madam who'd recently been released from jail for pandering and tax evasion. She wanted to meet me.

I slipped into a custom-made suit I had recently bought, threw my prop bag over my shoulder, and dabbed a different cologne on each wrist. I had a feeling this was not a casual call.

When I arrived, Grimble was standing next to her at the bar. He was wearing the exact same floral-print button-down shirt I had met him in, except the silver had faded to gray from so many washings. Three buttons were open, and his hairless chest was thrust further out than ever. Like a baseball player, he seemed to believe it was his lucky shirt.

"This is Style," Grimble told her, flashing a shady smile that was a little unnerving to a friend, but to a certain type of girl was no doubt a turn on. "The guy I was telling you about."

Heidi was attractive but hard, like only women who've had to fend for themselves in Los Angeles can be. I wondered if he was trying to set me up with her. She seemed like an odd choice. I try to avoid women who've served time.

She reached out and shook my hand firmly. "So," she said. "Show me your stuff."

"What are you talking about?" I asked.

"Grimble here says you're a pickup artist. He was telling me about what you teach. Let's see what you've got."

I flashed Grimble a dirty look. He'd sold me out. "Why don't you show her?" I asked Grimble.

"I have a girl here," he said, flashing a cruel smile and nodding to a petite Hispanic woman in four-inch heels. "Besides, she can see me on *Elimidate*."

Grimble had told me months ago that he was going to test his seduction skills by auditioning for the dating show *Elimidate*. I just didn't realize he'd gone through with it—and actually been accepted.

"When's it airing?" I asked.

"Tomorrow night."

"Who won?"

"I'm not allowed to talk about it. You'll have to watch."

I searched his face for a clue, but he betrayed nothing.

"Well." Heidi prodded. "Go pick up a girl. I bet I can get anyone you can."

It looked like I would be competing in my own *Elimidate* that night. I was exhausted from months of travel and constant pickups, but I wasn't going to pass up the challenge.

Heidi spun around and approached three girls who were sitting on the patio smoking. The battle had begun.

I opened a nearby three-set—two men and a lady who looked like an anchorwoman in search of a camera—with the cologne opener. Afterward, I asked the usual fact-finding question: "How do you all know each other?" Unfortunately, she was married to one of the guys in the set.

Just as I was about to eject, Heidi marched in.

"So," she asked my former target. "How do you know Style?"

"We just met him," she said.

"You looked like old friends," Heidi told her with an obsequious smile. Then she turned to me and whispered, "They're boring. Let's move on."

As we left, I asked how her three-set had gone.

"The girls were all twenty," she said. "I could have turned them out in a half hour." Evidently, pickup to Heidi Fleiss meant recruiting girls as escorts.

Minutes later, she was in another group. I had to give her credit: She had no fear of approaching. I decided it was time to humble her with the awesome power of my newfound game.

She was kneeling on the ground in front of two women with gold glitter lightly dusting their cheeks, talking about local restaurants. I walked in with a new opinion opener I had made up about a friend whose new girlfriend won't let him talk to his ex-girlfriend from college.

"Is she being fair?" I asked. "Or is she being too possessive?"

The point was to get the glitter girls talking amongst themselves, but Heidi blurted, "The guy should just fuck both girls. I mean, I always put out on the first night."

The line must have been part of her routine; it was the second time I'd heard her say it. I also noticed that she always kneeled on the ground after approaching, so as not to intimidate the girls. I was glad Grimble had called: Heidi Fleiss was one of us.

In recent weeks, I'd figured out my own routine. It was a simple structure that allowed me to determine the direction in which I needed to take a girl: First, open. Then demonstrate higher value. Next, build rapport and an emotional connection. And, finally, create a physical connection.

So now that I'd opened the set, it was time to demonstrate value and blow Heidi out. I ran a piece I'd invented after meeting the fake sisters in Miami—the best friends test.

"I have to ask you guys: How long have you known each other?" I began.

"About six years," one of the girls said.

"I could totally tell."

"How?"

"Rather than explain, I'll give you two the best friends test."

The girls leaned in toward me, thrilled by the idea of an innocuous test. Guys in the community have an expression for this phenomenon: I was giving them "chick crack." Most women, they say, respond to routines involving tests, psychological games, fortune-telling, and cold-reading like addicts respond to free drugs.

"Okay," I said, as if I were about to ask a serious question. The girls huddled in closer. "Do you both use the same shampoo?"

They looked at each other to decide on an answer, then turned to me and opened their mouths to speak.

"The answer doesn't matter," I cut them off. "You already passed."

"But we don't use the same shampoo," one of the girls said.

"But you both looked at each other before you answered. See, if you didn't know each other well, you'd keep eye contact with me. But when two people have a connection, they look at each other first and communicate almost telepathically before answering. They don't even need to speak to each other."

The two girls looked at each other again.

"See," I exclaimed. "You're doing it right now."

They burst out laughing. Big points for Style.

As the girls started telling me how they'd met on the plane the day they'd moved to Los Angeles and been inseparable ever since, I looked at

Heidi Fleiss kneeling there uselessly. The girls seemed to have completely forgotten about her.

But Heidi was no quitter. "So," she announced loudly, "are any of you girls gonna fuck him?"

Ouch.

In one sentence, she had humiliated me. Of course none of the girls wanted to fuck me—not yet. I hadn't even made it halfway through my sequence, and even if I had, the comment still would have blown me out. "Hey, I'm not that easy," I responded, recovering a little too late. "I need trust, comfort, and connection first."

Heidi and I walked away together. She clapped a hand on my shoulder and smiled. "If I left here right now," she said, "they'd follow me out like a line of ducks."

Seconds later, she was in another two-set. I dashed in after her, and the competition was on again. She was sitting with a balding man who said he was a stand-up comic and a heavily peacocked woman with long gumball-blue hair, an impish voice, and a wickedly smart sense of humor. Her name was Hillary, and she said she was performing a burlesque show the following night at a club called the Echo. She was so interesting, I hardly needed to game her. We just talked, and I took her phone number right in front of her date. Then Heidi invited them to a party and gave Hillary her number. She wasn't going to let me walk away victorious.

"I could have her working in a day," she said. She always had to get the last word in.

Some people are born to be rock singers. Others are born to be teachers. "I was born to be a madam," Heidi said. "I'll always be one."

Every time she left a set, she was convinced she could have turned the girls into hookers or extracted them to her house—even though those days were now behind her. By the time we left the bar that night, we had competed for every girl in the place. And I'd learned that there's a fine line between pimp and player.

Grimble and his date came up to me laughing afterward. "That was the sickest thing I've ever seen," he said. "I can't believe how much you've changed. You're like a new man." He gave my forehead a slimy kiss and then negged me. "You held your ground pretty well, especially considering she had an advantage because everyone recognized her."

"Well," I replied. "Let's see if you do any better on *Elimidate* tomorrow."

It was a red-letter day for the seduction community. Tonight on *Elimidate,* Grimble would be paired with three other eligible bachelors to compete for the favor of a lingerie model named Alison. Our entire lifestyle was at stake. If he won, it would prove that the community really did have a social edge over the jocks and studs we'd felt inferior to all our lives. If he lost, then we were just self-delusional keyboard jockeys. The fate of PUAs everywhere was in his hands.

I sat on Grimble's couch and watched the episode with Twotimer. Where the other guys on the show tried to suck up to Allison, Grimble leaned back and acted as if he were the prize. Where the other guys bragged about how successful they were, Grimble took the advice of his new guru and claimed to be a disposable lighter repairman. He made it past the first elimination.

During the second round, a waitress brought a bottle of champagne to the table for Alison, courtesy of Grimble. She was shocked, especially since Grimble hadn't been trying as hard as the other guys. He made it past the second elimination.

The final round was on the dance floor, which I knew would seal it, because Grimble and I had taken salsa-dancing lessons together. When he dipped her to the floor and scooped her back up, taking her breath away, I could see it in her eyes. He had won.

"Congratulations," I told him. "You have vindicated the good name of PUAs around the world."

"Yeah," he said, with a cocky smile. "Not all models are stupid."

We went out that night to see Hillary perform. Since my crush on Jessica Nixon in sixth grade, one-itis had been a regular part of my life. But in the past eight months, I hadn't felt even a tremor of one-itis. In fact, every woman I met seemed disposable and replaceable. I was experiencing seducer's paradox: The better a seducer I became, the less I loved women. Success was no longer defined by getting laid or finding a girlfriend, but by how well I performed. The bars and clubs became, as Mystery had coached me at that first workshop, just different levels on a video game I had to get through.

I knew Hillary, in particular, would be a challenge. Not only was she sharp and cynical, but she'd seen me run around picking up women all night with Heidi Fleiss.

Grimble and I sat in the back of the Echo and watched Hillary strip. She was dressed as a gangster, with a machine gun water pistol and a form-fitting pinstripe suit over a garter and matching panties. She had a classically curvy body that suited the art form. When she saw me in the back of the room, she sashayed over, sat on my lap, and sprayed me in the face with the water pistol. I wanted her.

Afterward, I joined Hillary, her sister, and two of her friends for drinks at a Mexican bar called El Carmen. As we talked, I took Hillary's hand in mine. She squeezed back. IOI. Grimble was right: A new me had evolved.

She took a step closer to me. My heart began to hammer against my chest, as it always does during the two parts of a pickup that give me the most anxiety: the approach and the kiss.

But just as I was about to tell her about animals and evolution and hair-pulling lions, disaster struck. Andy Dick walked in the bar with a group of his friends. One of them knew Hillary, so they joined us at the table—and suddenly my game evaporated. Our connection was eclipsed. There was a brighter, shinier object in her field of vision. When we rearranged ourselves, Andy Dick somehow ended up between us, separating me from Hillary.

He was all over her in an instant. It happens in Los Angeles: Celebrities hit on your dates. In my AFC days, I stood by helplessly and watched one night at the Whiskey Bar as Robert Blake slipped my date his phone number. But I was a PUA now, and a PUA wouldn't stand by helplessly and watch a celebrity molest his date.

Why was I constantly battling tabloid stars for this girl?

I stood up and walked outside. I needed to think. I'd given Heidi Fleiss a run for her money the night before, so I ought to be able to take out Andy Dick. It wasn't going to be easy, though, because he was so loud and obnoxious. It was clear from the moment he arrived why he'd become a star: He loved attention.

The only chance I had was to become more interesting than he was.

Grimble was outside, talking to a woman with curly, unkempt brown hair. He reached into his pants pocket and pulled out a pen and paper. He was about to number-close.

Suddenly, the girl broke away from Grimble. "Style?!" She peered at me, incredulous.

I looked at her: She seemed familiar. "It's me," she said. "Jackie."

My jaw dropped. It was the stinky-footed comedian whose hotel room I had run out of. My first semi-success story. Either this was a miraculous co-incidence, or we were running out of fresh women to sarge.

I talked to her for a while about her comedy class, then excused myself. I couldn't lose any more time; every minute was an inch higher up Hillary's thigh that Andy Dick's hand was moving. And I had a plan to stop it.

I walked back to the table, sat down, and ran the best-friends test on Hillary and her sister, which diverted the attention to me. Then, after discussing body language, I suggested we play the lying game. In the game, a woman comes up with four true statements and one lie about her house or her car. However, she does not say them out loud; she merely thinks them one at a time. And by looking for a variation in her eye movements, you can usually tell which is untrue because people look in different directions when they lie than when they're telling the truth. All through the game I teased Hillary mercilessly, until her body language closed off to Andy Dick and opened up to me.

Andy asked me what I did for work (I didn't realize this at the time, but it was an IOI), and I told him I was a writer. He said he was thinking of writing his own book. Soon he completely forgot about Hillary and started barraging me with questions, asking if I'd help him. He was my fan. And, as Mystery says, own the men and you own the women.

"My biggest fear is being thought of as boring," he told me. That was his weakness. I had beat him by being more interesting than him—and by having value to him. The tactics had worked, even better than they had the night before with Heidi Fleiss. Only I didn't realize just how well they had worked.

Andy slid closer to me and whispered: "What are you? Straight, bi, or gay?"

"Um, straight."

"I'm bi," he said, breathing in my ear. "That's too bad. We could've had a lot of fun."

After Andy and his friends left, I cozied back up to Hillary. She instantly gave me the doggy dinner bowl look. I took her hand under the table and felt the warmth emanating from her palm, from her thigh, from her breath. She would be mine tonight. I had won her.

When I came home from Hillary's in the morning, Dustin was waiting in my apartment for me. The king of the naturals had returned.

But what was he doing in my apartment?

"Hi," he said in his soft, effeminate voice. He was wearing a tweed sportcoat with large brown buttons, straight-legged polyester black slacks, and a black skullcap.

I hadn't talked to Dustin in more than a year, since before I had joined the community. Last I'd heard, he was managing a nightclub in Russia. He had sent me photos of his girlfriends: one for each night of the week. He actually referred to them as Monday, Tuesday, Wednesday, and so on.

"How'd you get in here?"

"Your landlady, Louise, let me in. She's really a sweet person. Her son's a writer too, you know."

He had a way of making people feel comfortable with him.

"It's good to see you, by the way," he said as he gave me a big bear hug. When he pulled away his eyes were misty, as if it really were good to see me again.

The feeling was mutual. Dustin had been on my mind every day as I learned the pickup arts. Where Ross Jeffries needed spoken hypnotic patterns to convince a woman to explore her fantasies with him, Dustin was able to achieve the same result without uttering a word. He was a blank male canvas for a woman to project her repressed desires onto—even if she didn't consciously know what they were before meeting him. I never had the resources to understand how he operated before; but now, with my new knowledge, I could watch him work, ask questions, and eventually model his process. I could usher a whole new school of thought into the pickup community.

"I don't know if I told you what I've been doing the past year," I said. "But I've been hanging out with the world's greatest pickup artists. My whole life has changed. I get it now."

"I know," he said. "Marko told me."

He looked at me with big, wet brown eyes, the ones that had gazed into the souls of countless beautiful women. "I don't . . ." He paused. "I don't really do that anymore."

I looked at him—incredulously, at first. But then I noticed that the skullcap on his head was a yarmulke.

"I live in Jerusalem now," he continued. "In a yeshiva. It's a religious school."

"You're kidding."

"No. I haven't had sex for eight months. It's not allowed."

I couldn't believe what I was hearing: The king of the naturals had gone celibate. It couldn't be true. Wasn't that why prisons were invented? They offered men food, clothing, shelter, television, and fresh air but deprived them of the two things that really mattered—freedom and women.

"Are you allowed to masturbate, at least?"

"No."

"Really?"

He paused. "Well, sometimes when I sleep, I have wet dreams."

"See. God is trying to tell you something. It *has* to come out."

He laughed and patted me on the back. His gestures were slow and his laugh condescending, as if he had spiritually bypassed toilet humor. "I go by my Hebrew name now," he said. "It was given to me by one of the highest rabbis at the Yeshiva. It's Avisha."

I was stunned: How could Dustin transform so suddenly from nightclub player to rabbinical student—especially now that I needed him most?

"So what made you give up women?" I asked.

"When you can get any girl you want, every guy—even if he's rich or famous—looks at you in a different way because you have something he doesn't," he said. "But after a while, I'd bring girls home, and I didn't want to have sex with them anymore. I just wanted to talk. So we'd talk all night and bond on a very deep level, and then I'd walk them to the subway in the morning. That's when I started to leave it behind. I realized that I got my entire validation from women. Women became like gods to me, but false gods. So I went to find the real God."

Sitting in his Moscow apartment, he said, he searched the Internet for guidance, until he came across the Torah and started reading. After an eye-opening trip to Jerusalem, he returned to Russia and went to a casino party, where the mafia, corrupt businessmen, and materialistic hangers-on sickened him in comparison with the people he'd met in Israel. So he packed his bags, left his week's worth of girlfriends, and arrived in Jerusalem on the eve of Passover.

"I stopped by," he said, "to ask your forgiveness for some of my past actions."

I had no idea what he was talking about. He'd always been a great friend.

"I idealized a lifestyle and behavior that were corrupt," he explained. "I abhorred kindness, mercy, human dignity, and intimacy. Instead, I used, degraded, and exploited women. I thought only about my pleasure. I despised the good instincts within me and within others, and attempted to corrupt anyone I met."

As he spoke, I couldn't help thinking that all these things he was apologizing for were the very reasons I had befriended him in the first place.

"I promoted and dragged you into this whole pickup thing, as if what I was doing were the highest ideal a person could live for," he went on. "So, to whatever extent I am guilty of affecting the natural goodness of your soul, I am deeply sorry."

It all made sense intellectually. But I've never trusted extremes, whether it be drug addiction, religious fanaticism, or zero-carb diets. There was something odd about Dustin, or Avisha. He had a hole he was trying to fill—first with women, now with religion. I listened to him, but I had a different opinion.

"I accept your apology," I told him, "but with the caveat that you have nothing to apologize for."

He looked at me softly but didn't say anything. I could see why he was so seductive: It was those eyes that glistened like the surface of a mountain lake, that intense power of focus, that way of making you believe that nothing else existed for him except what you were saying at that very moment.

"Think about it," I continued. "If a guy wants to improve his odds of meeting women, he's going to have to make some changes to himself. And it just so happens that all the qualities women look for in guys are good things. I mean, I've become more confident. I started working out and eating healthier. I'm getting in touch with my emotions and learning more about spirituality. I've become a more fun, positive person."

He looked at me, listening patiently.

"And I'm not just more successful with women now, I'm more successful in every other human interaction, from dealing with my landlord to handling credit card overcharges."

Still looking.

"So I guess what I'm trying to say is that I'm learning how to pick up women, sure, but in the process, I'm becoming a better human being."

His mouth began to move. He was going to speak. "Well," he said.

Yes? What?

"I am eternally here for you as a true friend, and also to make up for what I did."

He wasn't convinced. Fuck him. I was going to take a nap.

"Mind if I stay over for a couple of days?" he asked.

"No problem, but I'm leaving for Australia on Wednesday."

"Do you have an alarm clock I can borrow? I need to pray with the sunrise."

After I found him a small travel clock, he reached into his bag and pulled out a book. "Here," he said. "I brought this for you."

It was a small hardcover edition of an eighteenth century book called *The Path of the Just* with a note he had written for me inscribed on the title page. It quoted the Talmud:

> *Whoever destroys a single life is as guilty as though he had destroyed the entire world; and whoever rescues a single life earns as much merit as though he had rescued the entire world.*

So he was trying to save me. Why? I was having fun.

Mystery and I were on another road trip. The sun was blazing, the map was accurate, and there was a surfboard strapped to the top of a brand-new rental car. We had five workshops sold out in three cities in Australia. Life was good, at least for me.

Mystery, however, was in low spirits. I made a mental note to never go on a road trip with him again. Before he left Toronto, his girlfriend, Patricia, had given him an ultimatum: marriage and children, or good-bye.

"I haven't been laid in five days because of this bullshit," Mystery said as we drove up the coast of Queensland. "But I've been jerking it mercilessly to lesbian porn. I guess I've been sort of depressed a bit."

After four years of dating, their goals were diverging. Mystery wanted to travel the world as an illusionist with two loving bisexual girlfriends; Patricia wanted to settle down in Toronto with one man and no bonus woman. Celebrity and alternative lifestyle be damned.

"I do not understand women," he complained. "I mean, I know exactly what to do to attract them. But I still don't understand them."

We'd come to Australia because Sweater, the older Australian student from Mystery's first workshop, had invited us to stay with him for a week in Brisbane. After four months of sarging, he had finally met the woman he wanted to marry.

"I'm like a smitten teenager," Sweater exclaimed when we pulled into his driveway. He looked nothing like the insecure middle-aged man I had met in the lobby of the Roosevelt Hotel. He was tan, healthy, and, most extraordinarily, an irresistibly welcoming smile was now plastered constantly to his face.

Helena Rubinstein once said, "There are no ugly women; only lazy ones." Since society holds men to less rigid standards of beauty than women, this is doubly true of guys. Give a man like Sweater—or any man—a tan, better posture, whiter teeth, a fitness regime, and clothes that fit, and he's well on his way to handsome.

"I just spent the week in Sydney with my girlfriend," Sweater said, walking us into his house. "We talk on the phone about seven times a day. I asked her to marry me before I left. It's sick, isn't it? And on top of that, I made half a million dollars this week on a real-estate seminar. So life is just amazing. Thanks to the community, I have health, fun, money, love, and great people all around me."

Sweater's place was a sunny, airy bachelor pad overlooking Brisbane River and the City Botanic Gardens. He had a large pool and Jacuzzi; there were three bedrooms upstairs; on the ground floor, four employees—all enterprising, fresh-faced Australian boys in their early twenties—sat at a large horseshoe-shaped desk, each working on his own computer. Sweater had not only trained each of them to sell his products—books and courses on real-estate investing—but he'd turned them onto the seduction community as well. By day, they made Sweater money; by night, they went sarging with him.

"I'm still having fun helping the guys here get girls, but I'm off the market," Sweater said when we asked how he felt about his decision to settle down with one woman. "And as far as I'm concerned, I'm getting out at the top. I've come to understand that without commitment, you cannot have depth in anything, whether it's a relationship, a business, or a hobby."

In many ways, I was jealous. I hadn't met any woman yet I could say that about.

Mystery's workshop had changed all of our lives. Sweater was filthy rich and in love; Extramask had recently moved out of his parents' house and finally orgasmed in coitus; and I was traveling the world teaching men a skill I'd never even possessed a year ago.

Mystery was even more blown away than I was by Sweater—less by his engagement than by his home office. When he wasn't grilling Sweater and his employees on how they ran their business, he was silently watching them work.

"I want this," he kept telling Sweater. "You have a good social environment, and it creates a good working environment. I'm rotting away in Toronto."

As we drove to the airport, tan and flush with excitement, Mystery and I plotted our next adventure.

"I have a one-on-one workshop booked in Toronto next month," Mystery said. "The guy is paying me fifteen hundred dollars."

"How'd he get the money?" Most of Mystery's clients were college kids who could barely scrape together the standard fee, which he'd raised to six hundred dollars while reducing the number of nights from four to three.

"His dad's rich," Mystery said. "Exoticoption, from the Belgrade workshop, told him about me. He's a student at the University of Wisconsin. He just started posting online under the name Papa."

Most conversations with Mystery involved plans: organizing workshops, performing a ninety-minute magic show, creating a porn website in which we'd have sex with girls disguised as clowns. His latest scheme was the PUA tattoo.

"Everyone in the Lounge is going to get the tattoo," he said as we parted ways at the airport. "It'll be a heart on the right wrist, directly over the pulse. It'll allow us to identify each other in the field. And it'll be great for an illusion; I can teach you how to stop your pulse for ten seconds."

A couple of PUAs had already run out and gotten the tattoo—including Vision, which was somewhat of a surprise considering he'd moved to Los Angeles to make it as an actor. He'd e-mailed us a photo. But there was a problem: He'd put the tattoo in the wrong place and upside down. The heart was supposed to go over the vein where the pulse can be felt. But he had put it in the center of his wrist, an inch too high, and facing inward.

Nonetheless, it was a vote of affirmation, a pact that this PUA society was for life.

The day had arrived. This would be the most monumental trip of my seduction career. First, I was going to Toronto for Papa's one-on-one workshop with Mystery. Then we were going to get our PUA heart tattoos, take the bus to New York for Mystery's first classroom seminar, and finally, fly to Bucharest so Mystery could implement what he called Project Bliss. He wanted to return to Eastern Europe, find two young bisexual women searching for a better life overseas, and seduce them. He planned to get them student visas, take them back to Canada, and train them to become strippers, girlfriends, and, eventually, magic assistants.

Tattoos and white slavery: That's where self-improvement had led me.

On my way out of the house, I checked my mailbox. Along with the usual overdue bills and raised car insurance notices was a postcard of the Wailing Wall in Jerusalem. "Your Hebrew name is Tuvia." The writing was Dustin's. "It comes from the word Tov, or good. Its opposite is Ra, or evil. And in Hebrew, Tov also means that which endures and Ra is that which is short-lived. So your essence is connected to a desire to search out and connect to that which endures—the good. But sometimes you get stuck at the bad along the way."

On the flight, I reread the postcard. Dustin was trying to give me a message from God. And maybe he had a point. But, on the other hand, I'd had an enduring wish ever since adolescence for the power to seduce any woman I wanted. Now I was getting my wish. This was good. This was Tov.

Mystery had recently gotten his own place in Toronto with a PUA named No. 9, a Chinese software engineer who, thanks to Mystery's ever-present advice, had turned himself into a relatively cool-looking guy. They lived in a cramped two-bedroom apartment above a cybercafe near the University of Toronto.

Since No. 9 was out of town, I put my bags in his room and joined Mystery in the kitchen. Patricia had broken up with him, for good this time. And he'd been staying in his room a lot, playing a video game called Morrowind and downloading lesbian porn. Getting out of the house for these upcoming workshops would be good therapy for him.

There were three types of people who signed up for the workshops. There were guys like Exoticoption from Belgrade, who were normal and well-adjusted socially, but wanted to have greater flexibility and choice in meeting girls. There were guys who were uptight and set in their ways, like Cliff, who couldn't even handle having a nickname like everybody else. They tended to gather as much knowledge as they could but had trouble making even the smallest behavioral change. And then there were people like Papa—approach machines who compensated for a lack of social skills with a lack of social fears. Approach machines tended to improve the fastest, simply by following the flowchart of material they were given. But once they ran out of material, they floundered.

And this was going to be Papa's challenge. He was a soft-spoken Chinese pre-law student. He wore a checkered button-down shirt and jeans that were a size too large. They always seemed to arrive in a checkered button-down shirt and oversized jeans. And they always left in a loud shiny shirt, tight black synthetic pants, silver rings, and sunglasses pushed up on their heads. It was the player uniform, designed to convey sexuality, which was evidently synonymous with cheesiness.

Mystery and I sat down with Papa at a café and asked the usual questions: What's your score? What would you like it to be? What are your sticking points?

"Well, I used to be the social chair of my fraternity," he began. "And I come from a lot of money. My father is the president of a major university."

"Let me cut you off right there," I said. "You're qualifying yourself to us. Instead of gaining our admiration, all you're doing is displaying lower status. A rich man doesn't have to tell you he's rich."

Papa nodded stupidly. His head seemed to be surrounded by a dense invisible fog, which made his reaction time just a little slower than most people's. It gave the impression that he wasn't all there.

"Is it okay if I record everything you're saying?" Papa asked, struggling to pull a small digital recorder out of his pocket.

There are certain bad habits we've groomed our whole life—from personality flaws to fashion faux pas. And it has been the role of parents and friends, outside of some minor tweaking, to reinforce the belief that we're okay just as we are. But it's not enough to just be yourself. You have to be your best self. And that's a tall order if you haven't found your best self yet.

That's why the workshops were so life-transforming: We told each student the first impression he made. We weren't afraid of hurting his feelings. We corrected his every gesture, phrase, and item of clothing, because we knew he wasn't living up to his potential. None of us is. We get stuck in old thought and behavior patterns that may have been effective when we were twelve months or twelve years old, but now only serve to hold us back. And, while those around us may have no problem correcting our minor flaws, they let the big ones slide, because it would mean attacking who we are.

But who are we, really? Just a bundle of good genes and bad genes mixed with good habits and bad habits. And since there's no gene for coolness or confidence, then being uncool and unconfident are just bad habits, which can be changed with enough guidance and will power.

And that was Papa's asset: will power. He was an only child and used to taking any measure necessary to get what he wanted. I demonstrated some of my best routines on him—the jealous girlfriend opener, the best friends test, the cube, and a new piece I'd made up involving C-shaped smiles, U-shaped smiles and the personality characteristics each conveyed. Papa recorded every word on his digital recorder. He would later transcribe them, memorize them, and ultimately use my exact words to pick up Paris Hilton.

I should have recognized the signals then. I should have realized what was going on. This wasn't teaching; it was cloning. Mystery and I were traveling around the world making miniature versions of ourselves. And we would soon pay for it.

Our first stop was a lounge on Queen Street. After watching Papa crash and burn in a couple of sets, I started interacting. For some reason, I was on fire. It was just one of those nights. Every woman's eye was on me. A redhead who was there with her fiancé even slipped her number into my pocket. I figured this must be what they call seducer's aura: I was emanating something special. And what a perfect evening to do it, too—in front of a student.

I noticed Papa talking to a cute girl with short brown hair and a round face that perfectly matched his. However, she wasn't paying attention to him; her eyes kept twinkling in my direction. This was what the PUAs, in their worst acronym ever, call pAImAI, which basically translates as an unspoken invitation to approach. (Literally, it's a pre-approach invitation, male approach invitation.)

When Papa walked away, I said something to her. Afterward, I couldn't remember exactly what I said—and that was a good sign, because it meant I was internalizing the game, that I was getting away from canned material, that I could ride a little without the training wheels. After two minutes, I noticed she was giving me the doggy dinner bowl look. So I popped the question: "Would you like to kiss me?"

"Well, I wasn't thinking about it before," she said, holding eye contact.

I took that as a yes and moved in for the kiss. She responded enthusiastically, thrusting her tongue into my mouth and grabbing my knee with her hand. I saw a flash in the background; Papa was taking a picture.

When I came up for air, she smiled and said, "I don't have any of your albums, but my friends like your music."

My response: "Umm, okay."

Who did she think I was?

Then she smiled and licked my face, like a dog. Maybe David DeAngelo was right with his whole canine-training advice.

She looked at me expectantly, like I was supposed to talk about my music. I didn't want to correct her and rob her of the story she thought she'd earned by kissing me, so I politely excused myself. She gave me her phone number and told me to call when I got back to my hotel room.

On the way out, the hostess of the lounge pulled me aside and said, "Thank you very much for coming. Here's my card. Let me know if we can ever do anything for you."

"Who does everyone think I am?" I asked.

"Aren't you Moby?"

So I wasn't having an on night after all. Apparently, because of my shaven head, the hostess had thought I was Moby, and she'd told half the people in the room. All that time I'd put into seduction could be subverted simply with fame. To truly get to the next level, I'd have to find a way to flip the same attraction switches a celebrity does—chiefly validation and bragging rights—without being famous.

I suppose a lesser man would have taken advantage of the situation and continued the charade. But I never called the girl. I got into the game not to deceive women, but to make them like me for me—or at least for the new me.

In the clubs that followed, we watched Papa work. Every piece of material we gave him, he used. Every error we pointed out, he corrected instantly. With each successful set, he seemed to grow an inch taller. Instead of summer school, he told me, he'd spent three months working on Speed Seduction skills. He was even studying to get a hypnotist's certification with one of the field's most respected teachers, Cal Banyan. But until this workshop, he'd never seen real PUAs in the field before. He was so blown away he signed up for another workshop on the spot.

On our last day with Papa, we went to a club called Guvernment. I pushed him into sets and watched him repeat, like a robot, the openers, routines, and negs Mystery and I had taught him. And women were responding to him now. It was amazing how effective just a few simple lines could be—and it was also a little depressing. The first thing aspiring stand-up comics do is develop a tight five-minute routine that can win over any audience. But after seeing hundreds of rooms fill with laughter on cue at the exact same points, they begin to lose respect for their audience for being so easily manipulated. Being a successful pickup artist meant risking the same side effect.

When Papa left to get some sleep before his flight home, Mystery and I stayed at the club to continue sarging. Grimble had recently given me the idea of taking all the scraps of paper with phone numbers I'd collected and putting them under glass on a coffee table for decoration. But as I was sharing the idea with Mystery, he cut me off. "Proximity alert system!" he announced.

When women stand near a man but facing away from him, especially when there's no real reason for them to be hanging out in that particular spot, it trips what Mystery calls the proximity alert system. It means they're interested; they want to be opened.

Mystery wheeled around and started talking to a delicate blonde in a strapless dress and a muscular brunette in a do-rag. When he introduced me, he told them I was an amazing illusionist. We'd been winging together for months now, so I knew just what to do: fake them out with a couple of the practical jokes and pseudomagic tricks I'd learned in elementary school. In the field, one quickly learns that everything that was funny at age ten is funny all over again.

Mystery had brought along a video camera, so he began taping the interaction. The girls didn't seem to mind. As he isolated the brunette, I talked to the blonde. Her name was Caroline; her friend was Carly. Caroline lived in the suburbs with her family. Her goal in life was to be a nurse, but she was currently working at Hooters, despite having breasts the size of SweeTarts and a shy, withdrawn personality.

From two feet away, Caroline's face seemed alabaster; from one foot away, I noticed it was dappled with pinprick freckles. One of her teeth was crooked. She had a red mark on the skin over her collarbone, as if she'd been itching it. She smelled like cotton. She had gotten a manicure in the last twenty-four hours. She weighed no more than one hundred pounds. Her favorite color was probably pink.

I observed all these things as my mouth moved, reciting the routines I'd told to hundreds of girls before. What was different about Caroline was that the routines didn't seem to be working. I just couldn't reach what I call the hook point, which is when a woman you've approached decides she enjoys your company and doesn't want you to leave. Though I stood just a foot away from Caroline, a mile-wide chasm separated us.

After watching the movie *Boiler Room*, about ruthless cold-calling stockbrokers, Mystery had decided that phone numbers were wood—in other words, they were a waste of paper. Our new strategy was no longer to try to call a girl for a date, but to take her on a date right away—an instant date—to a nearby bar or restaurant. Changing venues quickly became a key piece in the pickup game. It created a sense of distorted time: If you went to three different places with a group you'd just met, by the end of the night it felt as if you'd known each other forever.

"Why don't we all grab a bite to eat?" Mystery suggested.

We walked to a diner nearby, arm-in-arm with our instant dates. During the meal, everything suddenly clicked in the group. Carly felt comfortable enough to unleash her biting wit, and Caroline began to radiate empathy and warmth. We didn't need any routines or tactics. We all just made fun of ourselves and each other. Juggler was right: Laughter was the best seduction.

Afterward, Carly invited us to call a cab from her apartment around the corner. She had just moved in and the rooms were bare of furniture, so Mystery and I sat on the floor. We didn't call a cab—and the girls didn't remind us to, which we took as an IOI.

Carly soon left the room with Mystery, giving Caroline tacit permission to fool around with me. As we wrapped ourselves around each other, the chasm that had separated us in the bar disappeared. Caroline's touch was soft and gentle, her body frail and forgiving. Now I understood why it had been so difficult to get rapport with her when we'd first met. She didn't communicate with words; she communicated with feelings. She'd make a great nurse.

After Caroline brought in some blankets to make the hardwood floor a little more comfortable, I went down on her. I stacked her orgasms as Steve P. had taught me, until it seemed like her body was melting into the ground. But when I reached for a condom afterward, I heard the five words that had taken the place of "let's just be friends" in my life: "But I just met you."

It was a much sweeter sound, and there was no reason to push for sex with Caroline. I knew I'd see her again.

She lay on my shoulder, and we enjoyed the afterglow. She was nineteen, she said, and hadn't had sex in almost two years. The reason: She had a one-year-old child at home in the suburbs. His name was Carter, and she was determined not to be another neglectful teenage mother. This was the first time she'd been apart from him for a weekend.

When we awoke the next afternoon, awkward from the passion of the night before, Caroline suggested having breakfast at a restaurant next door.

In the days that followed, I must have watched Mystery's video of that breakfast a hundred times. At the diner the night before, Caroline's blue eyes were flat and distant. But at breakfast in the morning, they glittered and danced when she looked at me. Whenever I made a joke, even one that wasn't funny, a broad smile spread across her face. Something inside her heart had opened. It was, I realized, the first time I'd made a real emotional connection with a woman since I'd started picking them up.

I don't have a particular type of girl I'm attracted to, the way some guys are Asian fetishists or chubby chasers. But of all the women in the world, the last type I ever thought I'd fall for would be a nineteen-year-old single mom who waited tables at Hooters. But the great thing about the heart is that it has no master, despite what reason may think.

After the girls dropped us off at home, Mystery and I broke down the events of the previous night, trying to figure out what we did right and wrong. Despite what Caroline and I had thought, Mystery hadn't even gotten a kiss from Carly, though not for lack of trying. She had a boyfriend.

She was clearly attracted to Mystery, however, despite having resisted his advances. So we concocted a plan: the freeze-out. It was based on my Moby experience. If women have sex for validation, Mystery figured, why not take validation away from her? His plan was to be cold and ignore her, until she became so uncomfortable that she wanted to cozy up to him just to make things normal again.

We loaded the footage of Carly and Caroline into Mystery's computer and proceeded to spend the next six hours self-indulgently editing it into a six-minute video. When we finished, I called Caroline and she picked us up that evening.

Juggler was in town, running his own workshop. He'd met a preternaturally bright jazz violinist named Ingrid and had started dating her exclusively. So we all went to dinner together.

"I'm going to get out of the seduction business," Juggler said. "I want to devote the time to my relationship." Ingrid squeezed his hand approvingly. "Some people may say I'm pussy-whipped, but I say it is my choice. These workshops are too stressful for Ingrid."

It was good to see Juggler again. He was one of the few pickup artists who wasn't needy, who didn't scare away my real-life friends, who made me laugh, who was normal. And for that very reason I didn't believe he was truly a pickup artist: He was simply a funny, masterful conversationalist. He seemed especially witty in comparison to Mystery, who was freezing us all out and making dinner somewhat uncomfortable. If Mystery's plan worked, it would be worth it; if not, then he was just an asshole.

Afterward, Mystery said decisively, "We're heading back to my place, and I'm going to show you the video I made of last night." Victory belongs to the person with the strongest reality and the most decisive actions.

As we watched the video at Mystery's house, Caroline couldn't stop smiling. Afterward, I brought her into No. 9's room, and we lay on the bed and slowly undressed each other. Her body trembled with so much emotion that it seemed to dissipate beneath me. It felt like making love to a cloud. When she came, she didn't make a sound.

As we lay together afterward, Caroline rolled away from me. She stared at the wall and grew distant. I knew what she was thinking.

When I asked her about it, she burst into tears. "I gave it up too fast," she sobbed. "Now I'm never going to see you again."

They were such sweet words, because they were so honest. I slid my arm under her and placed her head on my shoulder. I told her first of all that every passionate relationship I've ever had began passionately. It was a line I'd learned from Mystery, but I did believe it. Second, I told her that maybe she shouldn't have, but she wanted to and needed to. It was a line I'd learned from Ross Jeffries, but I did believe it. Third, I told her that I was more mature than a lot of the people she'd been with before, so not to judge me by her past experiences. It was a line I'd learned from David X, but I did believe it. Finally, I told her that I'd be sad if I never saw her again. It wasn't a line.

When we finally emerged into the front room, we found Carly and Mystery wrapped around each other in a blanket. Judging by the clothing strewn across the floor, Mystery's freeze-out had been a success.

Caroline and I spooned on the couch next to them, and together we watched an episode of *The Osbournes* on Mystery's computer, each basking in our own post-coital glow. It was a beautiful moment. And it wouldn't last.

There is nothing more bonding than successfully picking up girls together. It is the basis for a great friendship. Because afterward, when the girls are gone, you can finally give each other the high-five that you've been holding back since you met them. It is the sweetest high-five in the world. It's not just the sound of skin hitting skin; it's the sound of brotherhood.

"You know what's so fucked up?" Mystery said. "I feel so bad, and then a girl sleeps with me and likes me and, bam, I'm on top of the world again."

Smack.

"So?" Mystery asked.

"So."

"Are you ready to commit to this lifestyle?"

"I thought I was committed."

"No, for life. It's in your blood now. You and me, we have to challenge each other. Of all the guys I've met, you're my only competition. No one else has the chance to reach the throne except you."

When I was a teenager, I'd lie awake in bed, praying to God, "Please don't let me die before having sex. I just want to see what it feels like." But now I have a different dream. At night, I lay in bed and ask God to just let me have the opportunity to be a father before I die. I've always lived for experience: traveling, learning new skills, meeting new people. But having a child is the ultimate experience: It's what we're here for. And despite my rakish behavior, I hadn't lost sight of that.

Yet, at the same time, living for experiences also means wanting the novelty and adventure of dating different women. I can't imagine ever choosing one person for life. It's not that I'm scared of commitment; it's that I'm scared of arguing with someone I love over whose turn it is to do the dishes, of losing the desire to have sex with the woman lying next to me every night, of taking a back seat in her heart to our children, of resenting someone for limiting my freedom to be selfish.

This pickup thing had never been about sowing my wild oats. My oats are always going to be wild. And that's not necessarily something I relish. I'm screwing up my chances of being a cool dad. If I'd married my first girlfriend and had kids with her, they'd be, say, eight and ten now. And I'd be an excellent father, able to relate to them on nearly every level. But it's too late for me now. By the time my kids are ten, I'll be well into my forties. I'll be so out of touch they'll make fun of my taste in music and beat me at arm-wrestling.

And now I was really going to screw up my chances of getting married: I was about to brand myself a player for life.

An hour later, Mystery and I were outside Fineline Tattoo on Kingston Road. I was smarter than this, I thought. But it's easy to get caught up in the moment, in the hand slap, in the brotherhood.

I turned the handle of the door and pushed. It didn't open. Though it was three o'clock on a Monday afternoon, the shop was closed.

"Damn," Mystery said. "Let's find somewhere else."

I'm not a superstitious person, but when I'm on the fence about an idea, it only takes a slight draft to push me in either direction.

"I can't go through with this," I said.

"What's wrong?"

"I have problems with commitment. I don't think I can even commit to a tattoo that signifies a lack of commitment."

My neurotic nature had saved me for once.

The next night, Caroline drove to Mystery's house, and we all went out for sushi.

"Where's Carly?" Mystery asked.

Caroline flushed and looked into her tea. "She, um, couldn't make it," she said. "She says hi, though."

I could see Mystery's body language change. He slumped in his chair and pressed further.

"Did she say why? Is there a problem?"

"Well," Caroline said. "She's . . . well, she's with her boyfriend."

Mystery's face went pale. "And she wouldn't come?"

"Carly said you and she were very different anyway."

Mystery went quiet. He didn't speak for another ten minutes. Whenever we asked a question to draw him out, he responded monosyllabically. It wasn't that he loved Carly; he just hated rejection. He was experiencing the downside of seducing a woman with a boyfriend: She usually went back to him afterward. And seeing Caroline and I enjoying each other's company so much only rubbed it in.

"I'm the world's greatest pickup artist," he grumbled in my direction. "How come I don't have a girlfriend?"

"Well, maybe because you're the world's greatest pickup artist."

After a long period of silence, Mystery asked Caroline to drive him to the strip club where his ex-girlfriend Patricia worked. She dropped him off in the parking lot, and then took me to spend the night at the house in the suburbs where she lived with her mother, sister, and brother. It would be my first time meeting her family.

Her mother greeted us at the door. In her arms was a crying baby—my teenage girlfriend's baby.

"Do you want to hold him?" Caroline asked. I suppose the stereotypical reaction would be to say that I was scared, that reality sunk in, that I wanted to get out of there.

But I didn't. I wanted to hold him. It was kind of cool. This was what I got into the game for—to have these kinds of adventures, to hold a baby in my arms for the first time and wonder, "What does his mother expect of me?"

While I was playing daddy with Caroline, Mystery was spiraling.

Dropping him off at the club was a bad move. Seeing Patricia had fucked him up. Not only would she not take him back, but she also told him that she'd started dating other people.

"She's been working out three hours a day," he said over the phone. "She lost fifteen pounds and her ass is a 10, dude. The things a chick will do when she's angry. Damn."

"Don't think about how good she looks," I advised. "Look for the flaws and blow those up in your mind. It'll make it easier."

"I know that intellectually, but emotionally I'm fucked up. I feel like I'm being raked over coals. It all came crashing down on me when I saw her again. That hot body, the tan lines. She was the hottest stripper in the place. And I can't have her. Carly's back with her boyfriend. And I'm beat from trying to make my new place livable. For what?"

"Dude, you're a pickup artist. There are hundreds more just like Patricia out there. And you can get them in a night."

"I'm not a pickup artist. I'm a lover. I love women. I swear, I don't even think about threesomes anymore. I would be so happy to settle for Patricia now. I've got Patricia withdrawal on the mind. I miss her every minute of the day."

Mystery had hardly thought about Patricia or talked about her until she rejected him. Now he was obsessed. His own theories on attraction had come back to slap him in the face. Patricia was doing a takeaway. But for her it wasn't a technique—it was for real.

As a magician used to exploiting the gullibility of others, Mystery had no patience with anything spiritual or supernatural. His religion was Darwin. Love, to him, was simply an evolutionary impulse that enabled human beings to fulfill their two primary objectives: to survive and replicate. He called that impulse pairbonding.

"It's strange how strong pairbonding is," he said. "I feel so alone now."

"I'll tell you what. We'll pick you up tomorrow, and you can play in the suburbs with us. It'll cheer you up."

Caroline and I put Carter in his stroller and pushed him around the block to a park. As I sat down on the bench, I thought about what a pathetic couple of pickup artists Mystery and I were. Kids around the world thought we were in hot tubs surrounded by bikini-clad models. Instead he was alone in his apartment, probably crying and watching lesbian porn, and I was in the suburbs pushing a baby around in a stroller.

In the morning, Caroline and I fetched Mystery from the city. He hadn't shaved since I'd last seen him, and thin patches of stubble dappled his baby-white skin. He wore a gray T-shirt that hung loosely over faded jeans.

"Just make sure your family doesn't ask me to do any magic for them," he told Caroline.

Yet that night, when Caroline's mother asked him what he did for work, Mystery launched into a spectacular performance. He introduced each illusion—mind reading, bottle-levitating, self-levitating, sleights of hand—with ten minutes of patter and panache that put every other illusionist I'd seen to shame. He charmed everyone in the room: Caroline's mom was flabbergasted, her younger sister was attracted, and her brother wanted to learn how to levitate chalk to freak out his teachers. In that moment, I realized that Mystery actually had the skills to achieve his dream of being a superstar daredevil illusionist.

After Caroline's family turned in for the night, Mystery asked her if she had any sleeping pills.

"All we have is Tylenol #3, which has codeine," Caroline told him.

"That'll work," Mystery said. "Just give me the whole bottle. I have a high tolerance."

Already thinking like a nurse, Caroline brought him just four pills. But they weren't enough to knock him out. So while Caroline and I slept, Mystery, on a codeine high, stayed up all night writing posts on Mystery's Lounge.

Chapter

MSN GROUP: Mystery's Lounge
SUBJECT: Life Goals
AUTHOR: Mystery

I'm staying at Caroline's place right now because I've been upset over Patricia. Caroline is Style's Toronto girlfriend, and it must be tough for him. She is really beautiful, but she's got a kid. Style and Caroline look great together, but I understand the limitations too. Damn.

Solution: Be fair. Love her, dude. Be true to your feelings and don't hurt her but also know that you are polyamorous and want more. The idea of having many girls in many ports can be wholesomely nurtured.

She has a great family. I did magic for her eighteen-year-old sister, who's a cutie, and her brother and mom for like forty-five minutes. It was fun. I did a rune cast for the mom. Caroline is like my sister. I get that feeling of caring for her and her baby. And it's great to have Style here!

Then I took codeine to sleep because they all went to bed at normal hours, and I'm fucked up with my sleeping. But I didn't sleep. I just felt love. Don't get me wrong. I'm fully aware it's the Tylenol I took but, hey, the feeling is good nonetheless. I love this lounge. You guys are super bright. I hope we can all have a huge party one day.

And all this will wear off when the codeine gets pissed out, haaa.

This is what I want to see happen in the future: I want us to become closer friends—you think we can manage that? Grimble and Twotimer, your game is so different from mine. I want to sarge with both of you sometime to legitimately attempt to understand where you are coming from.

Papa, the game you played was fucking mint when you were up here. It was great to do a workshop with you, and you are welcome anytime, man. I don't even mind that you call me every day.

I envision this lounge as not being about pickup, but rather about something bigger: life goals. Women are a huge part of that, and we work together to help each other obtain them. However, I'd like to extend our topics to money, social status, and other ambitions.

I think one of life's biggest difficulties is not being able to share your problems honestly. So, state your issues here, and you have a hundred intelligent, trustworthy men who can assist you.

Also, tell us your goals and objectives. If you don't have any, now is the time to make them. I want to see all of us get our shit together and reach self-fulfillment. Travel, women, money, social status, whatever. Let's assist each other along the way. Let's all work on the same projects and synergize our efforts like a corporation.

I want to see Vinigarr[5] in his own apartment with a kickass car, coin in the bank, a hot nanny to help care for his kid (a nanny he gets to boink), and a couple girls who love him to death. He should own sections of New York—nightclubs or whatever. He should be driven around in his own limo. He should run his own escort agency.

Papa, you sponge off daddy. And the enemy of the best is the good. I want to see you focus as much on wealth as you do on relationship mastery. You have the drive to become a multimillionaire. You need to step out from daddy's financial shadow and dwarf his success. Imagine harnessing your sex drive and using it to create a successful business.

This is what I need: I need to complete promotional material to pitch to networks for a one-hour magic special. I need major funding to produce this. I'm not bullshitting or having fame fantasies when I say I can do it. People who have met me know I can play the role all the way. Once I have the special on the air, I can put on a Vegas show. I've designed the show in detail already.

Anyone interested in helping? Think of the after-parties! Let's build something. Let's exploit the fact that I need attention (must do shows) every day or I don't feel normal.

This isn't a freebie thing either. I don't believe in that. Work with me, and you'll get paid. Just tell me what your objectives are first so we can work on all our shit together! Gentlemen, let's get down to business.

—Mystery

---

[5] A former workshop student from Brooklyn, Vinagarr is a single father who earns a living as a driver for an escort service.

P.S. I've been reading Napoleon Hill's *Think and Grow Rich,* and I want to suggest something related. If you regularly masturbate, you can easily become addicted. This addiction comes in the form of daily regularity that curbs your desire to go out. It also does not allow you to harness your sex drive, which can be used to motivate yourself to work on wealth-building projects.

If you aren't getting laid on a regular basis (which happens to all of us from time to time), then don't just choke 'til you're broke. Set a date with yourself. Only jerk it once a week. If you jerked it today, set the jerk date for seven days from now. If you don't get a girl between then and now, you'll have something to look forward to. Make it a good jerk! Use the best porn and hand lotion. Look forward to it and this will keep you from wasting your life away jerking it daily and focusing constantly on the pain of not having a girlfriend.

In the meantime, harness your sex drive and build something.

The morning after his codeine-high post, Mystery lay slumped in the back-seat of Caroline's car, wrapped in a blanket and shrouded by a hat pulled low over his eyes. Beyond asking us to drop him off at his family's condo, he didn't say a word, which was rare for him. It reminded me of our Eastern European road trip. Except this time, Mystery wasn't sick—at least not physically.

We parked and took the elevator to his sister's apartment on the twentieth floor. It was a cluttered two-bedroom hovel crammed with people. Mystery's mother, a zaftig German woman, sat on a beat-up flower-patterned sofa chair. His sister Martina, her two children, and her husband, Gary, were crammed into a couch next to her. Mystery's father was shut up in his apartment four floors above them, sick with liver disease from a lifetime of drinking.

"Hey, how come you don't have a girl with you?" Mystery's thirteen-year-old niece, Shalyn, chided him. She knew all about his girls. He often used his nieces as a routine to convey his vulnerable, paternal side to women. He truly loved his nieces and seemed to come back to life a little when he saw them.

Mystery's brother-in-law, Gary, played us some pop ballads he had composed. The best of these was a song called "Casanova's Child," which Mystery sang along with at a near-deafening volume. He seemed to identify with the title character.

Caroline and I left afterward. The girls chased us all the way to the elevator bank, laughing and screaming, followed by Mystery. Suddenly, a door swung open and a man in a clerical collar gave the girls a steely, condescending stare.

"You shouldn't be making so much noise in the hallway," he said.

Mystery turned crimson. "What are you going to do about it?" he asked. "Because I think we should. These are young girls. They're having fun."

"Well," the reverend said. "They can have fun in a place where they're not disturbing other residents."

"I'll tell you what," Mystery snapped. "I'm going to get a knife, and we'll find out just who exactly should be in the hall when I get back."

Mystery marched back to the house as the rest of us exchanged concerned looks. Again, I recognized the behavior from our road trip: It reminded me of when he'd snapped at the border crossing after I'd told him what to do, triggering his father issues.

The reverend slammed the door shut, and Caroline and I slipped away in the confusion.

I didn't really want to go back to Caroline's. I've lived in cities my whole life. I hate the suburbs. Like Andy Dick, my biggest fear is being bored or boring. Weekend nights weren't made for sitting around watching videos from Blockbuster. But Caroline couldn't stay in Toronto. She didn't want to be away from her son; she didn't want to be a typical teenage mother.

So while Caroline played with Carter the next day, I checked my e-mail. Mystery and I had posted a field report about Carly and Caroline a few days earlier, and my inbox was full with messages from kids in North Carolina, Poland, Brazil, Croatia, New Zealand, and beyond. They were looking to me for help just as I had once looked to Mystery.

There were also two e-mails from Mystery. In the first, he wrote that he'd gotten into a fight with his sister over the hallway incident: "She proceeded to punch me several times. I had to restrain her by grabbing her throat and flipping her to the ground. I then left to go back to my house. I wasn't angry. I just wanted to stop her from attacking me. Weird, huh?"

The second one read simply: "I'm crackin' up. I'm hungry, my head hurts, my skin aches, and I've been choking it all day to Kazaa porn. I'm going to get sleeping pills because if I stay up all night alone, I'll go nuts. I can't wait to disappear. I'm so close to saying fuck it and ending it all. This living thing isn't fun anymore."

He was losing his mind. And I was stuck in bumblefuck, Ontario, watching Britney Spears in *Crossroads* with three teenagers, one of whom was supposedly now my girlfriend.

The next morning, I had Caroline drive me to Mystery's place.

"Can you stay with me?" I asked.

"I should really get back to Carter," she said. "I haven't been paying enough attention to him, and I don't want my mom to think I'm being neglectful."

"Your mom wants you to go out and be with your friends. You're putting this pressure on yourself."

She agreed to come inside for an hour.

We walked upstairs to Mystery's apartment and opened the door. He was sitting on his bed watching Steven Spielberg's *AI* on his computer. He was wearing the same gray T-shirt and jeans I had last seen him in. There were scratches on his arms from his fight with his sister.

He turned to me and began to speak. His voice was cold and dispassionate. "I've been thinking," he said. "The robots in this movie have motivated self-interest. They set objectives and then work to accomplish them. The child robot seeks protection from his mommy. The sex robot chases women. When he's freed from a cage, he sets out to mate with real women again because that's his objective."

"Okay." I leaned against a computer desk pushed flush against his bed. The room was the size of a large closet. The walls were bare. "What's your point?"

"The point is," he said, in the same deadened voice, "what is my objective? And what is yours? I'm a child robot, a sex robot, and an entertainer robot."

On the floor in front of his bed was a half-eaten plate of uncooked spaghetti. Shrapnel from the spaghetti sticks was scattered around the room. Nearby were the remnants of a black cordless phone that had been smashed against the floor. The battery dangled helplessly out of the open back.

"What happened?" I asked.

"I blew up at my sister and my mom. They wouldn't shut up."

When Mystery—or any PUA—was in a funk, there was only one cure for it: to go out sarging and meet new options.

"Let's get peacocked and go to a strip club tonight," I suggested. Strip clubs were Mystery's weakness. He had a list of strip club rules that pretty much guaranteed him at least a phone number every time: among them, befriend the DJ; never pay for a dance or a drink; do not hit on, compliment, or touch a stripper; stick to your material; and change the subject whenever a stripper starts reciting the stories she tells every other guy.

"I don't want to go out," he said. "There's no point."

He stopped the movie on his computer and began working on a half-finished e-mail.

"What are you doing?" I asked.

"I'm e-mailing the students in New York and telling them the seminar's canceled." He spoke as if he were on autopilot.

"Why are you doing that?" I was pissed. I'd put a month of my life on hold so we could go to New York and Bucharest together. I'd already bought the plane tickets. And now, because of some mixture of Steven Spielberg and codeine after effects, he was bailing out.

"Not enough people. Oh well."

"Come on," I said. "You're already making eighteen hundred dollars. And I'm sure more guys will sign up at the last minute. It's New York, for chrissake. No one commits to anything in advance."

"Living," he sighed, "costs too much."

It was all too melodramatic for me. The guy was a black hole sucking up attention. Fuck him.

"You are so fucking selfish," I seethed. "What about our tickets to Bucharest?"

"You can go if you want. I'm canceling all shows, all agents, all seminars, all workshops, all trips. I'm stopping everything. I don't want to be known for being a Ross Jeffries."

I gave his dresser a mule kick from behind. I have a long fuse, but when it hits bottom I explode. Though my father may not have taught me much about women, he did teach me that.

An orange prescription bottle hit the floor, scattering pills. I picked it up and looked at it. The word Rivotril was on the label.

"What are these?"

"They're my sister's anti-depressant pills. They really aren't about dealing with depression so much as making me sleep." Cold. Clinical.

I figured they couldn't be doing much good. So I left three in the bottle and stuffed the rest in my pocket. I didn't want him overdosing.

Mystery logged on to Party Poker, an online gambling site, and started playing mechanically. The Mystery I knew was too logical to gamble.

"What are you doing?" I said. But I didn't wait for an answer. "Never mind."

I slammed the door behind me and found Caroline in the front room.

"Let's go back to your house," I told her.

She smiled weakly, sympathetically. She didn't know what to say. In that moment, I hated her. She just seemed so useless.

So I went back to Caroline's house in the suburbs—to her mother and her brother and her sister and her son and her Britney Spears movies.

I could tell I was becoming a burden to her and a distraction from her son. And she could tell she was becoming a bore to me. It wasn't her constant fretting over her son I minded; it was her complete lack of initiative. The days and nights spent imprisoned in her house doing nothing were getting to me. I refuse to take time for granted.

One of the primary rules of pickup is that a girl can fall out of love with you as quickly as she falls in love with you. It happens every night. The girls who start rubbing your chest and making out with you in a club in two minutes will leave you just as quickly for a bigger, better deal. That's the game. That's life in the field. And I understood that.

During a workshop in San Francisco, I'd spent the night at the house of a lawyer named Anne. On her nightstand there was a thin book by a guy named Joel Kramer. Unable to sleep, I picked it up and leafed through the pages. He explained the emotions Caroline and I were feeling best: We have this idea that love is supposed to last forever. But love isn't like that. It's a free-flowing energy that comes and goes when it pleases. Sometimes it stays for life; other times it stays for a second, a day, a month, or a year. So don't fear love when it comes simply because it makes you vulnerable. But don't be surprised when it leaves, either. Just be glad you had the opportunity to experience it.

I'm very loosely paraphrasing, but his ideas reverberated in my head as I spent yet another night in bed with Caroline. I had originally memorized the passage to use as a routine. I never thought it would actually apply to my own life. Love was supposed to be something women chased, not men.

I spent the next day juggling airplane tickets and travel plans. I kept my flight to Eastern Europe, but instead of watching Mystery hunt for bisexual slave girls, I decided to meet a group of PUAs operating out of Croatia. I'd been corresponding with one of them, named Badboy, since the day I'd joined the community.

One of the reasons I became a writer is that, unlike starting a band, directing movies, or acting in a theatrical production, you can do it alone. Your success and failure depend entirely on yourself. I've never trusted collaborations, because most people in this world are not closers. They don't finish what they start; they don't live what they dream; they sabotage their own progress because they're afraid they won't find what they seek. I had idolized Mystery. I had wanted to be him. But, like most everyone else—perhaps more than most—he was his own worst enemy.

When I checked the seduction boards that day, there was one new message from Mystery. Its title: Mystery's Last Post.

I won't be posting here anymore. Just wanted to say thanks for the memories and good luck to you all.

Your friend,
Mystery

I went to Mystery's website, and it had been taken down already. It's impressive how quickly years of work and effort can be dismantled.

An hour later, my cell phone rang. It was Papa.

"I'm scared," he said.

"So am I," I told him. "I don't know whether this is just a cry for attention or the real thing."

"I feel the same way as Mystery." His voice was distant and weak. "My life is going all the way down. All I am is game. I haven't opened a book since school started. And I need to get accepted into law school."

Papa wasn't an exception. There was something about the community that took over people's lives. Especially now. Before Mystery started doing workshops, it was just an online addiction. Now everyone was flying around the country meeting and sarging together. It wasn't just a lifestyle; it was a disease. The more time you devoted to it, the better you got. And the better you got, the more addictive it became. Guys who had never been to clubs could now walk in, be superstars, and leave with pockets full of phone numbers and girls on their arms. And then, as icing on the cake, they could write a field report and brag about it to everyone else in the community. There were people who were quitting their jobs and dropping out of school in order to master the game. Such was the power and lure of success with women.

"One of the things that attracts a woman is lifestyle and success," I told Papa. "Imagine how easy the game would be if you were a high-powered entertainment lawyer with celebrity clients. By getting into a good law school, you'll be improving your game."

"Yeah," he said. "I need to prioritize. I love the game, but it's become too much of a drug for me now."

Mystery's depression was affecting not just his own life, but the lives of the kids who looked up to him and modeled themselves after him. Some, like Papa, were still modeling him, even in his downward spiral.

"Everyone who gets too absorbed in the game is depressed," Papa said. "Ross Jeffries, Mystery, me. I want Mystery's game, but not at the expense of life."

The problem was that this epiphany was coming too late for Papa. He'd already signed up for seminars with David X and David DeAngelo. All of it, of course, meant blowing off days of classes.

"My dad called yesterday," Papa continued. "He's really worried about me. All I've been doing is game for half a year while ignoring my education, finances, and family."

"You have to learn balance, man. Pickup should just be a glorified hobby."

It was wise advice—advice I should have been following myself.

After I hung up, I called Mystery. He wanted to give me his motorcycle. He wanted to give Patricia his computer. And he wanted to give the illusions he had designed for his ninety-minute show to a local magician.

"You can't give away the magic tricks you've worked so hard on," I protested. "You may want them later."

"Those are illusions. I'm not good at anything but bullshitting people. I never meant to be a bullshitter, so I'm stopping now."

I didn't need to be a high-school guidance counselor to recognize the warning signs. If I didn't take them seriously, I might regret it later. I couldn't turn the other way while my mentor walked off a cliff—even if it was a cliff of his own making. I once had a friend whose ex-boyfriend was always threatening to kill himself. One day she didn't respond to his cry for help. He shot himself on his front lawn an hour later.

As Mystery had noted in his codeine-high Lounge post, we had a valuable network at our disposal. The Lounge linked together surgeons, students, bodyguards, movie directors, fitness trainers, software developers, concierges, stockbrokers, and psychiatrists. So I called Doc.

Doc had discovered the community when Mystery signed up, on a lark, for a dating seminar Doc was conducting at the Learning Annex. Mystery listened patiently as Doc shared tips and tactics that were AFC stuff compared to the technology in the community. Afterward, he talked to Doc, who confessed to not being much of a ladies' man. So Mystery took him out for a night on the town, schooled him in Mystery Method, and gave him access to the Lounge. Now Doc was a machine, with his own harem of women. His nickname came from his doctorate in psychology, so I called him and asked for advice.

He suggested asking Mystery the following questions, in exactly this order:

· *Are you so down that you just feel like giving up on everything?*

· *Are you thinking about death a lot?*

· *Do you think about hurting yourself or doing something destructive?*

· *Are you thinking about suicide?*

· *How would you do it?*

· *What keeps you from doing it?*

· *Do you think you would do it within the next twenty-four hours?*

I wrote down the questions on a sheet of paper, folded it in quarters, and put it in my back pocket. This would be my cheat sheet. My routine.

When I arrived at Mystery's place, he was in the process of dismantling his bed. His movements were mechanical. So were his responses.

STYLE: What are you doing?

MYSTERY: I'm giving my bed to my sister. I love her, and she deserves a better bed.

STYLE: Are you so down that you just feel like giving up on everything?

MYSTERY: Yes. It's the futility of it. It's memetic. If you understand memetics, then you understand that it's all futile. There's no point.

STYLE: But you have a superior intellect. It's your duty to breed.

MYSTERY: It doesn't matter. I'm going to weed my genes out of existence.

STYLE: Are you thinking about death a lot?

MYSTERY: All the time.

STYLE: Do you think about hurting yourself or doing something destructive?

MYSTERY: Yes. This living thing is fubar.

STYLE: Are you thinking about suicide?

MYSTERY: Yes.

STYLE: How would you do it?

MYSTERY: Drowning, because it's what I'm most afraid of.

STYLE: What keeps you from doing it?

MYSTERY: I have to give away all my stuff. I dropped Patricia's computer and broke it. So I want to give her mine. She needs a computer.

STYLE: Did she care?

MYSTERY: No, not really.

STYLE: Was she mad that you broke it?

MYSTERY: No.

STYLE: Do you think you would take your life in the next twenty-four hours?

MYSTERY: Why are you asking me all these questions?

STYLE: Because I'm your friend, and I'm worried about you.

[Doorbell rings]

STYLE: Who is it?

VOICE ON INTERCOM: Hi, this is Tyler Durden. I'm here for Mystery. I'm a fan of his posts, and I want to see if I can meet him.

STYLE: It's probably not a good time right now.

VOICE ON INTERCOM: But I came all the way from Kingston.

STYLE: Sorry, man. He can't see anyone. He's, um, sick.

I left Mystery in his room, went to the kitchen, and dialed information for his parents' number. His real-world name was Erik von Markovik, but that was just another illusion. He'd legally changed it from his birth name, Erik Horvat-Markovic.

The phone rang once, twice, a third time. A man picked up. His voice was gruff, his manner curt. It was Mystery's father.

"Hi, I'm friends with your son, Erik."

"Who are you?"

"I'm Neil, Erik's friend. And I wanted to . . ."

"Don't call here again!" he barked.

"But he needs . . ."

Click. The asshole hung up.

There was only one other person I could call. I returned to Mystery's room. He was washing a pill down with a glass of water. His face was red and twisted, as if he were crying invisible tears.

"What did you just take?" I asked.

"Some sleeping pills," he said.

"How many?" Fuck. I was going to have to call an ambulance.

"Two."

"Why'd you take them?"

"When I'm awake, life sucks. It's futile. When I'm asleep, I dream." He was starting to sound like Marlon Brando in *Apocalypse Now*. "I dreamed last night that I was in a flying DeLorean. Like the one in *Back to the Future*. And there were all these wires around us. I was with my sister. And she was driving. We went above the wires. And I saw my life below them."

"Listen," I said. "I need Patricia's phone number."

The tears came now. He looked like a big baby. A big baby who was about to kill himself.

"Can you tell me Patricia's phone number?" I asked again slowly, gently, as if speaking to a child.

He gave it to me—slowly, gently, like a child.

I hoped that Patricia wouldn't hang up on me, that she hadn't cut Mystery out of her life entirely, that she'd have a solution.

She answered on the first ring. As a girlfriend, she had been taken for granted by Mystery. But in reality she was part of an invisible support system. Her stabilizing effect wasn't noticed until she was gone.

Patricia's voice was a little masculine, with a light Romanian accent. She didn't seem overly intelligent, but she cared about Mystery. There was compassion and concern in her voice.

"He's tried to kill himself before," she said. "The best thing you can do is call his mother or his sister. They'll probably put him in an institution."

"Forever?"

"No, just until he gets through it."

The door to Mystery's room swung open. Mystery emerged.

He walked past me toward the door.

"Hey!" I yelled at him. "Where are you going?"

He turned back for a moment and looked at me through blank, emotionless eyes.

"Good knowing you, buddy," he said, then turned away.

"Where are you going?" I repeated.

"I'm going to shoot my father and then kill myself" were his last words as he opened the front door to the house and closed it gently behind him.

I chased after Mystery. He was descending the stairs slowly, as if sleepwalking. I shot ahead of him and barred the lobby door in front of him.

"Hey." I tugged at his sleeve. "Let's go back upstairs. I talked to your sister. She's coming to get you. Just wait a couple more minutes."

He hesitated for a moment, unsure whether to trust me or not. He was so docile, he didn't seem like he would hurt a fly. I shooed him upstairs with gentle whispers of encouragement. As he turned and walked, I called his family again.

"He'll be okay," I thought, "as long as his father doesn't answer."

His mother answered. She said she'd be there within a half hour.

Mystery sat on a futon in his kitchen and waited. The sleeping pills must have kicked in. He stared at the wall and mumbled strands of evolutionary philosophy, memetics, and game theory. The conclusion of his mutterings was always the same: the words "futile" or "fubar."

His mother arrived with his sister in tow. The moment they saw him, they went ashen.

"I had no idea it had gotten this serious," Martina said.

She packed him a suitcase while his mother brought him downstairs. He followed passively, dead to the world.

They left the building and headed toward a car that would soon take him to the psychiatric ward of the Humber River Regional Hospital. As Mystery's mother opened the door for him, a four-set of girls poured out of an SUV parked in front of them. For a moment, a spark of life flickered in Mystery's eyes.

I watched him, hoping to hear him say those six magical words: "Is this your set or mine?" Then I'd know everything would be okay.

But his eyes went dead again. His mother helped lower him into the car. She picked up his legs and moved them inside, then slammed the door shut.

I saw him through the glass, the smiling blonde four-set reflected against his face. His complexion was pale and bloodless. He stared blankly ahead, his mouth closed, his jaw set, his sharp labret piercing angrily glinting in the cold afternoon light.

The girls were looking at the menu of a sushi restaurant. They giggled. It was a beautiful sound. It was the sound of life. I hoped Mystery could hear it.

Mystery's breakdown triggered a crisis of faith and self-examination in the community. We were all submerged so deep in the game that it was fucking with our lives.

Papa was failing out of school. A San Francisco PUA named Adonis had been fired from his advertising job when they discovered how much time he'd been spending on Mystery's Lounge. And my writing had come to a near-standstill. Even Vision had become so addicted to the seduction newsgroups that he gave his DSL cable to his roommate and ordered, "Don't give these back to me for two weeks."

Meanwhile, the community was growing exponentially. More and more newbies were flocking to the boards. They were young kids—some of them still in high school—and they looked to us PUAs for advice on not just seduction and socializing but everything. They wanted to know what college to apply to; if they should stop taking prescribed psychiatric medication; if they should masturbate, wear condoms, do drugs, run away from home. They wanted to know what to read, think, and do to be like us.

One of those lost souls was a short, well-muscled Lebanese student in his early twenties known as Prizer. He was from El Paso and had never even kissed a girl. He wanted advice on how to get comfortable around women, so we told him that first he needed to make female friends. And, second, he needed to experience sex, and not be too picky about a partner. He took us a little too literally.

Witness a few choice excerpts from his field reports:

MSN GROUP: Mystery's Lounge
SUBJECT: Field Report—Losing My Virginity in Juarez
AUTHOR: Prizer

I decided to see how it actually felt to have sex, so I crossed the border to Juarez. Since she was a hooker, I guess it's not technically a pickup. But I think this will help my game because I'll be less desperate. I had trouble keeping hard, except I got excited when I was going down on her and doing sixty-nine. It was my first time for all of that. Now that I'm not a virgin, do you think girls will find me more attractive?

MSN GROUP: Mystery's Lounge
SUBJECT: Field Report—Another Night in Juarez
AUTHOR: Prizer

I had sex again in Juarez. This makes four hookers for me now. She even swallowed my cum, but I still haven't been able to ejaculate during intercourse. Is this normal? Anyway, what I did this time to help my game is I pretended like she was my girlfriend. But when I wanted to eat her ass out, she charged me an extra five bucks. That was lame. Anyway, I'm writing this report because I'm thinking that it might improve my sarging more if I spend my money on hookers in Juarez for maybe six months instead of on workshops and e-books and shit. It's much more direct. Do you think that having more sex can raise your game and your confidence level?

After everyone in the community chastised Prizer for posting field reports about prostitutes, he was the first to turn to me for help. Then came a note from Cityprc in Rhode Island. Then came pleas from a dozen others I'd never met. They were all offering me money to teach them seduction. They wanted to fly in; they wanted to fly me out; they were willing to pay any price just to watch a real PUA in action.

With Mystery confined to the psychiatric wing of Humber Hospital and Juggler so deep in his LTR that he had taken down his website, the students were hungry. And somehow I had become their new guru. All those posts where I'd explained my routines and discussed my nights out hadn't just been a way of learning and sharing; they'd also been a form of advertising.

But seduction is a dark art. Its secrets come with a price and we were all paying it, whether in sanity, school, work, time, money, health, morality, or loss of self. We may have been supermen in the club, but on the inside we were rotting.

"I was modeling myself after you and Mystery," Papa said when I called to check on him. "I need to be me. I have so much potential for success, and I'm blowing it all. I used to be a straight A student."

He planned to go cold turkey on seduction and, for starters, cancel the seminars he'd already signed up for. "I'll also stop calling HBs until I get my life in order," he said. "If they call me, I'll tell them I need to get my life straight before I sarge them. I choose life. I will not be game."

"You have to treat school and studying like you treat seduction."

"Yes," he said, as if he'd just had an epiphany. "I will make school wings. I will make study pivots. I will fuck-close my tests."

"That may be taking it a little too far. But, um, good for you."

"I feel free," he said. "Whoa."

And I'd like to say that's how we all felt, that we all realized we'd become too consumed and came to our senses, that we put our lives in balance and got our priorities straight, that we relegated seduction to a glorified hobby.

But there is a concept in hypnosis called fractionation. And it states that if a person under hypnosis is brought out of trance and then put back under, the trance will be even deeper and more powerful.

And so it was with seduction. We all came out of it for a moment—we opened our eyes and saw the light of the real world. But then we went back under, deeper than we ever were before—and to an extent beyond what any of us could have imagined.

STEP 6
CREATE AN EMOTIONAL CONNECTION

PEOPLE USED TO LOOK OUT ON THE PLAYGROUND AND SAY THAT THE BOYS WERE PLAYING SOCCER AND THE GIRLS WERE DOING NOTHING. BUT THE GIRLS WEREN'T DOING NOTHING—THEY WERE TALKING. THEY WERE TALKING ABOUT THE WORLD TO ONE ANOTHER. AND THEY BECAME VERY EXPERT ABOUT THAT IN A WAY THE BOYS DID NOT.

—CAROL GILLIGAN,
In a Different Voice: Psychological Theory and Women's Development

Petra was a nineteen-year-old Czech with long chestnut hair, a thin golden-brown model's body, and no more than a dozen words of English in her vocabulary. I met her and her cousin on the island of Hvar in Croatia with a Seattle PUA named Nightlight9. We showed them our magic tricks. They showed us their popcorn. On a piece of paper, we drew a picture with a clock and a time on it to rendezvous that night. They met us and led us by the hand to a small, deserted beach. They took off all their clothes except their panties and tennis shoes, and ran into the water. We followed and made love to them as they chattered away in Czech to each other.

Anya was a whip-smart twenty-two-year-old Croatian who was vacationing with her younger sister. She oozed confidence, sensuality, and good breeding; her sister was the opposite. Nightlight9 and I met them on the beach in the Croatian town of Vodice. That night they slipped away from their parents, and we wandered along the waterfront until we found a docked sailboat. We snuck on board and had sex in the galley. I left twenty euros for the bottle of wine we drank.

Carrie was a nineteen-year-old waitress at Dublin's in Los Angeles. She approached me and complimented me on my dreadlocks; I neglected to tell her I was wearing a Rastafarian wig as a joke. I met her the next day completely bald, but we still ended up in bed together. When I e-mailed her the next day to tell her she'd left her rings at my house, she responded, "I don't wear rings. They're not mine."

Martine was a free-spirited blonde I met in New York, with milky skin, smeared red lipstick, and an iron-on T-shirt. I'd opened so many sets that I can't even remember what I said to her. The next night, we went to a bar. I brought along two other girls so she'd have to work for me. For a second I felt guilty about that. But only a second. In the bar, I asked her how good she was in bed, on a scale of one to ten. In my hotel room, I found out. She was a seven.

Laranya was a JAP in the body of an Indian woman. I'd met her when I was in college and we were both interning at the same weekly newspaper.

She was the hot intern; I was the shy intern. But when I ran into her years later in Los Angeles, Style took her out on the town. The first thing she said when we woke up together was, "I can't believe how much you've changed." Neither could I.

Stacy was a twenty-eight-year-old anorexic I met in Chicago. During a lengthy e-mail correspondence, she seduced me with her intelligence, candor, and poetry. When she finally came to visit, I was disappointed to discover that she was awkward and ineloquent. She probably felt the same way about me. Nonetheless, I brought her directly to my bedroom, and we began to make out. I put a finger inside her and felt a fleshy cord bisecting her vagina like a tennis net. It was her hymen. I told her I didn't want to be the one to take her virginity. That's when I realized that being a PUA sometimes meant saying no.

Yana was an older Russian woman with chiseled features and a great boob job. I met her at a bar in Malibu. She told me it was her birthday but wouldn't say her age. I guessed forty-five, but not out loud. As a present, I told her I'd be her boy toy. She grabbed my butt; I told her I charged extra for that. Two nights later, we had a cocktail and adjourned to my house. She said she didn't put out anymore, that she was looking for something deeper. We had sex that night. We role-played. I was the teacher; she was the naughty schoolgirl. It was her idea.

She was a drunk Asian girl with large breasts, surrounded by three sober Asian girls with small breasts. I can't remember her name. She thought I was gay. We talked for fifteen minutes, then I took her by the hand and led her to the bathroom. We gave each other oral sex and never spoke again. It was overrated.

Jill was an Australian businesswoman a fellow pickup artist set me up with. She had spiky blonde hair, leopard-print pants, and a voracious sexual energy. When she danced—if you could call it that—every man's head turned. We fucked in her BMW, with the top down and our legs out the door. When I asked her when she had first wanted to kiss me, she said, "As soon as I saw you." No woman had ever said that to me before.

Sarah was a fortysomething casting agent I met at the lounge of the Casa Del Mar hotel in Santa Monica. She looked clean and radiant, like she had stepped out of a shampoo commercial—even in the harsh light of my elevator, where, an hour after meeting, we made love. She kept asking if there were cameras. I couldn't tell if she was afraid of being caught or excited by the possibility. Probably both.

Hea and Randi were girls I met at the club Highlands. Hea was a teeny indie-rocker nerd with a boyfriend. Randi was a cute actress with the most mischievous smile I'd ever seen, and a boyfriend. It took a month to convince Hea to cheat on her boyfriend; it took a day to convince Randi.

Mika was a Japanese girl I met at Jamba Juice. She was an orange dream machine with energy boost. I am an orange dream machine with protein boost. I was intrigued. When we had sex, I discovered that she didn't believe in shaving her pubic hair. The next morning she told me, "I grow my hair out because I donate it to children with cancer." I was astonished: "They wear your pubes on their head?" She replied that she'd been talking about the hair on her head.

Ani was a stripper who worked out two hours a day and was addicted to plastic surgery. She had metallic red hair and lipstick tattooed on to match. After we had sex, she told me, "I have mastered the art of visualization." When I asked her to elaborate, she told me that since men are so visual, she makes sure that everything she does in bed looks hot. But when she developed feelings for me, she discovered that she was no longer able to have sex because the emotions opened wounds from childhood abuse. The visualizations ended.

Maya was a black-haired goth belly dancer I flirted with at one of her performances. When our paths crossed months later, she still remembered me. I invited her over the next night. Her car was in the shop, so I offered to pay for a cab. She was there in a half hour.

Alexis was a clothing store manager who looked like she should have been in an eighties new-wave band. Susanna was a recently divorced designer who wanted to rediscover her sexuality. Doris was a married woman whose sex life had died. Nadia was a librarian who had the skills of a porn star; I guess you can learn a lot from books. All four were the result of an experiment: I tried to concoct the perfect routine for the personals. After several failures, I succeeded. The secret, I learned, was to seem like a selfish prick in the ad, and then be a fascinating, laid-back gentleman on meeting.

Maggie and Linda were sisters; they're no longer talking to each other. Anne was a French girl who didn't speak a word of English. Jessica was a bookworm I met on jury duty. Faryal helped me call a tow truck when my car broke down. Stef was handing out flyers for a strip club on Sunset Boulevard. Susan was a friend's sister. Tanya was a neighbor.

My wish had come true. Women were no longer a challenge. They were a pleasure.

In the months since Mystery's breakdown, I'd turned a new corner in my game. Once I'd gotten the number of a woman, it was easy to meet and have sex with her. In the past, I was too obsessed with trying to get some to actually take a step back, assess the situation, and act appropriately. Now, after a year of accumulating knowledge and experience, I had finally gotten out of my own head. I understood the process of attraction and the signals women gave. I saw the big picture.

When talking to a woman, I could recognize the specific point when she became attracted to me, even if she was acting distant or felt uncomfortable. I knew when to talk and when to shut up; when to push and when to pull; when to tease and when to be sincere; when to kiss and when to say we were moving too fast.

Whatever test, challenge, or objection a woman threw my way, I knew how to respond. When Maya the belly dancer wrote and said, "Thanks for the multiple orgasms. Call and we can discuss when you'll be taking me out for dinner. You owe me for the cab ride, and I feel like being taken out on a real date," I didn't assume she was a bitch or pushy at all. She just trying to get validation for having put out so quickly and testing to see how much she could control me. I didn't even need to think about the response.

"I'll tell you what," I wrote. "I'll pay you back for the cab, like I promised, and then you can take me out to dinner in exchange for all those orgasms." She took me out to dinner.

I saw the matrix.

I *was* Mystery.

Chapter

WHO IS THE BEST PUA?
BY THUNDERCAT
FROM THUNDERCAT'S SEDUCTION LAIR

Okay, so the debate has been raging for a while now over who is the best pickup artist out there.

Obviously, a lot of egos are involved in this assessment, and everyone has their own opinions about who the best really is. In fact, it's so subjective that I don't really think there will ever be a clear and honest answer on the subject. It's like asking who the best warrior or soldier is in a war. But that doesn't stop some people from categorizing the guys in our little community as the best. So I've decided to rate the top PUAs operating out there.

Style is definitely, hands down, the best operating in the game today. This guy is probably the most evil, sneaky, manipulative bastard I have ever seen in operation. The thing is, this guy comes in totally under the radar, and that is why he is so dangerous. His subtlety is so amazing that before you know it, you are qualifying yourself to him and he has you right where he wants you. And the thing is, he does it with both girls and guys. No one is safe.

To give you an idea of how incredible Style is, he's invented most of the techniques a lot of the top guys are using and teaching. He is practically Machiavellian in nature and is someone I both admire and fear. Add to this the fact that he's a rather average-looking guy, and you have the most powerful of the Jedi, bar none.

It was when I went to Croatia after Mystery's breakdown that I realized everything had changed. I was no longer in the game to meet women; I was in the game to lead men. Two of the Croatian pickup artists I was staying with had even shaved their head in emulation of pictures of me they had seen online.

Despite my aversion to being a guru, I had clearly become one. When I talked to a woman, the room went silent. The guys leaned in close to hear what I was saying, pulling out notebooks to write my words down and commit them to memory.

On returning home, I watched Ross Jeffries run a variation of my jealous girlfriend opener (about the woman who doesn't want her boyfriend to speak to his ex from college), followed by a false time constraint. Afterward, he even e-mailed and asked for a copy of my evolution phase-shift routine. He was modeling me. And he planned on sharing these techniques in his seminars.

Then Thundercat's PUA ranking came out, and I was number one. I could no longer claim to be a student. Neil Strauss was officially dead. In the eyes of these men, I was Style, the king of the unnaturals. All over the world people were using my jokes, my comebacks, my lines, my words to meet, kiss, and fuck girls.

I had overshot my goal.

In the old days, I was just Mystery's wing or Ross's disciple or Steve P.'s hypnotic subject. Now I had to prove myself every time I went out. Guys in the community would ask behind my back, "How is Style? Is he any good?" If I didn't walk up to a group of girls and make out with the hottest one within fifteen minutes, they'd think I was a fraud. Before I joined the community, I had been afraid of failing in front of women. Now I was afraid of failing in front of men.

And the pressure ran both ways: I also began to develop unreasonable expectations of myself. If I was at an Italian restaurant and there was an alluring woman five tables away, I felt like a failure if I didn't sarge her. If I was walking to the dry cleaners and an aspiring actress-model-waitress passed by, I felt like a hypocrite if I didn't open her. And where simply talking to a stranger was enough to elate me in my AFC days, now I needed to have her in my bed within a week.

Though I knew my new mindset was seriously warped, I felt more ethical in many ways as a PUA than I had been as an AFC. Part of learning game was not just memorizing openers and phone game and rapport-building tactics, but learning how to be honest with a woman about what I expected from her and what she could expect from me. It was no longer necessary to deceive a woman by telling her I wanted a relationship when I just wanted to get laid; by pretending to be her friend when I only wanted to get in her pants; by letting her think we were in a monogamous relationship when I was seeing other women.

I had finally internalized the idea that women don't always want relationships. In fact, once unleashed, a woman's physical needs are often more ravenous than a man's. It's just that there are certain barriers and programming walls to be overcome in order for her to feel comfortable enough to surrender to them. I got good at the game because I understood that the goal of the PUA was simply not to trigger a woman's shutdown or flight responses.

[As I write this, I look up and, I swear to God, there is a girl on top of me. She has blonde hair and a sleeveless undershirt with a black bra underneath. She is smiling at me. I am inside her.

She is biting her lower lip as she rubs her clit against my pelvic bone. I can hear her gasping. She is supporting herself with one hand on my thigh and the other lightly resting on the top of the computer.

"You know it turns me on when you click the typewriter," she just said. "Can I put you in my mouth for a minute?"

So fuck the stereotypical image of the writer. This is the new one. I can get work done and play at the same time. It reminds me of sometlkhing Steve P. said, about alwyas being in your own reality. Everyone is jus a guest in it. So if it's my work tiem, and you want tohave sex with me, well,e welcome to my reality.

I think she's about to come. Sh e is coming allksd;Good for her.][6]

---

[6] This portion of the text has not been edited in order to preserve its authenticity.

So every part of the pickup is designed simply to anticipate and disarm objections—at least, when we're talking about solid game as opposed to fool's mate.

The opener, for example, is casual. It is not perceived as a pickup attempt. You are just being a friendly stranger when you walk up and ask her and her friends, "My neighbor just bought two dogs, and she wants to name them after an eighties or nineties pop duo. Do you have any ideas?"

When you start talking to a group of people, their first concern is, "Are we going to be stuck with this guy all night? How do we get rid of him?"

So you give yourself a false time constraint. "I can only stay for a minute," you tell them as you join their group, "because I need to get back to my friends."

As you interact, you pay attention to the people who seem most likely to shut you out—the jealous men, the overprotective friends. You make them feel good about themselves as you challenge, tease, and neg the target. If she interrupts you, for example, say, "Wow. Is she always like that? How do you deal with her?" If she looks shocked, you reel her back in with a light compliment. This is what I call push-pull—keeping her guessing by pushing her away and then quickly pulling her in closer.

After they're finished giving opinions on names for the dogs (Milli and Vanilli, Hall and Oates, Dre and Snoop—I've heard them all), then you demonstrate value. You give the girls the best friends test or teach them something about their body language or analyze their handwriting. Then you pretend like you have to get back to your friends.

Now they don't want you to leave. You are in. You've shown them that you're the most interesting, fun person in the room. This is the hook point: You can now relax and enjoy their company. You can listen to them, find out about their lives, and make a real connection.

In a best-case scenario, you can take the group or your target on an instant date to another bar, club, café, or party. Now you're part of the group. You may relax, tease, enjoy, and bond with your target, who is becoming attracted to you after the negging and after leading her group. When it comes time to leave, tell the group you lost your friends and need a ride home. This will give the woman an opportunity to be alone with you without letting her friends know she plans to sleep with you. (If the logistics are too difficult, get her number and make a plan to hang out later in the week.)

When she pulls up to your house, invite her in to show her that thing you were talking about (a website, a song, a book, a movie clip, a shirt, a bowling ball, whatever). But first, give her another false time constraint: Tell her you have to get to sleep early because you have a lot of work tomorrow. Say, "You can only come in for fifteen minutes, and then I'm going to have to kick you out." By this point, you both may know you're going to have sex, but you still have to play solid game so she can tell herself later that it just happened.

Show her around the house. Get her a drink. Tell her you're dying to play her a really funny five-minute video clip. Unfortunately, the TV in your living room is broken, but there's one in your bedroom.

Of course, there are no chairs in your bedroom, only a bed. When she sits on the bed, position yourself as far away from her as possible. Allow her to feel comfortable, perhaps even confused that you're not hitting on her. If you touch her, pull back afterward. Continue using a combination of time constraints and push-pull to amp her attraction. Keep telling her she has to leave soon.

Then, at your leisure, tell her she smells nice. Sniff her slowly, from the bottom of her neck to just below her ear. This is when you use the evolution phase-shift routine: smell her, bite her arm, let her bite your neck, bite her neck, and then kiss. Unless she attacks you with lust, as you physically escalate continue talking to keep her mind occupied and pulling back just before she starts to get uncomfortable. You should always be the first one to object. This is called stealing her frame. The goal now is simply to arouse her without making her feel pressured, used, or uneasy.

You make out, you remove her shirt, she removes your shirt, you start to remove her bra. What's this? She's stopping you from going any further? The PUAs have a name for this—last minute resistance, or LMR. Back up one or two steps, then continue. Wash, rinse, repeat. It's not real. It's just ASD—anti-slut defense. She doesn't want you to think she's easy. So you cuddle, you talk. She asks dumb questions like how many siblings you have; you answer honestly and make her feel comfortable again. Then you start from the top: You make out, then remove her bra. She lets you this time. You suck her breasts. She arches her back. She is aroused now. She gets on top of you and starts grinding. You are hard. You are excited. You want her.

You lift her off and begin to unbutton her pants. She pulls your hand away. "You're right, this is so bad," you agree, breathing heavily into her ear. "We shouldn't be doing this."

You make out more. You reach for the pants again. Wash, rinse, repeat. But she still stops you. So you blow out the candles, turn on the light, turn off the music, and ruin the atmosphere. Then you grab your laptop computer and check your e-mail while she lies there confused. This is called a freeze-out. She was feeling good a moment ago, enjoying your attention, your touch, and the intimacy of the room; now you're taking it all away.

She rolls over and starts kissing your chest, trying to reel you back in. You put down your computer, turn off the light, and return her affection. You reach for her pants. She stops you. She says you just met. You tell her that you understand. You turn the light on again. She asks what you're doing. You tell her that when a woman says no, you respect that, but it just pushes a button in you that turns everything off. You are not upset. You tell her this in a matter-of-fact voice. She rolls on top of you and whines, playfully, "No."

She wants to have sex. All she wants to know is that you're going to call her afterward, so that she feels good about what she did—even if she doesn't actually want to see you again. You let her know that.

You tell her, "Take off your pants."

She does. You enjoy yourselves and give each other many orgasms over the course of the night, the morning, and perhaps even for years afterward.

One morning, she asks you how many women you've been with.

This is the only time you're allowed to lie.

Chapter

As a community, we had reached a new height of arrogance.

"I'm starting to feel like I'm hunting rabbits with a howitzer," Maddash, a former student, told me.

He had just returned from pulling off one of the most unlikely sarges in community history. A Chicago office worker named Jackie Kim had accidentally forwarded her highly judgmental review of a date to her entire address book. It was just as shallow as the field reports of some PUAs.

"So where do I stand on . . . the date," she wrote. "The car, the money, the job, the cute apartment, the boat—which by the way only seats six people, so I really don't consider that really amazing—his mannerism, and his great kiss will probably lock in another date. But I can tell you now, unless he cuts his hair and sends me gifts, it won't lead me to seek anything more than my first thirty-year-old friend."

The post became an Internet phenomenon, forwarded around the globe and chronicled in the *Chicago Tribune*. One person who received the e-mail was Maddash, who promptly sent her a sympathetic response. Jackie wrote him back, saying the e-mail made her day and she read it every time she received a hate letter. A few e-mails, an exchange of photos, and one date later, she was in Maddash's bed. It took no gifts, no boats, no haircut. Just pure seduction.

Maddash's success set off a rash of copycat sarges in the community. Suddenly, just going out to a bar and bringing a girl home seemed too ordinary and easy.

Vision called an escort and paid her $350 for an hour. His goal was to be so interesting and seductive that she would pay him to spend the next hour together. He managed to tease her out of eighty dollars at the rate of twenty dollars per hour. They continued to see each other afterward, free of charge.

Grimble seduced a nineteen-year-old girl who came to his door selling magazines. Despite the fact that he was wearing boxers and a dirty sweater, he fucked her within an hour. And he didn't even buy a magazine.

After hearing about Maddash, Vision, and Grimble's latest antics, any PUA who had been disillusioned with the community after Mystery's breakdown was soon back in the game full throttle. And the most full throttle of them all was Papa.

Papa's pledge to study for law school had lasted a month. Then he went on a road trip around the country, visiting all the PUAs he could. Every week he sent me his schedule: He was driving to Chicago on Wednesday to spend time with Orion and Maddash; then he was going to Michigan to meet Juggler; finally, he was spending the weekend in Toronto with Captain BL (a deaf PUA) and No. 9. The next week he was in Montreal hanging out with Cliff and David X. The week after, he was working his way down the California coast, from San Francisco to Los Angeles to San Diego. As for PUAs in other countries—London, Tokyo, Amsterdam—he was constantly talking to them on the phone or online.

After a while, I couldn't tell whether he was still learning game or just trying to build his social circle. I don't think he knew either. He was simply imitating what he'd seen me do: travel around the world, meet different PUAs, and become the best.

There was one fledgling PUA, in particular, whom Papa bonded with: a twenty-two-year-old Canadian who had discovered the pickup scene when his mother stumbled across a seduction website. He called himself Tyler Durden, after the seditious character in *Fight Club*. And like a virus or a demagogue (choose your simile), he would eventually change the course of the community and everyone in it.

He was a philosophy student at Queens University in Kingston, Ontario. Beyond that, not much else was known about him—or would ever be known about him. He claimed to have been one of the biggest drug dealers in Kingston. He claimed to come from a rich family. He claimed to have written rigorous philosophy papers for academic journals. He claimed to have been a bodybuilder. But no one really knew.

Tyler hit the seduction boards like a hurricane. Before anyone had even met him, one thing was clear: He was obsessed to a degree beyond what any of us had seen before. He read the posting archives—thousands of pages long—of every master PUA in the game. And he was whipping through the list of recommended books—from *Introducing NLP* to *Mastering Your Hidden Self*—at a furious rate. He was a knowledge junkie.

Within a couple of months, he had consumed nearly every piece of rel-

evant information on seduction and reinvented himself as a self-styled authority, delivering stream-of-consciousness essays and field reports full of
impressive feats and braggadocio.

Like thumbtacks to a magnet, the seduction boys were up his ass. He
was a manic new voice, an instant do-it-yourself guru. And, soon, he was
Papa's trusted wing. He joined Papa on his journey to spend face time with
every seducer with a silly nickname. And one of them, naturally, was me.

Tyler Durden e-mailed me constantly. He was a persistent little brat, as
I suppose I had been. He seemed to pride himself on being a provocateur.

For years, nervous AFCs who were new to the community were told to
take the newbie mission. It involved simply showering, putting on nice
clothes, going to the nearest shopping center, and smiling and saying "hi"
to every woman who passed by. Many AFCs found that this not only
helped them overcome their shyness, but that some women actually
stopped to talk.

Tyler Durden advocated a new mission. He called it Project Mayhem, in
honor of *Fight Club*. And the directive was to run up to an attractive woman
and—before even uttering a word—lightly body check her, whack her on the
head with something soft, or physically accost her in some other playful
manner.

On the seduction boards, the majority of people didn't think. They
obeyed. I could have posted that snorting birth control pills helped my
game, and they all would have been lining up outside Planned Parenthood.
So after reading about Project Mayhem, hundreds of sargers around the
world were suddenly knocking into women with grocery carts and smacking
them with gym bags. It wasn't seduction, it was elementary-school recess.

And therein lay his appeal: Tyler Durden made seduction seem playful
and subversive—unlike, say, Speed Seduction, which required homework,
rote memorization, and even meditation exercises.

Yet, at the same time, there was something off about Tyler Durden. Vision had kicked him out of his house after finding him a snotty and un-
grateful guest, constantly demanding to be shown new routines. And
though Tyler's field reports were fun and compelling, every time he had the
option of getting laid, he seemed to back down.

Chapter

MSN GROUP: Mystery's Lounge
SUBJECT: Field Report—Speed Closing
AUTHOR: Tyler Durden

Okay, this just happened not even fifteen minutes ago, and I can't tell anyone other than you guys about it.

I was pretty bored today, so I went to the Rideau Centre shopping mall in Ottawa, hoping to meet some new HBs to hang with tonight because my AFC friends were all with their girlfriends.

I cruised the mall, and I couldn't find any HB higher than a 7.5, so I was pretty pissed.

I was about to leave when I saw this new Booster Juice place with a cute little redhead working there—about a 7.5 like every other damned Rideau Centre chick.

I ordered a juice, and here's what happened:

TD: Which mango is better: mango hurricane or mango breeze?
HB: Mango hurricane.
TD: Awesome. I'll have the breeze.
HB: Ha ha, okay. Which booster do you want?
TD: What are boosters?
HB: Those things on the sign on the wall.
TD: Ooh, so I can get like vitamins and energy and shit in it. Awesome! I'll be like a new man after I drink this. This is the shit!
HB: Ha ha.
TD: High-five!
HB: Okay! (*She high-fives me.*) Wow! That was like the coolest thing that's happened to me all day.
TD: Pretty bored, huh?
HB: Yeah, it sucks here.
TD: Hmm, well, guess what?
HB: What?

TD: I love you.

HB: Ha ha. Um, okay. I love you too.

TD: Awesome! We're going to get married. Wow, you can really find love in the strangest of places, like right here at the Booster Juice.

HB: Ha ha.

TD: Wait a sec. I know, close your eyes.

HB: Why?

TD: Just do it.

HB: Are you gonna steal my cash register or something?

TD: No, nothing like that. I swear. Remember, I love you.

HB: Okay. (*closes eyes*)

The counter was pretty wide. I leaned way over, so that I was Superman-style horizontal over the top, and kissed her.

As soon as I kissed her, she started screaming like fucking crazy.

HB: Aaaaaaaahhhh! Aaaaaaaahhhh!

All these people started looking over at me. She was freaking out, screaming her head off like a banshee, flailing her arms around and shit.

I was thinking, "Fuck, fuck, fuck. I knew this shit would backfire someday. Fuck. I should have waited for more IOIs or something. Fuck. I thought I had the IOIs! I'm never doing this ever again!"

TD: Um, I said I loved you first.

HB: Aaaaaaaahhhh! Aaaaaaaahhhh!

TD: Um, are you okay?

HB: Aaaaaaaahhhh!

TD: Uh-oh.

HB: Um, okay. That will be five dollars and thirty-one cents. Aaaaaaaahhhh!

She was trying to regain her composure by talking, but she kept screaming intermittently.

TD: Please calm down.

HB: Um, yeah. I'm okay. What's your name?

TD: Please don't call the police on me.

HB: No, no. It's just for the computer. I ask everyone.

TD: Okay. It's Tyler.

HB: Wow, that's an awesome name.

TD: Um, thanks. What's your name?

HB: Lauren.

TD: I like that.

HB: Oh my God, that was the most awesome thing that's ever happened to me in my entire life!

TD: Cool!

HB: Oh my God, you rock. Oh my God, I love you! That was fucking awesome!

TD: Glad to be of service. I promise I'll come back. I'll make you close your eyes again.

HB: Will you do more next time? (*winks, implying sex, I suppose*)

TD: I won't let you down. You know I love you.

HB: I'm looking forward to it.

TD: Wow, it looks so cool back there. Give me the backstage tour.

HB: Okay, c'mon back.

I was thinking, "Holy shit, I can't believe this!" I felt inside my jacket pockets, and I still had these two LifeStyles Tuxedo Black condoms that Orion had given me last weekend, so I could go for it if I wanted to.

Then I totally chickened out. I was like, "I can't handle this shit! I met this girl not even two minutes ago!"

There were literally fifty people all staring at me, watching the chick open the door for me to come back there with her. They were all looking like, "What the fuck is going on?" And it was making me really uncomfortable. With hindsight now, I would have done it. But at the time, I was so taken by surprise.

So I said:

TD: Um, actually I'm in a major rush.

HB: Will I see you again?

TD: Well, I'm leaving town tomorrow.

HB: Okay, what about after work?

TD: Um, I have to go hang out with my friends. I'll come back tomorrow and we'll go out then.

HB: Okay. Oh my God, that rocked! Wow!

Then I turned around and walked off.

—TD

Chapter

Mystery was back.

No. 9, his roommate, called and told me Mystery had been released from the hospital and was staying with his family. He was expecting him back at the apartment the following week, when Tyler Durden would be driving in to take a one-on-one workshop. It was probably too soon to be teaching again, but Mystery needed to pay the rent—and Tyler was determined to meet him.

"I came out of this strange emotional journey with some incredible cognitive models," Mystery told me a few days later.

His voice was Anthony Robbins clear again, his mind lucid. Life appeared to matter once more. However, something seemed different. He was in manic mode—more so than ever—but it was a new type of manic mode. He hadn't exactly returned; he had transformed.

"I have my life goals set," he continued. "The motivational carrots are all dangling properly in front of me. This year, I will build the foundation to take down Copperfield. I've decided to beat him. I am a superstar. My brain pupated into a butterfly."

I asked him if he was on any medication. He said he wasn't.

"I've given it a great deal of thought," he went on. "I only get depressed when I isolate myself. Look at what got me there: the pair-bond break with Patricia, new hotties staling and blurring,[7] no career momentum, and being alone in the apartment with no one to talk to. So we need to design a social environment with people to motivate me—something like Sweater's place in Australia. We can all motivate each other. While I was at the hospital, I took a lot of notes on this idea. I showed them to my psychiatrist. Even he was impressed. I'm calling it Project Hollywood."

That moment was the first time I heard the phrase Project Hollywood. I didn't think much about it at the time. I figured it would end up like Project Bliss: another stillborn scheme consigned to the trashcan of mental masturbation.

---

[7] Staling and blurring occur when a woman stops returning phone calls. See glossary.

"I shine," he went on. "I see this now. I'm a superstar, just like I'm tall. I'm simply a superstar who's been holding himself back. And I'd like you to come be a star with me."

It was good to have Mystery back. Flawed though he was, he had a certain charm. Some would call it narcissism, and they wouldn't be wrong, but at least he saw greatness reflected not just in the mirror but also in the potential of those around him. That's what had made him such an influential teacher.

"Dude, I'm already a star, at least in the community," I told him. "While you were gone, I was voted number one pickup artist—above even you. It's insane. A guy from England I've never even met before called the other day and said he pretends to be me when he's fucking girls. It makes him feel more powerful. What do you think of that?"

It was getting harder to live up to my name. One of our former students, Supastar, a ruggedly handsome teacher from South Carolina, had recently posted, "When I die and go to pickup heaven, Style will be there waiting for me because he is a pickup god."

Mystery laughed when he heard it. "That's something you're going to have to come to grips with," he said. "You've created an alter ego that you are."

Chapter

Mystery wanted to book me for three months straight. He planned to schedule workshops in London, Amsterdam, Toronto, Montreal, Vancouver, Austin, Los Angeles, Boston, San Diego, and Rio.

But I couldn't commit to the time. I needed to resuscitate my career. There was something I used to do before I was a full-time pickup artist—or, as the kids now called me, an mPUA (master pickup artist). It was called writing. Somewhere, in another life, I used to wake up in the morning, sit at a desk before even eating or showering, and stew in my own filth as I sat typing on a computer and not getting laid.

Now that I was mastering this whole girl thing, I needed to put the other pieces of my life back in balance. All the sarging was starting to scramble my brain. I was becoming too dependent on female attention, allowing it to be my sole reason for leaving the house besides food. In the process of dehumanizing the opposite sex, I had also been dehumanizing myself.

So I told Mystery that I was going to cut back on the whole sarging thing. I was currently seeing eight girls in L.A. My dance card was full. There was Nadia and Maya and Mika and Hea and Carrie and Hillary and Susanna and Jill. They had needs, and there were no strings attached. They knew I was seeing other women. And they were probably seeing other guys. I didn't know, didn't care, and didn't ask. All that mattered was that when I called them, they came. And when they called me, I came. Everybody came.

What I didn't tell Mystery was that I didn't trust him anymore. I wasn't going to set aside time and buy plane tickets only to have him break down on me again. I wasn't a babysitter. Trust, I always told women, is something you must earn. And he would have to earn my trust again.

It didn't take Mystery long to find two willing and enthusiastic wings to replace me: Tyler Durden and Papa. I wasn't surprised. Since Mystery had gotten out of the hospital, the pair was constantly in Toronto, staying at his apartment and vacuuming every shred of pickup information from his brain.

Mystery would call every day to fill me in on their progress.

He'd say, "I've humbled Tyler Durden with my game. He was an asshole at first, but we've broken through that and he's allowed himself to be taken under my wing as a proper student."

He'd say, "I've finally figured out the formula for getting rapport with a woman. Are you ready?" Big pause. "Rapport equals trust plus comfort!"

He'd say, "When you meet Tyler Durden, don't expect to like him. Only expect to tolerate him. He makes rationalizations constantly."

"Then why do you hang out with him?"

"He'll call and say he's coming for the weekend, and I just let him. He's like a thorn in my side that gets me out of the house."

"So should I let him stay at my place when he comes to town with Papa?"

"He's part of the PUA family. Just think of him as the annoying cousin who farts a lot."

One week later, Papa and Tyler Durden were on my doorstep.

Papa actually looked somewhat cool. He wore a leather jacket, sunglasses pushed up on his forehead, and an expensive cotton dress shirt untucked over jeans. Behind him was the palest non-albino human being I had ever seen. A shock of orangey blond stuck straight up from his ovoid head like a toy troll. His head was cocked upward; his smile seemed like a plastic snap-on attachment, and his features were flattened as if pressed back by an invisible stocking. Though he claimed online to be an avid weight-lifter, his body and face were doughy. Technically, he was a small person. He just had a certain genetic softness.

This was Tyler Durden. He reminded me of Heat Miser from *The Year Without A Santa Claus*.

He nodded at me when he walked in. No word of greeting—and, a pet peeve, no eye contact. I don't trust people who don't look me in the eye when they meet me. But I gave him the benefit of the doubt. Maybe he was nervous about making a good first impression. In his writings, he constantly referenced my posts and techniques. He looked up to me. They all did. But most were humble about it. Tyler Durden reacted to being uncomfortable by acting aloof and arrogant. Fine. Bono from U2 does that too. That's their thing.

When we went out to dinner, Tyler opened up. In fact, he talked nonstop, without even pausing between sentences. It was difficult to get a word in edgewise. He liked to talk in circles around a point rather than getting directly to it. He was the victim of a disease called thinking too much. My head spun listening to him.

"I was busting on this girl Michelle," he was saying. "I was busting on her hard. Hard fucking busting, dude." And here he pulled his head back, pursed his mouth, raised his eyebrows, and started nodding. The gesture was meant to convey how hard the busting was, but it looked strange and artificial. "Then this dude comes up to her and is like, 'Michelle, you are so cute. You are the bomb.' And she looks at me and goes"—here he smirked and spoke in a whiny falsetto to imitate her—"'I hate it when guys do that. Now I will never ever like him. I only want a guy who doesn't want me. I hate guys who want me. I hate it.'"

After an hour of blather, I started to understand Tyler Durden. Human interaction to him was a program. Behavior was determined by frames and congruence and state and validation and other big-chunk psychological principles. And he wanted to be the Wizard of Oz: the little guy behind the curtain, pulling the strings that made everyone around him think he was a big and powerful master of the realm.

I got it. I liked getting it.

Now here's the context: He grew up physically small and mentally slow for his age, he said. His father, a football coach, imposed high standards on him that he could never meet. This was all the biographical detail I was able to gather. It felt like a lot of hard information coming from him. And I still didn't know if it was truthful.

Every time the waitress came to the table, Tyler Durden wanted me to demonstrate a routine on her.

"Do the jealous girlfriend opener," he'd say.

"Show me an IVD,"[8] he'd say.

"Do Style's EV,"[9] he'd say.

I thought about how Tyler Durden had constantly pestered Vision for routines and material. Now I understood why Vision had kicked him out of the house. He didn't seem to see the humanity in us. He didn't care about what we did for work; where we were from; or what our thoughts on culture, politics, and the world were.

There was a distinction he didn't seem to understand: We weren't just PUAs. We were people.

---

[8] An acronym for interactive value demonstration. See glossary.
[9] An acronym for eliciting values. See glossary.

After dinner, I had a special evening planned for Tyler Durden and Papa. Hillary, the blue-haired burlesque dancer I'd battled Heidi Fleiss and Andy Dick for, was performing at the Spider Club in Hollywood. So I called a few other women to join us there, including Laurie, the Irish girl who had inspired me to invent the evolution phase-shift routine. I figured Tyler would want to meet Grimble, so I invited him as well.

When we arrived, Laurie and her girlfriends were sitting at the bar. Nearly every male in the room was staring at them, trying to work up the courage to approach. I introduced them to Tyler. After saying hello, he proceeded to sit down and not speak another word. For ten minutes, he sat there in uncomfortable silence. It was the first time he had shut up all night.

When I introduced them to Papa, he immediately came to life. He took the sunglasses off his head and put them on Laurie—a move Mystery had taught him in Toronto when he asked how to keep the target from wandering off while being ignored. He then started running my value-demonstrating routine about C-shaped smiles versus U-shaped smiles.

I liked watching Papa's progress. Arbiters of cool like to say that some people have *it* and other people don't. And you can tell in an instant, just from looking at someone, whether they have it. I'd thought my whole life that it was something one was born with. However, the whole community was predicated on the idea that it was something people could learn. Though there was still something mechanical about Papa, he was starting to get it. He was like an *it* robot.

While Papa entertained the girls, Tyler Durden and I went to the other room to watch Hillary dance. She was in a birdcage, waving two massive feathered fans in front of her body. A glimpse of shoulder here. A glimpse of leg there. She had a spectacular body. Too bad I'd never sleep with her again.

"Why didn't you say anything to Laurie and her friends?" I asked Tyler.

"I didn't know what routines you had used on them," he replied. "I didn't want to repeat anything."

"Dude, don't you have a personality of your own that you can use?"

Hillary was wearing just feathered pasties and matching panties now. She had such soft skin. Her nose looked like a beak, though. The last time I saw her, she told me she'd had a herpes outbreak. I couldn't bring myself to have sex with her.

"Let's go somewhere else?" Tyler nudged me.

"Why? There are plenty of girls here."

She had done the right thing by telling me she had herpes. It's better than keeping it a secret and letting me catch it. I couldn't punish her for honesty. But now I was too paranoid to sleep with her.

"I want to see you work in a place where you don't know anyone," Tyler prodded.

She covered her body with a feather, reached under her legs, and threw her panties into the audience. A flying herpes rag. A hipster with mutton-chop sideburns caught it. He crumpled it in his fist and thrust it into the air excitedly. His little venereal prize.

A hand clapped my shoulder. It was Grimble, in his lucky pickup shirt.

"So what's up, man?" he asked

"Nothing much. How do you feel about accompanying Tyler Durden here to the Saddle Ranch?"

"You're not coming?" Tyler Durden asked. "I really wanted to see your game."

"I'm tired, man."

"If you come, I'll do my Mystery-talking-about-how-much-he-misses-his-soul-mate-Style imitation for you. It's a real crowd pleaser."

Thanks but no thanks.

I walked to a booth and grabbed a seat opposite Hillary.

"Who are those losers you're with?" she asked.

"They're pickup artists."

"Could have fooled me."

"Well, they're young. And they're still learning. Give them time."

She pinched her left eyelash and slowly peeled it off. "Want to go to El Carmen?" she asked. Then her right eyelash.

If I went, I'd have to sleep with her. That was part of the contract. "No. I should really go home."

I wanted to get myself tested for everything. I was too neurotic to be so promiscuous.

Despite everything, I wanted to like Tyler Durden. Everyone else seemed to.

As he and Papa traveled the country winging workshops with Mystery, the reports of his skills were stellar. Perhaps he'd just been nervous around me. Or maybe he'd improved after being forced to perform for so many students, as I had. I decided to give him the benefit of the doubt.

There were trends in the community. Ross Jeffries and Speed Seduction had ruled the seduction boards when I arrived over a year ago. Then Mystery Method took over, followed by David DeAngelo and cocky funny. Now, Tyler Durden and Papa were on the rise.

The funny thing was that although the methods kept changing, women weren't. The community was still so underground that few women, if any, knew what we were up to. These were trends that had nothing to do with females and everything to do with male ego.

And one of the biggest egos of them all, Ross Jeffries, was getting left behind. Though Speed Seduction still had a lot to offer, it seemed as archaic to the new generation of community members as buying a girl flowers and sharing a malt at the soda shop. And Ross wasn't happy about it. He wasn't happy about much. I found that out one night when I returned home to find the following message on my machine:

Hey Style, it's Ross. I'm in a cranky mood. It's ten after twelve. Normally when I'm in a cranky mood, I call people I don't like and chew them out. But I'm not going to do that. I'm just going to tell you that it's uneven. It won't kill you to take me to more than one party, buddy, though I think you owe me a lot more than that.

If you don't come through, I won't get mad. I'll just cut you out of the Speed Seduction community and everything else. I really will. So think about how my work has changed your life, and think about what you've given in return and what you've promised to give. It's just not fair. I'm hoping there's more to you than that. If it sounds like a challenge I'd issue to a girl, so be it.

I understood where Ross was coming from. I had been completely ignoring him since our last party together. He'd have to hypnotize the image of him sniffing Carmen Electra's butt out of my head if I was ever going to take him to a party again.

However, I called Ross a couple of nights later and invited him to dinner for old-time's sake. He wasn't as angry as I thought he'd be, chiefly because his mind was consumed by someone else: Tyler Durden.

"The guy gives me the willies," Ross said. "There's something creepy about his lack of ordinary human warmth. I wouldn't be surprised if sooner or later he breaks from Mystery and just teaches totally on his own. He's uncomfortable around people who are more powerful than him. Besides, he's already claiming to be better than Mystery."

Though I wrote the comment off as more of Ross's competitive paranoia, Tyler Durden soon proved him right.

And it was my fault, according to Mystery.

"The workshops aren't fun anymore," Mystery complained. He was calling from New Jersey, where he was rained in with Tyler Durden and Papa at the home of a PUA named Garvelous, who invented toys for a living. "They're just work. These things are only fun when you come with, because then we get to wing each other."

I was flattered, though workshops weren't supposed to be fun; as the name implied, they were work.

"Besides, my goals are changing," he continued. "It started with wanting attention. Now I think I'm looking for love. I want to be in a relationship where I can feel butterflies in my stomach. I want a woman I can respect for her art, like a singer or a super-hot stripper."

The inevitable split came soon after.

Mystery flew to England and Amsterdam with Tyler and Papa to teach another round of workshops. When he left with glowing reviews and numerous requests for an encore performance, Tyler Durden and Papa stayed behind to run a few workshops of their own to satisfy the demand. They were on break from college, and teaching men how to pick up women seemed a lot more appealing as an interim job than scooping ice cream or working at the local Baby Gap.

Mystery phoned as soon as he returned to Toronto. "My father has lung cancer, so he's on his way out," he said. "It's strange, but the first person I wanted to call was you."

"So how do you feel about it?"

"I'm not upset, but my mom was crying and it's the first time I've ever seen her cry. Dad always wanted whiskey poured on his grave, so my brother said, 'I just hope he doesn't mind me filtering it through my bladder first.'"

Mystery laughed. I tried to force a chuckle out for his sake. But it didn't come. The image wasn't funny to anyone who didn't hate the guy.

Meanwhile, Tyler Durden and Papa were running wild in Europe. At first, they pretty much taught Mystery's material. But that all changed one night in London, when they came into their own in the great outdoors of Leicester Square, ground zero for backpackers, clubbers, tourists, players, and drunks. It was here that AMOGing was born.

The AMOG is the alpha male of the group, a constant thorn in the side of sargers. There's nothing more humiliating than having a lumbering high school quarterback who reeks of alcohol pick you up from behind and make fun of your peacocking gear in front of the girls you're trying to game. It's a constant reminder that you are not one of the popular kids, that you're just a closet nerd faking it.

Tyler Durden may have been the biggest closet nerd of us all. But what he lacked in coolness and grace, he made up for in analysis. He was a social deconstructionist and behavioral micromanager. He could watch a human interaction and break it down to the physical, verbal, social, and psychological components that powered it. And AMOGing—or cutting a competitive male cockblock out of a set—appealed to his subversive side; stealing a woman from the jocks who used to pick on him in school was a taste far sweeter than simply seducing a woman sitting alone in a café.

So he watched the body language AMOGs used to lower his status in sets; he observed the eye contact they used to signify to girls that he was a creep; he analyzed the way they'd pat him on the back with so much force that he'd lose his balance. Soon he was spending more time in the field studying AMOGs than sarging women, until he slowly and painstakingly laid out a new social order—where, to paraphrase the musician Boyd Rice, the strong live off the weak and the clever live off the strong.

Now nothing could stop the PUAs. They could steal girls right out from under the disbelieving eyes of boyfriends the size of refrigerators. They were stepping into dangerous territory.

Chapter

MSN GROUP: Mystery's Lounge
SUBJECT: AMOG Tactics
AUTHOR: Tyler Durden

Here's some stuff I've been up to lately that is pretty funny.

I learned most of this from European naturals while trying to steal sets from them and prevent them from stealing sets from me. The guys here are not pushovers like most guys in North America. Many have game. So I've been figuring out how to out-game them.

All of this has been field-tested probably hundreds of times.

AMOG: Hey girls, what's up?
PUA: Hey dude (*put your hands in the air like you give up*), I will pay you a hundred dollars right now to take these girls away from me.

(The girls will go, "No, no. We love you PUA." And they'll giggle and crawl on you, which is immediately deflating to the guy.)

AMOG: (*Shows signs that he wants to fight*)
PUA: Ha ha, dude. Are you like trying to pick a fight with me? Ha ha. Okay, okay. Hold up, hold up. Wait a sec. We'll do even better. First, we'll have an arm-wrestling competition. Then, we'll do one-armed push-ups. And last, pose-down!

(Then start flexing and go, "Ladies?" They'll start saying how you're so strong. The AMOG will look like a tool because you're making him seem like he's trying too hard to impress the girls with his physical superiority.)

AMOG: Hey man, keep talking. Let's hear your pitch. Pick these girls up, man. You're doing awesome.
PUA Hey, you know I've gotta try to impress you cool London guys (or

rugby-shirt-wearing guys or shiny-shoes guys or whatever). You guys fucking rock.

(The point is to cut him down on whatever limited amount of knowledge you have of him, even if it's not relevant. He'll feel uncomfortable and his body language will show it.)

> **AMOG:** Is that design on your shirt a sphincter? Man, you're going to need somebody to protect you, mate. You're going to have all the guys into you.
>
> **PUA:** Dude, that's why I rolled up on you. I need you, man. Help me, please, man. I look at you, and I just know that you were born to protect my sphincter.

(Somebody actually said this to me. And, to be honest, it was a good diss. So when you have an AMOG who knows the game, you have to go further. Put him in the position of trying too hard to be your friend or joke about hiring him to do jobs that are beta to you. Say, "You're like a comedian, but you don't have to be funny for me to like you." Or, "Man, that's great. You should like design my website or something.")

> **AMOG:** (*Starts touching you to show dominance*)
>
> **PUA:** Ha ha, dude. I'm not into guys, man. Dude, the gay club is over there. Hands off the merchandise, buddy.

(The girls laugh at him, then he starts qualifying himself to you that he's not gay.)

> **AMOG:** (*Gets in your face*)
>
> **PUA:** (*Silence*)
>
> (Don't respond. Just stand there quietly. If he keeps trying to out-alpha you and you don't answer, eventually he looks beta because he is trying too hard to get your attention. Another trick is to make let's-get-out-of-here motions with your eyes to the girls—mimic what they do to each other when you're running a bad set—and they'll leave with you.)

Here are some other pointers.

If an AMOG is with the girls I'm sarging, the goal is to neutralize him. If he's just met the girls, the goal is to blow him out.

AMOGing works best with the right body language. When you say these lines, you want to have a big smile on your face. If you can, elbow him hard in the chest or slap him on the back hard enough to make him spit up his drink. All this has to be under the guise of being friendly. And then (and this happened to me) tell him, "Fair play, mate," and offer him your hand. When he reaches to shake your hand, pull away at the last minute. Tool him constantly.

Also, you can use an AMOG's work for yourself. He lines 'em up, you knock 'em down. This is something I do a lot. I let a guy pick a girl up and increase her buying temperature, then I go in and out-alpha him. I say he's creepy to the girls, and then remove them from him. The girls are already aroused, so they are still in state based on what the AMOG did. I can do this on maybe 90 percent of sets I approach where a natural AMOG is talking to a girl.

Have fun.

—TD

When the reviews of Tyler Durden and Papa's London workshops hit Cliff's List, Mystery was outraged. He wasn't upset about AMOGing. You had to give the pair credit for that. He was upset because Tyler Durden and Papa had set up their own website and rival company. Mystery had called his classroom seminars Social Dynamics. They called their in-field workshops Real Social Dynamics.

Papa was as robotic about setting up his seduction business as he had been about sarging. He copied Mystery's model to the letter. Mystery charged six hundred dollars. So did Tyler and Papa. Mystery scheduled his workshops for three nights. So did Tyler and Papa. Mystery started his lessons at 8:30 P.M. and ended them at 2:30 A.M. So did Tyler and Papa.

Though Tyler Durden and Papa said Mystery gave them permission to run their own workshops, Mystery claimed they used his client list and never asked him. When they exhausted that, they went around and spoke to the Speed Seduction lairs, drumming up business from Ross Jeffries's disciples. And when Ross began to smell a rat, they started their own lair in each region, beginning with P-L-A-Y (for Player's Los Angeles Yahoo group) in Southern California.

Where Mystery limited his workshops to six people, Papa and Tyler Durden packed in dozens. It was sarging anarchy, but they were rolling in money. At nearly every workshop, Papa handpicked a student—even if he happened to be a virgin—and made him a guest instructor at the next workshop. Soon, Papa had his own gang of wings—Jlaix, a San Francisco karaoke champ; Sickboy, a square-jawed New Yorker in the fashion industry; Dreamweaver, a University of California senior and former Mystery student; and even Extramask—that he was flying around to each workshop.

Despite all this, Mystery continued to let Tyler and Papa stay at his house and pick his brain whenever they were in Toronto. When I asked him why, he answered, "Keep your friends close and your enemies closer." With a wonderful cliché like that, I assumed he knew what he was doing.

In the meantime, after seeing Tyler and Papa's success, two things dawned on the rest of the community. The first was that anybody could run a workshop. It didn't take any special talent to point two girls out to a guy and say, "Go approach them." The second was that the demand for seduction schooling was elastic. Guys would throw any amount of money at the problem to solve it.

Mystery had made a crucial mistake: He didn't give his students nondisclosure agreements. And now the genie was out of the bottle. One by one, everyone woke up to the notion that all those hours they had spent studying and practicing seduction—more time than they spent with family, school, work, and real-life friends—had more applications than just keeping the prophylactic industry healthy. We were the creators and beneficiaries of a body of knowledge that was light years beyond the rest of the mating world. We had developed an entirely new paradigm of sexual relations—one that gave men the upper hand, or at least the illusion of having the upper hand. There was a market for this.

Orion, the spazz who had made the *Magical Connections* videos, started leading daytime workshops in shopping malls and on campuses.

Next, two PUAs named Harmless and Schematic began advertising their own workshops, which was a surprise to everyone considering that Schematic had only lost his virginity a month beforehand.

One of the Croatians I had met, Badboy, a charismatic PUA who limped and had only partial use of his left arm after getting hit by sniper fire during the war, started a company called Playboy Lifestyle. Students flew to visit him in Zagreb for training in how to become an alpha male. Exercises included punching Badboy in the stomach and yelling, "Fuck you, Badboy!" as loud as they could. The average monthly salary in Croatia was $400; his workshops cost $850 per student.

Wilder and Sensei, both Mystery Method graduates, led Pickup 101 workshops out of San Francisco. A mysterious website appeared offering a book called *Neg Hits Explained*. Vision quit his job to run one-on-one workshops. One of Sweater's employees put together a seduction website and line of products. Three college students in London—Angel, Ryobi, and Lockstock—started teaching workshops called Impact Interaction. And even Prizer, the border-crossing hooker-fucker, put out a rambling DVD course, *Seduction Made Easy*, that doubled as unintentional comedy.

Finally, Grimble and Twotimer jumped into the fray, each developing his own method of seduction and writing an e-book on it. Grimble made fifteen thousand dollars the week his was released; Twotimer took in six thousand.

The community was blossoming with enterprise.

I realized that it was time for me to move. This was getting too big. The lid was going to blow.

I'd been in the community for a year and a half since taking Mystery's first workshop. It was time to stake a claim on the seduction subculture before another writer beat me to it. It was time to reveal myself. It was time to remind myself that I wasn't just a PUA; I was a writer. I had a career. So I called an editor I knew at the Style section of the *New York Times*. It seemed like an appropriately named section to write for.

No one ever posted their real names online; we called each other by our nicknames. Even Ross Jeffries and David DeAngelo were pseudonyms. Our real-world jobs and identities were unimportant. Thus, everyone in the community knew me as Style. Few, if anyone, knew my real name or that I wrote for the *Times*.

It wasn't easy to get the story into the newspaper. It took two months of going back and forth with editors, writing draft after draft. They wanted more skepticism. They wanted proof of the powers of the various gurus. They wanted the inherent weirdness of the techniques to be acknowledged. They seemed to have trouble believing that these people—and this world—really existed.

The night before the story on my double life as a pickup artist was published, I slept fitfully. I had created this character Style; now, in two thousand words of newsprint, I was going to kill him. I was sure everyone in the community would be pissed off that there had been a traitor in their midst. I had nightmares of sargers gathering outside my house with torches to burn me alive.

But no amount of fretting and worrying could have prepared me for the response: There was none.

Sure, there was a little bit of bellyaching about the community being exposed and potentially ruined. A few people didn't like the tone of the story, and Mystery resented being called a pickup artist rather than a "Venusian artist," his latest neologism. But Style's credibility was safe: He had become so entrenched in the community that to the sargers of the world, he was a pickup artist first and a journalist second. Instead of being upset at Neil Strauss for infiltrating their community, they were proud of Style for getting an article in the *New York Times*.

I was flabbergasted. I hadn't killed Style at all. I'd only made him stronger. Sargers Googled my name and ordered my books on Amazon, writing long posts detailing my career. When I asked them to keep my real-world and my online identities separate—especially since I didn't want women I met looking up field reports I'd written about them—they actually agreed. I was still in charge.

Even more surprising, I didn't want to leave the subculture. I was a mentor now to these kids, and I had a role to fill. I had friendships to maintain. Though I'd more than attained my goal as a pickup artist, along the way I had accidentally found the sense of camaraderie and belonging that had eluded me my whole life. Like it or not, I was an integral part of the community now. The kids were right not to feel shocked or betrayed. I was one of them.

As for the women in my life, the article also had little effect. I'd already told them about the community and my involvement in it. And, in doing so, I'd discovered a curious phenomenon: If I told a woman that I was a pickup artist before sleeping with her, she'd still have sex with me, but she'd make me wait a week or two longer just to ensure that she was different from all the other girls. If I told a girl I was a pickup artist after sleeping with her, she was usually amused and intrigued by the whole idea, and convinced that I hadn't been running game on her. However, her tolerance for the community lasted only until we broke up or stopped seeing each other, at which point it was used against me. The problem with being a pickup artist is that there are concepts like sincerity, genuineness, trust, and connection that are important to women. And all the techniques that are so effective in beginning a relationship violate every principle necessary to maintaining one.

Shortly after the article came out, I received a phone call from Will Dana, the features editor at *Rolling Stone*.

"We're doing a cover story on Tom Cruise," he told me.

"That's great," I said.

"Yeah. He wants you to do it."

"Would you mind specifying the pronoun? Who do you mean by *he?*"

"Tom Cruise asked for you specifically."

"Why? I've never interviewed an actor before."

"He read that article you wrote in the *Times* on the pickup guys. You can ask him about it when you see him. He's in Europe right now scouting for locations for the next *Mission: Impossible.* But he wants to go to wheelie school with you when he gets back."

"What's wheelie school?"

"It's where you learn to do motorcycle wheelies."

"Sounds cool. I'm in."

I neglected to tell Will that I'd never ridden a motorcycle in my life. However, it was high on the list of seduction-related skills I still wanted to learn—just above improv classes and below self-defense.

EXTRACT TO A
SEDUCTION LOCATION

AMONG OUR STRUCTURALLY CLOSEST ANALOGUES—THE PRIMATES—THE MALE DOES NOT FEED THE FEMALE. HEAVY WITH YOUNG, MAKING HER WAY LABORIOUSLY ALONG, SHE FENDS FOR HERSELF. HE MAY FIGHT TO PROTECT HER OR TO POSSESS HER, BUT HE DOES NOT NURTURE HER.

—MARGARET MEAD,
Male and Female

Chapter

He was the first person I'd met since joining the seduction community who didn't let me down.

His name was Tom Cruise.

"This is going to be great, man," he greeted me when I met him at wheelie school. He smiled, complimented my adventurousness, and smashed a friendly elbow into my chest. It was the exact same AMOGing gesture that Tyler Durden had written about in London.

He wore black bike leathers with a matching helmet tucked under his left arm and two days of stubble on his chin. "I'm training to jump a trailer," he said. He pointed to a mobile home sitting just off the track. "It'll be bigger than that one. But it's not that hard."

He squinted at the vehicle for a moment, visualizing the feat. "Well, the jumping's not that hard. It's the landing that's difficult."

He cocked his right hand and slugged me in the shoulder.

Tom Cruise was the perfect specimen. He was the AMOG that Tyler Durden and Mystery and everyone else in the seduction community had been trying to emulate. He had a natural ability to remain dominant, physically and mentally, in any social situation without seeming to exert any effort. And he was the living embodiment of all six of Mystery's five characteristics of an alpha male. Nearly everyone in the community had studied his films to learn body language and regularly used terminology from *Top Gun* in the field. There was so much I wanted to ask him. But first I needed to confirm something.

"So what made you pick me for this article?"

The dust lifted off the track and blew around us as we clutched our bike helmets under our arms.

"I dug your *New York Times* piece," he replied. "You were writing about the dating guys."

So it was true.

He paused and his eyes narrowed to slits, indicating that he was speaking about a serious topic. His left eye closed a little more than the right one, giving the appearance of deep intensity. "Now is that guy you wrote about in your article really saying that the character in *Magnolia* is based on him? Is he saying that?"

He was talking about Ross Jeffries. One of Ross's claims to fame was that he was the inspiration for Frank T. J. Mackey in Paul Thomas Anderson's film *Magnolia*. Mackey was the character Cruise played: an arrogant seduction teacher with unresolved father issues who wears a headset during his seminars and orders his students to "respect the cock."

"He shouldn't," Cruise continued. He swallowed a salt pill and chased it down with a long swig of bottled water. "That's not okay. It's not true. Really. That is an invention that PTA had." PTA is Paul Thomas Anderson. "That guy is not Mackey at all. He is not Mackey." It seemed important for Cruise to establish this. "I worked on creating that character with Paul Thomas Anderson for four months. And I didn't use that guy at all."[10]

Cruise sat me on his 1000 CC Triumph motorcycle and taught me how to start the engine and shift gears. Then he raced around the track, popping wheelies, while I wiped out going five miles an hour on his top-of-the-line bike. Afterward, he brought me into his trailer. The walls were covered with pictures of the children he and his ex-wife Nicole Kidman had adopted.

"Has this Jeffries guy turned his character more Mackey-ish since the movie?" Cruise asked.

"He's arrogant and megalomaniacal like Mackey. But he's not as alpha male as Mackey."

"I'll tell you something," Cruise said as he sat down at a table spread with finger sandwiches and cold cuts. "When I did that monolog as Mackey, we didn't tell the audience anything about what we were doing. And the guys just started getting pumped up as I was talking. So at the end of the day, PTA and I had to get on stage and say, 'Look, man. We just want to tell you that where this character is going and what he's saying is not good. And it's not okay.'"

Here came the lecture. First Dustin; now Tom Cruise. I couldn't understand it. What was wrong with learning how to meet women? That's what we're here for. It's how the species survives. All I wanted was an evolution-

---

[10] When asked how he had come up with the character of T. J. Mackey in an interview in *Creative Screenwriting* in 2000, however, Paul Thomas Anderson did mention researching Ross Jeffries.

ary edge. So why not work at it and learn to do it well, like I'd done with everything else in my life? Who says you're allowed to take lessons in motorcycle riding but not in interacting with women? I just needed someone to show me how to start the engine and shift to higher gears. And I wasn't hurting anyone. No one was complaining after I slept with them, no one was being lied to, no one was being hurt. They wanted to be seduced. Everyone wants to be seduced. It makes us feel wanted.

"We made this whole speech, because the guys were taking what we were saying and going with it and getting into it. So PTA and I were saying, 'Hey man, oh my God. Easy.'"

See, I wanted to tell him. Seduction is seductive. But I couldn't, because as he remembered that moment, Cruise let out a laugh. And Cruise doesn't laugh like ordinary people do. His laugh takes over a room. It comes on just fine, a regular laugh by any standards. You will be laughing too. But then, when the humor subsides, you will stop laughing. At this point, however, Cruise's laugh will just be crescendoing. And he will be making eye contact with you. *Ha ha HA HA heh heh.* And you will try to laugh again, to join him, because you know you're supposed to. But it doesn't come out right, because it's not natural. He will squeeze out a couple words sometimes between chuckles—"It's not real," in this case. And then he will stop, as suddenly as he started, and you will be relieved.

"Well," I told him, squeezing out the last breath of an awkward laugh. "That's easy for you to say."

We spent the next week together visiting various Scientology buildings. It's no secret that Tom Cruise is a member of the Church of Scientology—a religion, self-help group, charity, cult, and philosophy started by the science fiction writer L. Ron Hubbard in the 1950s. But Cruise had never taken a journalist into that world before.

The more I learned about L. Ron Hubbard, the more I realized that he was the exact same personality type as Mystery and Ross Jeffries and Tyler Durden. They were wickedly smart megalomaniacs who knew how to synthesize great bodies of knowledge and experience into personality-driven brands, which they sold to people who didn't feel like they were getting what they needed out of life. They were obsessive students of the principles that guide human behavior. But the ethics of and motivation for their use of those principles made them controversial figures.

On our last day together, Cruise took me on a tour of the Scientology

Celebrity Center in Hollywood, where I saw a classroom full of students being trained to use e-meters, devices that measure skin conductance. When curious civilians come into the church, they are hooked up to e-meters and asked various questions. Afterward, the interviewer goes over the results with them and tells them why they need to join the Church of Scientology to fix their problems.

Students were paired up in the classroom, role-playing the various scenarios that can occur during an interview. They had large books spread out in front of them. Everything the interviewer (or auditor, in Scientology terms) utters—every response to every contingency—was contained in those books. Nothing was left to chance. No possible convert was going to slip through their hands.

What they were rehearsing, I realized, was a form of pickup. Without a rigid structure, rehearsed routines, and troubleshooting tactics, there would be no recruitment.

One of my main frustrations with sarging was repeating the same lines over and over. I was getting tired asking girls if they thought spells worked or if they wanted to take the best friends test or if they noticed how their nose wiggled when they laughed. I just wanted to walk into a set and say, "Love me. I'm Style!"

But after watching the auditors, I began to think that perhaps routines weren't training wheels after all; they were the bike. Every form of demagoguery depends on them. Religion is pickup. Politics is pickup. Life is pickup.

Every day, we have our routines, which we rely on to make people like us or to get what we want or to make someone laugh or to endure another day without letting anyone know the nasty thoughts we're really thinking about them.

After the tour, Cruise and I ate lunch in the Celebrity Center restaurant. He was clean-shaven and ruddy-cheeked, wearing a dark-green crewneck T-shirt that fit his body like a glove. Over a healthy slab of steak, he discussed his values. He believed in learning new things, doing the work required of him, and competing with no one but himself. He was strong-willed, centered, and resolute. Any thinking that must be done, any turmoil that must be resolved, any issue that must be handled was solved first and foremost in a dialogue between Tom Cruise and himself.

"I don't really keep counsel with others," he said. "I'm the kind of person who will think about something, and if I know it's right I'm not going to ask anybody. I don't go, 'Boy, what do you think about this?' I've made every decision for myself—in my career, in my life."

Cruise leaned forward in his chair, resting his elbows in his lap. He was low in his seat and his head was parallel with the surface of the table. As he spoke, he expressed himself through gestures as subtle as changing the aperture of his eyes. The guy was born to sell things: movies, himself, Scientology, you. Whenever I criticized myself or made an excuse for myself, he jumped down my throat.

"I'm sorry," I said at one point, when discussing an article I'd written. "I don't mean to sound like one of those writer guys."

"Why are you apologizing? Why not be a writer guy? Who are those guys? They're talented people who write about things that people are interested in." Then he continued, mockingly, "No, you don't want to be one of those guys who's creative and expressive."

He was right. I had thought I was done with gurus, but I needed one more. Tom Cruise was teaching me more about inner game than Mystery, Ross Jeffries, Steve P., or my father ever had.

He stood up and slammed his fist down on the table, hard—AMOG-style. "Why don't you want to be one of those guys? Be one of those guys, man. I mean it. That's cool."

Okay. Cruise says it's cool. Case closed.

As we talked, I realized that out of all the people I'd met in my lifetime, no one had their head screwed on more tightly than Tom Cruise. And this was a disturbing thought, because nearly every idea Tom Cruise expressed could be found somewhere in the massive writings of L. Ron Hubbard.

I discovered this when Cruise had his personal Scientology liaison bring a heavy red book to the table. He opened it to the Scientology code of honor, and we discussed it point by point—set a good example, fulfill your obligations, never need praise or approval or sympathy, don't compromise your own reality.

When Cruise promised to send me an invitation for the center's annual Scientology Gala, I began to worry that this wasn't about an article for *Rolling Stone* at all. It was about getting another convert to Scientology. If that was true, he'd picked the wrong person. At most, he was introducing me to a body of knowledge I could draw from, like the writings of Joseph Campbell or the teaching of the Buddha or the lyrics of Jay-Z.

After our meal and study session, Cruise invited me to the president's room to meet his mother, who was taking a course in the building. "Let me ask you something else about that article you wrote," he said as we walked. "A lot of that stuff is about trying to control people and manipulate situations. Can you imagine all the effort they're putting into that? If they took that effort and put it toward something constructive, who knows what they could accomplish."

The interview ended. The article was published. And Tom Cruise and I would meet again. I would be a different person then, but he would be the same. He would never change. He was an AMOG—and he had AMOGed me. However, he hadn't converted me.

He had his church. I had mine.

My church, however, still needed to be built.

Tom Cruise was right: all our effort did need to be put toward something constructive, something bigger than ourselves. I had felt after writing the *Times* article that my work was not done in the community, that it was all leading somewhere. Now I knew where: Project Hollywood, our church of the spread legs.

The epiphany came to me on my birthday. Some of the PUAs threw a party for me at a Hollywood club called Highlands. They called nearly everyone I knew and had met in the last year. About three hundred guests came, along with another two hundred who showed up at the club just because it was a Saturday night. Even the big boys from the community were there: Rick H., Ross Jeffries, Steve P., Grimble, Bart Baggett (who specializes in handwriting analysis), Vision, and Arte (who stars in his own line of sexual technique videos).

Despite such heavy-hitters working the room, I had zero competition because, for the night, I was the man at the club. I was dressed like a dandy, in a long black jacket with a single button at the top and a cream shirt with ruffled sleeves exposed at my wrists. And I was surrounded by women: fuck buddies, friends, strangers. I couldn't carry on a conversation for more than two minutes because people were constantly pulling me away to talk. I didn't have time to spit game.

Women complimented me on my looks, my body, even my ass. Four different girls handed me their phone numbers over the course of the night. One said she had to meet her boyfriend, but then wanted to escape and party with me; the other gave me not just her phone number, but also her address and apartment number. These were girls I didn't know before the party, and two weren't even there for my birthday. I didn't need routines, boyfriend destroyers, gimmicks, or wings. All I needed was a big pocket to hold all the scraps of paper.

In addition, two porn stars a friend had brought with him introduced themselves. One was either named Devon or Deven; the other had big teeth.

We talked for a half hour, and they supplicated to me the whole time. The night felt like the time in Toronto when everyone though I was Moby—except this time they knew I was Style.

Mystery had recently developed another theory of social interaction. It basically stated that women are constantly judging a man's value in order to determine if it can help them with their life objectives of survival and replication. In the microcosmic world we had created at the Highlands that night, I had the highest social value in the room. And just as most men are attracted in a Pavlovian manner to anything that is thin, has blonde hair, and possesses large breasts, women tend to respond to status and social proof.

In the end, I took a petite, mischievous stripper with big saucer eyes named Johanna back to my house. While she was on my bed, grinding me through my clothes, she asked, "What do you do for a living?"

"What?" I replied. I couldn't believe she would ask that, but she seemed to need that piece of information in order to explain my status at the party and her attraction to me.

"What do you do?" she asked again.

And that's when I had the epiphany: Sarging is for losers.

Somewhere along the line, sarging became seen as the goal of pickup. But the point of the game is not to get good at sarging. When you sarge, every night is a new one. You're not building anything but a skillset. What got me laid on my birthday was not sarging but lifestyle. And building a lifestyle is cumulative. Everything you do counts and brings you closer to your goal.

The right lifestyle is something that is worn, not discussed. Money, fame, and looks, though helpful, are not required. It is, rather, something that screams: Ladies, abandon your boring, mundane, unfulfilled lives and step into my exciting world, full of interesting people, new experiences, good times, easy living, and dreams fulfilled.

Sarging was for students, not players, of the game. It was time to take this brotherhood to the next level, time to pool our resources and design a lifestyle in which the women came to us. It was time for Project Hollywood.

Mystery flew into town to meet me. All he had needed was the word go.

He was the only person I could talk to who wasn't afraid to take chances and make changes to pursue his dreams. Everyone else I knew always said, "Later"; Mystery said, "Now," and that was an intoxicating word to me—because later, every time I'd ever heard it, translated as never.

"Now is the time, Style," he said when he arrived at my apartment in Santa Monica. "Let's build this shit. Sarging *is* for losers. I mean, sure, it's better to be a loser who gets laid than one who doesn't, but we're talking about a championship level of game now."

I knew he'd understand.

According to the books I'd read on cold-reading, all human problems fall into one of three areas: health, wealth, and relationships, each of which has an inner and an outer component. For the past year and a half, we'd been focusing solely on relationships. Now it was time to get every cylinder in our lives firing. It was time to follow through on Mystery's codeine-addled ramblings and join forces to work together for more than just HB10s. We were greater than the sum of our cocks.

The first step to making Project Hollywood a reality was to find a mansion in the Hollywood Hills, preferably with guest bedrooms, a hot tub, and a location near the clubs on Sunset. Next we needed to hand-select the best in the community to live with us.

Perhaps I shouldn't have trusted Mystery again. But this time, I wouldn't let myself be dependent on him. His name wasn't going to be on the lease. Neither would mine, for that matter. We'd find a third party to take the risk and the responsibility.

We found that third party living in the Furama Hotel. His name was Papa. His grades had kept him out of law school, so instead he'd enrolled at Loyola Marymount in Los Angeles to study business. The day he moved from Wisconsin to Los Angeles, he dropped his bags off in his hotel room near the airport and took a taxi to my apartment, where six foot five inch Mystery was sleeping on my five foot six couch.

"The three most influential people in my life," Papa told us as he sat down on the couch at Mystery's feet, "have been you two and my father."

Papa's hair was now spiked and gelled, and he looked like he'd been working out. I left him to talk with Mystery in my living room while I ran downstairs to a Caribbean food stand to get dinner for everyone.

When I returned, Papa was Mystery's manager.

"Are you sure you know what you're doing?" I asked Mystery. I couldn't believe he was going to let a protégé-turned-competitor manage him. Mystery was an innovator. If Ross Jeffries was the Elvis of seduction, Mystery was the Beatles. Tyler and Papa were merely the New York Dolls: They were brash, they were loud, and everyone thought they were gay.

"Papa likes the business and he can fill workshops every weekend," Mystery replied. "So all I have to do is show up."

Papa, in his networking mania, was in constant contact with nearly every major sarger. He knew all the lair presidents and was on all the seduction mailing lists. With just a few e-mails and phone calls, he could recruit a dozen students nearly anywhere in the world.

"It's win-win," Papa insisted. Ever since he'd gotten into the pickup business, that had become Papa's favorite phrase. He was smarter than I'd given him credit for. He was going to become the middle man for the biggest pickup artists in the community. And they were all going to let him, because most artists have the same fatal flaw: They're too lazy to deal with anything practical themselves.

We never actually invited Papa to join us in Project Hollywood that day. It just happened because he was willing to do the work. There was a Coldwell Banker office across the street from the hotel, and Papa walked in and found us a real estate agent named Joe. Real estate agents don't make much money on rentals, but Papa managed to talk Joe into working for us by promising to teach him the game.

"He's going to take us tomorrow to look at houses," Papa said when we met him in the lobby of the Furama Hotel one afternoon. "There are three places I really like. There's a mansion on Mulholland Drive; there's the former Rat Pack crib off Sunset; and there's the supermansion, which has ten bedrooms, tennis courts, and a built-in nightclub."

"Well, I'm for the supermansion," I told him. "How much is it?"

"It's fifty thousand a month."

"Forget it."

Papa's face clouded. He didn't like the word no. He was an only child.

He disappeared into his hotel room and emerged a half hour later with a sheet of paper in his hands. On it, he had sketched out a plan to earn $50,000 a month. We'd throw a weekly party in the club, and make $8,000 by charging admission and $5,000 in drinks per month; various pickup and lifestyle seminars would earn the house $20,000; we'd offer tennis lessons that would add up to $2,000 a month; and the ten residents of the house would pay $1,500 each in rent.

It was completely impractical. It wasn't worth spending all our income on overhead. But it was impressive. Papa was going to make Project Hollywood happen, no matter what it took. I began to understand why Mystery wanted to work with Papa. He was one of us: He was a go-getter. He had initiative. And, unlike Mystery, he was a closer.

As a pickup artist, Papa also seemed worthy of Project Hollywood. He'd proven his fearlessness in the field over and over since we'd met him in Toronto. And he would prove himself once more the following day, when he picked up Paris Hilton at a taco stand.

Chapter

MSN GROUP: Mystery's Lounge
SUBJECT: Field Report—The Seduction of Paris Hilton
AUTHOR: Papa

Today, I went with Style, Mystery, and our real estate agent to our prospective mansion, Dean Martin's old crib in the Hollywood Hills. I am in love with the place and can't wait to close the deal. We will be on top of the world, literally and figuratively. When you are in our crib, everything seems perfect.

It's a short walk to a popular Mexican fast-food restaurant, so we went over there for a late lunch. After ordering food, we found a table outside. Suddenly, our agent leaned over to me and whispered:

> **REAL ESTATE AGENT:** You know, I saw Paris Hilton walk inside the restaurant. I think she's ordering a burrito. Why don't you go pick her up?
> **PAPA:** Really?
> **STYLE:** Hey, if you are going to walk over there, don't look in her direction.
> **PAPA:** All right, it's playtime.

I got up, walked into the restaurant, and saw a hot blonde chick getting salsa. So I thought, "Salsa sounds good to me." I've been gearing my game up for this moment, and now it was time to take what I deserved. So I walked over to her side and pretended like I was just at the salsa bar by coincidence. I helped myself to some salsa, and then looked over my right shoulder at her and started the conversation with Style's jealous girlfriend opener.

> **PAPA:** Hey, I need a female opinion on something?
> **PARIS:** (*Smiles and looks up*) Okay.
> **PAPA:** Would you date a guy who was still friends with his ex-girlfriend?
> **PARIS:** Yeah. I think so. Sure.

I started to walk away, then turned back and continued the conversation.

PAPA: Hmm. Actually, this is a two-part question.

PARIS: (*Smiles and giggles*)

PAPA: Imagine you were dating a guy who was still friends with his ex-girlfriend. And you were going to move in with him but he had a drawer with pictures of his ex-girlfriend—not nudie pictures or anything, just regular pictures and some letters.

PARIS: Ooh. I would so get rid of them. I would put them in a box.

I cut her off and continued with the opener.

PAPA: Do you think it's unreasonable for her to want him to get rid of those pictures?

PARIS: Oh, for sure. I dated a guy who did that, and I tossed them.

PAPA: Wow! The reason why I asked was because I have a friend in the same situation, and she burned them.

PARIS: Yes. That's what I should have done. (*Smiles*)

PAPA: Hmm. Cool.

Paris finished getting her salsa, then took her salsa containers and started to walk away.

PAPA: Hey, you know, you look like a little cartoon version of Britney Spears. Oh, maybe it's just your teeth.

Paris put her salsa container back on the table, looked at me, and smiled. Then I told her Style's Cs versus Us routine.

PAPA: Yeah! You have Britney teeth. Well, that's what my ex-girlfriend said. I mean, she has a theory that girls who have teeth in a wide C-shape, like Britney Spears, are perceived as good girls, no matter how many guys they hook up with. You have the same kind of C-shaped teeth.

PARIS: (*Excited and smiling*) Oh, yeah?

PAPA: Hey, I mean, just look at the smiles of the cover girls on magazines. They have the same kind of teeth. Well, at least that's what she said. She even got surgery done to her teeth because she had U-shaped teeth, like Christina Aguilera. She said U-shaped teeth are perceived as unfriendly, and that's why Christina Aguilera has the bad girl reputation and Britney Spears doesn't.

PARIS: (*Smiles*) Wow.

We walked to the counter and she grabbed her food. I acted as if I were going to leave, but don't think I'm going to leave Paris without proper game. She had her food and was about to exit the restaurant, so I had to keep her there. I looked over my shoulder and continued the conversation.

PAPA: I have an intuition about you.
PARIS: What?

She put her food down and looked at me.

PAPA: You know, I can tell you deep insights about yourself just by asking three questions.
PARIS: Oh yeah?
PAPA: Yeah. Here, come over to this table.
PARIS: Okay, sure.

I sat down at a nearby table, and she placed her food on the table and sat across from me. When she sat down, she smiled. I knew I was set and that it was time to work solid game. For the next fifteen minutes, we shared some stories about Hollywood and talked about commonalities. I did some qualifying, gave her some Speed Seduction patterns, and told her some socially proofed higher-value stories.

PAPA: Well, my friend taught me this fascinating visualization technique called the Cube. He's over there right now, and we just finished shopping for a house over there (*pointing in the direction of the Holly-wood Hills*). I've been living in a hotel for the last ten weeks. Ugh.
PARIS: Oh yeah! Which one?
PAPA: The Furama.
PARIS: (*Nods*) Yeah, I live right up the street on Kings Road.
PAPA: Cool. I'll be your neighbor. I'm moving into a house on Londonderry. It's a great place, and I already have so much heart for it. My friend Style and I are talking about making it a place for after-parties.
PARIS: Cooool.
PAPA: Okay. Are you ready for the Cube?

PARIS: Yes. Sure. (*Smiles*)

PAPA: (*Escalating the yes-ladder*) Before I start, I need to ask you a few questions. Are you intelligent?

PARIS: Yes.

PAPA: Are you intuitive?

PARIS: Yes.

PAPA: Do you have a good imagination?

PARIS: Yes.

PAPA: Okay. Great! We'll continue then. Imagine you're driving in the desert and you see a cube. How big is the cube?

PARIS: It's really big!

PAPA: How big is that?

PARIS: As big as a hotel.

Though I knew who she was, I didn't give it away and acknowledge she was a Hilton.

PAPA: Hmm. Interesting. Okay, so what color is it?

PARIS: Pink.

PAPA: Cool. Is it something you can see through or is it solid?

PARIS: You can see right through it.

PAPA: Rock on! Now, let's add a ladder. Where is the ladder in relation to the cube?

PARIS: It's leaning against the cube, going into the middle of it.

PAPA: Ah! I would have expected you to say that.

PARIS: Yeah. (*Smiles and giggles*)

PAPA: Yeah. So let's add one more thing to your picture. Let's add a horse. Where is the horse in relation to everything in your picture?

PARIS: It's sleeping.

PAPA: Where is it sleeping? .

PARIS: In front of the cube.

PAPA: Wow. Interesting. (*Pause*) Okay. Are you ready to find out what all of this mean? (*Pause*) It doesn't mean anything! No, just kidding. The cube represents what you think of yourself. It's your ego. Now, your cube is pretty big. You have a lot of self-confidence. It's not super-huge. I mean, it's not like you have a huge ego, but you definitely carry yourself with a lot of confidence. Also, your cube is pink.

PARIS: Yeah. That's my favorite color.

PAPA: Well, pink is also a color that is playful and bright, and you chose that because you carry yourself with the same kind of energy. You are the kind of person who really likes to have fun and party, but you are also the kind of person who just enjoys being in other people's company.

PARIS: Yes.

PAPA: And your cube is something that you can see right through. Now, that represents how people interact with you because you are the kind of person who even when people first meet you, they can see right through you. You really connect with people and that rocks.

PARIS: What's your name?

PAPA: Papa. What's your name?

PARIS: Paris.

PAPA: Rock on. I feel like we have so much to talk about.

PARIS: Yes.

PAPA: We should definitely party it up together sometime.

PARIS: Yes. We should.

PAPA: Here.

I gave her a piece of paper and a pen. She wrote down her first and last name, and then handed it to me, expecting to impress me and get a wow response. But I didn't give her any response, as if I had no idea who she was. Then I handed it back to her.

PAPA: Here.

PARIS: Okay. Write it down right here?

PAPA: Yes.

PARIS: This is my cell phone.

PAPA: Cool.

PARIS: Yeah. We should definitely meet up.

PAPA: Yeah. Rock on. I'll see ya, kid.

I walked back to see the boys at the table outside.

STYLE: Nice job, man. Nobody give Papa a high-five or acknowledge it, in case she sees it. Well done, bro.

REAL ESTATE AGENT: High five, bro.

I explained to the boys what happened. This rocks. I know that this is the way things are going to be. It just makes sense that I would roll with Paris Hilton when I am in Project Hollywood.

Mystery, this is my set. So hands off when Paris comes by the crib to see Papa.

Cheers,
Papa

Every word Papa told Paris Hilton had come from me: the jealous girlfriend opener, the C-shaped versus U-shaped-smiles routine. Even his delivery of the Cube was the exact same as what he'd recorded at his first workshop with Mystery and me, down to the way he said, "Interesting" and "Cool." He was a great robot, and he had just outperformed his programmer.

We walked back to the house to meet the owners and sign the paperwork. The former home of Dean Martin (and later the comedian Eddie Griffin), the Rat Pack crib was just above Mel's Diner on Sunset Boulevard. It was $36,000 cheaper per month than the supermansion, and it was walking distance from the clubs on Sunset Boulevard.

The living room looked like a ski lodge. There was a fireplace, a sunken dance floor, a thirty-foot-high ceiling, a massive wood-inlay wall mural, and a large bar in the corner. The space could easily hold a few hundred people for seminars and parties. There were two bedrooms off the living room on the ground floor. Outside each of these rooms was a staircase leading up to another bedroom. And then there was a small maid's room off the kitchen.

The crown jewel of the house was the multitiered backyard. On one level, there were two patios shaded by palm and lemon trees. On the second level, there was a large brick terrace with a peanut-shaped pool, a Jacuzzi, a dining area, and a working barbecue and refrigerator. Beyond it lay a landscaped hill with a path winding up to a small, secluded deck at the top of the property. From there, we could see the glittering lights and ten-story movie billboards of Hollywood. The place was a chick magnet. There was no way we could fail here.

Papa put his name down on the lease. This, in addition to paying the larger of the rents, earned him the right to the master bedroom, which came equipped with a raised platform intended for a bed, picture windows, and a fireplace. The bathroom was decked out with a glass-encased circular shower, two walk-in closets, and a whirlpool bathtub built for three.

The possibilities were limitless. Papa had visions of renting the house for after-Grammy parties, movie premieres, and corporate events. He no longer sarged girls when he went out; instead he sarged promoters and celebrities, trying to make connections for Project Hollywood after-parties. He even used Speed Seduction and NLP tactics to try and hypnotize people into investing in the house.

In his spare time, he made bids for tanning beds, movie projectors, pool tables, and stripper poles on eBay. He wanted to make Project Hollywood a place Paris Hilton would want to come every weekend to party.

There were still two bedrooms that needed to be filled, so we issued a call for roommates on Mystery's Lounge. The response was terrifying: Everybody wanted in.

STEP 8
PUMP BUYING TEMPERATURE

ALL THE GIRLS LINE UP HERE,
ALL THE BOYS ON THE OTHER SIDE.
I SEE YOUR RANKS ARE
ADVANCING.
I SEE MINE ARE LEFT BEHIND.

—ANI DIFRANCO,
"The Story"

Chapter

The first night, we all sat in the Jacuzzi from midnight until the skin hung loosely from our bodies, gazing at the palm trees of our new place and the lights of the Hollywood clubs we would soon descend upon. Mystery sang the entire soundtrack of *Jesus Christ Superstar* to the night sky. Papa told us about his plan to use the house for A-list Hollywood parties. And Herbal served watermelon drinks from his blender. There were no girls, and we didn't need any to validate us. Tonight, it was just the boys. We had done it. Project Hollywood was not just a fantasy anymore.

"We'll make the house famous with our public exploits," Mystery predicted as we all sat there with smiles plastered to our faces. "People will drive by and say, 'This was the home of the Hollywood celebrities Style, Mystery, Papa, and Herbal. They built their careers here and had parties that were the envy of the world.'"

Herbal was our fourth roommate. He was a tall, pale, even-tempered twenty-two-year-old PUA from Austin who peacocked by painting his nails silver and wearing all-white clothing. Like the rest of us, he was a reformed geek. But he owned a house in Texas, a Mercedes Benz S600, a Rolex, an office on Sunset Boulevard that he never went to, and a robot vacuum cleaner. They were impressive holdings for someone his age. He had earned them in some kind of shady casino operation, in which he hired others to gamble for him. In his spare time—which was basically all his time—he explored caves, recorded extremely catchy rap songs, and surfed the Internet for unusual items to buy and then never use.

Mystery insisted that everyone in the home have an identity—so we had a magician, a writer, a gambler, and a businessman. It was a combination that would prove more dramatic than the most sensationalist reality show.

A few days later, Papa moved a fifth roommate, Playboy, into the maid's room. Playboy was a party promoter from New York who earned my admiration when he told me he'd worked for the Merce Cunningham Dance Company. He was genetically good-looking—tall and slender with thick black hair—but he had a bad habit of wearing long artsy scarves and pants pulled up to his belly button. He had quit his job to move in with us, so Papa hired him to work for Real Social Dynamics in exchange for rent.

Then there was Xaneus. He lived in a tent in the backyard.

Xaneus was a short, stocky, fresh-faced college soccer player from Colorado who had begged to live in the house. He said he'd sleep anywhere and do anything. So Papa pitched a tent for him, asked him to pay for utilities and house cleaning, and brought him into the Real Social Dynamics fold as an intern.

For the first two weeks, all we did was marvel at the house. We'd done it; we had beaten the system. We had the most desirable location in West Hollywood. And we had lucked out with our roommates. Herbal had already scheduled a Pickup Artist Summit—the first annual—to take place in our house in a month.

At our initial house meeting, we established a structure for Project Hollywood, putting Papa in charge of social activities and Herbal in charge of finances. Then we laid down the rules: No unapproved houseguests for more than a month; anyone conducting a seminar in the living room has to give the house fund a ten percent kickback; and no sarging women another PUA has brought into the house. All these rules would soon be broken.

I initially enjoyed living with roommates, leaving my introverted writer's world and being part of a whole that was greater than the sum of its parts. Every morning, I'd wake up and see Herbal and Mystery pitching quarters into an ice bucket in the middle of the living room or jumping off a stepladder into a pile of pillows. They were like two kids in search of a playground.

"I have a feeling that you and I are going to become great friends," Mystery told Herbal one morning.

When Playboy threw our first house party, five hundred people showed up. We were setting a great example—maybe not to the neighbors, but at least to the community. Within a month, we had franchised.

A group of PUAs moved into Herbal's old house and christened it Project Austin.

Some of our former students in San Francisco rented a five-bedroom house in Chinatown and held pickup seminars in their living room, giving birth to Project San Francisco.

Several college students in Perth, Australia, found a house together and started Project Perth, approaching one hundred women in their first three days on campus.

And four PUAs Mystery and I had trained in Sydney rented a beach apartment with an elevator that opened directly into a club below them. This was Project Sydney.

Nobody had understood the potential of this whole pickup community, the bonding power of dudes talking about chicks. We had manicures, we had mansions, and we had game. We were ready to infect the world like a disease.

Chapter

In my first month at Project Hollywood, entirely by accident, my sexual reality burst open. Just as Mystery's first workshop had opened my eyes to what was possible in a bar, this latest turn of events opened my eyes to what was possible in bed.

And it all happened because Herbal wouldn't let me sleep—for a week straight.

"Have you ever heard of a sleep diet?" Herbal asked as we sat at Mel's Diner one morning. "I discovered it on the Internet."

In his free time, Herbal discovered a lot of things on the Internet: a limousine on eBay he wanted to get for the house, dirt-cheap 1,000-thread-count sheets for our beds, a new and better way to fold shirts, and a business that sold penguins as pets (though when he ordered a penguin for the house, he learned that it was a joke website).

"Basically," he continued, "it's a way to train your body to survive on just two hours of sleep a day."

"How is that?"

"They did scientific research, and instead of sleeping for eight hours every night, what you do is nap for twenty minutes every four hours."

I was tempted. Having six extra hours in the day would give me time to write more, play more, read more, exercise more, go out more, and learn all the other PUA skills I never had time to.

"Is there a catch?"

"Well," Herbal said. "It takes about ten days to adjust to the schedule. And it's not easy. But once you make it over the hump, the naps become totally natural. People say they have more energy, though they also find themselves wanting to drink a lot of juice for some reason."

Just like when Marko suggested driving to Moldova, I didn't hesitate to say yes. I had nothing to lose if it didn't work, except ten days of sleep.

We stocked up on video games and DVDs, and instructed our housemates to help keep us disciplined. Oversleeping or missing even one nap would throw off the entire experiment, and we'd have to start over. As an extra incentive to stay awake, I invited girls to the house each day.

I was seeing about ten different girls now. They were what the PUAs call MLTRs—multiple long-term relationships. Unlike AFCs, I never lied to these girls. They all knew I was seeing other people. And, to my surprise, even if it didn't make all of them happy, none of them left me. One of the most important realizations I'd had in the game came from a Huna self-improvement book that Ross Jeffries had recommended, *Mastering Your Hidden Self.* It taught me the idea that, "The world is what you think it is." In other words, if you believe that you need to have a harem and having a harem is normal, women will agree to it. It's simply your reality. However, if you want a harem but secretly feel that it's cheating and unethical, you'll never have one.

The only woman who wasn't entirely comfortable with this arrangement was a short, curvy, effervescent Spanish girl named Isabel, who had a habit of twitching her nose like a rat in search of cheese. "I only sleep with one person at a time," she constantly told me. "And I wish you'd do the same."

On the fourth day of the sleep experiment, I invited Hea, the indie-rocker I'd met at Highlands, over to keep me awake. She was tiny, like a Chihuahua, and wore large black spectacles. Yet there was something profoundly sexy about her, as if she were just one glass slipper away from becoming a princess. Potential for beauty is as attractive to most men as actual beauty. When women go out with their hair, makeup, nails, and clothing meticulously arranged, it's equally for the benefit of other women. Men, though they certainly enjoy it, don't require fashion-magazine grooming from a stranger: We have active imaginations. We are constantly stripping every woman naked as well as dressing her up to see if she meets our feminine ideal. Hea, then, was a girl who other women ignored yet every man desired. We saw her potential.

When Hea arrived, Herbal and I greeted her at the door with bloodshot eyes, unshaven faces, and dragging feet. The sleep diet was taking its toll. Our manners and maturity were the first to go. We brought her into Herbal's room, sat her down on the floor, and played video games on the Xbox for an hour to keep ourselves awake.

When the doorbell rang again, I trudged to answer it and found Isabel standing on the doorstep. "I was dancing with some friends at Barfly," she said, nose a-wiggle. "So since I was in the neighborhood, I thought I'd drop by."

"You know I hate drop-bys." I had always told my MLTRs to call before coming over, in case something like this happened. I sighed and let her in. It seemed rude to turn her away. "But good to see you, I guess."

I brought her into Herbal's room and introduced everyone. Isabel sat on the floor next to Hea. Her intuition tingled. She looked Hea up and down, then asked, "So how do you know Style?"

I had a feeling this wasn't a casual visit but a sneak attack. So I left them alone in the room and went to find Mystery. I was too tired for drama. "Dude," I said. "I'm screwed. Isabel and Hea are catfighting. How do I get rid of one of them?"

"I've got a better idea," he said. "You should threesome them."

"You're joking."

"No. One of my students was telling me about a technique he once used to get a threesome started. You should try it. Just suggest an innocent three-way massage. See what happens."

"Sounds like a gamble." I didn't want another disaster, like the Porcelain TwinZ bathtub incident.

"You're not gambling. You're taking a risk. Gambling is completely random; a risk is calculated. If two girls are at your house listening to you and giving you IOIs, the odds are in your favor that something will happen."

Mystery could be very persuasive. Throughout this whole pickup process, I'd been trying on clothes and behaviors I'd never thought were me. Some of them worked, so I kept them; others didn't, so I discarded them. I decided to take a chance. I was willing to risk losing them.

I dragged my feet back to Herbal's room. "Hey, guys," I told the girls between yawns. "I have to show you these home movies that Mystery and I made. They're hilarious." Inspired by our video of Carly and Caroline in Montreal, Mystery had started filming our trips and adventures, editing them into humorous ten-minute shorts.

I brought them up to my room. I had no chairs there, of course, just a bed. So we all lay on the comforter while I showed them a video Mystery had made of our trip to Australia.

As it ended, I steadied my nerves and took the risk. "I just experienced the most amazing thing," I told the girls. "I went to San Diego and hung out with my friend Steve P., who's a guru and a shaman. And he had two of his students perform what he called a dual-induction massage on me. Their hands were moving in perfect synchronization on my back. And because your conscious mind can't process all those movements, it disconnects and you feel like there are thousands of hands massaging you. It was amazing."

If you describe anything with enthusiasm and congruence, people will want to try it—especially if you don't give them the opportunity to say no.

"Get on your stomach," I told Isabel. Since she was the girl most likely to be jealous, I knew we'd need to massage her first. I kneeled on her right side and positioned Hea on the left, telling her to follow my movements exactly.

When we finished kneading her back, I pulled off my shirt and lay on my stomach. The girls positioned themselves on either side of my back and began massaging me—tentatively at first, then with more confidence. As the two of them leaned over me, their hands tracing circles around my shoulder blades, I could feel the energy in the room begin to charge. The sexual nature of the situation was beginning to dawn on them, if it hadn't already.

This was quite possibly going to work.

When it was Hea's turn, she took off her shirt and lay on her stomach. This time I made the massage more erotic, rubbing her inner thigh and the sides of her breasts.

After her massage, Hea remained on her stomach while Isabel and I kneeled over her. This was the deciding moment. I had to escalate.

I was so nervous my hand started shaking, just like at my humiliating high-school lunch with Elisa. I pulled Isabel's face close to mine and began making out with her. As we kissed, I lowered our bodies until we were practically lying on top of Hea, who was trapped under us. Then I turned Hea's face toward me and began kissing her. She responded. It was working.

I gently pulled Isabel into the kiss. Once Hea and Isabel's lips met, the spark of sexual tension that had hung in the room during the massage exploded. They were all over each other, as if they'd been wanting to do this all along. But they hadn't. They'd been bitter rivals less than an hour earlier. I didn't understand it—but then again I didn't need to.

Hea removed Isabel's shirt, and we both began sucking on her breasts. We pulled off her pants and began licking up her thighs until her back began to arch. I pulled off Isabel's panties while Hea crawled behind me and struggled with my pants.

As I helped her with the button-fly, I glanced at the clock. It was 2:00 A.M. My heart froze. It had been four hours since my last nap. I couldn't just go to sleep in the middle of the first threesome of my life. But if I didn't, the last four days of sleep deprivation would have been in vain.

"Hey," I told them. "I hate to do this, but I need to take my twenty-minute nap now. You can join me if you want."

With Isabel on one side and Hea on the other, I fell asleep instantly. I dreamed that the streets were water, and I was swimming through them. When the alarm went off, I pulled both girls into me, and we began fooling around again.

But this time Isabel pulled away. "This is weird," she said.

"It's totally weird," I replied. "I've been thinking the same thing. But it's a new experience, so I'm just going with it."

She nodded and smiled, and pulled my boxer briefs off. Both women put their hands around me, and I leaned back and watched. I wanted to keep the image in my head for future use.

However, when Hea began to give me a blowjob, Isabel's body tensed. I remembered something Rick H. had said about threesomes at David DeAngelo's seminar: The experience has to be about your girlfriend's pleasure, not yours. She has to be the lead sled dog—as he put it—and your main objective is to make sure she's always comfortable and feeling good.

"Is this making you uncomfortable?" I asked the lead sled dog.

"A little," she said.

I guided Hea's head back up, and we lay together, talking and fooling around, until my next nap. I didn't have sex with Hea that night; I knew Isabel wouldn't be able to handle seeing me inside another woman. This had already been a big step for her.

The next night, I was even more exhausted. Herbal and I sat in the living room watching *Dangerous Liaisons* to stay awake, but we kept drifting into daydreams that lasted fractions of a second. These are called microsleeps: Our bodies needed rest so badly that they were sneaking naps whenever we weren't paying attention.

"This sleep diet thing was a terrible idea," I told Herbal.

"Just stick with it," he said. "It'll pay off in the long run."

I'd bought several bottles of vitamins to help bolster my immune system, but I kept forgetting which ones I had taken and when. Fortunately, Nadia was coming over soon. She was another one of my MLTRs, the sexy librarian I had met during my personals experiment. She showed up after a Suicide Girls burlesque show at the Knitting Factory, accompanied by a girl named Barbara whose black bangs reminded me of Bettie Page.

I poured them a drink and we sat on a couch together. Though Barbara had a boyfriend, I noticed that she was very touchy-feely with Nadia. She seemed to have a crush on her. So I thought I'd give her the opportunity to act on it.

I excused myself for my much-needed nap—I dreamed I was stranded naked in an endless snow-covered field—and then called them up to my room to watch my home movies. Afterward, I initiated the dual-induction massage. And, to my surprise, it worked again. The moment they started kissing, the girls devoured each other just like Isabel and Hea had. So it hadn't just been a lucky accident the night before.

Unlike Isabel, Nadia was a lead sled dog with no jealousy issues. When I fucked Nadia, Barbara knelt behind me and licked my balls. I wanted to wait and fuck Barbara too, but there would be no waiting. What was occurring was so far beyond my wildest expectations when I'd first joined the community that I just lost it. I couldn't hold out any longer. And I never got to have sex with Barbara.

This is what the PUAs call a quality problem.

Over the last year and a half, I'd spent a lot of time working on my appearance, my energy, my attitude, and my state. Yet now, when all those qualities were at their lowest—when I looked and felt like shit—I'd had the most sexually decadent two days of my life. There was a lesson here: The less you appear to be trying, the better you do.

The next day, Herbal and I sat in the living room with a bowl of ice cubes, which we rubbed on ourselves every few minutes to shock our systems into staying awake. The sleep adjustment process was proving to be more difficult than we had imagined. I began to worry that we were wasting our time. After all, this whole sleep diet hadn't even been scientifically proven.

"There better be a rainbow at the end of this tunnel," I babbled to Herbal. "I mean, we're chasing after the pot of gold at the end of the rainbow. And we don't even know if it's there, or if the rainbow even has an end."

Herbal looked startled; I'd snapped him out of a microsleep. "I had a dream about gummy worms," he slurred. "Someone was chopping up gummy bears to make gummy worms."

After another two nap cycles, my head began to hurt and my eyes refused to raise any higher than half-mast. We bathed in cold water, we slapped ourselves in the face, we ran around the living room chasing each other with brooms. But nothing worked.

When I felt my teeth to check my braces, I knew I'd passed over the edge of reason. I hadn't worn braces since junior high.

"I'm going to sleep," Herbal finally said.

"We can't," I told him. "If you go to sleep, I won't make it by myself."

"Watch out for the toothpicks," he said.

We both started cracking up. He'd just had a microsleep. Dreams and reality were blurring.

"Just try to make it through one more sleep cycle," I told him.

But after the next twenty-minute nap, I couldn't get Herbal out of bed. He refused to even open his eyes. I couldn't continue on my own, so I dragged my feet upstairs and drifted into the sweetest slumber of my life. And though I had failed the sleep experiment, I'd reached a new plateau in my game.

I know I should be humble about the dual-induction massage and pretend like it was another step down a degrading path. But discovering the secret to threesomes was like finding the Rosetta Stone of pickup. Once the dual-induction massage routine was developed and shared, PUAs all over the world started having threesomes. It was like breaking the three-minute mile. The dual-induction massage would ultimately ensure my ranking as the number one PUA on Thundercat's list for a second year running.

Project Hollywood was already a success.

And then Tyler Durden arrived.

He looked like he'd been spray-tanning. "I know I didn't make a good impression in L.A.," he said. He shook my hand. He even looked me in the eye for a microsecond.

He wore a trendy black-and-white shirt with ropes hanging from the rib cage area like a corset. It wasn't peacocky; it was the kind of shirt I would have bought. "Social intelligence is something that hasn't come easy for me," he continued. I think he was apologizing. "I'm still working at it. I can come across as self-centered when I slip. Not cool. I suppose I should be more equipped to, as Mystery always tells me, learn how to sarge guys."

It was humble of him. He'd done dozens of workshops since we'd met, and I'd been watching his progress online. His students said he now rivaled Mystery in his pickup prowess. I was willing to give him a second chance: maybe he really had done some serious work on himself. That's the idea This community was predicated on, after all. Since we would both be going to Las Vegas to wing one of Mystery's workshops that weekend, I was looking forward to seeing if the stories about his prowess in the field were true.

Tyler slung his bag over his shoulder and walked up to Papa's room. Between Papa's newfound passion for business and Tyler Durden's quest to be the community's best pickup artist, they made a perfect team.

Our house now had the most admired PUAs in the game. Of course, to the best of my recollection, Tyler Durden had never been approved as a resident. There wasn't room for anyone else. However, Papa had taken it upon himself to invite him, converting one of his bathroom closets into an extra bedroom by putting a mattress on the floor.

We didn't have furniture yet. Just a collection of fifty throw pillows we'd bought to cover the sunken dance floor. That night, Playboy rigged his movie projector to show films on the ceiling, and we all lay in the pillow pit and watched *Carnal Knowledge*.

Afterward, Tyler Durden turned to me. "Your archive has been really influential in my game," he said. My collected posts on the seduction newsgroups had been compiled into a large text file and posted online along with the archives of Mystery and Ross Jeffries. "A lot of my best shit I took from there."

It was hard to get out of a conversation with Tyler Durden. Whenever he wasn't playing the game, he was talking about it.

"I've been experimenting with telling people I'm you in the field," Tyler said.

"What do you mean?"

"I tell them I'm Neil Strauss, and that I write for *Rolling Stone.*"

"And does it get results?" The idea of this pasty little freak running around telling people he was me turned my stomach, but I tried to act nonchalant.

"It depends. Sometimes they think I'm lying. Sometimes girls instantly say, 'Oh my God, we should hang out'. And other girls, if you tell them that shit, you're blown out because it looks like you're bragging."

"Let me tell you something. I've been writing for over a decade, and it hasn't gotten me laid once. Writers aren't cool or sexy. There's no social proof to be gained by hanging out with a writer. At least, that's been my experience. Why do you think I joined the community? But I'm flattered that you tried."

That weekend, Tyler Durden, Mystery, and I went to Las Vegas. Papa had booked ten students for Mystery, which was pretty good for a six person workshop. We took them to the Hard Rock Casino. Generally, on the first night, the students watch the instructors work.

As a PUA, Tyler Durden had improved drastically since I'd last seen him in Los Angeles, where he didn't talk to any women. When I noticed him sarging a bachelorette party, I inched closer to listen. He was talking about Mystery.

"See that tall guy in the top hat?" he was telling them. "He needs a lot of attention, so he'll say hurtful things to people just to make them like him. So humor him, because he needs help."

He was giving away Mystery's game—neutralizing his negs.

"He likes doing magic tricks to get people to accept him," he continued. "So just be nice and pretend like you're excited. He does a lot of children's birthday parties."

Now he was neutralizing Mystery's value-demonstrating routines.

After Tyler Durden left the set, I asked him what he was doing. "Papa and I have developed a lot of new techniques to blow you and Mystery out," he said.

"So what do you say about me?" I asked, trying to pretend I wasn't disturbed.

Tyler Durden started laughing. "We say, 'There's Style. He's actually forty-five years old, but he looks pretty young to me. He's so cute. He's like a little Elmer Fudd.'"

I stared at him in disbelief. He was AMOGing his fellow PUAs. It was diabolical.

"You can get me," Tyler said. "You can say I look like the Pillsbury Doughboy."

I choked back my disgust and thought, "What would Tom Cruise do?"

"But I don't want to get you, man," I replied, keeping my own counsel and giving him a big smile like I thought it was all very funny. "Here's the difference between you and me: I like to surround myself with people who are better than me because I enjoy being pushed and challenged. You, on the other hand, like to become the best person in the room by eliminating anyone who's better than you."

"Yeah, maybe you're right," he said.

Later, I would realize I was only half right. Tyler Durden did like to eliminate competition. But not before he'd squeezed every piece of useful information out of them.

For the rest of the weekend, whenever I talked to a person, male or female, Tyler Durden was hovering behind me, listening to every word. I could see him thinking, trying to figure out the rules and patterns behind everything I said that kept me dominant in a group. He had studied my archive. He was studying my personality. Soon, he would no doubt know more about me than I did. And then, as with the AMOGs in Leicester Square, he'd turn my own words and mannerisms against me.

At the end of the night, I saw a two-set sitting at the bar in the Peacock Lounge: a tall, creepy, bespectacled brunette with incongruously large fake breasts and a short blonde tomboy with a white beret and a small, thick, curvy body.

"That blonde girl's a porn star," Mystery said. He was the expert. "Her name's Faith. That's your set."

Despite the year and a half I'd spent in the community, despite being supposedly the best, I was still intimidated when I saw a beautiful woman.

My old AFC self was always threatening to snap back, whispering that everything I'd learned was wrong, that I was bowing before false gods, that all this game talk was just mental masturbation.

But I pushed myself to enter the set anyway, just to prove that little AFC voice in the back of my head wrong. As soon as I opened my mouth, I went into autopilot.

I opened with jealous girlfriend.

I gave myself a time constraint.

I negged the target about her hoarse voice.

I did the best friends test.

C-shaped smiles versus U-shaped smiles.

ESP experiment.

"There's so much I can learn from you," Faith said.

"We love you," gushed her creepy friend.

They were eating out of my hands. I'm a nerdy Elmer Fudd spouting bullshit tests I made up, and these two girls whose collective breasts weigh more than me were staring at me rapt. I had nothing to be afraid of. No guy out there had the tools we did.

I must kill off that inner AFC. When will he die?

I signaled to Mystery to wing the obstacle. As he sat next to the creepy girl, I went back on autopilot.

Evolution phase-shift.

Smell.

Pull hair.

Bite arm.

Bite neck.

"How do you rate yourself as a kisser on a scale of one to ten?"

Suddenly, Faith jumped out of her seat. "I'm getting too turned on," she said. "I have to leave."

I couldn't figure out if she was just giving me an excuse because I had made a mistake at some point in the sarge, or if I was really that good.

I approached a nearby set—two hippie girls on a bender—and was in with them instantly. Ten minutes into our conversation, however, Faith returned, grabbed my hand, and said, "Let's go to the bathroom."

We walked into the restroom on the side of the Peacock Lounge, and she lowered the toilet seat and sat me down on it. As she unbuttoned my pants, she said, "You so turn me on, intellectually and sexually."

"I know," I told her.

"How?"

"I felt our connection all night. Even when I was talking to those two other girls, I saw you looking at me."

She kneeled on the floor, circled her hand around my limp father of thousands, and lowered her mouth over it. But I couldn't get hard. I was overwhelmed.

I stood up and pushed her roughly against the wall. I circled my hands around her throat and made out with her, as I'd seen Sin do to women in his house when I was still an AFC. Then I pulled her pants down, sat her on the toilet seat, fingered her, and went down on her. She arched her back, fluttered her eyelids, and moaned, as if she were about to cum; but instead she suddenly switched positions and went down on me again.

"I want you to cum in my mouth," she said.

I still couldn't get hard. This had never happened to me before. I mean, I'm hard right now as I'm remembering this.

"I want to be inside you," I told her, in a last-ditch effort to get my blood flowing to the right place.

She stood up and turned around. I pulled a condom out of my pocket and thought about every beautiful woman I had approached that night. I started to get a little harder. She sat down on me, her back against my stomach, which was the worst position for a semi-erect dick to reach around. As soon as I was partway inside her, I went soft again. I couldn't figure out if it was the two Jack and Cokes I drank that night, the lack of foreplay, the intimidation factor of being with a porn star, or the fact that I'd masturbated earlier that day.

When we walked out of the bathroom, half the workshop students were standing there waiting for a lay report. One of the hippies I had been talking to before went to the bathroom and emerged afterward with my condom wrapper in a Kleenex. Evidently, I had left it on the floor, and she felt obliged to show it around. Everyone was celebrating a feat that hadn't actually happened.

I couldn't look Faith in the eye afterward. I had built myself up as such a mysterious, fascinating, sexually powerful guy. And then, in the moment of truth, the lies had come crashing down, revealing a skinny bald guy with a limp dick.

On the last night of the Las Vegas workshop, Tyler Durden picked up a hostess named Stacy at the Hard Rock Café. She was a vampirish blonde who listened to new metal. When her shift ended, Stacy met us at the casino and brought along her roommate, Tammy, a quiet beauty with a touch of baby fat and a scent of grape Bubblicious.

I was wearing a ridiculous snakeskin suit; Mystery was dressed in a top hat, flight goggles, six-inch platform boots, black latex pants, and a black T-shirt with a scrolling red digital sign that said "Mystery" on it. Even for Vegas, he looked like a freak.

Within minutes, Tyler Durden was AMOGing him to Stacy. "He wears these weird signs and people laugh at him," he told her. "I always tell him he doesn't need to do that for people to accept him."

The students fanned the room to talk to women as I leaned against the bar and watched them. After awhile, Stacy sidled up next to me. She had been watching me lead the workshop and, from sheer social proof (lead the men and you lead the women), she had become interested. As we talked, she held eye contact with me. She played with her hair. She looked for excuses to touch my arm. She leaned in when I leaned back. All the IOIs were there. I could feel the air around us tingle, as it always does when a potential kiss is accumulating energy.

I knew it was wrong. She was Tyler Durden's girl. There's a PUA code of ethics: The first one to approach a set gets to game the target, until either she submits or he gives up. But a PUA also doesn't AMOG his wing. If Tyler Durden was going to tell girls I was Elmer Fudd, then Elmer Fudd was going to hunt his rabbit.

I stroked her hair. She smiled.

Would she like to kiss me?

She would.

We did.

Then a shock of orangey blonde hair appeared in the periphery of my vision. It was Mr. Heat Miser. And he was pissed.

"Come with me," Tyler Durden said, grabbing her arm.

I started to apologize. What I had done was wrong, and I knew it logically. But when that bubble of connection and passion builds around you and a girl, logic goes out the window and instinct takes over. I had fucked up. Sure, he'd been AMOGing me. But two wrongs don't make a right. I felt like shit.

However, consolation was only a few steps away. Tyler took Stacy to our hotel room, leaving her roommate, Tammy, behind. We were making out within five minutes. I couldn't believe how easy this was. She was the sixth girl I'd made out with that weekend.

Mystery, in the meantime, had picked up a scantily clad stripper named Angela who, in his estimation, was a 10.5. So we decided to ditch the workshop—it was 2:00 A.M. and they'd gotten their money's worth—and take our dates to an after hours club called Dre's.

As we walked to the cab stand, Mystery paused and looked at himself in the casino mirror. "Winning feels good," he said, grinning to his reflection, which grinned right back at him.

In the taxi, Angela sat on Mystery's lap, facing him, with her skirt spread over his knees. Before we were even out of the parking lot, they were making out. She bit her lip before they kissed. She softly moaned every time their lips separated. She sucked his index finger in and out of her mouth. She was performing for him, for us, for the less attractive masses outside, for God above. Everyone we drove past yelled and whistled at the lip-locked pair. In response, she arched her back and pulled her white panties to the side, revealing a patch of pubic hair shaved into a perfect teardrop. Mystery put a finger inside her. He was validated. She was validated. They validated each other. They were a perfect pair, each completely unaware of the other.

At 5:00 A.M., when Angela left to drive back to Los Angeles, Mystery, Tammy, and I took a cab to the hotel room we were sharing with Tyler Durden at the Luxor. I collapsed onto the bed with Tammy, and we started making out. Mystery was on the other bed. Tyler was in a chair, with Stacy in his lap.

Tammy took off her top and bra, and then lowered my pants. She wrapped her hand around me, and started working it up and down while twisting her wrist. Her mouth joined her hand. This time my equipment worked, no problem. I guess something about the combination of whisky, porn stars, and public bathrooms was too cliché even for me.

Tammy took her pants off, and I reached into my jeans pocket and put a condom on. But after having sex with her for a minute, I stopped. The boys were there. They were watching, or maybe they were trying not to watch. I had no idea; I was too scared to look at them. I've never had sex with other guys in the room, let alone PUAs.

Tammy didn't seem to have any qualms about it. I admired her for that. Nonetheless, I picked her up, brought her into the shower, and turned on the water. I pressed her against the shower door, smashing her breasts against the glass, and took her from behind. After five minutes of thrusting, the bathroom door burst open and a flash went off. Mystery, Tyler Durden, and Stacy were standing there, taking photos.

All I could think was, "They have dirt on me now." I didn't realize until later that to them it was just a souvenir of good times in Las Vegas. Just as with the *New York Times* article, I was the only one worried about being exposed. Everyone else was simply having fun at a friend's expense. I had to get it through my head that these guys didn't care about the writer Neil Strauss. They were so entrenched in the community that nothing outside of it mattered or seemed real. Newspapers only came across their radar if they happened to run a science article about animal mating habits. If a disaster struck somewhere in the world, it was just material for a pattern about taking advantage of the moment because you never know what will happen tomorrow.

Afterward, the girls invited us to their place for breakfast. We packed our bags, drove to their apartment, and ate the best bacon and eggs of our lives. Tyler Durden and Mystery sat on the couch and talked openly about their pickup business: I could see they were squaring off. Mystery kept calling him a former student; Tyler Durden felt like he had surpassed his master and was offering an entirely new and original method of seduction.

The sun was up, and I didn't feel like talking about pickup when I had a real live girl I could be sleeping with. So Tammy took me to her room and gave me a blow job, and then I slept for two hours before my flight home.

There was something about her bed—the way it filled the room, the immaculate whiteness, the softness of the sheets, the thickness of the comforter, the tightness of the tucked-in bedding—that was intoxicating. I've always loved women's bedrooms: They're soft and sweet-smelling, like heaven must be.

Mystery and Tyler Durden weren't leaving Vegas until the evening, so they stayed with the girls and I took a cab to the airport alone. On the flight home, I had a dream:

I pick up a woman and go back to her house. She takes me to her room, and I struggle with last minute resistance for hours. All night long, it's push-pull, submit-resist. Finally, I give up and go to sleep.

In the morning, I'm sitting on a couch in her living room. Her room-mate, a Latin woman with bright red lipstick, saunters up to me and says, "I'm sorry my roommate isn't putting out, but you can be with me instead if you want."

She sits on the couch and spreads her legs in the air. She isn't wearing anything below the waist. She repeats her offer. I accept.

Her lipstick smears across my face as we make out. But when it comes time to have sex, though my dick looks hard, it isn't rigid. I feel like I'm try-ing to stuff a Twinkie inside her.

Afterward, my original target walks in. That's what I call her in my dream: my target. I try to hide my lipstick-stained mouth as we talk. I can hear her roommate laughing from somewhere behind me. And I know I've just failed a planned test by cheating on the girl who brought me home. Now she'll never like me, because she knows what I'm really like.

That night, the girls have a party. Mystery is hitting on my target. He gives her a garage-door opener as a gift. When no one is looking, I grab it and walk outside. I keep pressing it, figuring that a door will open some-where with a spectacular present for her.

While I am investigating, Mystery comes outside, looking for the girl. It turns out that the gift was part of a routine—a way to get her outside in pri-vate. By pressing the button, I had paged him. I run down the street at top speed, but within seconds Mystery catches up to me. His legs are so long it isn't even a challenge for him.

"I'm pissed at you for hitting on my target," I say.

"You had your chance with her and nothing happened," he replies. "The window closed and now it's my turn."

When I woke up, I understood the part of the dream about the test right away. I'd failed it by making out with Tyler Durden's target. And after my disaster with the porn star, the impotence was self-explanatory. But I couldn't understand the part about Mystery hitting on my target—that is, until I returned home and Mystery called.

"I hope you don't mind," he said, "but Tammy just gave me a blow job. She swallowed my load."

Somewhere in her stomach, my sperm was mingling with Mystery's.

"I don't mind," I said. And I didn't. It was part of being friends—a playful competition between PUAs. "Just remember that I was there first."

Tyler Durden, however, didn't see it that way. It wasn't playful competition to him. It was his life.

He would never forgive me for making out with his target.

The point was women; the result was men.

Instead of models in bikinis lounging by the Project Hollywood pool all day, we had pimply teenagers, bespectacled businessmen, tubby students, lonely millionaires, struggling actors, frustrated taxi drivers, and computer programmers—lots of computer programmers. They walked in our door AFCs; they came out players.

Every Friday when they arrived, Mystery or Tyler Durden stood in front of the pillow pit and taught them pretty much the same openers, body language tips, and value-demonstrating routines. On Saturday afternoon, they all went shopping on Melrose. They bought the same four-inch-platform New Rock boots and black-and-white striped shirt with bits of rope hanging from the sides. They bought the same rings, necklaces, hats, and sunglasses. They went to the tanning salon.

We were breeding an army.

At night they descended on the Sunset Strip, a swarm of player bees. Even when the seminar and workshop ended, students lingered in the clubs on Sunset for months afterward, working on their game. You could spot them from behind by the matching boots and the rope dangling from their shirts. They clustered in groups, prowling for open sets and sending in emissaries to say, "Hey, I need to get a female opinion on something."

Even on nights when there weren't workshops, badly peacocked guys from a hundred-mile radius gathered in our living room before going out. At 2:30 A.M., they reconvened at the house—either accompanied by drunk, giggling girls from Orange County, who they brought to the Jacuzzi, the terrace, the closets, and the pillow pit, or empty-handed and breaking down their approaches until dawn. They couldn't stop talking about this stuff.

"Do you know why my skill set is better than all my friends?" Tyler Durden said one afternoon, as he plopped down in the booth at Mel's next to me. "There is only one fucking reason."

"You're more sensitive?" I asked.

"No, because I plow!" he said with a triumphant flourish. By "plowing," he meant blitzing a girl with line after line, routine after routine, without even waiting for a response. "The other night, this girl was running away, and I screamed the routine at her. She came back like a fucking tractor beam. I have no regard for social conventions: I'll pummel their asses down. You have to plow it. No situation can't be plowed."

"I don't plow," I told him. There were guys who won girlfriends by chasing them until they relented and agreed to meet. But I wasn't a chaser. I wasn't a plower. All I did was give her the opportunity to like me, and either she did or didn't. Usually she did.

"You just fucking push push push, and it can't not work," Tyler Durden went on. "If the girls get mad at me, I'll change my voice tone and apologize and tell them I'm not well socially calibrated."

I watched Tyler Durden as he spoke. For all his talk about women, I rarely saw him in the company of one.

"Maybe the reason I'm not getting into a lot of relationships," he said as we left the diner, "is that I don't like oral sex."

"Giving or receiving?"

"Both."

That's when I realized that Tyler Durden wasn't in the community to get laid. He wasn't motivated by sex. He was motivated by power.

Papa's motivations were harder to determine. Originally, he was in the game for the girls. When we moved into Project Hollywood, he envisioned turning his room into a high-tech sultan's lair, with a harem just a phone call away. He talked about getting a bed like a throne, a high-end home entertainment center, a bar next to the fireplace, and drapery hanging from the ceiling.

But that's not what his room became. When I returned from Mel's with Tyler, Mystery was in Papa's room, arguing.

"You're giving Tyler Durden more students than you're giving me," Mystery was saying.

"I'm trying to make this win-win for everyone," Papa protested. The expression seemed hollower every time he used it.

As I looked around his room, I was appalled. There was hardly any furniture, just sleeping bags and pillows strewn across the floor. Women have one word for bedrooms like this: dealbreaker.

"Who's living here?" I asked.

"Some of the RSD[11] guys."

"How many people?"

"Well, right now, Tyler Durden and Sickboy are in the closets in my bathroom. And I have three boot camp students sleeping in the room."

"If anyone's staying more than a month, they need to be approved, like we agreed at the house meeting. There are enough guys in the house as it is."

"Outstanding," Papa said.

"If they're using the resources of the house, they should be paying," Mystery said.

Papa looked at him blankly.

"I can't talk to that guy," Mystery complained to me. "He just sits there and stares at you and says, 'Outstanding.' He's so fucking passive."

"That's not true," Papa said. "You think you can push me around because I was a former student." I'd never seen Papa upset before. He didn't get loud, like most people; instead, his voice became very stuffy. Somewhere inside, there was a living, breathing, emotional person waiting to be set free.

After that day, Papa stopped entering the house through the front door. Instead, in order to avoid Mystery, he walked all the way around the back to the patio and climbed a staircase that led to a door in his bathroom. All his guests did the same.

---

[11] An acronym for Real Social Dynamics. See glossary.

My father died when I was forty
And I couldn't find a way to cry
Not because I didn't love him
Not because he didn't try
I'd cried for every lesser thing
Whiskey, pain, and beauty
But he deserved a better tear
And I was not quite ready

The lyrics boomed through the living room. Mystery was lying in the pillow pit with his computer on his chest. He was playing the song "The Randall Knife" by Guy Clark over and over.

He seemed to be in need of attention. So I walked over and gave him some.

"My dad died," he said. His voice was flat and even. It was hard to tell if he was sad or not. "It's about time. It happened very quickly. He had another stroke, and then he died at 10:00 A.M. today."

I sat down next to him and listened to him talk. He was a passive observer of himself, analytically deconstructing his emotions as he felt them.

"Even though I was ready for it, it's strange. It's like when Johnny Cash died. You knew it was going to happen, but it was still a shock."

Mystery had hated his dad his whole life and wished death on him countless times. But now that it had happened, he didn't know how to feel. He seemed confused that he felt a little sad, despite himself.

"The only times we ever bonded were when a hot woman came on TV," he said. "Then he'd look at me and I'd look at him, and we'd quietly appreciate it together."

A few days later, we hosted the first annual Pickup Artist Summit at our house. PUAs from around the world flew in to speak, and several hundred rAFCs (recovering average frustrated chumps) gathered in our living room to hear them. Our housemates Playboy and Xaneus, who Papa and

Tyler Durden had been training to become instructors, opened the proceedings.

As Playboy discussed body language, I thought back to Belgrade and the first workshop I'd taught with Mystery. I remembered too-cool Exoticoption, Sasha skipping down the street with his first e-mail-close, and Jerry's sense of humor. I loved those guys. I cared about them. I wanted them to get laid. I e-mailed them for months afterward, checking on their progress.

Now I looked around the living room and saw neediness and hunger and desperation. Bald guys with goatees—miniature and super-sized versions of myself—asked me to pose for photos with them. Good-looking guys who could have been models clamored for advice on hairstyles and clothes to buy, and then asked me to pose for photos with them.

Two gangly brothers at the convention—both virgins—brought their sister along. She was a quiet nineteen-year-old imp with large eyes, gumdrop breasts, and a hip-hop fashion sense. Thanks to her brothers, she knew everything about the game. When guys approached her with cocky funny lines, she told them, "Don't try that David DeAngelo stuff on me. I've read it all." She introduced herself as Min, and then asked me to pose for a photo with her.

"I'm a big fan of your posts," she said.

"You've read them?" I asked, shocked.

"Yeah." She bit her lip.

For my presentation, I brought in five of the girls I was dating. I ran routines on them, and then used them as a panel of experts to critique the clothing and body language of various wanna-be players in the audience. I received a standing ovation.

Afterward, I sat on our newly purchased blood-red couches surrounded by Papa, Tyler Durden, and a few of their students. They were discussing the video of Mystery and I picking up Caroline and Carly. Somehow, Gunwitch had gotten hold of it and put it on the Internet, shattering what was left of my anonymity.

"It's so genius," Papa was saying. "Tyler Durden has broken down everything Style does to a science. He calls it Stylemogging."

"What's that?" one of the students asked.

"It's a type of frame control," Tyler Durden replied. A frame is an NLP term: It is the perspective through which one sees the world. Whoever's frame—or subjective reality—is the strongest tends to dominate an interaction. "Style has all these really subtle ways of keeping control of the frame and getting people to qualify themselves to him. He makes sure that the focus is always on him. I'm writing a post about it."

"That's awesome," I said.

Suddenly, Papa, Tyler Durden, and the students laughed. "That's one of the things you do," Papa said. "Tyler's writing about that."

"What? I just said 'awesome.' That's because I think it's hilarious. Seriously, I can't wait to read it."

They all laughed again. Evidently I was Stylemogging them.

"See," Tyler Durden said. "You'll use curiosity as a frame to get rapport and make the other person lose social value. When you show approval like that, it makes you the authority and makes other people want to seek your validation. We're teaching that."

"Shit," I replied. "Now, every time I say something, people are going to think I'm running a Real Social Dynamics routine."

They all laughed again. And that's when I realized that I was fucked: Everything Tyler Durden was writing about wasn't anything I had learned in the community. That was all part of me and who I really was. And even though he had my intentions wrong—that was his frame, his way of looking at the world—he had my mannerisms down. He was taking the building blocks of my personality, giving them names, and turning them into routines. He was going to take my soul and spread it all over the Sunset Strip.

On the last day of the summit, Mystery had a brainstorm: He was going to raise the price of his workshop from six hundred dollars to fifteen hundred. He wanted Papa to change the website to reflect the increase.

"That doesn't make sense," Papa protested. "The market won't support that." Papa rarely went out anymore. Instead, he spent his nights working on the Real Social Dynamics website and Internet affiliate program. Since we'd moved into the house, I'd seen him with a woman exactly once.

"It's my method," Mystery said. "People will pay. I've worked it all out."

"It's not practical." Papa stared straight through Mystery's chest. He didn't like confrontation.

"This is unacceptable!"

Mystery stomped through the living room, where Extramask was giving a presentation. Extramask had arrived in town a week before the seminar and was sleeping somewhere in the house—I wasn't sure exactly where, since Papa had run out of closets to stuff people into. I had hardly talked to Extramask since he'd arrived. He was always either in Papa's room working for Real Social Dynamics, winging a workshop with Tyler Durden, or working out.

I watched him for a few minutes. He was buff now, wearing a torn T-shirt and a loosely knotted tie. He was telling the students that he hadn't lost his virginity—or even held a girl's hand—until he was twenty-six-and-a-half. It was a gimmick now, part of his routine for guys. He had become a guru too. And, along the way, he'd lost the innocence he had when we first met.

"I do a lot of things with this cell phone, and it doesn't even work," he said, holding it up. "I just like to talk into it and pretend that I'm the man, especially if I feel uncomfortable at a club. Your cell phone is your best wingman."

Extramask had great stage presence and an oddball sense of humor. I wished he'd spend more time working on his stand-up comedy career than teaching seduction. Unlike Mystery and Tyler Durden, he wasn't born for this.

I followed Mystery into the kitchen. He was leaning against a counter, waiting for me. "Papa's been doing workshops behind my back," he fumed. "Someone told me they saw him at the Highlands with six guys last weekend."

I hopped onto the counter and sat at eye level with him.

"Let me catch you up to speed on what else has been going on," he said. I assumed he was going to complain about Papa, but instead he wanted to talk about Patricia. She had started dating an African-American jock she'd met at her strip club, and now she was pregnant with his baby. Though she had no plans to marry him, she wanted to keep the child. Her biological alarm clock was still ringing.

"I'm trying to look at this objectively," Mystery said, straddling a chair at the breakfast table that no one used. "I'm not angry. But I am hurt. It makes me want to kill the baby and kill him."

Among the required reading for all PUAs were books on evolutionary theory: *The Red Queen* by Matt Ridley, *The Selfish Gene* by Richard Dawkins, *Sperm Wars* by Robin Baker. You read them, and you understand why women tend to like jerks, why men want so many sexual partners, and why so many people cheat on their spouses. At the same time, however, you understand that the violent impulses most of us successfully repress are actually normal and natural. For Mystery, a Darwinist by nature, these books gave him an intellectual justification for his antisocial emotions and his desire to harm the organism that had mated with his woman. It was not a healthy thing.

Tyler Durden walked into the kitchen and saw Mystery moping at the table.

"You know what you need to do?" he told Mystery. "You need to sarge."

Sarging was Tyler Durden's solution for everything: He truly believed in it. Picking up women could cure all problems—depression, inertia, animosity, colitis, lice. Though I'd moved into the house to build a lifestyle, for Tyler Durden sarging was the only way to live. He never went on dates. Instead he brought women to the clubs on Sunset, and then usually ditched them to pick up more girls.

"You need to get out of the house," Tyler continued. "Go out with Style tonight. You guys have super-tight game. You can find a new girlfriend twice as hot as Patricia."

Next, the virgin brothers came into the kitchen, with their sister Min and a shaven-headed PUA in tow. It seemed like wherever I was during the convention, a small group gathered, and I wound up holding court.

"You had the best presentation of the day," the bald PUA said. "You were so gentle and elegant with those girls. It was like watching a beautifully choreographed dance."

"Thanks, man. What's your name?"

"I'm Stylechild."

For the first time in months, I was speechless.

"I named myself after you."

As he told me about his luckless life and his discovery of the community and my posts, I saw Min looking at me with her impish eyes. And I made the conscious decision not to game her, because that's what all the other guys at the seminar were doing. Besides the girls I had used in my presentation, she had been the only woman in the house all weekend.

That night at the Saddle Ranch, Min's eyes were still burning a hole in my head. I had to say something—but it couldn't be anything she'd read online or heard from her brothers.

"Listen," I finally told her. "I'm about to sign up to ride the mechanical bull. Why don't you join me?"

It wasn't a line: I still had designs on that mechanical bull. In many ways, it reminded me of the game. It had eleven settings, from ridiculously easy to fiendishly difficult. And ever since I'd first set eyes on the bull, it had been my goal to get to the top setting—the mythical eleven. So far, I'd only made it to ten.

It was a completely pointless ambition, with no practical application whatsoever. But if you sit the average male down in front of anything halfway intriguing and explain to him that it has a system of rankings that he can get better at over time, he'll become obsessed. Hence the popularity of video games, martial arts, Dungeons and Dragons, and the seduction community.

I asked the bull-wrangler to set the machine to eleven, gave him a five-dollar tip to make sure he went easy on me, then climbed through the gate and mounted the bull. I was wearing leather pants—not to peacock, but to help me stick to the sides of the machine. The first time I rode it, my thighs were black-and-blue the next day, and I could hardly walk. I understood then what a woman must feel like after sex with a three-hundred-pound guy.

I pressed my crotch firmly against the front of the saddle, clamped my legs against the flank of the bull, and raised my hand to signal I was ready. In an instant the machine shuddered to life, vibrating me so quickly that my eyes lost focus. I remember feeling my brain about to fall out of my skull, my hips rocking faster than they'd ever moved before, my legs losing their grip, and my crotch jackhammering into the saddle handle in time with the bull. But just as I was about to slide off the side, the bull stopped. I had lasted seven seconds.

At first, I was elated. I felt like I had accomplished something—even though it was really nothing. It wouldn't change my life, or the life of anyone around me in the least. I began to wonder why I had cared so much. Within minutes, I already had buyer's remorse.

Afterward, Min said she was tired and asked me to walk her back to Project Hollywood.

I understood the subtext.

As we ambled back to the mansion arm-in-arm, she talked about her older brothers and their difficulty learning the game. "They're real protective and get mad when I go on dates," she said. "But I think they're jealous because they're not going on dates themselves."

When we returned to Project Hollywood, I brought her to the Jacuzzi.

"My last boyfriend was the sweetest guy, and he did everything for me," she went on. "But I didn't like him. He got on my nerves. After I started reading my brothers' pickup stuff, I understood why I wasn't attracted to him or any of the other guys at school. They're all so boring. They don't understand cocky funny."

I stripped down to my boxers and jumped in the water, soothing my bull-bucked wounds. She joined me in her bra and panties. She was thin and delicate, like a marionette. I took her hands and pulled her toward me. She straddled my legs, and we began making out. I took her bra off and put her gumdrops in my mouth. Then I carried her naked and dripping to my bedroom, put on a condom, and slowly entered her. There was no LMR. By looking up to me so much, her brothers had driven her into my arms.

She was my first groupie. And she would not be my last. This whole PUA thing was getting too big. With so many new competing seduction businesses aggressively marketing their services online, the community was growing exponentially, especially in Southern California, where the Sunset Strip was transforming before our eyes.

No woman was safe. Workshops of fifteen people wandered the street like gangs. Bands of former students patrolled every club—the Standard, Dublin's, the Saddle Ranch, Miyagi's. When the bars closed at 2:00 A.M., they'd invade Mel's, walking up and down the aisles, seating themselves at any table with a female. They carted women into the house by the truckload.

And they were all using my material. They were running around Style-mogging and delivering the best-friends test like they were Spanish flys. In every club, I saw their shaven heads, their diabolical goatees, their shoes that looked like the pair I'd bought in the Beverly Center a week before. Mini-mes were everywhere. And there was nothing I could do about it.

Chapter

MSN GROUP: Mystery's Lounge
SUBJECT: My Approach Schedule
AUTHOR: Adonis

After getting fired from my job (too much time in the lounge, lol), I moved to
L.A. last week to devote myself full-time to getting this game handled. I've always felt like the odd guy out here because I'm still a virgin and kind of a keyboard jockey, so I have locked off Saturday and decided to do a hundred
approaches in a single day. I am going to start out on Melrose between La
Brea and Fairfax in the afternoon. I figure I can do ten approaches per hour for
five hours, yielding fifty approaches. (Does anyone know the name of the store
where they sell the New Rock boots?) Afterward, I'm going to shower up, hit
Sunset, and cover four bars (Dublin's, Miyagi's, the Saddle Ranch, the Standard), making twelve to fifteen approaches in each. A hundred approaches
should be no problem. Even if I crash and burn every time, at least I will conquer my fear of rejection.

—Adonis

MSN GROUP: Mystery's Lounge
SUBJECT: 125 Approaches!
AUTHOR: Adonis

Guys, this Saturday rocked. I got through 125 approaches. It was phenome-
nal. Before I left, I listened to Ross Jeffries's Unstoppable Confidence tapes.
They really help. I pictured myself forty feet tall and made of diamond, so no
one could hurt me.
     The opinion opener I used was the RSD classic, "Who lies more, men or
women?" At first, HBs gave me funny looks, like I was taking a survey. It really
started clicking for me at the Saddle Ranch. I think I opened every woman
there. One HB8 offered me an e-mail address, but I pushed for a number close
and lost it completely. Fuck! Lesson learned. Afterward, I went to the Standard,

and there were already two workshops there. Practically every set there had been approached already with the "who lies more" opener, so I started opening people in the street outside.

I would recommend that anyone starting out go and do this. (But make sure you've broken in your New Rocks first, lol!) I have now decided to try to get 1,000 approaches under my belt before the end of the month. My opening game is going to be supertight, and I will no longer be resentful of women and fear their power to make me feel inadequate.

—Adonis

MSN GROUP: Mystery's Lounge
SUBJECT: My Thousandth Approach
AUTHOR: Adonis

I have kept score of every approach I have done and, as promised, I just got through my thousandth approach—and still with four days left in the month!

I can say after a thousand approaches, there are only so many ways to get rejected or ignored. It doesn't hurt at all anymore because why should someone who's a complete stranger have any control over your sense of self-worth?

The other thing I learned is to challenge or intrigue HBs right away instead of trying to be logical or factual. I can stay in sets now for ten or fifteen minutes. I have been Stylemogging too, which was hard at first. But now I'm finding it easier to control a set, despite my size (I'm 5'4"). I am even isolating and doing the cube sometimes, and getting the odd phone number. I feel like I've become a new, more confident person, with no social fears. Before, I was so insecure and self-conscious that people avoided me; now when I walk down the street, I radiate. HBs can just sense it. I strongly recommend that everyone try this. It's worth it.

Next month, I'm going to master phone game—a thousand phone calls, lol. If I keep this up, I should be getting laid by the end of the year.

—Adonis

MSN GROUP: Mystery's Lounge
SUBJECT: Are You A Social Robot?
AUTHOR: Style

Have you ever noticed that there's something strange about a lot of guys in the community?

It's as if just by looking at them, you can tell that something is missing. They don't seem entirely human.

Some of these guys even do well in the field. They get great reactions—sometimes even numbers and lays—but they never seem to have a girlfriend.

Are you one of these guys?

To find out, ask yourself the following questions:

* Do you panic if you run out of "material" during a conversation with a woman?

* Do you think that everything a woman says to you that isn't 100 percent positive is a "shit test"?

* Do you see every other male who is interacting with a woman as an AMOG who must be destroyed?

* Are you unable to discuss a woman without first asking, "What's her rating?"

* Do you call women in your life who you are not sleeping with "pivots" instead of friends?

* If you are around a woman in a non-social setting, such as a business meeting or a nursing home, do you get a strange shot of adrenaline and feel obligated to sarge her?

* Have you stopped seeing value in things that are not pickup related, such as books, movies, friends, family, work, school, food, and water?

* Is your self-esteem constantly at the mercy of the reactions of women?

Then you may be a social robot.

Most of the sargers I know are social robots. This is especially true among those who found the community in their teens or early twenties. Because they haven't had much real-world experience, they have learned to socialize almost entirely through rules and theories they've read online and learned in workshops. They may never be normal again. After a great twenty-minute set with many of these social robots, a woman begins to realize that they don't have anything more going for them. And then they post online complaining that women are flakes.

The Internet newsgroups and the pickup lifestyle can give you so much—I know it's given me so much—but it can take away a lot too. You can end up becoming a one-dimensional person. You start to think that everyone else around you is a social robot too and begin to read too much into his or her actions.

The solution is to remember that the best way to pick up women is to have something better to do than to pick up women. Some guys give up everything—school, work, even girlfriends—to learn the game. But all these things are what make one complete and enhance one's attractiveness to the opposite sex. So put your life back in balance. If you can make something of yourself, women will flock to you, and what you've learned here will prepare you to deal with them.

—Style

"I can't just tell students not to come to your workshop."

Mystery and Papa were arguing again.

"You booked too many students," Mystery said, throwing his hands up, exasperated. "It's not fun for me. And it's not fair to them."

"And you're making my business look bad." Papa's voice was stuffy with pent-up frustration.

"Fine," Mystery yelled. "Then take my name off your website. Our business relationship is through. I don't want anything to do with Real Social Dynamics."

It was a doomed partnership to begin with.

The next day, Herbal offered to be Mystery's business partner. It seemed as if he'd been laying low the whole time, waiting for his moment to get involved in the pickup business. Since he'd arrived at the house, he hadn't been with a single woman besides Sima, an ex-MLTR of Mystery's who had moved to Los Angeles from Toronto. When Mystery and Sima started getting on each other's nerves shortly after her arrival in town, she started showing IOIs to Herbal. Instead of getting upset, Mystery sat Herbal down and told him everything he needed to do to sarge her. Sima and Herbal ended up fooling around that night. Afterward, it only served to strengthen Mystery and Herbal's friendship. But they seemed unaware of something that everyone else around them realized: a bad precedent was being set.

Once Herbal started working for Mystery, we truly became a house divided: There was Real Social Dynamics, encamped in Papa's room, and Mystery Method, which had the rest of the house.

I was the only person under the roof who wasn't on the payroll of either. But that didn't stop Papa from snubbing me along with Mystery and Herbal. I was guilty by association. If Papa and I happened to bump into each other as he snuck around the back of the house, he'd walk past with a brusque hello, staring vacantly through me.

He wasn't angry. He was just operating on some sort of program that didn't include me. The curious thing is: Most robots don't program themselves.

In the meantime, every single rule we had laid down at the house meeting—requiring approval for guests, giving the house a percentage of seminar money, not hitting on another PUA's woman—was bypassed and ignored. We had no idea how many students, sargers, and instructors Papa was packing into his room. They scurried around the house like peacocked rats. We didn't even bother to lock the doors anymore.

His latest recruits were two interns who looked like younger versions of himself. No one knew their names. They were known simply as the mini-Papas.

The mini-Papas were just as cold to me as Papa was, but they were constantly around. They watched my every move, as if it were an assignment they'd been given. Sometimes I'd see them sitting at Mel's Diner with Tyler Durden. The three of them would be talking about me.

"He'll reposition his body to steer the conversation in his direction."

"He'll leave at times to show scarcity."

"If you make a joke, he exaggerates it to steal the glory."

"If someone asks him to do a routine, he'll say, 'In the field,' so that it's on his time and the person appreciates it more."

They weren't criticizing me. They were trying to model me. Yet, oddly, they never hung out with me as friends. They just wanted to listen and absorb and take notes. It was dehumanizing. But then again, no one in that house seemed entirely human to begin with.

I needed to get out of there.

Fortunately, *Rolling Stone* wanted me to tackle another tough subject. Her name was Courtney Love.

The interview was scheduled to take place for one hour at the Virgin Records office in New York. Courtney was at the peak of her infamy at the time. That week she'd bared her breasts to David Letterman on network TV; appeared on the front page of the *New York Post* with one of her mammaries in the mouth of a stranger outside Wendy's; and been arrested for allegedly hitting a fan in the head with a microphone stand during a concert. On top of all that, she was facing drug charges and had recently lost custody of her daughter. The *Rolling Stone* story was the first interview she'd agreed to do since all the trouble went down.

When I met her at Virgin, Courtney was wearing a black dress with a sash wrapped tastefully around her torso. Her lips were painted red and full. Considering the number of ugly tabloid headlines featuring her name, Courtney looked good—pale, thin, statuesque. Soon, however, the sash was loose and dangling behind her like a tail and the lipstick was smeared. It seemed like a metaphor for her life: constantly unraveling.

"If you guys are waiting for me to die, you're going to have to wait a long time," she began. I was the press; I was the enemy. "My grandmother didn't die until she was a hundred and two."

This is what PUAs call a bitch shield. It was nothing personal, just a protective mechanism. I couldn't let it faze me. I had to get rapport and show her I was human, not just another bloodsucking journalist.

"I still have nightmares about my grandmother," I told her, "because the last time I had the chance to see her alive, we had plans to go to the Art Institute of Chicago. And I blew her off because I wanted to sleep late."

We fluffed for a while about our families. She didn't like hers very much.

Now we were getting somewhere.

As the interview continued, I hit the hook point. She looked up at me and the walls came down. Her face flushed, the muscles in her cheeks clamped, and the tears started dripping. "I need to be saved," she sobbed. "You need to save me."

Now we had rapport.

Rapport equals trust plus comfort.

When our hour was up, Courtney suggested exchanging phone numbers. She said she'd call me later that night to continue the interview. I was relieved, because an hour-long discussion in a record company office wouldn't have made for a very interesting profile. At least Tom Cruise had taken me motorcycle-riding and Scientology-sightseeing.

That night, I met some old college friends at Soho House, a private club in the meatpacking district of Manhattan. I hadn't seen them since I'd joined the community, and they hardly recognized me. They spent a half hour discussing how awkward and introverted I used to be. Then their conversation turned to work and movies. I tried to contribute, but I had trouble focusing on the words. They just floated into my ear and accumulated there like wax. I felt like I didn't fit in with them anymore. Fortunately, an Amazonian woman with tree-trunk thighs and a lethal boob-job soon stumbled past the table. She was a foot taller than me and somewhat drunk.

"Have you seen a girl in a black cowboy hat?" she asked in a staccato German accent.

"Hang out with us," I said. "We're more fun than your friends."

It was a line I'd learned from David DeAngelo. And it worked. My friends looked on in shock as she sat down and asked for a cigarette.

For the rest of the night, the Amazon and I talked. Every now and then, she'd drag me to the bathroom, where I'd watch her inhale cocaine like a human Dustbuster.

"Do you watch *Sex in the City?*" she asked as we left the bathroom for the third time that night.

"Sometimes," I told her.

"I just got a pearl," she said, with Teutonic pride.

"That's great." I had no idea what a pearl was.

"It's cool," she said. "With those little beads."

"Oh, the beads. Those things are great."

I was totally confused. But I liked listening to her, enjoying the mismatch between her harsh accent and her spongy lips. Maybe she was talking about anal beads. Good for her.

I stopped and leaned against the wall of the corridor we were walking through. "How good of a kisser are you, on a scale of one to ten?"

"I'm a ten," she said. "I like soft, slow, teasing kisses. I hate it when someone rams their tongue down my throat."

"Yeah, I had a girlfriend who did that. It was like making out with a cow."

"I give amazing blow jobs," she said.

"Respect."

That one-word answer had taken me months to figure out. Some women like to make extremely sexual comments after meeting a man. It is a shit test. If the guy becomes uncomfortable, he fails; however, if he takes the bait and gets excited or says something sexual in response, he also fails. After watching the British television character Ali G, I discovered the solution: Just look her in the eye, nod approvingly, and, with a slight smile creeping across your face, say, "Respect," in a smart-ass tone. I had responses now for nearly every challenge a woman could throw my way. But this was hardly a challenge—it was fool's mate. My job was simply to not do anything wrong.

I fell silent and did what the PUAs call triangular gazing, looking slowly from her left eye to her right eye and then to her lips to create suggestive sexual tension.

She threw herself against me. The next thing she did was ram her tongue down my throat, like a cow. Then she pulled away. "Talking about kissing got me excited," she said.

"Let's get out of here," I replied, peeling myself off the wall.

We took the elevator downstairs and hailed a cab. She gave the driver an address in the East Village. I guess we were going to her place.

She straddled me in the back seat and pulled a heavy breast out of her tank top. I guess I was supposed to suck it.

We arrived at her house and climbed the stairs to her apartment. She turned on a lamp, which cast a dull brown glow over the room, and slipped the Rolling Stones' *Goats Head Soup* into her stereo.

"I'm just going to put my pearl on," she told me.

"I can't wait," I said. And I couldn't.

As I lay there, I realized I'd forgotten to say good-bye to my friends. In fact, I'd ignored them all night. Sarging had dropped a polyester curtain between me and my past. But when my new friend emerged in her pearl, I decided, in the heat of the moment, that it was worth it. The pearl wasn't anal beads at all. It was a pair of panties with an exposed crotch and a chain of small metal balls connecting the front side to the back, running over her pussy.

She'd probably left the house that night hoping to find someone to take home to show it off to. Obliging, I rubbed the balls gently against her labia and her clit. I figured that was what it was for, though I wasn't really sure because, a minute later, the chain of balls snapped off the underwear. It dangled between her legs like a tampon string.

So much for her new pearl.

"I'm going to change," she said. She didn't seem upset. Inhaling an eight ball of cocaine will do that to someone.

She re-emerged in knee-high black leather boots, lay down on the bed, and took another Dustbuster snort from a burgundy vial of coke. Then she lifted the vial over her chest and tapped a small pile of powder onto the crest of her left breast.

I'm not a fan of drugs. Part of being a PUA is learning to control your own state, so you don't need alcohol or drugs to have a good time. But if I were ever going to do cocaine, now would be the time.

Every woman is different in bed. Each has her own tastes and quirks and fantasies. And someone's surface appearance never accurately indicates the raging storm or dead calm that lies beneath. Reaching that moment of passionate truth—of surrender, honesty, revelation—was my favorite part of the game. I loved seeing what new person emerged in bed, and then talking with that new person after our mutual orgasms. I guess I just like people.

I leaned over her breast and plugged my left nostril. I was really dreading this: I didn't want to be up all night, and I had a feeling that coke wasn't good for a gentleman's staying power.

Not that I was a gentleman.

And then the phone rang. My phone.

"I have to get this," I told her. I jumped up, spilling fairy dust all over the sheets, and grabbed my cell phone. I had a feeling I knew who was calling.

"Hey, can you come over?" It was Courtney Love. "See if you can get some acupuncture needles in Chinatown—the big ones that hurt the most. And get some alcohol and cotton swabs."

Chapter

"This one's for the gallbladder," Courtney Love said as she slammed an acupuncture needle into my leg.

"Um, shouldn't this be done by a licensed professional?"

"I've been doing this since I was young," she replied, "but you're the first person I've done it to in a while." She wiggled the needle around. "Tell me when you feel it."

There. An electric shock to the leg. Okay. Enough.

My scheduled one-hour interview with Courtney Love had turned into a surreal slumber party. Outside of food runs, I didn't leave her Chinatown loft for seventy-two hours. It was five thousand square feet with nothing in it but a bed, a television, and a couch.

Dressed down in a T-shirt and sweatpants, she was in hiding: from the paparazzi, from her manager, from the government, from the bank, from a man, from herself. I was stripped down to my boxers on her couch, with a dozen needles sticking out of me. Over time the floor around her bed grew dense with crumbs, cigarette butts, clothing, food wrappers, needles, and root beer bottles; meanwhile, the color of her fingers and toes changed from flesh to blackened ash. She was too scared even to answer her phone, in case someone called her "with some bullshit news about some fucking thing."

It was just the two of us: journalist and rock star, player and playette.

She put *Boogie Nights* into her DVD player, then climbed into her bed and threw a stained blanket over herself. "I always ask the guy I'm dating, 'What's your biggest fear?'" she said. "My last boyfriend said it's drifting, which he's doing now. The video director I'm currently obsessed with said failure. And I'm living mine: It's loss of power."

Of all the problems in Courtney's life, the one that seemed to consume her most was romantic. The video director wasn't returning her calls. It was a problem common to all women, no matter what they looked like or how famous they were.

"I have a theory," she said. "You have to sleep with a guy three times for him to fall in love with you. And I only slept with him twice. I need one more night to get him."

This director had captured her heart by playing push-pull. He'd walk her home, make out with her, and then tell her he couldn't come inside. Whether by accident or design, he was following David DeAngelo's technique of two steps forward and one step back.

"If you want to get him," I said, "read *The Art of Seduction* by Robert Greene. It'll give you some strategy."

She stubbed her cigarette out on the floor. "I need all the help I can get."

The Art of Seduction was classic PUA reading material, along with Greene's other book, *The 48 Laws of Power*. For the former, Greene studied the greatest seductions of history and literature in search of common themes. His book classified different types of seducers (among them rakes, ideal lovers, and naturals); targets (drama queens, rescuers, crushed stars); and techniques, all of which jibed with community philosophy (approach indirectly, send mixed signals, appear to be an object of desire, isolate the victim).

"How do you know about that book?" she asked.

"I've spent the last year and a half hanging out with the world's greatest pickup artists."

She sat up in her bed. "Tell me, tell me, tell me," she squealed like a schoolgirl. Talking about pickup was better than the alternative: Whenever the discussion veered toward her legal, media, and custody problems, her eyes filled with tears.

She listened rapt as I told her about the community and Project Hollywood. It wasn't easy to have a serious conversation with a dozen acupuncture needles sticking out of my body. "I want to meet them," she said excitedly. "Do you think they're as good as Warren Beatty?"

"I don't know. I've never met him."

Courtney climbed out of bed and rubbed patchouli oil around the needles in my feet, legs, and chest. "Let me tell you, he's smooth."

"I would love to know how he operates."

"He's great. He once called me and said, 'Hey, it's me,' as if I should have known who it was. Then he tried to convince me to come over to his house that night. When I finally say yes, he laughed and said he was in Paris. It's a total mindfuck. He'll blow his nose and then hand the dirty tissue to his date."

It was a neg. Warren Beatty negged women. Every PUA—whether he's aware of it or not—uses the same principles. The difference between those in the community and lone wolves like Warren Beatty (when he was single), Brett Ratner, and David Blaine is that we name our techniques and share our information.

"I don't know what this director's problem is," Courtney was saying. "I have a magic pussy. If you fuck me, you become a king. I'm a kingmaker." (Translation: If you fuck her, you become famous.)

She began pulling the needles out of my body. Relief. "You have to get one in your head. It's the best feeling."

Fumbling around the floor, Courtney grabbed a dirty needle. She aimed it just above my eye.

"No thanks. I've had enough for today."

"You gotta try it. It's great for the liver."

"My liver's fine, thanks."

She dropped the needle back to the floor. "Fine. I'm going out to get some Rice Krispie Treats then."

She wriggled out of her pink shirt and stood in front of me topless.

"These are natural breasts but with a silicone lift," she said, hovering over me and revealing a scar underneath her left mammary. "Do you know how much a shot of my tits is worth? Nine thousand dollars."

"Then your problems are solved," I suggested.

"That won't even get me in the door at the lawyer's office," she snapped, slipping into a black-and-white baby-doll dress.

When she returned from the store, she was flushed with excitement. She pulled a coffee cake out of her bag and split it in half, leaving a trail of crumbs behind her as she made for the safety of her bed. "Let's make a bet," she said.

"What?"

"I will bet you that I can get this director back."

"I doubt you can. If he's not returning your calls, he's not interested."

"He even denied he'd slept with me in the *Post*." She handed me half of the coffee cake in her blackened fingers. "But I like a challenge."

"Well, if you can get him back, you're a better pickup artist than I am."

"Then let's bet," she insisted.

"What are the stakes?"

"If I can't get him back, I will give you a one-week stand with me—wherever you want."

I looked at her blankly. I was so taken aback by the notion that I had trouble processing the words.

"Or you can pick the middle name of my next child. It's your choice."

"Okay."

"But I have one condition: I get an hour of advice with each pickup artist you're living with."

When it came time for me to leave and catch my plane, Courtney climbed out of bed and kissed me good-bye.

"I just need to be fucked," she said as I waited for the elevator that would take me out of her loft. "I just need a bossy guy to come here and fuck me."

I knew I could have been that guy. The IOIs were there. But there's a PUA's code of honor, there's a gambler's code of honor, and there's a journalist's code of honor. And having sex with her would have been violating all three.

What I had told Dustin that morning in my apartment really was true: Learning pickup had enriched so much more than just my sex life. The skills I had amassed in the community made me a much better interviewer than I'd ever been. I discovered just how good when I was assigned an interview with Britney Spears.

Chapter

Was there a lot of pressure on you while making this album?
What, now?

Was there a lot of pressure from yourself or the label to have a major hit this time around?
I have no idea.

You have no idea?
I have no idea.

I heard you did a track with the DFA that wasn't included on your new CD. Why was that?
What's the DFA?

They're two producers from New York, James Murphy and Tim Goldsworthy, who call themselves the DFA. Does that ring a bell?
Yeah, maybe they did something.

My interview with Britney Spears was going nowhere. I looked at her, crossing her legs and fidgeting on the hotel-room couch next to me. She didn't give a shit. I was just an amount of time blocked off on her calendar, and she was tolerating it—poorly.

Her hair was tucked under a white Kangol hat and her thighs pushed at the seams of her faded blue jeans. She was one of the most desired women in the world. But in person, she looked like a cornfed Southern sorority girl. She had a beautiful face, lightly and perfectly touched with makeup, but there was something masculine about her. As a sexual icon, she was unintimidating and, I imagined, lonely.

A gear slammed down in my head.

There was only one way to save this interview: I had to sarge her. No matter what country I was in or what age or class or race of woman I was talking to, the game always worked. Besides, I had nothing to lose by gaming Britney Spears. The interview couldn't get any more boring. Maybe I'd even get a decent quote I could actually print.

I folded my list of questions and put them in my back pocket. I had to treat her like any club girl with attention deficit disorder.

The first move was to hook her attention.

"I'll tell you something about yourself that other people probably don't know," I began. "People sometimes see you as shy or bitchy offstage, even though you aren't."

"Totally," she said.

"Do you want to know why?"

"Yeah." I was creating what's called a yes-ladder, capturing her attention by asking questions that require an obvious affirmative answer.

"I'm watching your eyes when you talk. And every time you think, they go down and to the left. That means you're a kinesthetic person. You're someone who lives in her feelings."

"Oh my God," she said. "That's totally true."

Of course it was. It was one of the value-demonstrating routines I'd developed. The eye goes to one of seven different positions when someone thinks: Each position means the person is accessing a different part of their brain.

As I taught her how to read different types of eye movements, she clung to every word. Her legs uncrossed and she leaned in toward me.

The game was on.

"I didn't know this," she said. "Who told you this?"

I wanted to tell her, "A secret society of international pickup artists."

"It's something I observed from doing lots of interviews," I answered. "In fact, by watching the direction peoples' eyes move when they speak, you can tell whether they're telling the truth or not."

"So you're going to know if I'm lying?" She was looking at me entirely differently now. I wasn't a journalist anymore. I was someone she could learn from, someone who offered value. I had demonstrated authority over her world.

"I can tell from your eye movements, from your eye contact, from the way you speak, and from your body language. There are many different ways to tell."

"I need to do psychology classes," she said, with endearing earnestness.

"That would be so interesting to me, studying people." It was working. She was opening up. She kept talking and talking: "And you could meet some-body or be out on a date and be like, 'Are they lying to me right now?' Oh my gosh."

It was time to pull out the heavy artillery.

"I'll show you something really cool and then we'll get back to the in-terview," I said, throwing in a time constraint for good measure. "It'll be an experiment. I'm going to try to guess something that's in your thoughts."

Then I used a simple psychological gambit to guess the initials of an old friend she had an emotional connection to—someone I wouldn't know and hadn't heard of. The initials were G. C. And I got one letter out of two cor-rect. It was a new routine I was still learning, but it was good enough for her.

"I can't believe you did that! I probably have so many walls in front, so that's why you didn't get them both," she said. "Let's try it one more time."

"This time, why don't you try it?"

"I'm scared." She put her knuckle in her mouth and pinched the skin between her teeth. She had great teeth. They really were a perfect C-shape. "I can't do that."

She was no longer Britney Spears. She was just a one-set, a lone target. Or, as Robert Greene would classify her in his breakdown of seducer's vic-tims, she was the lonely leader.

"We'll make it easier," I said. "I'm going to write down a number. And it's a number between one and ten. What I want you to do is not to think at all. You need to trust your instincts. There's no special ability required to read minds. Just quiet your internal chatter and really listen to your feelings."

I wrote a number on a piece of paper and handed it to her face down.

"Now, tell me," I said, "the first number that you feel."

"What if it's wrong?" she asked. "It's probably wrong."

This was what we called in the field an LSE girl—she had low self-esteem.

"What do you think it is?"

"Seven," she said.

"Now, turn over the paper," I told her.

She slowly turned it over, as if she were afraid to look, then moved it up to eye level and saw a big number seven staring right back at her.

She screamed, leaped off the couch, and ran to the hotel mirror. Her mouth hung agape as she looked her reflection in the eye.

"Oh my God," she said to her reflection. "I did that."

It was as if she had to look at herself in the mirror to make sure that what had just happened was real.

"Whoa," she gasped. "I did that." She was like a little girl seeing Britney Spears for the first time. She was her own fan.

"I just knew that it was seven!" she announced as she galloped back to the couch. Of course she knew. That was the first magic trick I learned from Mystery: If you have someone chose a number between one and ten randomly, seventy percent of the time—especially if you rush their decision—that number will be seven.

So, yeah, I had tricked her. But her self-esteem needed a good boost.

"See," I told her. "You already know all the answers inside. It's just that society trains you to think too much." I really believed that.

"Cool interview!" she exclaimed. "I like this interview! This has been the best interview of my life!"

Then she turned her face toward mine, looked me in the eye, and asked, "Can we stop the tape recorder?"

For the next fifteen minutes, we talked about spirituality and writing and our lives. She was just a lost little girl going through a late emotional puberty. She was searching for something real to hold onto, something deeper than pop fame and the sycophancy of her handlers. I had demonstrated value, and now we were moving on to the rapport phase of seduction. Maybe Mystery was right: All human relationships follow the same formula.

Rapport equals trust plus comfort.

However, I had a job to do. I started the tape recorder and asked the questions I'd given her at the start of the interview, plus all the other questions I had. This time she gave me real answers, answers I could print.

When the hour was up, I stopped the tape recorder.

"You know," Britney said. "Everything happens for a reason."

"I truly believe that," I told her.

"I do too." She touched my shoulder and a broad smile spread across her face. "I'd like to exchange numbers."

After our hour was up, Britney left the room to change for an MTV interview. She returned ten minutes later with her publicist.

As she sat down in front of the cameras, her publicist looked at me strangely.

"You know, she's never done that with a writer before," she said.

"Really?" I asked.

"She said it was like the two of you were destined to meet."

The publicist and I stood next to each other in silence as the MTV interview began.

"So you had a crazy time out the other night," the interviewer asked.

"Yeah, I did," Britney answered.

"What was the energy level like in the club when you walked in and surprised everyone?"

"Oh, it was just crazy."

"And how much fun did you have?"

Suddenly, Britney stood up. "This isn't working," she told the crew. "I'm not feeling this."

She pivoted on her heels and walked toward the door, leaving the crew and her assistants befuddled. As she passed me, the corners of her mouth turned upward, forming a conspiratorial smile. I had gotten to her. There was something deeper to Britney Spears than what the pop machine required of her.

The game, I realized, works better on celebrities than ordinary people. Because stars are so sheltered and their interactions limited, a demonstration of value or the right neg holds ten times the power.

In the days that followed, I thought often about what had happened. I had no illusions: Britney Spears wasn't attracted to me. She wasn't considering me as a potential mate. But I had interested her. And that was a step in the right direction. Pickup is a linear process: Capture the imagination first and the heart next.

Interest plus attraction plus seduction equals sex.

Of course, maybe this was all just self-hypnosis. For all I knew, she exchanged phone numbers with every journalist to make him feel special and ensure a good story. She probably had an answering service set up at that number specifically for gullible writers who thought they were pickup artists. Or perhaps it was a scheme of the publicist's to make journalists think they had a special connection with her artist. Maybe I was the one being sarged, not her.

I would never know the truth.

I stared at that number every day, but I couldn't bring myself to dial it. I told myself that it was crossing a journalistic line: If she didn't like the piece I was writing (which was quite possible), I didn't want her to go on record saying I had written a bad article because she hadn't phoned back.

"Just call her," Mystery constantly prodded me. "What do you have to lose? Tell her, 'Can you not look like Britney Spears? We're going to do some crazy shit, and we can't get caught. We're going to wear wigs, climb up to the Hollywood sign, and touch it for good luck.'"

"If I had met her socially, fine. But this is a work assignment."

"You're playing the game at another level now. When the article is finished, it isn't an assignment anymore. So call her."

But I couldn't do it. If it had been Dalene Kurtis, the Playmate of the Year, I would have called her back in a second. I had no fear of women like that anymore. I felt worthy. I'd proven that over and over since meeting her. But Britney Spears?

One's self-esteem can only grow so much in a year and a half.

MAKE A PHYSICAL
CONNECTION

AND DO YOU THINK

THAT LOVE ITSELF,

LIVING IN SUCH AN UGLY HOUSE,

CAN PROSPER LONG?

....

—EDNA ST. VINCENT MILLAY,
"And do you think that love itself"

It took just one woman to bring Project Hollywood down.

By all appearances, Katya was a standard-issue party girl. She liked to drink, dance, have sex, and get high, not necessarily in that order. But Katya—perhaps out of innocence, perhaps out of revenge, perhaps out of true love—would outgame every PUA in the house. All those years of study, all those memorized routines and learned patterns of behavior, all those New Rock platform boots were no match for a woman scorned.

When I returned from New York, Mystery had a workshop scheduled in Los Angeles. He was charging fifteen hundred dollars now—and people were paying. He had five students, guaranteeing a healthy profit for a week-end of talking and sarging. Katya's was just one of several numbers he had collected while demonstrating his game during the workshop. He'd met her at a Hollywood bar called Star Shoes. She was very drunk at the time, and quite possibly high.

Monday was telephone day at Project Hollywood. Everyone called the numbers they'd collected the previous weekend to see which leads were hot and which had staled. When Mystery made his calls, the only person who picked up the phone was Katya. If Katya hadn't been home and another one of Mystery's numbers had answered instead, all our lives would have been different.

Despite our supposed skill, mating is largely a game of chance. Women are at different places in their lives when we meet them. They may be look-ing for a boyfriend, a one-night stand, a husband, or a revenge fuck. Or they may be looking for nothing at all, because they're in a happy relationship or recovering from an emotionally destructive one.

Katya was probably looking for a place to live.

When Mystery called, Katya couldn't remember having met him. Nonetheless, after a half hour of talk (or comfort-building, as Mystery put it), she agreed to come over.

"Dress casual," Mystery told her. "I'll only be able to hang out for an hour or two."

Using words like "casual" and "hang out," and the time constraint, were all part of a strategy to make the visit a low-pressure event. It's a much better way to get someone to commit to time with a stranger than AFC-style dinner dating, which can be a painful, drawn-out affair that involves two people who may have nothing in common stuck together for an entire night of awkward conversation.

Katya arrived that evening wearing a pink sweatsuit and dragging along a scrappy little terrier named Lily. Both Katya and Lily instantly made themselves at home. The former collapsed into the pillow pit and the latter took a shit on the carpet.

Mystery popped out of his room in jeans, a long-sleeved black T-shirt, and his hair in a ponytail. "I'm just going to hook my computer up to the projector and show you some movies I made," he told her.

"No worries, no troubles," Katya replied in an upbeat Russian accent. She had a button nose that wiggled, puffy cheeks that flared, and blonde hair that bounced to maximize her cuteness.

Mystery dimmed the lights and showed her our home movies. They were becoming a popular routine around the house because they allowed us to convey positive qualities about ourselves and our friends without even talking. After movie time, Mystery and Katya massaged each other and made out. On their second meeting, three days later, after much LMR, they closed the deal.

"I'm moving out of my apartment," she told Mystery afterward. "So is it okay if Lily stays here while I go to Las Vegas this weekend?"

Leaving Lily at the house was a cunning tactic because, while Katya was gone, we all grew attached to the cheery, lovable dog—and, by extension, to its owner as well. Their personalities were similar: They were both bouncy and energetic and liked licking Mystery's face.

When Katya returned from Las Vegas, Mystery helped her move out of her old house. "I think it's completely ridiculous for you to rent a new apartment, knowing that you'll be spending most of your time with me," he told her. "So why don't you just move into my room?"

All she had to her name were two duffel bags, a makeup kit, Lily, and a Mazda SUV stuffed with clothing and shoes. As far as anyone knew, she had no job or source of income, though she'd modeled for a couple of low-budget swimsuit calendars. In the evenings, she went to school to learn special-effects makeup. Every night after class she'd prance around the house with fake rope burns around her neck or artificial brain spilling out of a flesh wound in her forehead or the wrinkles and liver spots of a ninety-year-old woman.

Katya quickly wove herself into the fabric of the house. She volunteered to be a pivot for Papa's workshops; she put eyeliner on Herbal before he went out for the night; she cleaned the kitchen that we were all too lazy to deal with ourselves; she went shopping with Xaneus; and she played hostess to Playboy's parties. She had an amazing ability to befriend anyone, though her motivation was unclear: Maybe she was genuinely a people-loving person, maybe she enjoyed the free rent. Either way, she was giving the home its first rays of warmth and camaraderie since the night we'd moved in and sat in the Jacuzzi, dreaming of the future together. I liked her. We all liked her. We even let her brother, a shaggy-haired sixteen-year-old with Tourette's syndrome, sleep in the pillow pit for a few weeks.

Mystery was particularly happy with himself. He hadn't dated anyone seriously since Patricia.

"I actually have a crush on my own girlfriend," he said with pride one evening, showing Katya's swimsuit-calendar picture to a group of random sargers. "I think of her constantly, like when you have a baby. I have a very strong nurturing instinct. I need to take care of this girl and make sure she's safe."

Later that night, as Herbal cooked steak on the barbecue, Katya and I sat in the Jacuzzi, sharing a bottle of wine.

"I'm really scared," she said.

"Why?" I asked, though I really knew why.

"I'm starting to fall in love with Mystery."

"Well, he's a talented and amazing guy."

"Yeah," she said. "I never let myself fall in love like this. I don't know enough about him yet. I'm worried."

Then she sat there quietly. She wanted me to say something, to warn her if she was making a mistake.

I didn't say anything.

A few days later, Mystery, Katya, and I flew to Las Vegas. As we changed to go out for the night, he rattled on about his favorite subject. "I am so into this girl." He smudged on black eyeliner and smeared white concealer beneath his eyes. "She's even bi. She has a couple she sleeps with in New Orleans." He centered a black cowboy hat he had bought in Australia on his head and admired himself in the mirror. "I feel like I'm pairbonding."

We had dinner at Mr. Lucky's at the Hard Rock Casino, where Katya put away two glasses of champagne; then crossed the street to Club Paradise, a strip club, where she put away two more glasses of champagne.

When the waitress came to the table, Katya commented to Mystery, "She's really hot." Mystery looked the waitress over. She was a perky Latina with long black hair that reflected the stage lights and a densely packed body that threatened to burst through her clothing.

"Ever seen the movie *Poltergeist?*" Mystery asked her. He made her straw move. He told her they wouldn't get along. He asked her what she was famous for—"everybody's famous for something." Soon the waitress was stopping by our table every few minutes to flirt with Mystery.

"I would love to see that girl," Mystery told Katya, "eating you out."

"You just want to fuck her," Katya slurred. I suppose it was difficult for any woman—especially a drunk one—to see the same routines that had ensnared her being used on another woman. And effectively.

Katya leapt to her feet and stormed to the bar. Mystery followed to appease her. But when she refused to acknowledge him, he stomped out of the club like an angry child. Although Katya was bisexual, Mystery still wasn't getting threesomes. He made the same mistake every time: He pushed too hard. He needed to follow Rick H.'s advice and make the experience her fantasy, not his.

When I woke up, I took a plane home, leaving the two of them alone in the hotel room until their flight in the evening.

A few hours later, I received a phone call: "Hey, it's Katya."

"Hey. Is something wrong?"

"No. Mystery wants to marry me. He got down on his knees at the Hard Rock pool and proposed. Everyone applauded. It was so sweet. What should I do?"

The only reason I could come up with to explain Mystery's desire to get married was so he could get a U.S. citizenship. But Katya wasn't a U.S. citizen. She still had a Russian passport.

"Don't rush into anything," I advised. "Just get engaged. Or, if you want, they have commitment ceremonies at the chapels there. Do that. Then spend some more time together and see if this is something you both really want to do."

Mystery grabbed the phone. "Hey, man, you're going to get really mad at me. We're getting married. I love this girl. She's crazy. We're on our way to the chapel. Okay, bye."

The guy was an idiot.

That evening, Mystery carried Katya over the threshold of Project Hollywood humming "Here Comes the Bride."

They'd known each other for three weeks.

"Look at my ring," Katya cooed. "Isn't it beautiful?"

"Our rings cost eight thousand dollars," Mystery said with pride. That was basically all the cash he had. Though he was raking in money from his workshops, he was a fan of man toys—computers, digital cameras, electronic organizers, basically anything with a chip.

"This whole marriage thing," Mystery told me while Katya was in the bathroom, "is the best routine ever. She loves me now. She gets off on calling me her husband. It's like a time distortion."

"Dude, it's the worst routine ever," I replied, "because you can only do it once."

Mystery took a step toward me and removed his ring. "I'm going to tell you a secret," he whispered, putting the ring in my hand. "We're not really married."

If any other PUA had told me he'd gotten married in Vegas to a girl he'd just met, I would have known it was a joke. But Mystery was so headstrong and unpredictable that I had given him the benefit—or, more accurately, the detriment—of the doubt.

"Yeah, after you left, we walked by a jewelry store in the Hard Rock and decided to fake our marriage. So I bought two rings for a hundred bucks. She's such a good liar. She totally fooled you."

"You're both great illusionists."

"Don't tell Katya I told you. I think she's really enjoying the role-play. On an emotional level, it's the same as really being married for her."

Mystery was right: Perception is reality. In the days that followed, their entire relationship changed. They actually started acting like an old married couple.

Now that he was living with a woman, Mystery didn't feel the need to go out anymore. To him, clubs were for sarging. To Katya, though, they were for dancing. So she started going clubbing without him. After a while, Mystery hardly left his room or, for that matter, his bed. It was hard to tell whether he was just being lazy, or if a depression was coming on.

There's a pattern the pickup artists have called rocks versus gold. It's a speech a man gives a woman he's dating when she stops having sex with him. He tells her that women in a relationship want rocks (or diamonds) while men seek gold. Rocks, for a woman, are wonderful nights out, romantic attention, and emotional connection. Gold for a man is sex. If you give a woman only gold or a man just rocks, neither will be satisfied. There must be an exchange. And Katya was giving Mystery the gold, but he wasn't giving her the rocks. He wasn't taking her out at all.

It wasn't long before they began to resent each other.

He'd say, "She gets drunk every night. It's driving me crazy."

She'd say, "When I met him, he had all these plans and ambitions. Now he never leaves his bed. What's the point?"

He'd say, "She never shuts up. She's constantly yapping about something pointless and bouncing off the walls."

She'd say, "I'm getting wasted every night because I don't want to be in a reality that's so sad."

Mystery needed a more passive girl. Katya needed a more active man. And it saddened the rest of us; after living in a house full of men for so many months, we'd grown attached to her positive energy and high spirits.

Mystery had taught himself everything there was to know about pickup, but nothing about how to maintain a relationship. He had this beautiful creature, full of sparkle and life, and he was just throwing it away.

Soon, another woman, with a very different kind of sparkle, would move into Project Hollywood.

I received the text message at 11:39 P.M.: "Can I stay at yr house? They repoed the car and worse. U don't wanna know. Need to not be alone."

It was Courtney Love.

I knocked on the door of Courtney's corporate apartment in West Los Angeles.

"Come in. It's open."

Courtney sat on the floor in the middle of a sea of American Express bills and bank statements with a yellow highlighter in her hand. She wore a black Marc Jacobs dress with buttons running down the side. One was missing

"I can't look at these anymore," she moaned. "There are so many loans here that I never knew of or approved."

She stood up and slammed an American Express bill on the table. Half the items were highlighted, with notes in black ink scribbled in the margins. "If I stay here, I'll do drugs again," she cried.

She didn't have a manager, and taking care of her own affairs was proving to be more than she could handle.

"I don't want to be alone," she begged. "I need somewhere to stay for a couple days. Then I'll be out of your hair. I promise."

"That's fine." I guess she didn't have a problem with the story I'd written in *Rolling Stone*. "Herbal said you could sleep in his room. I just want to warn you, though, that you're not going into an ordinary house."

"I know. I want to meet the pickup artists. Maybe they can help me."

I walked her downstairs and strapped her sixty-pound suitcase to the luggage rack on the back of my Corvette.

"You should also know that Katya's brother is staying with us," I said. "And if he seems a little off, it's because he has Tourette's."

"Is that like when you yell 'Shit! Balls!' uncontrollably?"

"Yeah. It's sort of like that."

I parked in the garage and dragged her suitcase upstairs to the house. The first person we saw inside was Herbal, who was coming out of the kitchen.

"Hi shit balls," Courtney said to him.

"No," I told her. "That's not Katya's brother."

Her brother walked out of the kitchen a moment later, sipping a Coke.

"Hi shit balls," Courtney said to him.

She took a step backward and stepped on Lily, who yelped loudly. Courtney turned around. I assumed she was going to apologize.

"Fuck off," she told the dog.

This was going to be an interesting couple of days.

I showed her around the house and then bid her goodnight. Two minutes later, she marched into my room.

"I need a toothbrush," she said as she breezed through to my bathroom.

"There's a clean one in the medicine cabinet," I yelled after her.

"This will do," she snapped back, grabbing my gnarly used toothbrush off the sink.

There was something endearing about her. She possessed a trait nearly every pickup artist desired but lacked: She just didn't give a fuck.

The next morning, I came downstairs to find her in the living room, smoking a cigarette and wearing nothing but a pair of expensive Japanese silk panties. Her body was covered with black marks, as if she'd been rolling around in charcoal.

In that state of dishabille, she met the rest of the house.

"I used to ride horses with your dad," Papa told her when I introduced them.

Courtney scowled. "If you call that man my father again, I'll punch you in the face!"

She wasn't trying to be mean—she just lived in and reacted to the moment—but Papa didn't take well to aggression. All Papa had wanted from the day he'd signed the lease to Project Hollywood was to hang out with celebrities. But now that he was living with one—in fact, the most notorious woman in the country at the time—he was petrified of her. He avoided her from that day forward, like he did everyone else who wasn't part of his pickup business.

Next, Courtney met Katya. "I just took a pregnancy test," Katya told her, puckering her lips into a childish expression of self-pity. "It came out positive."

"You should have the baby," Courtney said. "It's the most beautiful thing in the world."

I was living *The Surreal Life.*

Mystery kneeled in front of Katya and kissed her belly. "If you want to keep the baby, whether we are together forever or not, I will support your decision. It would be a beautiful baby."

The sun poured into the kitchen from the patio, illuminating a thin, orderly chain of ants that ran from the brickwork outside to the overflowing trashcan. Before he stood up, Mystery licked his finger and wiped a thin stripe of saliva through the middle of the chain. The ants went scurrying in every direction at the point of rupture.

"I can't even believe you'd think of keeping the baby," Katya replied, her voice chirpy but scornful. "You are weird. You're acting like we're married."

The ants began to fall back into line. Soon, order was restored. It was hard to tell there had ever been a catastrophe.

"I love you," Mystery said, without emotion. "And you know my mission in life: survive and replicate. So I don't see any harm in having the baby. I'm willing to fulfill my half of the obligation."

Our house wasn't self-organizing like a line of ants. There was no chain of command or unspoken structure. The invisible chemical path we were all following smelled like male hormones. And its natural state was disorder.

All afternoon, Mystery and Katya fought with each other over whether she should have an abortion and who should pay for it. These matters, however, are not group decisions. Katya and Mystery went to an abortion clinic three days later.

"Guess what?" Katya squealed when she returned. "I'm not pregnant."

She jumped into the air and clapped her hands together in praise of luck. Mystery stood behind her, giving her the finger. The look on his face was pure hatred. I'd never seen him display such malevolence toward a woman before.

A few hours later, I found Katya at the bar pouring herself a glass of Chardonnay. Then another. Then another.

"Mystery doesn't come out of the room, and he doesn't fuck," she complained. "So I'm going to have a good time tonight without him."

"You deserve it."

"Come drink with me," she cooed.

"That's all right."

"No worries, no troubles." She took a slow sip of wine and sat next to me on the couch.

"Wow," she said. "You really have been working out. Your arms look good."

"Thanks." One of the things I'd learned in the past year and a half was how to take a compliment. Just say, "Thank you." It's the only response a confident person can make.

She sidled up to me and squeezed my biceps. "You're the only person in the house I can talk to." Her face was inches away from mine.

I felt that tingle of energy, the one I'd felt just before I kissed the hostess Tyler Durden had picked up at the Hard Rock.

"Look at this," she said. She was lifting her top now. "I got a scratch."

"That's nice."

"Here, feel it."

She took my hand and pulled it toward her breast. I really had to get going.

"Well, it's been fun talking, but I have to go to my room and floss my cat now."

"But you don't have a cat," she whined.

I circled around to the back of the house and entered Mystery's room through the patio. He was lying on top of his bed in jeans with a laptop computer resting on his bare stomach. He was watching *Back to the Future II*.

"When I was in tenth grade, I wanted to kill myself because I had nothing left to live for," he said. "Then I heard that *Back to the Future II* was opening in twenty-three days. I had a calendar, and I would mark off each day until I could see the movie. It's the only thing that kept me from killing myself."

He paused the movie and lifted the laptop off his stomach. "When I saw it and heard the opening music, I cried, dude. It was my reason to live. I know all the props." He held up the DVD box and showed me the cover. "I touched this car."

I sat down at the foot of his bed. No one wants to be the bearer of bad news. I picked up the DVD box and looked at it. Mystery enjoyed movies like *Real Genius* and *Young Einstein* and *The Karate Kid*. I liked Werner Herzog, Lars von Trier, and Pixar. It didn't mean I was better than him: It just meant we were different kinds of nerds.

"Dude," I told him, "your wife is hitting on me."

"I'm not surprised. She hit on Playboy earlier tonight."

"Aren't you going to do anything about it?"

"I don't care. She can do what she wants."

"Well, at least she's not pregnant."

"Get this," he said. "She's such an idiot. That wasn't a pregnancy test at all. It was an ovulation test. She bought the wrong box at Rite Aid. She took the test three times and each one was positive. So all she discovered was that at twenty-three, she's still ovulating."

"Listen, man." I noticed that there were scratches on his arm. "You're driving her away. If she's hitting on everyone in the house, it's only because she's trying to get revenge on you. It's rocks versus gold, man. You haven't been giving her rocks."

"Yeah. She's a brainless alcoholic." He paused, shut his eyes for a moment, and nodded wistfully. "But that body: Her ass is a 10."

When I left Mystery's room, Katya was no longer in the living room. Papa's door was open, and she was cuddled next to him on his bed—with her top off.

I retreated to my room and waited. An hour later, the storm came. Voices yelled, doors slammed, glass smashed.

There was a knock on my door.

It was Courtney. "Are your roommates always this loud?"

She was one to talk.

I followed Courtney to Herbal's room. Herbal had been sleeping in the pillow pit while Courtney commandeered his room. Clothes, books, and cigarette ash were spread across the floor. A candle sat burning at the foot of the bed, its flame licking just an inch below the comforter. One of her dresses was draped over a hot, exposed light bulb for mood lighting. And all four of the house phone books were spread across her bed, with pages torn out of each. I examined the ripped scraps: They were listings for lawyers.

The noises coming from Mystery's room grew louder.

"Let's see what's going on," she said.

I didn't want to be involved. I didn't want to clean up anyone's mess. This wasn't my fucking responsibility.

We walked into Mystery's bathroom. Katya was kneeling on the floor with her hands clasped around her neck, as if she were choking. Her brother was leaning over her, holding an asthma inhaler in her mouth. Mystery stood a few feet away, staring daggers at Katya.

"Should I call an ambulance?" I asked.

"They'll arrest her because she has drugs in her system," Mystery said contemptuously.

Katya looked up and glared at him.

If she had the presence of mind to glare at Mystery, then she clearly wasn't dying.

When Katya finally emerged from Mystery's room, her face red and damp, Courtney took her by the hand and led her to a sofa in the living room. She sat down next to her, still gripping her hand, and told her about the abortions she had been through and about the beauty of childbirth. I looked at the unlikely pair sitting there. Courtney was both Project Hollywood's child and its mother.

She was also probably the sanest person in the house. And that was a scary thought.

Chapter

The next morning, Courtney burst out of her door at an atypically early hour. She was wearing an Agent Provocateur nightie.

"What? What's going on?" she asked, rubbing the sleep out of her eyes. "I had a bad dream. I didn't know where I was." She looked around: at me, at Katya sleeping on the sofa, at Katya's brother and Herbal snoring inches apart in the pillow pit. "Everyone's nice," she observed with relief. "No one's mean. Okay."

She returned to her room and shut her door. A few minutes later, a driver arrived at the house.

"Where's Courtney?" he asked.

"Sleeping," I said.

"She's got a court date in an hour."

He knocked on her door and walked inside. Shortly afterward, a slew of dresses came tumbling out of Courtney's room, followed by their owner.

"I need to find something to wear to court," she said as she slipped on various outfits, running in and out of the bathroom to check them in the mirror. Eventually, she left the house in a strapless black cocktail dress of Katya's, Herbal's eight-dollar sunglasses, and Robert Greene's *The 48 Laws of Power* book tucked under her right arm.

"It's a silly dress because it's a silly case," she told court reporters that day.

While she was gone, we inspected the damage. There were cigarette burns in Herbal's bedspread, and the wall behind the door was destroyed from the constant slamming. There were slicks of unidentifiable liquid on the floor, candles still burning, and clothing flung over every light fixture.

In the kitchen, the refrigerator and cabinet doors all hung open. Two peanut butter jars and a jelly jar sat on the counter top, with their caps scattered on the floor. Globs of peanut butter dripped from the counter, the cabinets, and the refrigerator shelves. Rather than open bags of bread using the twist tie on the end, she had torn the tops of the plastic bags open like an animal. She didn't give a fuck. She was hungry; she ate. It was another quality that pickup artists admired: She could go caveman.

When Courtney returned from court, she sat with the house's cabal of pickup artists and planned her appearance that evening on *The Tonight Show with Jay Leno.* Mystery and Herbal taught her about concepts like social proof, and NLP ideas like framing. She needed to be reframed. The current frame everyone saw her through was that of a crazy woman. But having lived with her for two weeks, we knew she was just going through a bad period. She was eccentric, but not crazy. In fact, she was incredibly smart. She understood and internalized every concept they taught her.

"So my new frame, then, is that I'm a damsel in distress," she said.

That evening, she shone on *The Tonight Show.* Unlike during her tabloid-headline-making *Letterman* appearance, she was composed and well-behaved on camera—and her performance with her all-female band, the Chelsea, was a reminder that she wasn't just a celebrity, she was a rock star.

I had driven to the show in Katya's car with Herbal, Mystery, Katya, and Kara, a girl I'd met in a bar a couple of days before. After the show, we went upstairs to Courtney's dressing room, where she was sitting on a stool surrounded by the Chelsea. I was stunned by her guitarist: She was a tall, gorgeous bleached-blonde rock-and-roller oozing attitude. Why couldn't I ever find girls like that in the clubs?

"Can I stay in your room for two more weeks?" Courtney asked Herbal.

"Sure," he replied. Herbal never had a problem with anything or anyone. While Mystery had been moping in his room, he was out helping Katya keep her brother entertained.

"It may be a month," Courtney called after us as we left the room.

In the parking lot, Mystery climbed into the driver's side of Katya's car. He hadn't spoken a word to her all day. She sat in the passenger seat and slipped a dance mix by Carl Cox into the CD player. Her musical taste was confined to house and techno; Mystery listened almost exclusively to Tool, Pearl Jam, and Live. That should have been a warning sign.

As we pulled out of the parking lot, Mystery's phone rang. He turned the music off to answer it.

Katya reached over and turned the music on quietly.

Mystery angrily turned it off again.

And so it went: on, off, on, off—each twist of the knob with more venom than the last until, finally, Mystery slammed on the brakes, screamed "fuck you," and jumped out of the car.

He stood in the middle of Ventura Boulevard blocking traffic, with his right arm thrust out and a middle finger in the air, directly in line with Katya's face.

Katya crawled into the driver's seat and drove to the intersection, then turned around to fetch Mystery, who had started walking along the sidewalk. When she pulled up next to him, he stopped, shot her a scornful look, crossed his arms into the fuck-you position, and then continued walking.

She drove off without him. She wasn't angry; she was just disappointed by his childishness.

That night, Mystery didn't return home. I called him several times, but he didn't answer. When I woke up the next morning, he still hadn't returned. Every time I dialed his number, the call went straight to voice mail. I began to worry.

A few hours later, there was a knock on the door. I answered it, expecting Mystery, but found Courtney's driver standing there instead. One of Courtney's many talents was the ability to turn anyone within a hundred-yard radius into a personal assistant. Seduction students visiting the house for the first time found themselves running to Tokyopop for a manga book Courtney was in, picking up bedding from her corporate apartment, or sending e-mails to the financial expert Suze Orman.

"Shitballs!" she called to Katya's brother. "Can you go back to my apartment with the driver and get my DVDs?"

After he left, Courtney told Katya, "He's a nice kid, and kind of cute."

"You know, he's a virgin," Katya said.

"Sure," Courtney replied. She went silent, contemplating this piece of information for a few moments, then nodded her head and told Katya, "I'd give him a mercy fuck."

That night, Mystery returned. He had a stripper on each arm. They looked like they'd been working in the same dark club for twenty years; our hundred-watt lightbulbs weren't serving them well.

"Hey, buddy," he said, as if he'd just come back from the grocery store.

"Where were you?"

"I went to a strip club and spent the night with Gina."

"Hi," said a horse-faced brunette on his left arm. She lifted her waving hand meekly.

"Well, dude, you should have called. It's okay to have your little spat with Katya, but Herbal and I were really worried. That wasn't cool."

He paraded the girls through the house, making sure he introduced them to Katya, then sat on the patio with them.

Katya went about her business. She showered, she cleaned the daily explosion of peanut butter in the kitchen, and she did her special-effects-school homework on Herbal's face, giving him a lobotomy.

While Mystery's stripper gambit had failed to make her jealous, it did succeed in making everyone else's respect for him dwindle further.

Chapter

It was bound to happen. Katya eventually reached someone in the house. She'd been hitting on all of us since her pregnancy scare.

It was Herbal who ultimately cracked. He was laid-back. He never lost his cool. He liked to listen. He was modest and understated. In other words, he was the exact opposite of Mystery. All that time he had spent with Katya while Mystery was pouting or laying indolently in bed or sleeping with a stripper out of revenge had affected him. He had developed feelings for Katya. After watching her suffer through Mystery's manipulation and neglect, he'd even begun to believe that he was more worthy of her.

"It's getting harder and harder to say no," he told me.

"Just ask Mystery. He's probably over her by now."

"Yeah. After all, he was cool with the whole Sima thing." (Sima was Mystery's ex-MLTR from Toronto who Herbal had fooled around with.)

So Herbal asked Mystery. The answer was no. But that evening, after fighting with Katya again, Mystery found Herbal in the living room. "We're broken up," he said casually. "She's all yours."

They were words he would soon regret.

Within hours, Herbal had his dick inside her. Since Courtney was sleeping in his bed, he fucked Katya in Playboy's room off the kitchen.

When Mystery returned home that night from the Standard, he went to the kitchen for a Sprite. That was when he heard them. The moans that had been his exclusive nightly serenade were being sung to another man. He stood outside Playboy's door in shock, listening to them have sex. Katya seemed to be enjoying it. Loudly.

Mystery walked into the living room and collapsed on the floor. The blood drained from his face. Like his father's death, it affected him more than he could have predicted.

Never underestimate your own capacity to care.

"I love her," he said, as the first tear trickled down his cheek. "I love that girl."

"No you don't," I corrected him. "You said the other day that you hated her." The thoughts I'd been holding back for weeks came pouring out of me. "All you like about her is her body. The only reason you're upset is because you feel rejected."

"No. I'm pissed at her for not loving me back."

"She loved you more than any other girl I've seen you with. She sat with me in the hot tub one night talking about how scared she was to let go and really love you. And as soon as she did, you became a cold, shutdown, miserable bastard."

"But I love her."

"You say that about every girl you sleep with. That's not real love. It's fake love. It's an illusion."

"No it isn't," he screamed at the top of his lungs. "You're wrong!"

He stood up, stomped to his room, and slammed the door, splintering paint onto the carpet.

He'd been so neglected as a child that the withdrawal of love pulled all his emotional triggers, exploding the carapace of narcissism built by his childhood escapism.

As I walked back to my room, a scene from *The Wizard of Oz* sprung into my head in which the Wizard tells the Tin Man, "A heart is not judged by how much you love, but by how much you are loved by others."

I was looking forward to letting my dreams file away all my thoughts, worries, and aggravations so I could start the next day fresh. But I was waylaid by Courtney. She stood in my doorway, a sheaf of papers in her hand.

"You gotta get Frank Abagnale on the phone for me," she demanded. "He can fix this. And call Lisa and tell her I need to see her."

"You got it."

I had no idea what she was talking about. I didn't know how to get in touch with Frank Abagnale (the counterfeit artist whose memoir inspired the movie *Catch Me If You Can*) or, for that matter, Lisa, her guitarist. But by now I'd figured out how to deal with Courtney's constant demands: Just say yes and do nothing. She'd forget what she wanted in a few hours anyway.

In the morning, I checked on Mystery. He was sitting on his bed in his robe, shaking and convulsing. His face was red and his eyes were full of tears. I'd never seen him like this before. When he was depressed in Toronto, he'd simply shut down and become catatonic. This time, he seemed to be in real pain.

Evidently, Katya had come into his bathroom in the morning to get her toothbrush.

"Do you want to tell me about what happened last night?" Mystery had asked.

"Why should I? You basically gave me as a present to Herbal."

"Did you fuck him?"

"Well, let's put it this way," she had said, "I just had the most amazing sex of my life."

It crushed him.

"I want to kill her." He rolled onto his back and moaned like a dying dog. "Logically, I know I'm being controlled by my emotions. But my logic is just 2 percent right now. I feel emotionally raw." He clenched his bedsheet in his fist. "I feel strange and empty, like after a shit."

He rolled over and started sobbing again. "I feel shit empty."

I would have laughed if he were trying to be funny.

As he grieved, I kept thinking of one of Courtney's lyrics: "I made my bed/I'll lie in it." Mystery had made his bed. And now Herbal was lying in it.

He raised his hands to the ceiling and screamed in his Anthony Robbins voice. Suddenly, Courtney poked her head in the door. "Is it about me? I can sleep in the front room if you want."

She could be so sweet.

I walked into the living room and told Courtney what was going on. Katya was sitting on the patio outside, smoking a cigarette.

"I feel so bad," Katya said. "Poor Mystery." She made sympathetic sounds for him—*awws* and *mmms*—as if she were talking about her dog.

Herbal shuffled to the table with his head slumped forward. He was silent, trying to think of something to say. Neither of them seemed to regret sleeping together. They just didn't realize that Mystery would take it so hard. None of us did.

Courtney lit a cigarette and told Herbal about a threesome she'd experienced and how sharing can be caring and how she ran away to San Francisco to join Faith No More and how the Suicide Girls was her idea and how she tried to turn a groupie into an artist in Europe. Somewhere in her meandering speech there was a metaphor for Herbal's current dilemma—caught between his closest friend and the girl he was falling in love with—but we couldn't find it.

Just then, Herbal's phone rang. He answered it and, with a shocked expression on his face, handed it to Courtney.

"It's Frank Abagnale calling for you," he said. "I guess he got my message."

I left the three of them on the patio and called Mystery's sister, Martina.

"He's starting to crash again," I said.

"How bad is it?"

"It started off like normal heartbreak, but this morning he went over the edge. The situation seems to have triggered some kind of chemical reaction. He's crying uncontrollably right now."

"Well, if it gets any worse, I'll get him a ticket back to Toronto. If you can put him on the plane, we'll take care of him when he arrives."

"You realize that if he comes back to Toronto, everything will be lost. He's overstayed his visa here, so they'll never let him into the United States again. He'll have no chance of becoming a famous illusionist. And his pickup business will be destroyed."

"I realize that. But what choice do we have?"

"I'll try to handle it myself."

"Just send him home. Health care in Canada is free. We can't afford to take him anywhere in the States—especially if they institutionalize him."

"Let me try. If it gets worse, I'll send him back to you."

Watching Mystery's relationship with Katya unfold had been an eye-opener. He invited her to move in. He married her. He got her not-pregnant. He ignored her and resented her. He gave Herbal permission to sleep with her. He was no one's victim but his own.

In the meantime, ever since the *New York Times* article, half a dozen reality TV executives had called Mystery—including the producers of *American Idol*. VH1 had even sent him a contract for a show in which he turned losers into Lotharios. The stardom Mystery wanted so desperately was his for the taking. But he wasn't calling anyone back.

"This has happened before," Martina sighed when I told her about the reality-show offers. "Every time he gets close to making it, he breaks down and throws it all away."

"So do you mean . . ."

"Yes," she said. "He's actually scared of the success he wants so badly."

Chapter

The next night, Katya came home at 2:00 A.M. She was with Herbal and the couple from New Orleans she sometimes slept with. Mystery pushed open his door, sat on a pillow on the floor, and watched them as they drank in the common room. He was making an effort to hold himself together.

The woman in the couple was six feet tall, with a gym-taut abdomen, brown hair hanging down to a well-sculpted butt, brand new fake breasts, and a large nose that was next in line for the plastic surgeon's scalpel. When Katya leaned over and made out with her, Mystery's face scrunched up and reddened. If he'd just held onto Katya a little longer, he could have had his elusive threesome. Instead he was confined to his pillow, watching Katya laugh with the couple, watching Herbal sit there with a self-satisfied grin, watching the girls change into bikinis and prance out to the hot tub, watching Herbal join them.

Katya had given Mystery her love, and now he was paying for tossing it in the trash. Whether intentionally or not, she was rubbing her bisexuality, her youth, and her happiness in his face.

By morning, Mystery's sanity had decomposed further. When he wasn't crying on the couches, he was patrolling the house, trying to make sure Katya and Herbal were apart. If he couldn't find them, he'd call her. Whether she answered the phone or not, the result was the same: Mystery would fly off the handle and destroy whatever was within arm's or leg's reach. He pulled several bookcases to the ground; decimated his pillows, leaving feathers strewn across his room; and threw his cell phone against the wall, snapping the apparatus in half and leaving a deep black dent in the plaster.

"Where's Katya?" he'd ask Playboy.

"She's shopping for clothes on Melrose."

"Where's Herbal?"

"He's, um, sort of with her."

And then Mystery's heart would twist and his face would fall and his eyes would leak and his legs would give out from under him and he'd make some bizarre evolutionary justification for it all. "It's selfish genes," he'd say. "It's the nonexistent potential baby punishing me for leaving."

When Herbal returned from shopping on Melrose with Katya, I warned him, "You're being tooled. She's using you to get back at Mystery."

"No," he said. "It's not true. We have real feelings for each other."

"Well, can you do me a favor and just try not to see her until Mystery gets better? I'm going to ask her to leave the house for a while."

"Fine," he said, with some reluctance. "But it's not going to be easy."

That night, I took Katya and her brother to the movies. Plan A was to get her out of the house and away from Herbal so that Mystery didn't get any worse. Plan B was to fuck her in order to show Herbal that his connection with Katya wasn't so special.

Fortunately, plan A worked.

"You are destroying Mystery," I told her as I drove her back from the theater. "You need to leave the house. And don't come back until I say it's okay. This isn't about you anymore. Mystery has a serious psychological problem, and you've set it off."

"Okay," she said. She looked up at me like a child being disciplined.

"And promise me not to sleep with Herbal again. You're hurting one of my roommates, and you're about to break the heart of another. I can't stand by and watch it."

"I promise," she said.

"The fun is over. You've made your point."

"Okay," she said. "I'm done."

"Pinky swear?"

We locked pinkies.

I should have made her swear on something more serious.

Seduction was easy compared to this. Even if people were just programs designed by evolution, as Mystery believed, they were apparently too complicated for any of us to truly understand. All we had figured out were a few simple cause and effect relationships. If you lower a woman's self-esteem, she will seek validation from you. If you make a woman jealous, she will become more attracted to you. But beyond attraction and lust, there were deeper feelings that few of us felt and none of us had mastered. And these feelings—for which the heart and the word *love* are just metaphors—were tearing Project Hollywood, a house already divided, further apart.

And so it came to pass that Mystery scared everyone out of the house and he started talking about killing himself and I got him a Xanax from Katya and I put him in my car and I took him to the Hollywood Mental Health Center and he tried to run away twice and he wanted to hit on the therapist but couldn't.

Six hours later, he left the clinic with a package of Seroquel pills in his hand and another Xanax in his system. I'd never heard of Seroquel before, so when we returned the house I looked at the pamphlet that came with it.

"For the treatment of schizophrenia," it read.

Mystery took the pamphlet from my hands and looked it over. "They're just sleeping pills," he said. "They'll help me get to sleep."

"Right," I told him. "Sleeping pills."

BLAST LAST-MINUTE
RESISTANCE

WHAT IS SEXUAL IS WHAT GIVES A MAN AN ERECTION . . . IF THERE IS NO INEQUALITY, NO VIOLATION, NO DOMINANCE, NO FORCE, THERE IS NO SEXUAL AROUSAL.

—CATHARINE MACKINNON,
Toward a Feminist Theory of the State

Chapter

It was lemonade day at Project Hollywood. At least, that's what Courtney Love had decided. Mystery was recovering, Katya was in New Orleans for six weeks, and there were good vibes to be spread.

Cigarette hanging from her mouth, dropping ash onto her Betsey Johnson T-shirt, Courtney grabbed a giant mixing bowl from the cabinet. She opened the refrigerator and scanned for liquids, snatching two half-gallon cartons of lemonade and a quart of orange juice. She emptied them into the mixing bowl and, when that overflowed, several pots. Then she grabbed a handful of ice cubes from the freezer and dropped them into her brew. Finally, she plunged her black-charred fingers into each vessel and stirred. Juice sloshed onto the counter as ashes from the cigarette in her mouth fluttered into the mixing bowl.

Stubbing her cigarette out on the yellow tile countertop, she looked around frantically until she noticed an overhead cabinet. She swung the doors open and thrust her hands inside, sticking her fingers into four glasses and squeezing them together to pull them out. One by one, she dipped the glasses into the bowl and filled them. Then she grabbed the rest of the glasses, any clean coffee mugs she could find, and a Pyrex measuring cup, and sloshed lemonade into all of them.

In the living room, Mystery sat cross-legged on a couch, leading his first pickup seminar since returning from the mental-health center three weeks earlier. He wore a T-shirt and denim overalls. His feet were bare. Patches of unshaven hair dappled his chin, and his eyelids drooped lazily over unfocused eyes. He'd been taking the Seroquel regularly and sleeping out his depression. He was beginning to break through to the other side.

"There are three phases to a relationship," he told his students, speaking in a torpor. "There's a beginning, a middle, and an end. And I'm going through the end right now. I'm not going to lie to you. I've cried three times in the last week."

His six students glanced at each other, confused. They were there to learn to get laid. But for Mystery this wasn't just a seminar; it was therapy. He'd been telling them about Katya for two hours now.

"This is what you're building up to, and it can be difficult," he went on. "My plan for the next girl is to have a fake marriage again. The mistake I made last time was letting Katya and her mother know it was a joke. Next time, I'll have the wedding in the backyard. I'll have an actor be the preacher, and everyone except her and her parents will know we're not really getting married."

One of the students, a good-looking man in his thirties with a crewcut and a jaw like a block of cement, raised his hand. "But didn't you just get through telling us how the fake marriage was a disaster last time?"

"I was just field-testing it," Mystery said. "It's a great routine."

Whenever Mystery returned from his depressions, his mental bearings shifted a little. This time there was an anger lurking beneath the surface, along with a new bitterness toward women.

Suddenly, Courtney came careening out of the kitchen. "Who wants lemonade?"

The students looked at her dumbstruck. "Here you go," she said, forcing a glass on Mystery and another on Cementjaw. "What are you doing here?" she asked. "You're cute."

"I'm a self-defense instructor," he said. "Mystery is letting me sit in on the workshop in exchange for lessons in Krav Maga."

Courtney shot off to the kitchen and came back with two more glasses of lemonade, then two more, and two more, until there were more glasses than people in the room.

"I think we're set on lemonade," Mystery said as she returned with two coffee mugs in her hands.

"Where's Herbal?" she asked.

"I think he's showering."

Courtney dashed to the bathroom and kicked the door. "Herbal? Are you there?" She kicked the door again, harder.

"I'm showering," he yelled back.

"It's important. I'm coming in."

She pushed through the door, ran inside, and ripped the shower curtain open.

"What's going on?" Herbal asked, panicked. He stood there naked, his hair streaked white with shampoo. "Is the house on fire?"

"I made this for you," Courtney said. She thrust a mug of lemonade in each of Herbal's wet hands and dashed away. Herbal stood there silently. Ever since he'd promised to stop talking to Katya, he'd been drifting through the house in a forlorn cloud of silence. Though he was too proud to admit it, his heart ached. He loved her.

As Mystery's students broke for lunch, Courtney dashed past them and up the stairs to Papa's room, leaving a trail of lemonade drops on the carpet. She burst through the door. Inside, Papa, Sickboy, Tyler Durden, Playboy, Xaneus, and the mini-Papas were working on individual computers. Extramask was laying on Papa's unmade bed, reading the Bhagavad Gita. While staying at the house, Extramask had gotten bored and started reading Playboy's books on eastern religion, which had unexpectedly led him down a path of spiritual self-discovery.

"Courtney," Tyler Durden asked as she distributed drinks, "can you get us on the guest list for Joseph's on Monday?"

Courtney picked up the phone, walked into the bathroom with Tyler, and dialed Brent Bolthouse, the promoter who threw the Monday night parties at Joseph's, famed for their tight guest lists and crowds of gorgeous wanna-bes. "Brent," she said. "My friend Tyler Durden is a professional pickup artist." Tyler waved his hands frantically in a futile attempt to signal Courtney not to talk about it. "He picks up women for a living. It's really cool." Tyler dropped his head into his hands. "Can you put him on the guest list so he can come with some of his pickup artist friends and pick up chicks?"

Courtney picked a strip of six wrapped condoms off the edge of the sink and wrapped it around her wrist like a bracelet, then began exploring the bathroom. She poked her head inside the two closets—Papa's infamous guest bedrooms—that were on either side of the toilet.

"Let me ask you something," she said as she withdrew from Tyler Durden's closet, which contained a suitcase, a pile of dirty clothes, and a mattress on the floor. "Do you like women?"

On the other side of the bathroom's slotted windows, Cementjaw dragged a sandbag along the brickwork of the patio.

"I wasn't a misogynist when I started this," Tyler replied. "But you get good and you start sleeping with all these women who have boyfriends, and you stop trusting women."

A side effect of sarging is that it can lowers one's opinion of the opposite sex. You see too much betrayal, lying, and infidelity. If a woman has been married three years or more, you come to learn that she's usually easier to sleep with than a single woman. If a woman has a boyfriend, you learn that you have a better chance of fucking her the night you meet her than getting her to return a phone call later. Women, you eventually realize, are just as bad as men—they're just better at hiding it.

"I got hurt a lot when I first started picking up," he continued. "I'd meet an amazing girl I really liked, and we'd talk all night. She'd say she loved me and was so lucky to have met me. But then I'd fail one shit test, and she'd walk away and wouldn't even talk to me anymore. Everything we'd built up over the last eight hours would just go down the drain. So it hardened me."

There are men in this world who hate women, who do not respect them, who call them bitches and cunts. These are not PUAs. PUAs do not hate women; they fear them. Simply by defining oneself as a PUA—a title earned solely by the responses of women—one becomes doomed to derive his entire self-esteem and identity from the attention of the opposite sex, not unlike a comedian's relationship to audience members. If they don't laugh, you're not funny. So, as self-esteem defense mechanisms, some PUAs developed misogynist tendencies in the process of learning.

Sarging could be hazardous to the soul.

Outside the window, Cementjaw held the sandbag as Mystery flailed at it with long, limp punches.

"Harder," he yelled at Mystery. "I want to see more aggression!"

Chapter

Beyond Project Hollywood, the whole community appeared to have taken on a dangerous, unstable edge. Field reports became not just about meeting girls but about getting into fights and being kicked out of clubs. Community members began living vicariously through the drama taking place in Project Hollywood, as well as through the distinct writings of Jlaix, a shotgun-toting, karaoke-singing, Elvis-looking PUA whom Tyler Durden and Papa had discovered in San Francisco.

MSN GROUP: Mystery's Lounge
SUBJECT: FR—Jlaix's First Stripper (Drugs Sold Separately)
AUTHOR: Jlaix

I just flew back from Vegas, and I'm fucking exhausted. I was thrown out of a karaoke bar last night for rolling on the floor and crying during the bridge of Journey's "Separate Ways (Worlds Apart)."

But this post is not about karaoke. It is about fucking a stripper. So let's get right to it, shall we?

I got into town on Wednesday afternoon and began drinking. Some guys from work and I were staying at the Hard Rock, just like the characters on *The OC* did in this week's episode. We got ejected from the Hard Rock Café for making meat cocktails and daring each other to drink them. A typical meat cocktail contained beef, bacon, beer, mashed potatoes, more beer, ribs, ice, onions, mustard, A-1 Sauce, salt, pepper, Nutrasweet, and perhaps a little vodka. After one of my co-workers puked on the table, we all went to the strip club Olympic Gardens.

I was pissed because I wanted to sarge, not get some lame-ass lap dance. I'm always saying what a great pickup artist I am to the guys from work, and I needed to show them I wasn't just talking out of my ass. I'd been training for this thing hard and was frankly a little nervous that I'd look like a tool if I didn't pull on this trip. Furthermore, I don't like strip clubs because I refuse to pay for sex of any kind. But I went along for the ride and sat there with a beer while the guys had their fun.

So this girl sat down across the booth from me. It turned out she worked there, but decided to take the day off because there weren't enough customers and there were too many chicks in the place. I started running routines on her and busting her balls. My friends were looking at me like I was insane because I kept calling her a dork.

She kept saying, "You are so cocky!" and started really getting into me. My friends watched this happen with their jaws dropped open. I told her we were going back to our hotel and she should come and call some of her "hot ho friends." She got pissed that I called her a ho, so I instantly changed the subject. "Oh my God, my friend is so weird. She eats lemons whole, just like an orange blah blah." And this made her forget. More routines—boom, boom, boom. This went on for a while. We all left together.

Outside, the manager was trying to get her to go back in and work. But I pulled her away, and we got into a cab. She said, "I'm a stripper with a brain!" I ran Mystery's "we're too similar" on her, then Style's Cs versus Us.

When we got back to the hotel, I told her we should drop her shit off in my room. Up there, I did the cube on her. Then I told her, "When I did this on Paris Hilton at the taco shop, she said her cube was as big as a hotel. What an egomaniac!" So now she thought I was hanging with celebrities and models all the time, even though it actually happened to Papa.

I also did Tyler Durden's new stuff about having standards and said, "I'm so sick of dating these chicks who do drugs all the time and have plastic surgery. I mean, don't get me wrong, I love to blow rails off a shitty dive bar toilet tank as much as the next guy, but only once in while! I mean, you're not like that, are you?" She qualified herself. Then I asked her if she was a good kisser, and we kissed for a while. I stopped it and suggested we go downstairs for a drink.

In the casino. I started running comfort routines, filling in the empty canvas of my life. I ran Supercuts, Summer of Ripped Abs, Balloons in the Park, Stripper Babysitter, and My Cat Got Laid. They're all stories from my life and, trust me, the titles are more interesting than the actual content.

We walked around the casino looking for my friends for a while. Then I told her I was tired and needed to go to sleep, and she should come up and tell me a bedtime story and tuck me in. She asked, "What are we going to do? Bad things? I've only known you thirty minutes!"

I said, "Sheesh! I hope not! I have to wake up early so you better not keep me up! Besides, I have whiskey dick." This shit is classic; you guys have to use it.

We got to the room and three bozo co-workers were in there, wasted. I hurriedly pushed them out of the room, suggesting they go gamble. The chick looked at the desk and said, "Someone's been doing coke here. I can tell. I'm a stripper."

I serenaded the stripper. I sang "On the Wings of Love" by Jeffrey Osborne to her. I told her I wanted to cuddle, and we did and just talked for a while. I then told her I wanted to show her a trick. I got on her and initiated tonguedown. I told her, "I wanna lick it," and took off her pants. No panties. I inspected her for sores, then began the licking. She had a clit piercing, which I'd never encountered before. It clicked on my teeth weirdly. I put the fingers in after five minutes and licked her into submission. Then I said, "Too bad I have whiskey dick!"

She said, "It looks okay to me," and I fucked the shit out of her.

I had never seen real tits this big on a chick that skinny. Oh my fucking God, this was the hottest chick I've ever fucked: my first stripper and my first 9. I cuddled and snuggled with her afterward. She expressed shock at my many injuries and scars. I kissed this little-ass, adorable-ass stripper mothafucka tenderly and said, "I'm not an insane maniac. I'm a poser insane maniac. I'm just dealing with the absurdity of existence by shoving absurdity down existence's throat."

She gave me her number and told me to call her.

I used the *My Little Pony* opener the next night. ("Hey. Do you guys remember that shit *My Little Pony*? Yeah, well I was trying to remember, did they have powers? Blah blah.") By the end of the night, after I got thrown out of the karaoke club, I was just going up to chicks and drunkenly bellowing, "Maaaah lil poneee." I ended up getting thrown out of another strip club.

The last thing I remember is sitting up in my bed watching the TV, confused and screaming at nobody, "What the fuck am I watching? Is this *The OC*? What the fuck is this?" until I realized that it was just an episode of *Punk'd* where they were pranking *The OC* cast. Then I passed out.

—Jlaix

The first time I saw her, she was taking a shit.

I opened my bathroom door and she was sitting on the toilet.

"Who are you?" I asked.

"I'm Gabby."

Gabby was friends with Maverick, one of the many junior PUAs who or-bited our house and appeared in our living room every weekend uninvited. She had the attitude of a beauty queen but the body of a sack of tomatoes. I took a step back and started to close the door behind me.

"Hey," she said, flushing. "This is a nice house. What do you do for work?"

Those words were an instant dealbreaker. Sarging in Los Angeles, one develops a radar for women who are users. The less tactful among them will ask, within the first few minutes of a conversation, what kind of car you drive or what you do for work or what celebrities in the room you're friends with in order to determine your social ranking and how useful you might be to them. The more tactful ones don't have to ask questions: They look at your watch; they see how people respond to you when you talk, they listen for indicators of insecurity in your speech. These are the signals that PUAs call subcommunication.

Gabby belonged to the less tactful of the species.

As she washed her hands, she opened the medicine cabinet and in-spected the contents. Then she stepped into my room and continued her exploration. "Are you a writer?" she asked. "You should write about me. I have a really interesting story. I want to be an actress. And you know how some people are just born to be famous." She snatched a pair of Ray-Ban sunglasses from the top of my dresser and put them on. "Well, that's me. Not that I'm special or anything. It's just something you know from a very young age because people treat you differently."

A rich man doesn't have to tell you he's rich.

As she chattered away, she grabbed a muffin from a plate on my desk. Today had been muffin day. Courtney had run around the house giving everyone plates full of more muffins than they could eat.

Gabby took a bite, then dropped the muffin back onto the plate. I couldn't figure out who had invited her into the house. Maverick wasn't around, and she wasn't friends with anyone else here.

"I have to do some work," I told her. "But nice meeting you."

I figured she could find her own way out of the house. But she must have taken a wrong turn. Mystery later discovered her sitting on his toilet.

Both were such narcissists, I thought they'd repel each other like two positive ends of a magnet. Instead, they ended up having sex.

She spent the next week at the house, sleeping with Mystery and cat-fighting with Courtney after borrowing her clothing without permission. Like Mystery, Gabby's biggest fear in life was having no one around to hear her talk, so she was constantly running around the house, gossiping, complaining, and getting on Courtney's nerves.

One afternoon, as Courtney stood in the kitchen digging into a jar of peanut butter with two spoons, she asked Gabby, "Aren't you ever going home?"

"Home?" Gabby looked at her funny. "I live here."

It was news to Courtney, to me, to Mystery. The house attracted people like that. Eventually, it would expel them all.

Twyla was the next victim of Project Hollywood. She first apperared at the house when a stripper Mystery made out with several years ago was going through a major depression. Having some experience in the matter, Mystery offered to give her advice one night while Gabby was out clubbing. However, the stripper came over drunk and with Twyla in tow.

Twyla was no prize. She was a tattooed thirty-four-year-old Hollywood rock-and-roller with weathered skin, a body as hard as her face, black hair in a bird's nest of dreadlocks, and a heart of gold. She reminded me of a Pontiac Fiero, an old sporty model liable to break down at any moment.

When Mystery and Twyla started flirting, their drunk, depressed friend burst into tears. She cried in the pillow pit for a half hour, until Twyla and Mystery finally scampered off to his room. Gabby returned home that night and, without a word of objection, crawled into bed with the two of them and promptly fell asleep. Gabby and Mystery weren't in love; they just wanted each other's shelter.

That morning and the morning after, Twyla cooked pancakes for everyone in the house. Since she didn't appear to be leaving anytime soon, Mystery hired her as his personal assistant for four hundred dollars a week.

The more Mystery neglected Twyla, the more she began to believe she loved him. He hurt her over and over by chasing different women, and she kept coming back for more. Mystery seemed to enjoy the tears; they made him feel like he mattered to somebody. If Twyla wasn't crying in the house, it was Gabby. If it wasn't Gabby, it was someone else. From the chrysalis of Mystery's latest depression, a monster was emerging.

Project Hollywood was supposed to be a way to surround ourselves with healthy, helpful influences to better ourselves, our career, and our sex lives. Instead, the house had turned into a vacuum for needy males and neurotic females. It sucked in anyone with mental problems and scared away anyone of quality. Between permanent guests like Courtney, Mystery's women, and Papa's revolving door of new trainers, employees, and students, it was impossible to tell how many people were actually living in the house.

However, at least the way I rationalized it, I was continuing my learning and growing process. I've lived and worked alone most of my life. I've never had a strong social circle or a tight network of friends. I've never joined clubs, played team sports, or been part of any real group prior to the community. Project Hollywood was bringing me out of my solipsistic shell. It was giving me the resources I needed to be a leader; it was teaching me how to walk the tightrope of group dynamics; it was helping me learn to let go of petty things like personal property, solitude, cleanliness, sanity, and sleep. It was making me, for the first time in my life, a responsible adult.

I had to be: I was surrounded by children. Every day, someone ran up to me with a new crisis to be managed:

GABBY: Mystery's being a dick. He says this isn't my house, and I'm not wanted here.

MYSTERY: Courtney took eight hundred dollars from my room. She made it up to me by paying my rent, but her check bounced.

COURTNEY: That guy with his pants pulled up too high is bothering me. Can you tell him to leave me alone?

PLAYBOY: Courtney has her urine in our refrigerator. And Twyla's crying in my bathroom and won't come out.

TWYLA: Mystery's trying to mack on some chick in his room, and he told me to fuck off. And Papa won't let me sleep in his room.

PAPA: Cliff from Montreal has been staying in my room, and Courtney came up and took four of his books and three pairs of his underwear.

Every problem had a solution; every dispute had a compromise; every ego had a way to be stroked. I hardly had time to sarge anymore. The only new women I was meeting were the ones who came into the house. Keeping Project Hollywood from imploding was becoming a full-time job.

I left the house for an hour to get some groceries. Only an hour. And when I returned there was a red Porsche spewing smoke in the driveway, a thirteen-year-old girl in the living room, and two pissed-off bleached blondes smoking on the patio.

"What the hell is going on?" I asked as I kicked the door shut behind me.

"This is Mari," Mystery said.

"The cleaning lady's daughter?" We were never able to hold onto a maid. The task of cleaning a week's accumulation of dishes, overflowing trash cans, fast-food debris, spilt alcohol, and cigarette butts from a dozen guys and countless party girls was more than most could handle. Consequently, Project Hollywood tended to stew in its own filth for a month or more between maids. The latest had set a record: two consecutive weeks.

"The cleaning lady left the house for supplies, so I'm watching her." He took a few strides closer to me. "She reminds me of my nieces."

It was nice to see Mystery acting somewhat normal again. An adolescent in the house was a calming influence on him. As for the Porsche, Courtney had it brought to the house so that Mystery could drive her to rehearsal. But Mystery had taken the car for a test run and found out the hard way that he couldn't rely on his magical intuition to teach him how to drive a stick shift.

"And who are they?" I asked, pointing at the blondes.

"They're in Courtney's band."

I went out to the patio and introduced myself.

"I'm Sam," said a slightly tomboyish girl with a Queens accent. "I play drums with Courtney."

"We've met before," I told her.

"We've met before too," sneered the other girl. Her Long Island accent was so sharp that it startled me. She was two inches taller than me, her hair was pushed straight back over her head like a horse's mane, and her large brown eyes were framed with thick black mascara that reminded me of masturbating as a teenager to Susanna Hoffs in the Bangles video for "Walk Like an Egyptian." This girl was the epitome of rock and roll.

"Yeah," I stammered. "I saw you briefly at *The Tonight Show*?"

"Before that. At that party at the Argyle Hotel where you were talking to those twins the whole night."

"Oh, the Porcelain TwinZ." I couldn't imagine having forgotten her. She was so charismatic. Good posture is one of the things I find most attractive about a woman, and this girl's posture screamed confidence. It also screamed, "Don't fuck with me."

I went back inside and asked Mystery about her. "That's Lisa, Courtney's guitarist," he said. "She's a total bitch."

The girls were visiting because Courtney had planned to tape an acoustic performance at our house for a British television program. But Courtney was nowhere to be found, and Sam and Lisa were fuming. I sat down to pacify her bandmates. I felt so small next to them.

I picked up a CD case that belonged to Lisa and thumbed through the discs. I was impressed. She had music by Cesaria Evora, a diva from the Cape Verde islands. Her mournful songs, backed by a lilting Latin rhythm, are perhaps the best make-out music on the planet. As soon as I saw that CD, I knew I'd met someone I wanted to get to know better.

Somewhere in the back of my mind, I dimly recalled what enabled me to meet and interact with women before I'd discovered the seduction industry: commonalities. Simply finding out that you have a passion for something another person also likes and respects is enough to fire that strange emotion we like to call chemistry. Scientists studying pheromones claim that when two people discover they have things in common, pheromones are released and attraction begins.

Moments later, Mystery joined us. He dropped into a chair and sat there for a moment, a vortex of neediness sucking up any stray pheromones Lisa and I had managed to release. "I called Katya today," he said. "And we talked for a while. I still love that girl."

He looked at Sam and Lisa, as if trying to select a target. "Do they know about the drama with Katya?" he asked.

The girls rolled their eyes. They had their own drama to deal with.

"Well," I excused myself. "I'm going to grab a burrito at Poquito Mas. Nice meeting you—again."

I had to get away from there. I didn't want to be associated with the madness—even if I was part of it.

I walked down the hill to Poquito Mas, where I found Extramask sitting at a table outside, reading a book as thick as his skull. He was wearing shorts, a headband, and a torn white T-shirt with a fresh sweat stain from the gym.

It was the first time I'd seen him out of the house alone in months. Ever since meeting him at Mystery's first workshop, I'd felt like he was my younger brother in this whole endeavor—though, since joining the Real Social Dynamics crew, he'd been more like an estranged sibling. I decided to make an effort to reconnect with him.

"What are you reading?" I asked.

"*I Am That* by Sri Nisargadatta Maharaj," he said. "I like him better than Sri Ramana Maharshi. His teachings are more modern and easier to read."

"Wow—impressive." I didn't know what else to say; I wasn't particularly familiar with Indian Vedanta writing.

"Yeah, I'm starting to realize there's more to life than just girls. All of this stuff"—he gestured up the hill to Project Hollywood—"means nothing. Everything means nothing."

I half-expected him to burst out in laughter at any moment and start talking about his penis, like the old days. "So you're over sarging then?" I asked.

"Yeah, I was obsessed with it, but when I read your post about social robots, I realized I was becoming one. So I'm moving out."

"Are you heading back to your parents' house or getting your own place?"

"Neither," he said. "I'm going to India."

"That's amazing. For what?" When Extramask had come into the community, he was one of the most sheltered people I'd ever met. He'd never even been on a plane before.

"I want to figure out who I am. There's an ashram near Chennai called Sri Ramanasramam, and I want to stay there."

"For how long?"

"Six months or a year, or possibly forever. I really don't know. I'm just kind of rolling with it."

I was surprised but not shocked. Extramask's sudden transformation from pickup artist to spiritual seeker reminded me of Dustin. Some people spend their lives trying to fill a hole in their soul. When women don't absorb that emptiness, they look to something bigger: God. I wondered where Dustin and Extramask would turn afterward, when they discovered that even God wasn't big enough to plug the hole inside.

"Well, man, good luck on your journey. I wish I could say that I was going to miss you, but we've hardly even talked to each other for half a year now. It's been a little strange."

"Yeah," he said. "That's my fault." He paused, and his lips forced themselves into a curvy smile. For a moment, the old Extramask was back. "I used to be an insecure bitch," he said.

"So was I," I told him.

By the time I got back to the house, the TV producers from Britain had arrived, along with a prospective manager for Courtney and a stylist.

"I can't work with her anymore," the stylist said when it became clear that Courtney wouldn't be showing up in time for the shoot. "Ever since she's been doing drugs, she's become a nightmare to deal with."

We hadn't seen any evidence of drugs in the house, but considering Courtney's erratic behavior, perhaps Project Hollywood hadn't kept her away from them as she had hoped. I felt bad for her. She was allowing the problems of the house to distract her from the real-life issues she should have been dealing with. Perhaps we all were.

I awoke that night to see Courtney standing at the foot of my bed with a Prada shoe in her hand.

"Let's redecorate the house," she said excitedly. "This will be our hammer."

I looked at the clock. It was 2:20 A.M.

"Do you have any nails or tacks?" she asked. Without waiting for an answer, she ran downstairs and returned with a box of nails, a framed painting for my wall, a throw pillow for my bed, and a smashed pink box that looked like an old Valentine's Day present.

"This is *the* heart-shaped box," she said. "I want you to have it."

She picked up my guitar, sat on the edge of my bed, and played my favorite country song, "Long Black Veil."

"I'm going to a friend's birthday party tomorrow night at Forbidden City," she said, dropping the guitar to the floor. "I want you to come too. It'll be good for us to get out of the house together."

"I'll tell you what. I'll meet you there." I knew how long she could take to get ready.

"Okay. I'll go with Lisa."

"Speaking of Lisa," I said. "There were a bunch of people waiting for you here today and you were nowhere to be found. I think they're pretty upset."

Her face clouded, her lips puckered, and tears dripped from her eyes. "I'm going to get help," she said. "I promise."

I wore a white blazer over a black shirt emblazoned with a scrolling bank of LCD lights that could be programmed with a message. I input the words "Kill me." I hadn't been out sarging in at least a month and wanted the attention. My expectations for Courtney showing up to Forbidden City were low, so I brought Herbal along as a wing.

We had recently flown to Houston together to pick up the Project Hollywood limousine, a 1998 ten-passenger stretch Cadillac Herbal had found on eBay. Flush with the success of that scheme, Herbal had, against our better judgment, put down a deposit to buy a wallaby at an exotic pets website. On the way to the party, we argued about the practicality and humanity of having a baby marsupial in the house.

"They make the best pets," he insisted. "They're like house-trained kangaroos. They sleep with you, they bathe with you, and you can take them for walks by holding their tail."

The last thing we needed was a wallaby in the mix at Project Hollywood. The only bright side to the fiasco was that it made for a great opener. We ran around the party asking everyone for their opinion on having wallabies as pets. Between the opener and my shirt, within a half hour we were surrounded by women. It felt good to flex our skills again. We'd been so absorbed by the drama of the house that we had forgotten the reason we'd moved there in the first place.

As a tall, stoop-shouldered girl who claimed to be a model pawed at my shirt, I saw a mane of bleached-blonde hair sticking up out of the crowd. I looked closer. Though she was on the other side of the room, she seemed to glow. Her jaw was set, her face was chiseled, her eyes smoldered beneath a half-shell of heavy blue eye shadow. It was Courtney's guitarist, Lisa. Next to her, all the wanna-be models and actresses I had been talking to seemed insignificant. She dwarfed them with her style and poise.

I excused myself and ran up to her.

"Where's Courtney?" I asked.

"She was taking too long to get ready. So I came alone."

"I respect a person who isn't afraid to show up at a party alone."

"I am the party," she said, without blinking or smiling. I think she was serious.

For the entire night, Lisa and I sat side-by-side in a chair, the most pea-cocked couple in the room. The party seemed to come to us, as if we exerted some sort of gravitational pull together. The couches around us soon filled with models, comedians, reality TV has-beens, and Dennis Rodman. When the various women I had talked to during the night came by to flirt, Lisa and I drew on their arms with pens or fed them shots of Hypnotiq or gave them intelligence tests that they usually failed. This is what the PUAs call creating an "our world" conspiracy. We were in our own little bubble, where we were king and queen, and everyone else was our plaything for the night.

When a phalanx of paparazzi started taking pictures of Dennis Rod-man, who was standing nearby, I looked at Lisa's face, illuminated by the flashbulbs. And out of nowhere, my heart awoke from its torpor and body-checked my chest.

When the party broke up, Lisa put her arm around me and asked, "Will you take me home? I'm too drunk to drive." My heart slammed again, and then settled into a fast, arrhythmic throb. She may have been too drunk to drive, but I was too nervous to drive.

Without waiting for a response, she dropped the keys to her Mercedes into my hand. I called to Herbal and asked him to drive my car home. "I can't believe it," I told him. "It's on!"

But it wasn't on.

I drove Lisa back to her place. I recognized the building: It was directly across the street from the Hollywood Mental Health Center where I had taken Mystery. When we arrived, she went to the bathroom. I lay down on her bed and tried to look relaxed.

Lisa padded out of the bathroom, looked at me, and then said, with a withering look, "Don't think anything's going to happen between us."

Damnit, I'm Style. You have to love me. I'm an mPUA.

She changed, and we drove to my house to look for Courtney. All we found there, however, was Tyler Durden leading ten men in the living room through some sort of exercise that involved running around the couches, yelling loudly, and giving each other high fives. Tyler had been experiment-ing lately with a technique of physically pumping up his students' mood for a night out meeting women. He believed that whether or not they actually performed better, the shot of adrenaline and camaraderie would make them think they had fun, and thus give Real Social Dynamics good reviews in the seduction newsgroups. It was becoming a competitive industry.

Courtney seemed to have disappeared again. Maybe she'd been serious the other night and really was getting help, or maybe she was off getting into more trouble.

I took Lisa up to my room, lit some candles, put Cesaria Evora in the CD player, and went to my closet.

"Let's have some fun," I told her.

I pulled out a garbage bag full of old Halloween costumes: masks, wigs, hats. We tried them all on, taking photos with my digital camera. I was going to attempt the digital photo routine.

We took a photo smiling, then serious. For the third photo, the romantic pose, we gazed at each other. Her eyes seemed so happy. Behind that tough exterior was vulnerability and tenderness.

I held her eye contact and moved toward her for the kiss, holding the camera in front of us to capture it.

"I'm not kissing you," she barked.

The words scalded my face like hot coffee. There was no girl I couldn't kiss within half an hour of meeting her. What was her problem?

I froze her out and tried again. Nothing.

It is in these moments that, as a PUA, you start to question the work you've done on yourself. You begin to worry that maybe she sees the real you, the one who existed before the silly nickname, the one who wrote poems about this exact situation in high school.

I delivered a moving, impassioned performance of the evolution phase-shift routine. Somewhere in the distance, I heard a thousand PUAs applauding.

"I'm not biting you," she said.

I wasn't through. I told her the most beautiful love story ever written: "On Seeing the 100 Percent Perfect Girl One Beautiful April Morning" by Haruki Murakami. It is about a man and a woman who are soul mates. But when they doubt their connection for a moment and decide not to act on it, they lose each other forever.

She was ice cold.

I tried a hardcore freeze-out: I blew out the candles, stopped the music, turned on the lights, and checked my e-mail.

She climbed into my bed, curled up under the covers, and went to sleep.

Finally I joined her, and we slept on opposite sides of the bed.

I still had one trick left: going caveman. In the morning, without a word, I started massaging her leg, working my hand slowly up her thigh. If I could just turn her on physically, her logic would disengage and she would no doubt submit.

My intention wasn't to use Lisa for sex. I knew I wanted to see her again, no matter what happened. I just wanted to get the whole sex thing over with so we could be normal together. She wouldn't be trying to keep anything from me; I wouldn't be trying to get something from her. I always hated the idea that sex is something a woman gives and a man takes. It is something that should be shared.

But Lisa wasn't sharing. As I began to rub the warm crease where her thigh meets her pelvis, her voice rang shrill in the air like an alarm clock. "What are you doing?" She smacked my hand away.

We had breakfast together, and lunch, and dinner. We talked about Courtney and the PUAs and my writing and her music and our lives, and all kinds of other things that I can't remember but must have been fascinating because hours passed in the blink of an eye. She was my age; she liked all the same bands I did; she said something intelligent every time she opened her mouth; she laughed at my jokes that were funny and made fun of the ones that weren't.

She spent another night with me. Nothing happened. I had met my match.

After breakfast, I stood on the front stoop and watched Lisa leave. She walked uphill, climbed into her Mercedes, lowered the convertible top, and pulled away. I turned around to climb the stairs. I didn't want to glance back. I wanted to look cool, and not give her any more IOIs.

"Hey, come here," she yelled from her car.

I shook my head no. She was ruining my exit.

"No, seriously, come here. It's important."

I sighed and walked back down to her car. "I'm really sorry, don't be upset," she said. "But I think I might have accidentally dented your limo when I was pulling out."

My body went cold. It was our newest and most expensive possession.

"Just kidding," she said, stepping on the accelerator and leaving me in the dust with a wave. I saw her blonde hair streaming over the side of the car as she turned down Sunset, blasting the Clash.

I had been played by her—again.

I told Mystery about my frustration with Lisa as we sat in the hot tub one night. I'd turned to him so often in the past for advice on women, and he'd rarely steered me wrong. Though relationship management was clearly not his forte, he was flawless when it came to blasting through last-minute resistance.

"Start stroking yourself," he said.

"Now? Here?"

"No, next time you're in bed together, just take your cock out and start stroking it."

"Then what?"

"Then you take her hand and put it on your balls. And she'll start giving you a hand job."

"Are you serious?"

"Yes. Then you put your finger on your dick and put a little precum on it, and put your finger in her mouth."

"No way. This is like that bad joke advice you see in movies, where the friend does it and the girl freaks out and the guy who gave the advice goes, 'I thought you knew I was kidding.'"

"I'm totally serious. You've practically had sex after that."

Three days later, after the bars closed at 2:00 A.M., Lisa dropped by my house with Sam, Courtney's drummer. She was wasted.

We climbed into bed and babbled to each other for hours. "I don't know what my problem is," she slurred. "I never want to leave your room. I could just listen to you talk forever."

She rolled toward me. "Forget I said that," she snapped. "I didn't mean it. Alcohol is like a truth serum."

Now was my chance. Mystery's words ran through my head, and I considered the pros and cons of stroking myself and placing her hand on me.

I couldn't do it. Not because I was scared, but because there was no way it was going to work. Lisa would have laughed in my face and said something cutting like, "You might as well touch yourself, because I'm certainly not about to." Then she would have told all her friends about the cheesy guy who started rubbing his dick in front of her.

Mystery wasn't always right.

So we spent another platonic night together. It was driving me crazy. I knew she liked me. Yet she wouldn't get intimate. I was teetering on the border of being LJBF'ed.

Maybe I just wasn't her type. I imagined her with tattooed, muscle-bound, leather-jacketed Danzig types, not scrawny metrosexual guys who had to take pickup workshops. She was killing me.

For the first time since I'd learned the word one-itis, I had it. And I knew that I was doomed. No one ever gets his one-itis. He gets too clingy and needy and blows it. And, sure enough, I blew it.

The next night, Lisa left town to play a festival in Atlanta with Courtney. She called three times while she was gone.

"Are you free for dinner when I get back?" she asked.

"I don't know," I told her. "It depends on whether you can behave yourself or not."

"Fine, then," she said. "If you're going to be like that, I don't need to go."

I was just trying to tease her and bust her balls, like David DeAngelo had taught me. And in doing so, I had destroyed the moment. I sounded like an asshole.

"Don't be a troublemaker," I said. It was time to be straightforward. "I want to see you when you're back. I'm leaving town for two weeks, so it will be our last chance to hang out."

In the background, I could hear Sam speaking. "You're talking to him like he's your boyfriend," she told Lisa.

"Maybe I want him to be my boyfriend," Lisa said to her.

So I hadn't been LJBF'ed. I couldn't wait for her to come back. I wanted her to be my girlfriend too.

I spent the entire day of Lisa's return plotting the perfect seduction. I would pick her up from the airport in the limo. Herbal would drive, and I would wait for her in the backseat. Then I'd take her to the Whiskey Bar at the Sunset Marquis Hotel—walking distance from Project Hollywood.

Because women don't respect guys who pay for them but at the same time are turned off by guys who are cheap, I went to the Whiskey Bar ahead of time, gave the manager $100, and told him to make sure whatever we ordered was on the house. Afterward, I planned to take her home. On my computer, I wrote down all the patterns and routines I would use to combat her LMR. Now that I knew she liked me, I had the confidence to push this thing to the end.

If she still resisted, then she clearly had intimacy issues and I'd have to be the one to LJBF her.

Her flight was scheduled to arrive at 6:30 P.M. As Herbal drove the limo past the Delta terminal looking for her, I mixed Cosmopolitans at the bar in the back of the car.

When the flight arrived, however, she wasn't on it.

I was confused, but not disappointed—yet. A PUA must be willing to change or abandon any plan when confronted with the chaos and chance of reality. So Herbal drove me home, and I left a message for Lisa.

When she didn't call back, I left another message and then waited all night in vain to hear from her.

At five o'clock that morning, I was awakened by my cell phone ringing.

"Sorry to wake you up, but I need to talk to someone." The voice on the other end was a man's. The accent was Australian. It was Sweater.

Since I'd last seen Sweater, he had left the community and gotten married. I thought about him often. Every time someone asked if guys in the community were learning these skills just to have sex with as many women as possible, I pointed to Sweater as an example of someone who had gotten into the game for all the right reasons.

"I tried to kill myself today," he said.

"What happened?"

"My wife is expecting our first baby in ten days, and I'm miserable. I do everything for her, but it's not enough. She's driven me away from my friends. My business partner is leaving me. She spends all my money and all she does is complain." He paused to choke back his tears. "And now that she's having this baby, I'm trapped."

"But you were in love with her. How can she just change?"

"No. The problem is that I changed. It was too hard to be that person who Mystery and David DeAngelo taught us to be. That person wasn't a good guy. And that's not the kind of person I wanted to be. I like doing nice things for people. So I got her whatever she wanted. I sent her flowers three times a week. I tried it her way, but it didn't work."

I'd never heard grown men cry as much as I had in the last two years. "I sat in the garage today with the motor running and the windows up," he continued. "I haven't thought of suicide since 1986. But I just got to the point where I was like, 'Fuck.' I didn't see any purpose in living."

Sweater didn't need to be saved. He just wanted a friend to talk to. He had pretended to be someone he wasn't just to seduce a woman, and now he was suffering the consequences.

"When I first got in the community, I wrote down everything I wanted," he said. "And now I'm living the life I imagined. I have the money, the big house, and the beautiful girl. But I wasn't specific enough about the beautiful girl. I never wrote that she had to treat me with respect and kindness."

Later that morning, Courtney returned to the house. I could hear her screaming at Gabby in the living room.

I walked downstairs to discover Courtney carrying Gabby's bags out of the house, and I found myself saying the same three words that seemed to come out of my mouth every time I entered the living room: "What's going on?"

"Gabby got into a fight with Mystery, and she's moving out," Courtney said. "So I'm helping her."

Courtney could barely conceal her smile.

"Did the rest of the band get back from Atlanta yet?" I asked, trying to sound casual.

"Yeah. They came home on an earlier flight."

I turned away quickly. I knew if I said anything in response, my voice would betray my disappointment.

After Gabby left, Courtney threw a bundle of sage on the coffee table. "Let's clear the air in here," she said. Then she skipped off to the kitchen, explaining, "We need some rice for good fortune."

Unable to locate any rice, she returned with a package of jambalaya mix and a bowl of water. She poured the jambalaya mix into the water, planted the sage in the middle of it, and then ran to her room. She emerged carrying a blue-and-white-checkered flannel shirt.

"This will work," she said. "It's one of Kurt's shirts. I only have three of them left."

She carefully arranged the shirt underneath the table, safe from harm, so that it could bring good energy to the house. After lighting the sage, she sat Mystery, Herbal, and me down next to her makeshift altar, and we joined hands. Her grip was bone-crushing.

"Thank you God for this day and all that you have given us," she prayed. "We ask that you clear the energy of this house of all evil. Please bring peace and harmony and friendship under this roof. No more tears! And help me win my court case in New York and help clear up all my other problems. I will work with you, God. I really will. Give me strength. Amen."

"Amen," we repeated.

The next day, a driver came and whisked Courtney to the airport to go to New York. There, her prayers for herself would eventually be answered, but the atmosphere in the house would only grow darker in her absence. Courtney and Gabby, it soon became clear, weren't the cause of any problems: They had merely been the symptoms of something much larger that was eating away at our lives.

That afternoon, Lisa left me a short voice mail. "Hi, it's Lisa. I'm back. We took an earlier flight." That was it. No apology, no tenderness, no mention of the plans she had completely blown off.

I called her back, but she didn't answer. "I'm leaving town in a few hours to go to Miami with Vision," I told her voice mail. "I would really love to talk to you before I leave." It was an AFC message, and I never heard back from her. I checked my voice mail every day while I was away. Nothing.

I wasn't a plower, like Tyler Durden. If she were interested, she would have called. I'd been blown off. And by the first woman I had felt something for in a while. I figured she'd probably started dating someone else, someone who had been able to break through her LMR.

First I was angry at her, then I was angry at myself, and then I was just sad.

The PUAs had always advised that the best way to get over a one-itis is to fuck a dozen other girls. So I went on a rampage.

I didn't want to end up like Sweater, anyway. I had almost let myself get caught.

I went sarging every night in Miami, with more fire, drive, and success than I'd ever had. I've never been a fan of one-night stands. Once you've gotten that close to someone, why throw it away afterward? I'm more a fan of ten-night stands: ten nights of great sex, each one getting steamier, wilder, and more experimental as two people grow more comfortable together and learn what turns each other on. So after I slept with each woman, I mixed and matched them like jellybeans.

It was my reality.

The girls I was most looking forward to getting together were Jessica, a tattoo-covered twenty-one-year-old I'd slept with a few times in Los Angeles, and another Jessica, who I'd met at Crobar. She was also twenty-one, but the exact opposite of Jessica I. She was innocent looking, with a touch of baby fat. I knew they both liked porn, so I thought things might get interesting.

After a drink at the hotel bar, I brought them up to my room for a rune reading and then left them alone for a few minutes to get acquainted. When I returned, I showed them home movies on my laptop and then began the trusty dual-induction massage. It was all just a routine now, like the jealous girlfriend opener or the best friends test. And it worked just as consistently.

Once the girls' lips touched, they transformed from strangers to lovers. It shocked me every time to see two women get intimate so quickly in such an unusual situation.

The night was as nasty as I'd anticipated. We tried every position we could twist into, some more successfully than others. When Jessica I asked me to come in her mouth, I obliged. She spit the wad into Jessica II's mouth, and they started making out passionately. It was the sexiest moment of my entire life.

But afterward I felt empty and alone. I didn't care about them. All I really had was a memory and a story. Every girl in my life could disappear and never call me again, and I wouldn't have cared.

All the ten-night stands and threesomes in the world wouldn't be enough to get me over my one-itis.

The PUAs were wrong.

Male sexuality may seem on the surface like it runs rampant in society—there are strip clubs, porn websites, *Maxim*-style magazines, and titillating advertisements everywhere. But, despite all this, true male desire is often kept repressed.

Men think about sex more than they will ever let women, or even each other, know. Teachers think about fucking their students, fathers think about fucking their daughter's friends, doctors think about fucking their patients. And right now, for every woman with even an iota of sex appeal, there's probably a man somewhere in the world who's touching himself and thinking about what it would be like to fuck her. She may not even know him: He may be that businessman who walked past her in the street or the college student who sat across from her on the subway. And any man who tells a woman otherwise is most likely doing so because he's trying to get in her pants, or the pants of someone else within earshot. The great lie of modern dating is that in order to sleep with a woman, a man must pretend initially as if he doesn't want to.

Most appalling to women is the male obsession with strippers, porn stars, and teenage girls. It is abhorrent because it threatens a woman's reality. If all men really desire a woman like that, then where does that leave her marriage and happily-ever-after fantasies? She's doomed to live them with a man who really wants that Victoria's Secret model or the neighbor's daughter or that dominatrix in the videos he hides in his closet. As a woman ages, an eighteen-year-old girl will always be eighteen. Love is dashed on the rocks in the face of the possibility that a man doesn't want a person but a body.

Fortunately, this is not the entire story. Men are visual thinkers; thus we're often deceived by our eyes. But the truth is that the fantasy is often better than the reality. I had just learned that lesson. Most men eventually learn that lesson. Mystery may have thought he wanted to live with two girls who love each other as much as they love him, but chances are they'd get on his nerves, team up against him, and eventually make him just as miserable as he'd been with Katya.

Men are not dogs. We merely think we are and, on occasion, act as if we are. But, by believing in our nobler nature, women have the amazing power to inspire us to live up to it. This is one reason why men tend to fear commitment—and sometimes, as in Mystery's case, even rebel against it by endeavoring to bring out the worst in a woman.

While I was in Miami, Katya returned.

I dreaded the day and the terror it would unleash in the house. But Mystery was looking forward to it like a birthday. He had it all planned out.

Because I was away, I have reconstructed the story of the disaster that ensued from the accounts of those involved.

Project Hollywood had reached a new nadir.

MYSTERY: I met a nineteen-year-old hottie named Jen at an after-party at the house. I full-montied her, and it was amazing, like the shower scene in *9½ Weeks*. She had the softest, purest skin and the best ass I'd ever been with. And I was standing there just looking at that ass and that skin thinking, "I deserve this."

KATYA: Mystery called me every other day while I was in New Orleans, trying to sweet-talk me. He said, "I have this beautiful nineteen-year-old girl that you'll love." I asked him if he was giving her to me. He said, "No, we're sharing."

MYSTERY: The idea wasn't for Katya to be my girlfriend again, but to be a playtoy for Jen and me. My plan was to pick her up from the airport in the limo, grab some food at the Farmer's Market, and then go back to the house and do the dual-induction massage.

HERBAL: I ignored Katya for almost the entire month and a half she was gone, even though she kept sending me text messages. Mystery spent the whole time bragging about how he was going to get a threesome with her, which was like a knife being twisted in my heart. I told Mystery repeatedly just to ignore her and not let her back in the house to avoid problems. But he wouldn't do it.

KATYA: I flew into Los Angeles the day before, which Mystery doesn't know, to rent a studio apartment and hang out with some friends from New Orleans. I stayed in a hotel and called Herbal to talk, because at that point I really wanted to start dating him. The next morning, I just showed up at the house and told Mystery my plane got in early so I took a taxi.

HERBAL: When I came home from doing errands and saw Katya's suitcase, I went into my room to mind my own business. However, Mystery and Katya came in and started talking to me. Then we went to Mystery's bathroom and Katya painted our nails. She disappeared into Mystery's walk-in closet to get a sweater, then Mystery went in. After five minutes, they were still in the closet.

MYSTERY: She called me into the closet and said, "I want to date Herbal." I don't think she said it because she truly wanted to be with him. She just said it to bug me. I was being too kissy-kissy with Jen, and I believe that triggered jealousy in her. So I called Herbal into the closet and told Katya, "Why don't you say it to him?"

KATYA: I really liked Herbal. We talked on the phone throughout my entire visit to New Orleans, and I enjoyed his personality. He was so easygoing, and he never disagreed with anything.

MYSTERY: Herbal and Katya were hanging out, hugging and kind of awkward, so I said, "Why don't you two kiss and get it over with?" They did, and it instantly made me haywire. I didn't expect that to happen after so much time had passed. But, as David DeAngelo says, attraction is not a choice.

HERBAL: That night, we went on a double date. Mystery asked Twyla to drive us in the limo to the Santa Monica Pier. I guess I was naive, but I really thought everything would be fine.

TWYLA: I couldn't believe Mystery had the gumption to ask me to drive, to shove it in my face. He thought he was this grand manipulator. And it made me disgusted with myself for even liking this person.

MYSTERY: Jen and Katya ended up making out with each other in the limo that night. I have pictures of them sucking each other's tits in a phone booth at the pier. But it was getting complex. The moment Katya became Herbal's girlfriend, the threesome was off and I didn't want Jen touching Katya anymore. However, Katya was attracted to Jen, so she started talking trash about me to her.

KATYA: Mystery kept saying he really liked Jen and not to make him look like an asshole in front of her. I told him, "You guys are great. If anyone's going to put up with your shit, it's that girl." I was glad he had someone because I wanted Herbal.

MYSTERY: Jen went home to San Diego for a week after that, and Katya called her every day. One night while Jen was gone, I had a six-foot-tall model in bed with me and was dealing with last-minute resistance. I was fingering her and getting jacked off, but I couldn't get any further. So during a freeze-out, I went to the kitchen to get a Sprite. And I heard Katya having sex with Herbal again. The moaning triggered feelings of jealousy, and I started crying. I couldn't stop, even though I had a girl in my bed. I went back to my room and told the model how fucked up my life was. So she said she wanted to go home. I was going to drive her, but then Twyla started laughing at me.

TWYLA: I was sleeping in the pillow pit and Mystery walked by, upset. I kind of giggled a little bit because I was quite entertained by it all. At that point, I had to take it with humor, because if I didn't, I was going to end up hurt again. Then he flew off the handle and fired me. The girl he was with had to call a taxi home.

KATYA: The next week, Mystery wanted to use my car to pick up Jen from San Diego. On the way back to the house, Jen and I were chitchatting and having fun. Mystery felt left out so he started negging me.

MYSTERY: I felt that Katya was trying to steal Jen from me and share her with Herbal. So I got pissed at Katya in the car, and we had a blow-up. Jen saw this and said, "Just take me home." After that, she asked me never to call her again.

MYSTERY [Posted in Mystery's Lounge]: Be on the lookout for Herbal, Katya, and Jen. If anyone sees Herbal (easy to spot as he frequently peacocks) or his girlfriend Katya (a bi Russian 9.5, easy to spot) with Jen (a nineteen-year-old Mexican 9.5, also easy to spot), please call Mystery so I may administer punishment to Herbal without warning.

KATYA: He thought I was trying to turn Jen against him. But after that car ride, she didn't want anything to do with me either. She thought I was lying by saying all that good stuff about Mystery. It made me look like an ass.

MYSTERY: Herbal and I still had a business relationship. So we went to Chicago together for a workshop. Because I'm fascinated by the mind, I'd explain to him the jealousy I was feeling and we'd draw various boundaries on his relationship with my ex-girlfriend.

HERBAL: On the last day of the Chicago workshop, Mystery and I went to get food together. Mystery opened a four-set of girls next to us. During the sarge, he said, "Can you believe it? This guy actually took my ex-girlfriend."

He told them the whole story. I'd occasionally give my perspective, and he started getting really angry. He said, out of nowhere, "Katya is not allowed in my house ever again."

I said, "It's my house too. You created this situation."

He said, "If I see her in the house again, I will end you."

And I told him, "Do what you have to do."

MYSTERY: When we came back, Twyla had moved out of Project Hollywood, quit being my personal assistant, and moved in with Katya.

TWYLA: Katya and I became friends. We bonded over talking about what kind of a person Mystery was. She asked me if I wanted to be her roommate. So I said, "Right on."

HERBAL: Eventually, Mystery and I compromised. I said that Katya wouldn't spend more than half the week at the house. We shook hands and had an agreement.

When I came back from Chicago, I had a week in Los Angeles before going to Boston for a family reunion. I stayed at Katya's apartment the entire week, just to be cool.

KATYA: While Herbal was gone, I was helping Papa with his workshops. We finished late on Friday night, went to Mel's, and then came home and sat in the hot tub. I had to be up in the afternoon and look pretty. So he told me to sleep in Herbal's room. When I woke up, I saw Mystery.

He asked me what I was doing in the house and I said, "Papa and I were hanging out last night. We had fun."

Then I said, "I met one of your friends two nights ago."

He said, "Who did you meet?"

I said, "Sima."

And he freaked out.

MYSTERY: When Katya told me in a very glib way that she had hung out with my ex-girlfriend from Toronto, I was furious. I lost Jen because of her; I lost Twyla because of her; and now she was about to steal Sima, who was still an option.

KATYA: He ran past me and kicked Herbal's door off the hinges and said, "Where's Herbal?" Then he ran back to his room, grabbed a framed photograph of Sima, and threw it at the wall over Herbal's bed. He said, "I don't want you in this house when your boyfriend's not here."

MYSTERY: I knew I couldn't reason with Katya and I couldn't touch her, so I decided to frighten her. I kicked the door and told her I wanted her out of the house. She said, "This isn't your house." And I told her, "I pay rent. I live here. You're a guest, and your host is not here. This is not acceptable."

KATYA: Mystery started threatening that if he saw me in the house again, Herbal would get hurt. He threw candles around; he flipped

Herbal's mattress off the bed; he threw a flowerpot against the wall; and then he opened Herbal's balcony door and started throwing my stuff into the driveway. He busted my bottle of Kama Sutra oil. I was so pissed.

MYSTERY: I said, "Don't come back here or else!"

She said back to me, "Or else what? Are you going to kill me?"

And I said, "No. I love you. I will punish your boyfriend if you come back. Tell him to control his girl."

KATYA: I went upstairs to look for Papa, but he wasn't there. So I got in my car and drove to my apartment. Five minutes later, Papa called. He said, "It's not Mystery's house. My name is on the lease, and you're my guest. I'm going to pick you up right now." So he snuck me back into the house.

MYSTERY: Papa was breaking a cardinal rule. He was hiring my ex-girlfriend, who I trained, to be in his workshops, which was an idea he'd stolen from me.

HERBAL (to Mystery, via e-mail): I have been told that my bedroom and personal belongings have been "destroyed" because Katya was at the house. I don't know exactly what destroyed means, but now I do not feel safe in my own house. You seem to believe that the world revolves around you and that everyone else should bend to your wishes.

MYSTERY (to Herbal, via e-mail): I don't want Katya here and that is so final that there will be no need for you to reply to this e-mail in any way. Nor bring up the subject again, for it will arouse my anger so deeply that you will be thrown through glass. There will be no further warning. If she comes around when you return, I will instantly pound you—it will be fast, hard, unexpected, merciless, and repetitive. If you come by and she isn't around, then we can safely live in peace under the same roof. Either way, our business relationship is, obviously, finished.

TYLER DURDEN (via e-mail, to Mystery): You lost Katya for many reasons, but to me it appeared as though you emotionally leeched off of her. You are needy and like a black hole sucking in attention. You can't handle not being the center of attention for even one minute. That is your tragic flaw. Don't offer your girls to your friends. Don't try to make a party girl into your girlfriend. And don't underestimate the consequences of bringing recently converted AFCs into our lifestyle.

My phone rang every day while I was in Miami. I'd pick it up, and it would be Mystery or Herbal or Katya or Twyla or Tyler Durden. I even received phone calls about Project Austin, which was also falling apart: The gas and electricity had been shut off because the bills hadn't been paid, and the bedrooms were cluttered with candles, dirty clothing, and pornography. But the only person I really wanted to hear from was Lisa.

When I returned to Project Hollywood, Herbal's room was in tatters. There were holes in his wall; his door was propped up precariously against its hinges; his mattress lay over his television set; and glass and dirt were strewn across the hardwood floor.

From the perspective of a pickup artist, all Mystery was doing was strengthening Katya and Herbal's relationship by creating drama and a common enemy. But Mystery wasn't thinking like a pickup artist. He was unable to control himself.

That night, the doorbell rang. When Mystery answered it, he found a well-muscled man in his twenties standing in the rain with an angry look on his face. Katya's car was parked in front of the house.

"I'm Katya's brother," the man told Mystery.

"I don't think so. I know her brother."

"Well," he said, stepping past Mystery and into the house. "I heard you threatened to kill her. And that's not going to happen."

"I never threatened Katya." Mystery sized Katya's friend up. He was shorter than him but definitely stronger. "I threatened Herbal."

"Well, if you do anything to her, I will personally crack your skull wide open."

Mystery never responded well to provocation. Just like during our argument in the car at the Trans-Dniester border, Mystery snapped. The veins in his neck leaped to attention; his face ripened; he grew an inch.

"You want to go?" Mystery yelled. "Let's go then, because I'm ready to take this thing all the way."

"Fine," Katya's friend said. "Then step outside. I don't want to get blood on the carpet."

"No, let's do it right here. I want blood on the floor. I want something to remember you by."

In the periphery of his vision, Mystery spotted a cluster of large rocks he'd brought back from the beach and painted into runestones. He reached for one, prepared to smash his adversary's head in, then quickly changed his mind. He took three giant strides to Herbal's already-decimated door and kicked it to the ground again.

"Come on then," Mystery yelled. "I'm not making any apologies for what I'm about to do."

He grabbed a bookshelf and pulled it over.

Katya's friend saw the gleam of madness in Mystery's eyes—and in a fight the insane generally have a competitive edge. "You don't have to kick doors down and shit," he said, backing off. "All I want is the dog, man. Katya sent me to get her dog."

The guy scooped Lily into his arms, and Mystery paused and looked at him. The threat was gone. The cortisol, the adrenaline, the testosterone—all those hormones that were rushing through his body—began to ebb. His brain returned to logical mode. "Why didn't you say that in the first place instead of threatening me in my own home?"

The guy stood next to the door, befuddled, with Lily cradled in his arms.

"Do you need food for Lily?" Mystery asked.

"Um, yes. I guess."

Mystery walked to the kitchen, grabbed Lily's bag of dry food and several cans of wet food, and gave them to his would-be attacker.

On the way out, the guy dropped some cans on the steps. Mystery bent down, picked them up, handed them to him, and then patted him on the back.

"Respect," he told Katya's friend, using the line we'd appropriated from Ali G to use in the field.

I walked upstairs, collapsed on my bed, and stared at the ceiling.

Why was I here? It wasn't just about my envy of Dustin anymore. Along the way, I had gotten caught up in the social network and bonding rituals of the community—in the idea that we were the supermen of the future, the smoothest who would inherit the earth from the strong, the sole owners of the skeleton key to the female mind. I had moved in with these guys because I thought we had all the answers. I imagined working together to bring all the other areas of our lives up to a new plateau, beyond just women. I hoped we would be greater than the sum of our parts.

But rather than creating a mutual support system, we had created *Lord of the Flies.*

Something had to be done to resolve this. My faith in these guys—and this community—was hanging by a thread.

MANAGE EXPECTATIONS

NOT THAT IT was beautiful,
But that, in the end, there was
A certain sense of order there;
Something worth learning
In that narrow diary of my
mind.

....

—Anne Sexton,
"For John, Who Begs Me Not to Enquire Further"

Mystery and Herbal sat facing each other on opposite couches, their arms folded across their chests. It was not only a defensive position, but also a stubborn one. Between them stood Mystery's Krav Maga instructor and Roadking, a PUA who worked as a bodyguard. Herbal had refused to set foot in the house without someone there to protect him from Mystery.

The other permanent residents—Papa, Xaneus, Playboy, and me—sat on a third couch perpendicular to them. Tyler Durden didn't attend because he claimed to be a guest, although he'd been living in Papa's closet for months now.

We had called a house meeting to resolve the dispute between Mystery and Herbal once and for all.

We allowed each to present his side of the story without interruption. Mystery said he would not allow his ex-girlfriend to set foot in the house again. And Herbal said he would move out if his girlfriend couldn't come over. It took each of them half an hour to convey these simple points.

"Now, normally, I would just say that Herbal should move out if he wants to be with Mystery's ex-girlfriend that badly," I said, trying to play the role of peacemaker that had been foisted on me. "However, Mystery, you've damaged house property and threatened a tenant's well-being. You have neither apologized for your actions nor repaired the damages." Herbal's door was still lying on the floor, the dents were still in his wall, and his room still looked like a tornado had hit it. "And it makes us very reluctant to reward bad behavior by letting you get your way."

"I purposely left Herbal's room like that as a demonstration of what I will do if I see Katya in this house again," Mystery said sullenly. "It was a perfectly acceptable means of showing that I was willing to enforce my rules."

One of the problems with the PUA community was that it presented inflexible standards of behavior that men were supposed to follow in order to win a woman. And chief among them was the idea of being an alpha male.

The result was a bunch of men who'd been kicked around most of their lives trying to act like their former bullies, leading to immature behavior such as Mystery's.

"If I may say something?" Roadking interjected. "Herbal here broke an important rule."

"And what's that?" Herbal asked. There was no anger or resentment in his voice; only the red rings around his eyes betrayed the emotion he felt.

"It's the rule of bros before hos," Roadking said.

"No," Mystery said. "I'd like to agree, but sometimes it's hos before bros."

Herbal cracked a smile for the first time that afternoon: He and Mystery actually saw eye to eye on something.

Strip away the community bond and the seduction business interests that united us, and what was left? Six guys chasing after a limited subset of available women. Wars have been fought, world leaders shot, and tragedies wrought by males claiming territorial rights over the opposite sex. Perhaps we'd just been too blind to see that Project Hollywood was doomed from the start by the very pursuit that had brought it together.

After three hours of go-nowhere debate—during which Papa, oddly, didn't speak once—we asked Mystery and Herbal to give us some privacy to talk amongst ourselves and come to a house decision.

They both agreed to accept whatever we decided.

When we entered Papa's room, there was a flurry of activity. Several figures darted into his bathroom and shut the door. I hadn't seen his room in nearly a month. The carpet was barely visible beneath six convertible black foam chairs that had been unfolded into beds. On top of each was a pillow and bedding.

Where were the people who slept here? Who were they?

We folded the beds back into chairs, sat down, and prepared to reach a conclusion. That was when Papa spoke for the first time.

"I will not live in the same house as that guy," he said.

"Who?" I asked.

"Mystery!"

Papa's hands trembled from either hatred or nervousness. He was a difficult person to read. He hadn't been sarging in months, and much of the progress he'd made after working so hard to improve himself had disappeared. He was the same blank, introverted shell I had first met in Toronto. His passion was no longer pickup; it was Real Social Dynamics. Instead of going to seminars on meeting women, he spent most of his time flying around the country to marketing and business seminars.

"Mystery disrupts my workshops," Papa continued. His voice was distant and monotone, echoing from somewhere deep inside his head. "He damages the house. And I'm worried he's going to harm me."

"What are you talking about? He wouldn't do anything to you."

"I have nightmares that Mystery is coming into my room with a knife. I'm getting locks put on my doors because I'm scared he'll break in."

"That's ridiculous," I said. "He's not going to hurt you. That's your own issue: You need to learn how to deal with aggression and confrontation rather than just avoiding everyone and trying to kick them out of the house."

But no matter what I said to dissuade Papa, he kept repeating the same sentence—"I will not live in the same house as that guy"—in a robotic voice, as if he'd been programmed to say it.

"Have you ever stopped to think," Playboy finally asked me, "that the only reason you're defending Mystery is because he's your friend?"

Perhaps Playboy was right. I was giving Mystery special-circumstances treatment, because he had brought me into the community and because the house had been his idea. None of us would have been here without him. But he had screwed up. He had made his bed. I needed to consider what was best for the house.

"But," I said. "I'd still like to find a way to solve this without anyone having to leave the house."

"We'll trust whatever you decide," Papa said. "You're the house leader. Everyone looks up to you."

I found it strange that Papa, who was so adamant about having Mystery leave, was putting the decision in my hands. For the next two and a half hours, we discussed possible compromises. The more we talked about it, the more complex the dilemma seemed. There was no solution that was going to satisfy everyone:

Papa wouldn't live in the house with Mystery.

Mystery wouldn't live in the house with Katya.

And Herbal wouldn't live in the house without Katya.

Someone had to go.

"All the problems in this house can be traced back to one source," Playboy said firmly, "and that source is Mystery."

I looked at Xaneus. "Do you agree with Playboy and Papa?" I asked him.

"I do," he said. He too seemed to speak from somewhere deep in his skull, as if he weren't really present. He was turning as robotic as the rest of them. "I think Mystery needs to go."

We called Mystery and Herbal into the room to give them our decision. They sat on the edge of the step leading up to Papa's bed. Having come up with the only possible compromise for a complicated dilemma, I was proud of myself—mistakenly, it would turn out—for exercising my newfound leadership skills in a Solomon-like manner.

"Herbal," I began. "Katya will not be allowed in the house for two months. After that, if you're still dating her, she may return to the house."

Herbal nodded.

"Mystery, you have two months to get over Katya and find yourself a new girlfriend. In addition, there will be a zero-tolerance policy for violence in this house. If you threaten anyone's life, attack anyone, or damage property, you will be asked to leave the house immediately."

Mystery didn't nod.

"So basically you're saying you want me out of the house and that bitch gets to replace me," he snarled.

"Well," Playboy said. "There's always the chance Herbal and Katya will break up in that time."

"I don't see that happening," Herbal said.

Mystery threw his arms into the air. "Well, then you guys are kicking me out."

"No," I said. "We're giving you two months to come to grips with your emotions."

I was trying to help him. But he refused to be helped.

"If you give me at least two weeks notice before you leave," Papa said, "I'll refund your full deposit and find someone to fill the room."

Papa was happy. He was getting his way.

Mystery's forehead creased; his head twitched involuntarily. "You realize," he said, "that Papa is trying to get me out of the house because he's in competition with me. This is not about Mystery versus Herbal. It's about Mystery Method versus Real Social Dynamics. I gave Papa his entire business model. I told him to harness his sex drive and become a businessman.

He's even charging fifteen hundred dollars now for boot camps where he teaches my material." Mystery glared at Papa; Papa stared right through Mystery. "And now that he doesn't need me anymore, he wants to move me out and turn my room into a twelve-person dorm."

At the time, I thought Mystery was in denial, that he was still refusing to take responsibility for his actions. "It didn't have to turn out like this," I told him. "Every step of the way, you've made bad decisions, and now you have to live with them. We're not even kicking you out. You're deciding to leave."

Mystery folded his arms across his chest and looked at us disdainfully.

"Can't you see that the actions you think are alpha-male ways to solve a problem actually prevented you from getting the outcome you wanted?" I continued.

"It was a tactic designed to keep Katya out of the house, and it worked," he maintained. "She hasn't been back since."

I lost my cool. It was time for him to wake up and take a good look at himself.

"You need some tough love," I said, raising my voice for the first time all meeting. "You're the best illusionist I've ever seen, yet you haven't taken a single step toward your ninety-minute show—or any show, for that matter—since I've met you. Your pickup business is a mess, and your former students are raking in all the money that should be yours. As for your love life, ever since Katya, you've driven away every girl you've slept with. I would not recommend a girl ever dating you. You are a financial, mental, and emotional mess." With each sentence I felt like a weight was being lifted off my chest. "You have nothing: no health, no wealth, and no relationships. And you have no one to blame but yourself."

Mystery dropped his head into his hands. His shoulders started shaking. Big Mystery tears rolled out of his eyes. "I'm a broken man," he cried. "I'm broken."

The wall of sophistry and self-deception that had been propping him up came tumbling down. "What should I do?" He looked at me. "Tell me what to do."

Tears began leaking out of my eyes. I couldn't help it. I turned and faced the wall so Herbal and Papa wouldn't see. The tears ran faster. Despite all of Mystery's flaws, I still cared about the guy. After two years in the seduction community, I still didn't have a girlfriend, but for some reason I had bonded with this big blubbering genius. Perhaps it was really shared emotion and experience that creates relationships, not seven hours of routines followed by two hours of sex.

"You need therapy," I said. "You need treatment or counseling or something. You can't just keep doing this to yourself."

"I know," he said. His eyes filled with tears as viscous as mercury. He balled his hand into a fist and hit his head self-castigatingly. "I know. I fucked up."

I walked out of Papa's room and left the house. I had a headache. It had been a long day.

As I started down the hill to grab a burrito at Poquito Mas, a black Mercedes convertible whipped around the corner and began climbing the hill. Inside were two blondes.

The car screeched to a halt in front of me, and a voice yelled my name from the driver's seat. It was Lisa. My heart skipped a beat.

She wore a red Diesel jacket with a wide rainbow collar that made her look like a cross between a supermodel and a racecar driver. I was unshaven, wearing sweatpants, and frazzled from debating with my roommates all day. I felt so many emotions at once: embarrassment, excitement, resentment, fear, joy. I didn't think I was ever going to see her again.

"We're going to get a drink," Lisa yelled. "Do you want to join us?"

"What are you doing here?" I tried to keep my cool and appear unfazed by her sudden reappearance.

"Going to the Whiskey Bar."

"Didn't you just pass it?"

"Yeah. I came by to ask you to go with us. Do you have a problem with that?"

A touch of attitude. I still liked her. She was a challenge. She didn't let any sarcasm, neg, or cocky funny get past her without a verbal smackdown.

"Let me change," I said, "and I'll meet you there."

I slipped on a pair of Levi's Red jeans with fake cat scratches down the front and a military-collared button-down shirt I'd bought in Australia, and ran down the hill to join them.

I was anxious to talk to Lisa and find out why she'd disappeared after Atlanta. But when I arrived, Lisa and Sam were at a table with two stocky, heavily tattooed rockers. They were the type of guys I had imagined Lisa dating. I sat between them, dwarfed by ink and hair dye.

As they gossiped about local rock scenesters I neither knew nor cared about, an overwhelming anxiety took hold of my body. I didn't want to make small talk or pretend to enjoy it. I wanted to be alone with Lisa. I wanted to connect with her.

When the first drip of sweat rolled down my forehead, I jumped up. I couldn't take it.

"I'll be right back," I said. I needed to sarge—not because I wanted to pick up women, but because I wanted to get into a positive state and talkative mood. Otherwise I was going to just crack sitting there so awkwardly.

As I ordered a drink at the bar, I smelled lilacs behind me. I turned around to see two women in black evening dresses. "Hey guys, let me get your opinion on something," I began, with a little less enthusiasm than usual.

"Let me guess," one of the women said. "You have a friend whose girlfriend is jealous because he still talks to his ex from college."

"Like, every guy keeps asking us that," her friend said. "What's the deal?"

I grabbed my Jack and Coke and shuffled out to the smoking patio—the site of my pickup battle with Heidi Fleiss. With some trepidation, I delivered the spells opener to a two-set sitting on a bench. Fortunately, they hadn't heard it.

"Hey," I said afterward. I really wasn't feeling it, but I wanted to push myself to be talkative. "How long have you guys known each other?"

"About ten years," one of the girls said.

"I could tell. I have to give you guys the best friends test."

"Oh, we know that one already," she said politely.

It had finally happened: The Sunset Strip was sarged out.

The community had grown large and reckless; too many competing businesses were teaching the same material. And we had saturated more than just Los Angeles. PUAs in San Diego, Montreal, New York, San Francisco, and Toronto had been reporting the same problem lately: They were running out of fresh girls to sarge.

I walked back to Lisa and her friends. "I'm wiped out," I told Lisa. "I'm going to head home. But I'm driving to Malibu tomorrow to surf. You and Sam should join me. It'll be fun."

She looked up at me, and we connected for the first time all evening. For three extraordinary seconds, the rest of the club disappeared. "Yeah, all right," she said. "Sounds cool."

"Great. Meet me at the house at noon." Connection over.

When I returned home from the Whiskey Bar, Isabel was waiting for me. I was never going to get any sleep.

"Didn't I tell you to call first before dropping by?" I asked.

"I left you a message."

There was nothing wrong with Isabel. Five years ago, I would have given up writing for a year just to sleep with a girl like that once. But she offered nothing. She was all holes: ears to listen to me, a mouth to talk at me, and a vagina to squeeze orgasms out of me. We weren't a team; we were just a distraction for each other, a way to feel less lonely for a few hours in a big, uncaring world. We never had conversations; we had nonversations, where we just filled empty space with words. At least, that's what I thought. But sometimes, simply through the act of having sex with a man, especially if that man is a little more emotionally distant than she'd like him to be, a woman can develop feelings. She can start wanting more.

"Are you still seeing other girls?" Isabel asked in the morning, rolling on top of me and looking aggressively into my eyes.

It was a loaded question with only one right answer. I gave her the wrong one—the honest one. "Well, I met a girl named Lisa, who I'm developing feelings for."

"Well, you're going to have to choose between her and me."

In the past, I used to fall for ultimatums. But I'd since learned that ultimatums are expressions of powerlessness, empty threats designed to try to influence a situation someone has no control over.

"Just by asking me to make that choice," I said, "you're setting yourself up to be the loser."

She dropped her head onto my shoulder and cried. I felt bad for her. But that's all I felt.

An hour after she left, Sam and Lisa arrived. Mystery sat at the computer, typing furiously. He looked up at Lisa, who was wearing a Juicy Couture linen pullover with the hood over her head, and tried to neg her. "What kind of get-up is that?" he asked. It was the only way he knew how to relate to a beautiful woman.

Lisa slowly scanned Mystery's get-up. He was wearing a robe, boxer shorts, black toenail polish, and slippers. She gave him a withering look and sneered, deadpan, "Right back at ya, babe."

Lisa was neg-proof. Next to her, other girls seemed like incomplete human beings. For most of their childhood, females are conditioned to act subservient to male authority figures. Once they grow up, a certain subset of them—many of whom end up in Los Angeles—move through the world psychologically stunted, constantly dumbing themselves down in the presence of the opposite sex. They believe that the techniques they used to manipulate their fathers will work just as well on the rest of the world, and often they're right. But Lisa wasn't a doormat designed by the expectations and desires of the men in her life. She lived the advice that most women hypocritically give to men: She wasn't afraid to be herself.

Mystery was silent for once. He cleared his throat; announced, a little too loudly, "I'm busy"; then turned away to continue typing. I was sure he was posting in Mystery's Lounge, letting off steam after the previous day's house meeting.

Before we left for the beach, I showed Sam and Lisa the photos I had taken the first night Lisa slept over, when we had played dress-up with the wigs.

"Look at that," Sam said when she saw the photo of Lisa and me staring into each other's eyes, just before we didn't kiss. "I've never seen Lisa look so happy."

"Yeah," Lisa said, her lips spreading into a toothy smile. "I guess you're right."

Sam ran upstairs to use my bathroom while Lisa and I loaded the surfboards into the back of the limousine, which doubled as my surf car. As we drove to Malibu, I noticed Sam leaning over the seat divider to whisper something to Lisa, which wiped the smile off her face in an instant.

"What is it?" I asked.

They looked at each other hesitantly.

"What?" I persisted. I really wanted to know. I was sure it was about me, and I was sure it wasn't positive.

"It's not important," Sam said. "Just girl talk."

"Um, okay."

When I surfed in the past, I usually hung out close to the shore, riding the smaller waves while the more experienced surfers paddled further out for the big ones. I thought I was better than them because I got more waves. But after helping Sam and Lisa get comfortable on their boards, I paddled out with the expert surfers to try and catch a big wave.

As I waited, I looked on with envy as the surfers on the inside—closer to shore—caught wave after wave. After twenty minutes, the water finally swelled behind me and I began to paddle. As a wall of blue grew in my peripheral vision, my body tensed: I wondered if I could handle a wave this big. It grabbed my board with a crack, like pealing thunder, and I leapt to my feet. The blue stretched far overhead. I cut through the open face all the way to the top of the wave and maneuvered to shore. I felt alive, exhilarated, ecstatic. I didn't know I could do it before: I didn't think I had the knowledge and the skill to take a wave like that. For the first time since junior high, I felt like writing poetry.

As I triumphantly carried my board to the beach, I realized it was time, with girls, to take the big waves and stop messing with the mushy little inside ones, to go for the best rather than the most. I deserved it.

When we returned home, I pulled Lisa aside.

"I'd like to take you out for sushi on Saturday," I said.

It was so AFC of me. I was asking her out on a date.

She hesitated for a moment, as if she were deciding the best way to let me down easy. She pursed her lips and squinted. Then, finally, she spoke. "Okay, I guess."

"You guess?" I couldn't remember the last time I'd asked a girl on a date, and she was giving me attitude about it?

"No, it's just that. . . ." She stopped herself. "Never mind. Yeah, I'd love to go. I was wondering when you were finally going to ask."

"That's better. I'll pick you up at eight."

The girls left, and I went to the kitchen to sauté a chicken breast. The remains of countless meals made by scores of guests had congealed into a black crust that coated the stovetop. As I waited for my food to cook, Tyler Durden came in through the patio door, wearing running shoes and a Walkman. He lifted up his T-shirt, examined a roll of baby fat on his belly, and took his Walkman headphones off.

"Hey, man, I heard what happened with Mystery," he said. "I'm really sorry about how things turned out. Let me know if I can do anything to help convince him to stay in the house."

"He's very stubborn. I doubt there's anything you can do."

"If he leaves, there's no Project Hollywood anymore," he went on. "I guess it would sort of become the RSD mansion."

"I guess so." I scooped the chicken onto a plate and grabbed a fork and knife.

"By the way. I bought a Style shirt on Melrose today. It looks just like something you would wear. I have to show it to you."

"That's great, but kind of weird." There was something I'd been mean-ing to discuss with Tyler Durden for a while now. "I'd like to talk to you about paying a small rent or part of the utilities. You've been living here for months now, and we made a rule the day we moved in that long-term guests should contribute to the house."

"Sure, man," he said. "Just bring it up with Papa."

His words were agreeable, but not his body language. He shifted his head uncomfortably while he spoke, as if he didn't know where to look, then wheeled around and left. He always seemed to go unnaturally out of his way to make sure he wasn't actively involved in any house issue, drama, or meeting. Behind his smile I sensed something—not unlike what I'd felt when I'd kissed his girl in Las Vegas. By asking him to pay rent, I'd become a threat to him.

I took my food to the office area of the house, turned on my computer, and checked Mystery's Lounge. I wanted to read the masterpiece Mystery had been so furiously working on that afternoon.

MSN GROUP: Mystery's Lounge
SUBJECT: Mystery Moves Out
AUTHOR: Mystery

I will likely be moving out of Project Hollywood next month because it is no longer a suitable place for me. The invasive social environment has made living here uncomfortable.

As far as lifestyle goes, Project Hollywood is a bust. I don't see living here to be a positive experience for anyone. If and when my overpriced bedroom is made available, your unsavory roommates (save Style) will, at some point, undermine your happiness. This is something they have demonstrated on more than one occasion.

In my specific case, aside from the issues with having a competing business running out of the same home I live in (one of many breaches in trust between Papa and me), house members think that it's appropriate to intervene in my private sex life. This is an intolerable situation for me. I've been told that my ex-girlfriend, who has demonstrated numerous times that she is untrustworthy, will be allowed back in the house in two months.

If she comes back (which Papa hopes), then this forces me out of the house because I do not want such a toxic person near my friends or me. Unless the restraining order Katya is threatening to file against me keeps her out of my house, such involvement in my personal affairs will likely cause irrevocable bitterness.

As for those who say I need psychological help, the greatest solution to depression is not paying some stranger to listen to you or taking drugs, which is just a short-term fix for when things hit rock bottom. The long-term fix is a positive social environment filled with friends who will listen and share your challenges. That is what Project Hollywood was supposed to be. If anyone would like to talk to me openly about the situation and why I do not endorse living here, call me. I don't want anyone else to get ripped off and hurt as I have been. Know the culture before making any decision to move here.

'Nuff said.

—Mystery

P.S. If I move out, I will be selling my bed. I've only slept with ten girls on it so it's very clean. It's a California king-sized bed. The price is $900 cash and does not include comforter or sheets.

Here is a list of who's been bedded on the bed:

1. Joanne the stripper

2. Mary the blonde model

3. The hot bartender from the Spider Club

4. Sima the ex-girlfriend from Toronto

5. Katya the *&%!

6. Gabby the gabber

7. Jen the nineteen-year-old hottie

8. Vision's cousin (I know, but I still enjoyed her)

9. Twyla the personal assistant

10. The six-foot tall model I scared away (third base only)

I think that's everyone. It's a great bed. Firm. Eleven happy people.

MSN GROUP: Mystery's Lounge
SUBJECT: Field Report—Mystery Meets His Future Wife
AUTHOR: Mystery

I have met my future wife. And I have decided not to tell you about her. She is that important and that classy. She is my dream girl (at least I think she is so far).

Unlike the last girl, I will not make her public. This time I will start from scratch and not undermine my relationship by sharing it with you guys. I will be more loyal to her than to you because the bros before hos ethic only applies if you think of the girl as a ho.

Here is all you need to know: I met her briefly when I was in Chicago, doing my last workshop with Herbal. I met her for seven minutes and then number-closed. We have spoken on the phone since for hours and hours. I love her personality. And, yes, body- and face-wise, she is a 10. I have talked with her mom on the phone, and she likes me too. This girl is coming to Los Angeles to visit me for a week. I bought her a flight. My family will be arriving the same week and they will meet.

Though we have only been in each other's presence for seven minutes, I predict that I will marry her, live with her, and possibly have kids with her. How is that for a prediction, huh? From the world's greatest pickup artist.

You won't see her winging my workshops because I will refrain from exploiting her unless she wants to help out for shits and giggles. She is untouchable to this paltry gang of misfits. She isn't a party girl like the last five girls. She may look like one (mmm) but she is perfection, at least to me. My friends will meet her soon.

As for all the other PUAs, stay away from her because you know I bite.

Love,
Mystery

Chapter

Mystery sulked through the trash-strewn house in his robe, telling anyone who would listen about the former student who was stealing his business and the bitch who ruined his life. Any attempt to get him into therapy was dismissed with a long-winded explanation of how his emotions and actions were evolutionarily justified. The window of vulnerability and honesty that had opened when he broke down in the house meeting had closed. His frame had reasserted itself; his mind had rebuilt the tortuous walls separating rationalization from reality.

Though he wasn't upset with me, I felt guilty. The compromise that was effectively pushing him out of the house had been my decision. So much for my Solomon-like wisdom.

To make matters worse, Katya was twisting the knife. She'd given her landlord sixty days notice, and planned to move into Herbal's room once she was allowed back in the house. Her revenge, then, was complete.

That Friday, I drove with Mystery to pick up his sister, mother, and nieces from the airport. They piled into the back of the limo and surrounded him with the love he so desperately craved.

We then headed to the United Airlines terminal. Mystery had one more guest coming in for the week: Ania. She was the girl he'd met in Chicago, the one he'd claimed online would be the future Mrs. Mystery, the ultimate rebound. One of Mystery's specialties in sarging was what he called hired guns, such as bartenders, strippers, shot girls, and waitresses. Ania was a coatcheck girl at the Chicago Crobar.

We pulled outside the terminal and waited. "Get ready to meet my future wife," Mystery announced to his family.

"Don't scare her away like the last one," his mom chuckled. She seemed to have learned that the secret to surviving the stresses her husband and children had put on her was to never take anyone or anything too seriously. Life was an in-joke between her and God.

We recognized Ania the moment the automatic doors opened, revealing a short woman with bottle-blonde hair, a bosom disproportionate to her body, and a shrunken-apple face that betrayed, like Patricia and Katya before her, Eastern European origins.

Mystery greeted her, grabbed her bags, and brought her to the limo. Outside of a meek "hello," Ania didn't say a word during the entire trip home. Instead, she sat passively and listened to Mystery. She was just his type.

She may not have been a party girl like Katya, but Ania came with her own baggage, which arrived unexpectedly at the airport the next day. His name was Shaun.

On Saturday we discovered Shaun standing outside the house, dialing Ania's cell phone every five minutes. Ania had never told Mystery she was engaged. And, clearly, she had never told her fiancé she was flying to Los Angeles to visit a pickup artist she had met at work. Shaun had evidently checked her voice mail, discovered messages from Mystery, and decided to fly to L.A. to confront his rival.

The irony wasn't lost on Mystery. "I understand what Shaun's going through," he said. "I'm like Herbal to him. He wants to kill me and take his woman back." He paused for a moment and adjusted his posture into what would have been an alpha male pose if he had any pectorals. "I'm going out there to talk to him."

As Mystery swaggered outside, I waited in the living room with his sister and mother. We sat on the upholstery—so filthy now even the stains were stained—that was the backdrop to the tears, girls' bottoms, and house meetings that had been consuming my life for months. I felt a need to escape this trap I had set for myself; this trap Mystery kept setting for himself; the traps we all constantly set for ourselves, over and over, and never seem to learn from.

"You realize," I told them, "that Mystery is just building himself up for another fall with this girl."

"Yes," his mom said. "He thinks it's all about the girls, but it's not. It's about his low self-esteem." Only a mother could reduce a person's entire ambition and raison d'etre to the one basic insecurity fueling it all.

"What worries me is the violence," I said. "He's starting to think that violence is a solution to these problems, and it's a dangerous way of thinking."

"Butting heads with someone never works," his mom said. "I always say that you don't have to do the direct approach. You can just go around because there's always a back way."

"Now I know where he got Mystery Method from." In three sentences, his mother had unintentionally summarized Mystery's entire approach to meeting women: the indirect method.

Martina knitted her eyebrows and shifted her weight on the couch. "His depressions get worse every time," she sighed. "He was never violent before."

"Well, I remember one time when he was angry, he slammed a door and killed his pet rat," his mother said. "But I never saw him get mad about anything else. Even when the cat died, he just said, 'That's life.' "

"What I think is happening," Martina said, "is that with our father gone, he's starting to realize that Dad was never as bad as he remembered. So now he's allowing himself to be more like Dad."

I reflected back on my conversation with Mystery at the Trans-Dniester border. He'd made his dad out to be a monster. "So your dad wasn't as bad as Mystery always said?"

"The problem is that they were too similar," Martina explained. "Dad could take over any room he walked into. He was very charismatic but also very stubborn. They never got along. Mystery would always do things to antagonize Dad. And Dad, instead of acting like an adult, would blow up at him."

"We'd have to put them on opposites sides of the table," Mystery's mom cut in, "and if one so much as looked at the other wrong, a fight would break out."

"And now that Dad's gone," Martina said, "Mystery needs someone to take all his anger out on. So Katya has taken the place of his father. She's become the villain responsible for all the messed-up emotions he's feeling."

Now was my chance to bring up the question I'd wanted to ask ever since Mystery's breakdown in Toronto, the question that would free me of the inexplicable obligation I felt to save him from himself.

"So what do we do?"

We talked it through for a half hour. The answer, Martina finally decided, was to let him run free; to give him a chance to make something of his talent and genius; to give him time to quest after two 10s who will love him as much as they love each other. And to hope that he made some progress toward his life goals before the next crash, or the crash after that, or whichever crash would be so destructive he'd have to return home for good. He was walking on quicksand with helium balloons in his hands. In that respect, he was like all of us, except the air in his balloons was escaping faster.

We cut our discussion short when Mystery strode into the kitchen.

"Done," he said. "I had a long talk with Ania's fiancé at Mel's. I told him it was too late for him to fix things with her. Ania is now my girlfriend, and we are in love with each other. This is turning out to be the best pickup in the history of Mystery Method."

Martina gave me a knowing glance. Mystery's mother crossed her arms over her chest and chuckled to herself.

He slammed a tape recorder down on the kitchen counter. "I recorded the whole conversation," he said. "Do you want to hear it?"

"No," I told him. I'd had enough drama.

Besides, I had a date with Lisa to keep.

Chapter

I picked Lisa up at 8:00 P.M. and took her to a Japanese restaurant called Katana. It was one of the toughest dinners of my life. We'd spent so much time together already that I literally had no more material left. I was forced to be myself.

"There's something I've been meaning to ask you," I said as the heat lamps on the restaurant patio scalded our scalps and the sake warmed our stomachs. The question had been giving me insomnia for weeks. "What happened to you after Atlanta? We had plans and you broke them."

"You were rude on the phone," she said. "And I didn't think we had definite plans anyway." So it had been her version of cat-string theory, punishing me for bad behavior.

"I was being cocky funny. I wanted to see you."

"Whatever. You were rude. You were being too-cool-for-school and so laid-back and aloof about things that it was a turnoff. I thought, 'I can get anybody, and all of a sudden this guy is acting like Mr. Cool?'"

As we talked, I tried to figure out why I liked this girl so much, why after meeting so many people she had become my obsession. A cynical part of me said I was simply falling for the female equivalent of the tactics we use. The secret to making someone think they're in love with you is to occupy their thoughts, and that's what Lisa had done with me. She had blown me off and rebuffed me physically while stringing me along with just enough encouragement to keep me chasing her.

On the other hand, I wasn't a plower. If a woman I didn't care about had played this hard to get, I would have given up long ago. Of course, it was also possible that my obsession came from a misogynist, alpha-male streak I'd accidentally contracted as a side effect of sarging. Lisa was fiercely independent, someone I looked up to rather than down at. So perhaps the caveman in me just wanted to sleep with her and, thus, conquer her.

And then there was always the remote possibility that she had managed to touch a part of me that I kept hidden from everyone, even myself. It was a part of me that wanted to stop thinking, to stop searching, to stop worrying about what everyone thought of me and just let go and be comfortable and free and in the moment, the way I felt surfing that big wave in Malibu. And every now and then, when Lisa and I both dropped our defenses, I felt like that with her. I felt alone, together.

We drove back to my house. Lisa slipped into a white T-shirt and boxers, and we lay in bed as we had so many times before—under the covers, on separate pillows, heads turned toward each other, but no part of our bodies touching.

I wanted to continue our conversation from dinner. I wasn't trying to seduce her anymore. I just needed answers.

"So what made you drive up the hill the other day to see me again?"

"While you were gone, I realized how much I missed you." I loved watching her lips part over her front teeth when she talked. It made me think of salmon on rice. "My friends were making fun of me because I was counting down the days until you came home. I actually went grocery shopping while you were gone so I could cook you food. I don't know why." She hesitated and smiled, as if she were offering information she'd never planned to divulge. "I bought a fresh piece of swordfish and had to throw it away because it went bad."

A warm flush of confidence filled my chest. So I still had a chance with this girl.

"But it's too late," she said. "The window was open with me, and you blew it."

David DeAngelo would have said to go cocky funny here. Ross Jeffries would have said not to buy into her frame. Mystery would have said to punish her. But I had to ask: "How did I blow it?"

"First off, you didn't call me when you came home from Miami. I had to go to you."

"Hold on. I thought you were blowing me off. You never even called while I was away."

"Well, your voice mail said you were out of town and you weren't returning calls, so I didn't leave a message."

"Yeah, but I would have returned your call. I wanted to hear from you."

"Then you came to the Whiskey Bar and hardly talked. And the last straw was when we went to your house to go surfing. I told Sam I was starting to like you again and she said, 'Get over it. When I went up to his room to use the bathroom, I found a used condom on the floor.'"

My brain leaped up and slapped itself. I had been careless: I'd forgotten to throw away the condom I'd used with Isabel. So that's what Sam and she were whispering about in the car on the way to Malibu.

"So then why did you agree to go out with me tonight?"

"You asked me out on a proper date. And you were a little nervous, so I figured you must really be into me."

I propped myself up on the pillows. I was about to say the most AFC thing of my life. "Let me tell you something. The pickup artists have a word they call one-itis. It's a disease that people get when they become obsessed with just one girl. And they never end up with this girl because they get too nervous around her and scare her away."

"So?" she asked.

"So," I said. "You're my one-itis."

We were looking each other in the eyes now. I could see hers sparkle. I knew mine were sparkling. It was time to kiss her.

There were no lines, no routines, no evolution phase-shift—I'd tried them all unsuccessfully anyway. I leaned in. She leaned in. Her eyes closed. My eyes closed. Our lips met. It was just like I'd always thought a kiss was supposed to begin.

For hours, we lay there making out and dissecting the connections and misunderstandings of the past few weeks.

While Lisa slept in the morning, I crept downstairs with my phone book. I called Nadia and Hie and Susanna and Isabel and the Jessicas and every FB and MLTR and other acronym I was seeing and told them I had started spending time with someone I wanted to be faithful to.

"So you're choosing her over me?" Isabel asked angrily.

"It's not an intellectual choice."

"Is she better in bed or something?"

"I don't know. We've only kissed."

"So you made out with some girl," she said, with a weak attempt at a cruel laugh, "and you want to get rid of me now."

"It's not that I want to get rid of you. I'd still like to see you, but as a friend." I could hear the word pierce her heart like a dagger, as it had my own heart so many times before I'd joined the community.

"But I love you."

How could she love me? She needed to go fuck a dozen other guys to get over her one-itis.

"I'm sorry," I said. And I was.

There is a downside to casual sex: Sometimes it stops being casual. People develop a desire for something more. And when one person's expectations don't match the other person's, then whoever holds the highest expectations suffers. There is no such thing as cheap sex. It always comes with a price.

I had violated Ross Jeffries's only ethical rule of seduction: Leave her better than you found her.

Chapter

Steam rose from the water into the starless L.A. sky as Mystery and I sat opposite each other in the Jacuzzi. He draped one pale arm around the edge of the hot tub, and with the other took a birdlike sip from a glass that contained an orange liquid and ice cubes. It seemed like a cocktail, which was strange because Mystery never drank alcohol.

"I gave Papa my notice," he said. "I'm officially moving out next month."

He was abandoning me, just like he had during his breakdown in Toronto. Now I would be stuck living with the happy couple who had forced him out and the clone army being built in Papa's room.

"But you're letting your enemies win," I said, picking a cigarette butt out of the Jacuzzi and dropping it into an empty glass. "Just stay here and hold your ground. Katya wouldn't dare set foot in the house if you were here. Make a stand. Don't leave me alone with these guys."

"No. The anger and resentment I have is very great—great enough for me to move out so that I don't have to see them ever again."

He took another small swallow from his glass. "What's that you're drinking, by the way?" I asked.

"It's a screwdriver. I think I feel a little tipsy. You know, I've never been drunk before. I always avoided it because I didn't like my father. But now, with him gone, I figure it's okay to try it."

"Well, dude, now is a bad time to start. You're unstable enough as it is. You don't need to add alcohol to the mix."

"I enjoy it."

As usual, I was wasting my breath.

He took another sip, with a flourish this time, as if he were doing something glamorous and cool. "So Isabel stopped by here looking for you last night," he said.

"That's annoying. I tried to be clear with her about Lisa."

He leaned forward, stirring the foam in the water with the bottom of his glass. "You haven't even had sex with Lisa yet. So why not just have Isabel on the side? It's a shame to lose a body like that."

"No way, dude. I want to do this right. I don't want to lie in bed next to Lisa, feeling guilty for something I can't tell her about. It will break the trust we have."

I leaned over the edge of the Jacuzzi and dipped my hand into the pool. It was just as warm as the hot tub. Someone had left the heat on again. Our gas bill was going to be astronomical.

"Do you know the story of the frog and the scorpion?" Mystery asked.

"No, but I love analogies." I jumped into the pool and treaded water as Mystery leaned over the edge of the hot tub and recited the story.

"One day, a scorpion stood on the side of a stream and asked a frog to carry it to the other side. 'How do I know you won't sting me?' the frog asked. 'Because if I sting you, I'll drown,' the scorpion said.

"The frog thought about it and realized that the scorpion was right. So he put the scorpion on his back and started ferrying him. But midway across the stream, the scorpion plunged its stinger into the frog's back. As they both began to drown, the frog gasped, 'Why?'"

"The scorpion replied, 'Because it is my nature.'"

Mystery took a triumphant sip of his screwdriver, then fixed his gaze on me as I floated in the pool beneath him. He spoke slowly and deliberately, like the Mystery who'd first told me to snap and shed the boring skin of Neil Strauss. "It is your nature," he continued. "You are a pickup artist now. You are Style. You've bitten from the apple of knowledge. You cannot go back to the way you were before."

"Well, dude." I took a couple strokes backward. "That's very cynical talk from a guy who's talking about marrying and having children with a girl he just met."

"We're polyamorous," he said. "As a result, we have to cheat on our girl-friends. And if that threatens our relationships, so be it." He emptied his drink and held his temples, as if fighting off a dizzy spell. "Never underestimate the power of denial."

"No." I couldn't look at him. I wasn't going to let him ruin this. "I don't need any more advice."

I climbed out of the pool, threw a towel over my shoulders, and walked into the living room. Xaneus, Playboy, and Tyler Durden were sitting there. As soon as I entered, they walked up to Papa's room without even acknowledging my presence. It was odd behavior, but nothing unexpected after living in Project Hollywood this long.

I went up to my room, showered, and paged through a copy of the medieval legend *Parsifal* I had recently bought. People often read books to search for themselves and find someone who agrees with them. And, right now, the nature of *Parsifal* agreed with me a lot more than the nature of the scorpion.

As I interpreted the legend, it's the story of a sheltered mother's boy who meets some knights and decides he wants to be just like them. So he goes off into the world, has a series of adventures, and progresses from legendary fool to legendary knight.

The country, at the time, has become a wasteland because the grail king (who guards the holy grail) has been wounded. And it just so happens that Parsifal is led to the grail castle, where he sees the king in terrible pain. As a compassionate human being, he wants to ask, "What is wrong?" And, according to legend, if someone pure of heart asks that question of the king, he will be healed and the blight on the land will be lifted.

However, Parsifal does not know this. And as a knight he has been trained to observe a strict code of conduct, which includes the rule of never asking questions or speaking unless he is addressed first. So he goes to bed without talking to the king. In the morning, he wakes to discover that the grail castle has disappeared. He has blown his chance to save king and country by obeying his training instead of his heart. Unlike the scorpion, Parsifal had a choice. He just made the wrong one.

When I walked through the living room to get a drink from the kitchen, I saw Mystery nursing another cocktail in front of the TV. He was watching a video of *The Karate Kid* and crying. "I never had a Mr. Miyagi," he sobbed, wiping tears off his reddened cheeks. He was drunk. "My dad didn't teach me anything. All I wanted was a Mr. Miyagi."

I suppose we were all searching for someone to teach us the moves we needed to win at life, the knightly code of conduct, the ways of the alphamale. That's why we found each other. But a sequence of maneuvers and a system of behavior would never fix what was broken inside. Nothing would fix what was broken inside. All we could do was embrace the damage.

Chapter

Lisa and I spent the next day together, and the day after that, and the day after that. I kept worrying that I was going to ruin it, that we were spending too much time with each other, that she was going to get tired of me. Rick H. had always said, "Give her the gift of missing you." But we couldn't seem to part.

"You are so perfect for me," she said as we lay in my bed for the fourth night in a row. "I've never had sex with a guy I liked this much before. I'm afraid I'll get attached."

Beneath that tough exterior, she was scared. All her push-pull wasn't a pre-planned psychological tactic; it was her heart warring with her head. Perhaps the reason she'd been so reluctant to open up was that she was protecting something fragile inside. Like me, she was afraid to actually feel something for somebody else—to love, to be vulnerable, to give someone else control over her happiness and well-being.

When I slept with all those other girls, I just had sex with them once a night—and, if I liked them enough, a second time in the morning. But something amazing happened with Lisa when we had sex for the first time. After I had an orgasm, it didn't go down. It remained, as the old Extramask would say, rock-hard and luscious.

I did it with her a second time.

"Feel it," I said afterward. It was still ready to go.

We did it a third and a fourth time that night, and it never went soft. I couldn't understand it. My dick, which I had thought was a completely mindless animal desperate to stick itself in any hole, actually responded to emotion. It had feelings too. And it wasn't just built-up anticipation. It stayed up through three or four orgasms every time Lisa and I made love. We fucked in cars, in alleys, in restaurant bathrooms, and in the vending-machine room in a hotel hallway, where a maintenance man caught us and tried to extort twenty dollars from me.

When I'd gone impotent in the bathroom with the porn star, perhaps it didn't have anything to do with the whiskey. My body was responding to the lack of emotional foreplay: I neither cared about nor really desired her. And I'm sure she felt the same. It was just entertainment. Sex with Lisa was not entertainment. It was not about validation and ego-gratification, as with all those pickups I'd been so proud of. It was about creating a vacuum where nothing else existed except the two of us and our passion. It made the rest of existence seem like a distraction.

And then, one afternoon, just when I'd forgotten all about her, Courtney returned. She pulled up to the house in a limo and leaped out, looking radiant in a blue dress and white shawl.

"There's blood flow to my pussy again!" was the first thing she exclaimed.

"Did you land that director you were chasing?" I asked.

"No. I got a new man in New York. And it's going to be his fault for making me a slut, because now I want it all the time."

She danced toward me, light like a ballerina.

"Well," I said. "We had a bet about your director crush."

"That's right. I guess I lost."

"So that means I get to choose the middle name of your next child."

She smiled and stared at me expectantly, as if I were supposed to just select one on the spot.

I shuffled through a list of possible names in my head. "How about Style?" I finally decided. "I'm going to be retiring the name anyway, so I might as well pass it on." I thought about the idea for a moment. It was really a stupid moniker. Then again, her daughter's middle name is Bean.

She squealed and gave me a bone-crushing hug. "You know, I've found you sexually intriguing these last few months," she said.

I swallowed and prepared to tell her about Lisa. Before I opened my mouth, however, she continued. "But I heard all about you and Lisa. I think that's great. So some good came out of having me in the house after all?"

"Yeah. For you too, I hope."

"I don't even want to think about what went on in that house."

"Well, you look great. Getting laid has done wonders for your complexion."

"Well, that and rehab."

She winked at me and smiled. Her prayers had been answered. She was normal again.

"I'm going to get out of your hair and live at the Argyle hotel until I get my daughter back, which should be very soon," she said. "I came by to give you the money I borrowed from Mystery."

She handed me a check and bounded back into the limo. As I watched her leave, she unrolled the window and yelled, "And this one won't bounce."

I was really going to miss her.

A few days later, Lisa and I went to the Scientology Celebrity Center. We hadn't become Scientologists; we liked our income too much. Tom Cruise had kept his word and sent me an invitation to their annual gala. It was one of the most star-filled events I'd been to in Los Angeles.

After dinner, Cruise, clean-shaven in a perfectly pressed black tuxedo, walked toward the table. His approach was hypnotic: There was no doubt in his walk, no effort in his smile, no intricacy in his intentions. I stood to shake his hand, and he clapped my shoulder forcefully. I kept my balance. Barely.

"Is that your girlfriend?" he asked, looking Lisa up and down in a non-lecherous way. I couldn't imagine him ever being lecherous. "You didn't tell me how gorgeous she was."

"Thanks. I can't remember ever feeling this fulfilled by someone."

"So you got tired of picking up women?"

"Yeah, after a while it started to feel like filling a bucket with a hole in it."

"Exactly," he exclaimed. "Cameron Crowe and I, when we were doing *Vanilla Sky,* would talk about what a one-night stand is and what a fuck buddy is. And when you kind of get down to it, those things are a false intimacy. And they're unsatisfying. In a real relationship, sex means more. You just want to keep going, and you want to hang out all the time and talk about life. It's very cool."

"Yes, but the problem is that I don't want this to be the end of my journey in this subculture. It just reaffirms society's message of monogamy and true love conquers everything and all those Hollywood happy endings. It seems so cheesy."

"Who says it's cheesy?" Cruise asked, his eyes narrowing and his hands reaching out to attack me with a friendly gesture. "You know what? I got past that. Since when is it cheesy to be in love?"

He had AMOGed me again.

Ghosts.

We were just phantoms, drifting invisibly through a putrefying house that hadn't seen a maid or repairman in months.

Mystery wasn't talking to Herbal. Herbal wasn't talking to Mystery. Papa hardly spoke to anyone. And for some reason Sickboy, Playboy, Xaneus, and all the other Real Social Dynamics worker bees had stopped interacting with Mystery and me. Even the junior PUAs who hung out in the house—Dreamweaver, Maverick, and other former students—didn't say hello when I passed by. If I tried to engage them in conversation, they were curt. They wouldn't even look me in the eye.

The only person who spoke to everyone was Tyler Durden. But interacting with him was never a conversation; it was an interrogation, like someone might have with an actor who wanted to play him in a movie.

"I really want to ask you something," he said one afternoon as he emerged from the kitchen with Sickboy. I'd always liked Sickboy. Despite the name, he was a well-raised, mild-mannered New Yorker.

"What do you have that enables you to get Lisa?" Tyler Durden asked. "Because I go out every night and work so hard on myself, and I know that I couldn't get her as a girlfriend."

What was amazing about Lisa was that despite her toughness, she was one of the most generous women I'd ever been with. She'd make my bed every morning; she'd cook meals and bring them up to my room when I was working; and she rarely came over without a small gift—a tube of Origins face cleanser, a bottle of John Varvatos cologne, a copy of *Henry IV, Part I* I'd been looking for. Perhaps I had found my Caresse.

"I guess I have life experience," I told him. "All you do is sarge every night. You're only working on one aspect of yourself. It's like going to the gym every day and just doing bicep curls."

His brows knitted, and his mind began turning rapidly. For a moment, he appeared to take the advice to heart. Then he rejected it, and his eyes began to blaze. If it wasn't hatred they contained, it was at least resentment.

He resented me because I still didn't see him as an equal, because he still wasn't cool in my eyes, because he couldn't pick apart the idea of coolness to a subset of behaviors he could model. Lisa dated me because, to her, I was cool. Tyler Durden would never be cool.

He chewed my ear off for ten minutes about how good he was in the field now, and how he didn't need routines anymore to get IOIs, and how celebrities always tried to get him to go to parties.

Finally, he turned to walk up to Papa's room. Sickboy remained behind, standing next to me. "Aren't you coming?" Tyler asked Sickboy, nodding his head upstairs as if something important were occurring there.

"I just want to say good-bye to Style," Sickboy said.

"You're leaving?" I asked. I was surprised Sickboy was even acknowledging my presence.

The door to Papa's room slammed lightly overhead. Sickboy looked up nervously.

"I'm out of this whole thing," he said.

"What whole thing?"

"This house is toxic." The words burst out of him, as if they'd been slowly forming inside like a blister. "There are so many cool things to do in L.A., and all anyone wants to do is sarge. I haven't even seen the Pacific Ocean the whole time I've been here. These guys are losers. I wouldn't introduce any of them to any of my friends back in New York."

"I know what you mean. Lisa can't stand them."

"It's a joke," he continued. He sighed the tension out of his shoulders, as if relieved he'd found someone normal, someone who understood, someone who wasn't entirely brainwashed. "They bring girls back to the house all the time, but the girls get creeped out and leave. Tyler Durden can hardly get anyone to return his calls. I don't think he's been laid in two months. Papa's had sex with probably one girl in the last year. Mystery can't hold onto a girlfriend to save his life. And when Xaneus came here, he was a cool guy. But now he seems fake. All he talks about is sarging. You're the only guy I want to model. You have a great lifestyle, a good job, and a cool girlfriend."

Flattery will get you everywhere. "I'll tell you what. I'm going to give Lisa a surfing lesson tomorrow. Why don't you join us? It'll be good for you to get out of the house and see the ocean."

MSN GROUP: Mystery's Lounge
SUBJECT: Field Report—Life at Project Hollywood
AUTHOR: Sickboy

For those who don't know, I've been sleeping in Papa's closet at Project Holly-wood. Today was the best day I've ever had here, despite all the crazy drama that has been going on.

I woke up earlier than usual and went surfing in Malibu with Style and his girlfriend, who is really an amazing person. Seeing how cool they get along is really inspiring. He's one of the few people I've met in the game who has something great to show for all the effort he's put into it.

The surfing was amazing. I was so happy to go because I haven't gone yet this summer. I recommend taking up the sport to anyone who's never tried it. As soon as you hit the water, your mind clears and it's almost impossible to think of anything else. It's truly a relaxing experience.

Afterward, we ate at a fish stand right at the edge of the Pacific Ocean and had a great conversation about music, friends, traveling, life, and careers.

When I returned to the house, I did some work. Then I watched *The Last Dragon* with Playboy, whom I've become good friends with. During the movie, Herbal and Mystery talked outside and settled their differences. Though Mystery's still upset at Katya, he said he wouldn't hold it against Herbal for falling in love with her. And Herbal said that if Mystery paid for the damages to his room, he'd forgive Mystery for his behavior. Thank God. It's good to see this thing ended in a sane way. Mystery will be moving out of the house tomorrow anyway, which I think is a shame.

At about 2:00 A.M., Playboy, Mystery, and I sat in the main room smoking a hookah, listening to music, and talking about our goals in life.

I didn't have a single conversation today about sarging, pickup, or the community. My day was filled with real conversations with real friends. I didn't need to fuck some L.A. bimbo from the Saddle Ranch for validation. In fact, I didn't do a single set all day.

These are the days that make life worth living. These are also the days that I will miss when I move out of Project Hollywood.

—Sickboy

I sat uselessly in the living room and watched Mystery pack the last of his possessions: the platform boots, the ridiculous peacocking hats, the pin-striped suits he no longer wore, the lunch box with his picture emblazoned on the front, the hard drives filled with lesbian porn and episodes of *That '70s Show*.

I couldn't help feeling that maybe we'd made the wrong decision.

"So where are you going?" I asked.

"I'm moving to Las Vegas. I'm going to start Project Vegas. I've learned from my mistakes here, and Project Vegas will be bigger and better. There are hotter women in Vegas, and great opportunities for doing casino magic. I'm going to fly my brother-in-law to Vegas to record his songs, with me singing. Imagine"—he ran his hand along the air as if reading a line of type—"the world's greatest pickup artist releases an album of love songs. Who wouldn't buy that?" Mystery's manic sense of possibility was back. "Ania will be living with me there. And, since you're my best friend, once I get it set up, I'd like you to join me. We'll build it right this time. We will be in charge, and we'll carefully screen everyone we move into the house."

"I'm sorry, man." I couldn't just follow him around every time he fucked things up for himself.

"It'll be Mystery and Style, just like the old days," he persisted. He opened the front door of the house and carried a suitcase onto the landing as he delivered one of the many great aphorisms that he used to turn defeat into triumph. "Where there's a problem, there's an opportunity."

"I can't go through this again." The words, apologetic, came out accusatory.

"I understand," he said. "Sometimes events turn sour, and we follow bad threads in our lives. I want you to know that, even though we haven't seen eye to eye lately, I will always be your friend, for life and a day. You don't have to manage your relationship with me. Enjoy your girlfriend, and we will always have time to hang out together. You are the most important man in my life."

My face swelled and my eyes tingled with the first flush of tears.

"Try not to queer that up, okay?" he smiled weakly, choking back emotion himself.

A cab pulled into the driveway and honked, and Mystery slammed the door shut on Project Hollywood. The blank whiteness of the door wavered in the mist of my eyes. I felt like I was losing a piece of myself. For a moment, I couldn't figure out which of us was the bigger fool.

Within a week, Katya had moved into Herbal's room and Papa had moved two PUAs into Mystery's old room. One of them was Dreamweaver, a former student of mine; the other one I'd never met before. Papa planned to move a third PUA into Mystery's closet. With the influx of new, younger residents, Project Hollywood looked more like a frat house every day, though most frat houses were cleaner.

Without Mystery sitting in the living room, ready and willing to share the details of his latest drama with whoever passed by, the lack of communication in the house became even more uncomfortable. Whenever I walked through the living room, I'd find new roommates lying on their bellies on the carpet, playing video games. They never looked up or said a word, even when I greeted them. They weren't PUAs; they were vegetables. If someone had told me two years ago that this was the lifestyle I had to look forward to, I would never have joined the community. I would have realized that those who live by the joystick are doomed to die by the joystick.

At Papa's twenty-fourth birthday party, not a single woman showed up—let alone Paris Hilton, who, needless to say, had never come to party at Project Hollywood as Papa had hoped. His only friends were PUAs. And, for some reason, they all ignored me. I couldn't understand it.

In the week that followed, Tyler Durden, who'd never been directly hostile to me, started writing posts attacking me online. I decided it was time to have a talk with him about everyone's strange behavior in the house. I navigated through the overflowing trash bags in the kitchen; walked through the backyard, where just a small puddle of sludge lay at the bottom of the hot tub; and knocked on Papa's back door.

I found Tyler Durden sitting at a computer, posting on the seduction boards.

"I want to talk to you about what's been going on lately," I said. "Everyone in the house is acting weird—even weirder than usual. And you seem to have a chip on your shoulder. Are people pissed because I've been hanging out with Lisa too much and not going out sarging?"

"That's part of it," he said. "But a bigger part of it is that no one in this house likes you. Everybody thinks that you're a snob and that you're responsible for a lot of trouble in this house, because you talk about people behind their backs." Though these were strong words coming from Tyler Durden, who had never said a cross word to my face before, his voice wasn't venomous. He spoke almost obsequiously, as if he were trying to give me constructive advice from one PUA to another. "I'm just saying this because I'm your friend, and I don't want to see what happened to Mystery happen to you."

I didn't know how to respond because I was so taken aback. I had no idea the other guys in the house felt that way.

"Yeah," he went on. "Did you notice how Extramask used to be your friend, but then he started avoiding you? Well, that's because he didn't trust you. Dreamweaver told me he hates your guts. Maverick hates you too."

I thought about what he was saying. Maybe he was right. The enthusiasm I had brought to my first encounters with fellow sargers had dissipated as I saw routines sold instead of shared and perfectly normal men turn into creepy social parasites. So, though I was always friendly to everyone, maybe they were picking up on the fact that I was growing disillusioned with the community.

On the other hand, as Juggler had always pointed out, people tended to feel comfortable around me. I'd always been friendly and easy to get along with, even before I'd joined the community. I had no enemies, or so I thought.

When I left the room after another hour of talk, my head was spinning. I couldn't understand why these guys, who I'd spent the better part of two years getting to know, hated my guts. What had I done?

The answer, I soon found out, was nothing.

When I saw Playboy in the living room packing his books into boxes, I asked the usual: "What's going on?"

"I'm moving out."

First Extramask, then Mystery, then Sickboy, and now Playboy. I was on a sinking ship.

"Do you have a few minutes?" he asked. "I want to get something off my chest before I leave."

Playboy brought me into his room and shut the door.

"They're trying to freeze you out," he said.

"Who's trying to freeze me out?"

"Papa and Tyler Durden. They're using tactics on you."

"What are you talking about? What do you mean by tactics?"

"Wow, you really have no idea what's been going on up in Papa's room. Tyler Durden is telling everyone to ignore you. He wants you to think that everyone hates you. He's trying to make you uncomfortable in the house."

"Why would he want to do that?"

"He wants to take over. And he can't have you here because you threaten him."

This explained the head games Tyler Durden was playing the other day, the reason he was trying to make me think everyone was against me. He was attempting to drive me out. He was running game on me.

"He sees you as a threat to his power because he can't suck you in. You're not weak like Xaneus," Playboy continued. "He sees you as a threat to his finances because you want him to pay rent. And he sees you as a threat to his women because you made out with that girl he picked up in Vegas. He thinks that if he lets his girls get near you, they're going to lose attraction for him."

"He's still upset about that?"

"Yeah. But I think the main problem is that Tyler and Papa associate you with Mystery, and he's their competition. They have a gang mentality. They think in terms of alliances. So they pushed Mystery out, and now they're pushing you out. They want to make the whole house an office and dormitory for Real Social Dynamics."

"I don't understand. How could they have pushed Mystery out? He dug his own grave."

"But don't you see how they helped it along? How Papa invited Katya to sleep at the house and then brought her back after Mystery kicked her out? They were baiting him." Each sentence Playboy spoke was like a strip of gauze being removed from my eyes. "Everything Papa said in his room during the house meeting, he was instructed to say by Tyler Durden. He's a follower. And I made a mistake by going along with it too. If I could do it all over again, I'd vote for Mystery to stay. This house was his project. Even if his behavior was out of line, he had a right not to want his ex-girlfriend here."

I had played right into their hands. They were such masters of social manipulation that they had set up the meeting so I thought I was in charge. Papa even kept calling me the house leader. And thus, they'd managed to make it my decision to kick Mystery out. So much for the whole win-win idea.

"They played me like a puppet," I said, shaking my head in disbelief.

"They played me, too. That's a large part of the reason I'm leaving. Tyler Durden can get those guys to do whatever he wants. He's not motivated by girls. He's motivated by acquisition and power."

How could I have been so blind? In Las Vegas, I had even told Tyler Durden point blank that he was the kind of person who liked to rise to the top of a situation by eliminating his competitors. And he had agreed.

"All they do up in Papa's room is hang out in the bathroom and plot," Playboy elaborated. "Every word that comes out of Tyler Durden's mouth is calculated. Every post he writes is to serve an agenda. That guy's mind is all gears, turning and manipulating. He sees everything in life as a set. They even talk about 'guy sets' up in Papa's room now. They have routines worked out to make students give their workshops better reviews and routines to control guys in the house. Every time someone new comes up to their room, they inoculate him against you."

We had created a dangerous precedent by studying how to control social situations in clubs. It had led to a mindset that everything in life was a game that could be manipulated to a player's advantage with the right routines.

But there was one thing I still didn't understand. "If what you're saying is true," I asked Playboy, "why was Papa avoiding me and Mystery before there was even a plan to freeze us out of the house?"

"That came from Tyler Durden too," Playboy said. "He didn't want Papa representing Mystery's business as well as his, so he turned Papa against Mystery as soon as you guys moved in. Then, once Mystery and Papa started bickering, he told Papa to avoid you guys completely and use the back door to enter the house."

So many connections were firing in my head as Playboy spoke. All the weirdness that had been taking place in the house since day one had been orchestrated by a little man in the closet, the wizard of Project Hollywood. I felt like such a chump.

"The biggest mistake you and Mystery made," Playboy concluded, "was having Papa move into this house."

There was a lesson here, perhaps the last one this community would teach me. And that was always to follow my instincts and first impressions. I hadn't trusted either Papa or Tyler Durden when I'd first met them. I found Papa spoiled and robotic, and Tyler Durden soulless and manipulative. And though they'd made great leaps forward when it came to fashion and game, Mystery was right: The scorpion can't deny its nature.

Yet, at the same time, Mystery and I weren't entirely blameless. We had used Papa as a patsy to sign the lease and pay for the most expensive room. We had never attempted to befriend him or treat him as an equal.

When I was checking e-mail later on my computer in the office area of the house, I noticed a program called Family Key Logger. I would have ignored it if it weren't for the paranoia I'd developed as a result of my discussion with Playboy. So I Googled the name of the program. When I saw the results, anger swung through my body like a wrecking ball. Someone had installed software that was capturing every word typed on the keyboard and storing it in a text file. The computer was intended as a shared resource so that residents and guests could check the Internet. This meant that whoever had installed the program now had everyone's passwords, credit card numbers, and private e-mails.

Unbeknownst to me, there had been a war going on in the house from the moment we'd moved in.

Afterward, I called Sickboy in New York. I wanted a second opinion.

"Does that match your experience?" I asked after telling him everything Playboy had said.

"Totally. When Mystery was there, they did what they're doing to you now. Tyler Durden and Papa would say, 'Don't talk to Mystery; freeze him out.' Everything they do is a routine. The house meeting about Mystery was thought out for days. They'd constantly talk about how to get Mystery to move out so they could take control of Project Hollywood. The house is part of their business plan. I had to leave. I can't be around that shit."

In the days that followed, I talked to Maverick and Dreamweaver. They both told the same story: Mystery and I, supposedly the best players in the community, had been played. The worshippers were smashing their idols.

There was one pickup guru I still needed to meet. I didn't want advice from him on how to pick up girls; I wanted advice on how to stop.

Everyone in the community had mentioned his name. He was a sort of spiritual presence that hung over the pickup world, a mythological figure like Odysseus or Captain Kirk or an HB11. He was Eric Weber, the first modern PUA, the writer of the 1970 book that started it all, *How to Pick Up Girls,* and the subject of the movie with the same name.

I met him in a small post-production studio, where he was editing a film he had directed. He definitely wasn't peacocked; he looked like a middle-aged advertising executive, with gray hair, a starched shirt buttoned up too high, and featureless black pants. Only his eyes, which sparkled with energy, gave evidence that his youthful daring had not yet been extinguished.

Are you aware of the seduction community?
I am. But I look at it with the sense of being imitated. Part of what came along after my book was repellant to me. I don't believe in doing things that twist and turn a person. I was never interested in conquering women in a despotic way. I was interested in finding somebody to love. However, I didn't stay passionately interested in seduction. I felt like there were too many other things I wanted to do.

What made you get over it?
I lost interest after getting married, gaining more confidence in myself, and realizing that accumulating dozens of notches in my belt wouldn't cure my existential despair. What also helped was having two daughters who have occasionally accused me of being sexist, which I am mildly, I guess.

What was your existential despair?
I think the existential dilemma is: We're social animals, so we all wrestle with a sense of inadequacy. But when we realize that we're not as inadequate as we thought we were, and when we realize that everybody else also

thinks they're inadequate, then that ache goes away and the idea that we're not a person of value disappears to some extent.

And what about those people who don't get rid of their sense of inadequacy?
They become obsessed with sleeping with more and more women. And that's a problem.

    Then there are the kinds of guys who need to be in therapy sessions. I can't tell you how many people I've seen in bad clothes say, in a nasal voice, "Eric, I can't seem to pick up girls." I tell them, "You need new clothes, better posture, and a speech therapist." All these things are evidence of deep inner psychological wounds.

The phone rings. He answers it, speaks for a few minutes, then hangs up.

That was a girl I picked up thirty-eight and a half years ago—my wife. I was actually researching the book right around the time I met her and used a line on her. She walked past me in a bar and I said, "You're much too pretty to let get away." I thought this tough New York chick would be mad. But she said, "You think so." I couldn't get rid of her after that.

So how did you actually conceive of the book?
I had a friend who was a copy trainee with me at Benton and Bowles. One day we both looked through the window of the El Al office next door and noticed a girl working there. She was Mediterranean and gorgeous, like a Botticelli. The next day, he saw me and said that during his lunch break he'd followed her to a deli, where she got a sandwich, and then sat down in the park, talked with her, and made a date to have dinner that Friday.

    The next week, he came in and said that she was a virgin. He had to run out and find a tin of Vaseline because she was so tight. That's what gave me the idea of doing a book on picking up girls. I got interested in his brazenness and his ability to turn talking to strangers into a comfortable, everyday thing. I was very shy and unconfident growing up. I wrote about pickup because I couldn't do it, and I really, really wanted to be good at it.

Was there any precedent for it at the time?
In the mid-sixties, life was changing radically in America. Women had just started taking the pill; the Stones and the Beatles had hit; Bob Dylan was

becoming popular. A whole counterculture was taking shape. Life was very suddenly wildly erotic.

In the forties and fifties, if you grew up in your hometown, you met people at church socials or were introduced by an aunt. But in the sixties, all these people were moving out of their parents' homes into their own apartments in the city. They lived alone without the conventional means of meeting. So singles bars became popular. And people needed new tools to meet strangers.

What do you think is the difference between naturals and guys like us who need to learn analytically?
I think that naturals have the psychological power to do it. Toward the end of my singlehood, I found a boldness that was shocking. I developed the courage to tell a woman after a glass of wine, "I'd like to fuck you." There are some women looking for you to be bold and a leader. It took me a long time to learn that.

Something strange happened to Eric Weber when the conversation veered toward naturals and tales from the field. He came to life. The spark in his eyes brightened. For a half hour, we swapped stories and theories about the game. For all his talk of marriage and happily ever after, beneath the surface still seethed that awkward guy who was envious of his friends' success with women.

After we talked, he showed me a scene from the movie he was editing. It was about a pale, bald, unemployed middle-aged man shopping a terrible screenplay and sponging off his ex-wife, who was now married to a handsome, successful man.

"Is that screenwriter in the movie the way you really see yourself?" I asked as we walked out of the building together.

"That's the inner me," he admitted. "Inside I sometimes feel pathetic, awkward, and unloved."

"Even after all the confidence you acquired as a pickup artist, a husband, and a father?"

"Well," he said, opening the door to his car, "all you can do is put on an appearance of confidence sometimes. And after a while, others will start to believe it." He grabbed the door handle to pull it closed. "And then you die."

Slam.

At 2:00 A.M., Lisa burst into the house, making her nightly drunken entrance. She stomped up my stairs, shedding her purse and clothing on the way, and leaped onto my bed wearing nothing but a beer bottle.

"I'm attracted to you in every way," she blurted.

"Really?"

"Do you know what all the ways are?"

"Um, maybe."

"Do you want me to name them?"

"Sure."

"Emotionally, physically, and mentally."

"That's a lot of ways."

"I can elaborate."

"Okay. Let's start with the physical." That's probably the area where I still needed the most reassurance.

"I love your teeth, and your mouth especially." I listened for hesitation or doubt. There was none. "I love how broad your shoulders are and how narrow your hips are. I love the hair placement on your body. I love the color of your eyes, because they're the same as mine. I love the shape of your nose. I love the indents on the side of your head."

"Oh my God." I flipped on top of her and grabbed her shoulders. "No one has ever complimented me on my head indentations before. I love them too."

I laughed, a little too loudly, at the ridiculousness of what I'd just said. And then I confessed everything to her. I told her about the last two years of meeting players and learning about the game. I told her about the AFCs and PUAs, the FBs and MLTRs, the IOIs and AMOGs.

"I would love to have you dress super-hot one day," I said, caught up in the excitement of the game I had helped invent, "and then go to a bar. And I'll practice AMOGing all the guys who try to hit on you."

She rolled me off her, so that we were facing each other on our sides, our faces an inch apart. "You don't need to take their advice," she said, her breath intoxicating and intoxicated. "Everything I like about you, and everything that makes me think you're rad, is all the stuff you already had before you met those PUA guys. I don't want you wearing dumbass jewelry and Pee-wee Herman shoes. I would have liked you before all that self-improvement shit."

From outside, we heard the sounds of men climbing the hill, flush with the excitement of another night out almost getting laid. "All the things you learned from the PUAs almost made us not come together," Lisa continued. "I want you to just be Neil: balding, nerdy, glasses, and all."

Maybe she was right. Perhaps she would have liked the real me. But she never would have had the opportunity to meet him if I hadn't spent the last two years learning how to put my best foot forward. Without all that training, I never would have had the confidence to talk to and handle a girl like Lisa, who was a constant challenge.

I needed Mystery, Ross Jeffries, David DeAngelo, David X, Juggler, Steve P., Rasputin, and all those other pseudonyms. I needed them to discover what was me to begin with. And now that I had found that person, brought him out of his shell, and learned to accept him, perhaps I had outgrown them.

Lisa sat up and took a sip from the bottle of beer she had brought upstairs. "Everyone was hitting on me tonight," she giggled. Modesty was never her strong suit. "I hope you realize that you are dating the most fabulous girl in L.A."

In response, I wordlessly pulled open my bottom dresser drawer, grabbed two large manila envelopes from inside, and brought them to the bed. I turned the first envelope upside down and dumped its contents onto the comforter. Hundreds of paper scraps, matchbooks, business cards, cocktail napkins, and torn receipts spilled out. Each one contained the handwriting of a different girl. Then I emptied the second envelope onto the bed—full of more of the same—until there was a small mountain of paper scraps. They were all phone numbers I'd collected since taking that first fateful workshop with Mystery.

"I know you are," I finally answered her. "I've spent two years meeting every girl in L.A. And out of them all, I chose you."

It was the most beautiful thing I'd said in a long time. And, after I spoke it, I realized it wasn't entirely accurate. If there was anything I'd learned, it's that the man never chooses the woman. All he can do is give her an opportunity to choose him.

Herbal was the next to go.

I saw him from my bedroom window, stuffing his robot vacuum cleaner into a U-Haul van.

"I'm going back to Austin," he said with a wan smile when I ran out to talk to him.

He was the last person I expected to abandon the house. "Why? After all you went through with Mystery, you're going to leave?"

"I just feel like the house has been a failure," he said. "No one hangs out anymore. The RSD guys stopped talking to me when I started working for Mystery, and Papa keeps moving in guys I don't really like."

"What's Katya doing?"

"She's moving to Austin with me." I suppose if Katya were using him solely for revenge, she would have dumped him by now.

"Um, by the way, what should I do when your wallaby arrives?"

"I've already arranged to have it sent to Austin."

Watching Herbal pack his possessions into the moving truck, I was struck by a much more profound sadness than when Mystery had left. With Mystery, I had lost a friend and former mentor. But I had thought that perhaps without the drama, the house could unite. However, between Tyler Durden's plotting and Herbal's imminent departure, Project Hollywood was truly dead.

Outside of Papa and Tyler Durden, everyone seemed to be waking up from the spell the community had cast on them. Even Prizer—the sarger who had lost his virginity in Juarez—had stopped selling his pickup DVD course and become a born-again Christian. In his last post, he warned, "Snap out of your trance and stop handing your salary over to a bunch of losers who are only able to seduce gullible guys. There's more to life than sarging."

If the stupidest sarger of us all had outgrown the community, what was I still doing here?

Behind Herbal and me, a beer bottle shattered on the street, scattering fragments of green glass everywhere. I looked up and saw a teenager with a dyed-blond Eminem crewcut and a white tanktop sitting on our steps.

"Who's that?"

"I don't know," Herbal said. "He's been staying up in Papa's room."

I was alone here now. It was just me in my bedroom against the borg in the rest of the house trying to force me out. I was tired of fighting. I was tired of being disappointed in people. I didn't need to be here anymore. Besides, I had a girlfriend.

Still, I couldn't help thinking, "If I was so smart, how did Papa end up with the house?"

Lisa answered that question as we lay in bed together that night.

"Because you didn't want the house," she said. "It's not a life. It's a subculture you dipped into. How could something be good that's based on a false reality and a learned behavior? Walk away. These guys aren't helping you anymore. They're holding you back."

Watching *The Wizard of Oz* as a child, I was always disappointed when Glinda the Good Witch told Dorothy that she'd possessed the power to return home since the moment she had arrived in Oz. Now, twenty years later, I understood the message. I had possessed the power to leave the community all along, but I hadn't reached the end of the road until now. I still believed that these guys had something I didn't. Yet the reason all the gurus latched on to me—the reason Tyler Durden wanted to be me, even though he hated me—was that they thought I had something they lacked.

We were all searching outside ourselves for our missing pieces, and we were all looking in the wrong direction. Instead of finding ourselves, we'd lost our sense of self. Mystery didn't have the answers. A blonde 10 in a two-set at the Standard didn't have the answers. The answers were to be found within.

To win the game was to leave it.

Even Extramask had discovered that. After staying at a Vipassana meditation center in Australia and an ashram in India, he was coming home to, as he put it in an e-mail to me, "the way things were before."

In the morning, I was awakened by noises downstairs. Three new recruits for Real Social Dynamics—replacements for Playboy, Sickboy, and Extramask—were hauling boxes from Ikea into Herbal's room. Like those who came before them, they were former students turned interns and employees, working for free in exchange for pickup lessons and a closet to sleep in. They had quit their jobs; they had dropped out of school; they had left their hometowns for this.

I sat in the living room in my boxer shorts and watched them as they worked. They were diligent. They were efficient. They were automatons. Wordlessly, they set up three bunk beds with matching sheets, blankets, and mattresses. Herbal's room was being converted into a barracks to house this growing army. The troops would be sent to the Sunset Strip nightly to do battle—armed with my clothes, my stories, my mannerisms—while the generals in the bathroom plotted the last stages of their conquest of the community. Even Mystery's Lounge would soon be theirs, with Mystery himself purged.

There was nothing here for me now.

I returned to my room, pulled several duffel bags off my closet shelf, and started packing. Hanging over me were rows of peacocking garments: a fuzzy purple vest, a pair of tight black vinyl pants, a pink cowboy hat. Stacked on the floor were dozens of books on flirting, NLP, Tantric massage, female sexual fantasies, handwriting analysis, and how to be the jerk women love. I wouldn't need any of those where I was going.

It was time to leave the house, and the community, behind. Real life beckoned.

GLOSSARY

Below is a list of pickup terms and acronyms used or referred to in this book. Some are words coined by the community; others come from hypnosis and marketing jargon; and others are common words that have been appropriated by pickup artists. The definitions below pertain solely to each word's use in the context of seduction. Wherever possible, the person credited with coining the term has been cited.

AFC—*noun* [average frustrated chump]: a stereotypical nice guy who has no pickup skills or understanding of what attracts women; a man who tends to engage in supplicative and wimpy patterns of behavior around women he has not yet slept with. Origin: Ross Jeffries.

AMOG—1. *noun* [alpha male of the group or alpha male other guy]: a socially comfortable male who competes with a pickup artist for a woman or interferes with a pickup artist's game. Origin: Old_Dog. 2. *verb:* to remove a potential male competitor—through physical, verbal, or psychological tactics—from a group of women. *Also: outalpha.* Origin: Tyler Durden.

ANCHOR—1. *noun:* an external stimulus (a sight, sound, or touch) that triggers a specific emotional or behavioral response, such as a song that makes one happy because it's reminiscent of a positive life event. Anchors are used by pickup artists to associate themselves with a woman's feelings of attraction. 2. *verb:* the act of creating an association between an external stimulus and an emotional or behavioral response. Origin: Richard Bandler and John Grinder.

ASD—*noun* [anti-slut defense]: the maneuvers some women make to avoid taking responsibility for initiating or agreeing to sex; or in order to avoid appearing slutty to the man she is with, to her friends, to society, or to herself. This can occur before or after sex, or it can prevent sex from occurring. Origin: Yaritai.

BF—*noun* [boyfriend].

BF DESTROYER—*noun* [boyfriend destroyer]: a pattern, routine, or line a pickup artist uses with the intention of seducing a woman who has a boyfriend.

BITCH SHIELD—*noun:* a woman's defensive response to deter unknown men who approach her. Though her reaction to an opening line may be rude, this does not necessarily mean the woman herself is rude, or even impossible to engage in a conversation.

BLUR—*verb or adjective:* an occurrence in which a woman stops returning calls, although she was initially interested in the man phoning.

BUYING TEMPERATURE—*noun:* the degree to which a woman is ready to make intimate physical contact with a man. Unlike attraction, a high buying temperature generally appears and fades quickly. To maintain a woman's level of physical interest over a longer period of time, a pickup artist attempts to pump her buying temperature with fast-paced routines. Origin: Tyler Durden.

CALIBRATE—*verb:* to read the verbal and nonverbal responses of a person or group and accurately deduce what they are thinking or feeling at that moment. Origin: Richard Bandler and John Grinder.

CAVEMAN—*verb:* to directly and aggressively escalate physical contact, and progress toward sex, with a consenting woman; predicated on the idea that early human beings did not use intelligence and words but instinct and strength to mate. *Also: to go caveman.*

CHICK CRACK—*noun:* any spiritual or psychological subject that appeals to most women but does not interest most men, such as astrology, tarot cards, and personality tests. Origin: Tyler Durden.

COCKBLOCK—*noun and verb:* a person who interferes with or hinders a pickup artist's game, whether accidentally or on purpose. A cockblock can be a friend of the woman, a friend of the pickup artist, or a complete stranger.

CRASH AND BURN—*verb:* to be directly, and often rudely, rejected or turned away by a woman or group one has just approached.

DAY TWO—*noun:* a first date. *Also: second meeting.*

DHV—*noun or verb* [demonstration of higher value]: a routine in which the pickup artist displays a skill or attribute that raises his worth or appeal in the estimation of a woman or group; it is intended to make him stand out from the other, less interesting men in the club. *Antonym: DLV [demonstration of lower value].*

DOGGY DINNER BOWL LOOK—*noun:* the entranced expression a woman gets in her eyes when she is attracted to a man who is talking to her. *Also: DDB.* Origin: Ross Jeffries.

ELICIT VALUES—*verb phrase:* to draw out, through conversation, what is important to a person, usually with the intention of reaching a deep inner desire that motivates them. In terms of seduction, eliciting values may help a man determine that a woman who says she is looking for a rich husband is actually just looking for a feeling of safety and security. *Also: EV.* Origin: Richard Bandler and John Grinder.

FALSE TAKEAWAY—*see takeaway.*

FALSE TIME CONSTRAINT—*see time constraint.*

FB—*noun* [fuck buddy]: a woman with whom a man engages in casual, consensual sex without an emotional attachment or relationship expectations.

FIELD—*noun:* any public place where a pickup artist can meet women.

FIELD REPORT—*noun:* a written account of a pickup or a night out picking up women, usually posted online. *Also: FR.* Other types of reports include an OR (outing report), LR (lay report), FU (fuckup report), and TR (threesome report).

FIELD TEST—*verb:* to experiment with and perfect a pickup tactic or routine on a number of women in different social situations before sharing it with other pickup artists.

FLAKE—*verb:* an occurrence in which a woman cancels or does not show up to a planned meeting.

FLUFF—*verb:* to make mundane small talk, typically between two people who have just met; common subjects include where one lives, what one does for work, and general interests and hobbies.

FMAC—*noun* [find, meet, attract, close]: a rudimentary, sequential model of pickup. Origin: Mystery.

FRAME—*noun:* the context within which a person, thing, event, or environment is perceived. Origin: Richard Bandler and John Grinder.

FREEZE OUT—*verb or noun:* to ignore a woman to make her seek validation; usually used as a technique to counter last-minute resistance.

FULL-CLOSE—1. *verb:* to have sexual intercourse. 2. *noun:* sexual intercourse. *Also: fuck close, f-close,* or *!close.* Origin: Mystery.

GROUP THEORY—*noun:* the idea that women are usually accompanied by friends, and to meet her a man must simultaneously win the approval of her friends while actively demonstrating a lack of interest in her. Origin: Mystery.

HB—*noun* [hot babe]: a term used by members of the seduction community to refer to attractive women. When discussing a specific woman, it is often followed by either a numerical ranking of her beauty—such as HB10—or by a nickname, such as HBRedhead. Origin: Aardvark.

HIRED GUNS—*noun:* female employees in the service industry who are generally recruited for their attractiveness, such as bartenders, waitresses, shot girls, and strippers. Origin: Mystery.

HOOK POINT—*noun:* the moment in a pickup when a woman (or a group) decides that she enjoys the company of a man who has recently approached her and doesn't want him to leave. Origin: Style.

INSTANT DATE—*noun:* the act of taking a woman one has just met from one venue to another in the same day, typically from a bustling environment to one more conducive to getting to know each other, such as from a bar to a diner or from the street to a café. Origin: Mystery.

IOI—*noun* [indicator of interest]: a sign a woman gives a man that indirectly reveals she is attracted to or interested in him. These clues, generally unintentional and subtle, include leaning toward a man when he speaks, asking mundane questions to keep a conversation going, or squeezing his hand when he takes her hand in his. *Antonym: IOD [Indicator of Disinterest].* Origin: Mystery.

IVD—*noun* [interactive value demonstration]: a short routine intended to hook the attention and interest of a woman one has just met by teaching her something about herself. Origin: Style.

KINO—*verb* [from kinesthesia, *noun*]: to touch or be touched, generally with suggestive intent or the purpose of arousal, such as hair-stroking, hand-holding, or hip-grabbing; precedes actual sexual contact. Origin: Ross Jeffries.

KISS-CLOSE—1. *verb:* to kiss or make out, with passion. 2. *noun:* a passionate kiss or makeout. *Also: k-close or *close.* Origin: Mystery.

LJBF—*verb* or *adjective* [let's just be friends]: a statement a woman makes to a man to indicate that she is not sexually or romantically interested in him. One can hear an LJBF speech or get LJBF'ed.

LMR—*noun* [last minute resistance]: an occurrence, often after kissing, in which a woman who desires a man prevents him, through words or actions, from progressing toward more intimate sexual contact, such as removing her bra, putting his hand down her pants, or penetration.

LSE—*adjective* [low self-esteem]: used to describe a woman who is insecure and tends to engage in self-effacing or self-destructive behavior. Origin: MrSex4uNYC.

LTR—*noun* [long-term relationship]: a girlfriend.

MANAGE EXPECTATIONS—*verb:* to let a woman know before sleeping with her roughly how committed a relationship one intends to have with her, so that she does not expect too much or too little.

MLTR—*noun* [multiple long-term relationship]: a woman who is part of a harem, or one of many girlfriends a pickup artist is currently seeing and sleeping with. Ideally, the pickup artist is honest with his MLTRs and informs them that he is seeing other women. Origin: Svengali.

MM—*noun* [Mystery Method]: a school of seduction started by Mystery that focuses on indirect group approaches. Origin: Mystery.

MODEL—*verb:* to observe and imitate the behavior of another person, typically someone who possesses a trait or skill one wishes to acquire. Origin: Richard Bandler and John Grinder.

MPB—*noun* [male pattern blindness]: some men's inability to recognize that a woman is attracted to and interested in him until after she leaves and it's too late to act on it. Origin: Vincent.

MPUA—*noun* [master pickup artist]: a player who excels at the game, and whose skills put him in the top 1 percent of the seduction community.

MYSTERY'S LOUNGE—*noun:* a private, members-only online forum where many of the leading pickup artists in the community exchange techniques, photographs, and field reports. Origin: Mystery.

NEG—*noun:* an ambiguous statement or seemingly accidental insult delivered to a beautiful woman a pickup artist has just met, with the intent of actively demonstrating to her (or her friends) a lack of interest in her. For example:

"Those are nice nails; are they real?" 2. *Verb:* to actively demonstrate a lack of interest in a beautiful woman by making an ambiguous statement, insulting her in a way that appears accidental, or offering constructive criticism. *Also: neg hit.* Origin: Mystery.

NEWBIE MISSION—*noun:* an exercise designed to help shy men overcome their fear of approaching women. The newbie mission involves spending a day in a public area, such as a mall, and saying "hi" to every woman who passes by.

NLP—*noun* [neuro-linguistic programming]: a school of hypnosis developed in the 1970s based largely on the techniques of Milton Erickson. Unlike traditional hypnosis, in which subjects are put to sleep, it is a form of waking hypnosis in which subtle conversational cues and physical gestures are used to influence a person on a subconscious level. Origin: Richard Bandler and John Grinder.

NONVERSATION—*noun:* a conversation in which one person isn't paying attention to what the other person is saying, generally due to lack of interest or being distracted. Origin: Style.

NUMBER-CLOSE—1. *verb:* to obtain a correct phone number from a woman. Note that giving a woman one's own number does not constitute a number-close. 2. *noun:* a woman's phone number, obtained during the course of a pickup. *Also: #close.* Origin: Mystery.

OBSTACLE—*noun:* the person or people in a group whom the pickup artist does not desire, but whom he must win over in order to run game on the woman in the group he does desire. Origin: Mystery.

ONE-ITIS—*noun:* 1. an obsession with a girl whom one is not dating; pickup artists believe that such an extreme fixation on one woman significantly lowers a man's chances of dating or sleeping with her. 2. a girl with whom one is obsessed. Origin: John C. Ryan.

OPENER—*noun:* a statement, question, or story used to initiate a conversation with a stranger or group of strangers. Openers may be environmental (spontaneous) or canned (pre-scripted); and direct (showing romantic or sexual interest in a woman) or indirect (not showing interest).

OUTALPHA—*verb:* see AMOG.

PAIMAI—*noun* [pre-approach invitation, male approach invitation]: a nonverbal action or series of actions meant to induce a woman or group to notice a man and passively express interest in meeting him before he actually approaches her. Origin: Formhandle.

PATTERN—*noun:* a speech, usually scripted, that is based on a series of neuro-linguistic programming phrases designed to attract or arouse a woman.

PATTERN INTERRUPT—*noun:* an unexpected word, phrase, or action performed suddenly in order to halt a person's auto-pilot response before it's completed, such as cutting off a woman who's talking about her ex-boyfriend and quickly changing the subject. Origin: Richard Bandler and John Grinder.

PAWN—1. *verb:* to approach and talk to one group of people in order to meet a woman or group adjacent to it. 2. *noun:* a person one approaches in order to meet a nearby woman or group. A pawn can be an acquaintance or stranger. Origin: Mystery.

PEACOCK—*verb:* to dress in loud clothing or with flashy accoutrements in order to get attention from women. Peacocking items include bright shiny shirts, light-up jewelry, feather boas, colorful cowboy hats, or anything else that makes one stand out in a crowd. Origin: Mystery.

PHASE-SHIFT—*verb:* to make the transition, during a one-on-one conversation with a woman, from ordinary talk to slower, sexually-charged talk, touch, or body language; intended to precede an attempt to kiss. Origin: Mystery.

PIVOT—*noun:* a woman, usually a friend, used in social situations to help one meet other women. A pivot serves many functions: she provides social proof, she can create jealousy in the target, she can make it easier to open difficult sets, and she can brag about the pickup artist to his target. *Also: wingwoman.*

PROXIMITY ALERT SYSTEM—*noun:* the state of being aware of a woman or group of women who are standing awkwardly nearby in hopes of being talked to. Generally, the woman will have her back to the pickup artist, so as to make her presence there seem accidental. Origin: Mystery.

PUSH-PULL—*noun:* a technique used to create or increase attraction, in which a man gives a woman indications that he is not interested in her followed by indications that he is. This sequence can take place in a few seconds—such as taking a woman's hands and then dropping them as if you don't trust her yet—or over time, such as being very nice during one phone conversation but then very distant and abrupt during the next one. Origin: Style.

RAFC—*noun* [reformed average frustrated chump]: a seduction student who has not yet become a pickup artist or mastered the skills offered by the community.

REFRAME—*verb:* to alter the context through which someone sees an idea or situation; to change the meaning a person attributes to an idea or situation. Origin: Richard Bandler and John Grinder.

ROUTINE—*noun:* a story, scripted conversation, demonstration of skill, or other piece of prepared material intended to initiate, maintain, or advance an interaction with a woman or her group. Examples include the best-friends test, the evolution phase-shift, and the ESP value-demonstration.

RSD—*noun* [Real Social Dynamics]: a company specializing in pickup seminars, workshops, and products started by Papa and Tyler Durden. Origin: Papa.

SARGE—1. *verb:* to pick up women, or to go out to try and meet women. 2. *noun:* a woman who has been picked up. Origin: Aardvark.

SARGER—*noun:* a person who picks up women; a member of the pickup community.

SECOND MEETING—*noun:* a first date. *Also: day two.*

SET—*noun:* a group of people in a social setting. A two-set is a group of two people; a three-set is three people, and so on. Sets may contain women, men, or both (in which case they may be referred to as mixed sets). Origin: Mystery.

SHB—*noun* [super hot babe]: an extremely attractive woman.

SHIT TEST—*noun:* a question, demand, or seemingly hostile comment made by a woman intended to gauge whether a man is strong enough to be a worthy boyfriend or sexual partner. If he takes the question, demand, or comment at face value, he fails and generally loses the opportunity to move forward in his interaction with her. Examples include telling him he is too young or old for her, or asking him to perform an unnecessary favor.

SHOTGUN NEG—*noun:* a type of neg used in a group situation with a woman, intended to amuse the group at her expense. Origin: Mystery.

SNIPER NEG—*noun:* A type of neg used to embarrass a woman while talking one-on-one with her. Origin: Mystery.

SOI—*noun* [statement of intent or show of interest]: a direct comment intended to let a woman know that one is attracted to or impressed with her. Origin: Rio.

SS—*noun* [Speed Seduction]: an NLP-based school of pickup founded by Ross Jeffries in the 1980s. Origin: Ross Jeffries.

STALE—*verb* or *adjective:* an occurrence in which the phone number of a woman is no longer an effective means of making plans with her, usually because too much time has lapsed between interactions and the woman has lost interest; may also be used to describe a woman who has lost interest in a pickup artist.

STYLEMOG—*noun* or *verb:* a subtle set of tactics, mannerisms, backhanded compliments, and responses used to keep a pickup artist dominant in a group. Origin: Tyler Durden.

SUBCOMMUNICATION—*noun:* an impression, message, or effect created by a person's mannerisms, dress, or general presence; an indirect, nonverbal form of communication generally perceived better by women than men. Origin: Tyler Durden.

SUPPLICATE—*verb:* to put oneself in a servile or inferior position in order to please a woman, such as buying her a drink or changing an opinion in order to agree with her.

SYNESTHESIA—*noun:* literally, an overlapping of the senses, such as smelling a color; in seduction, a name given to a type of waking hypnosis in which a woman is put into a heightened state of awareness and told to imagine pleasurable images and sensations growing in intensity. The goal is to arouse her through suggestive, metaphorical talk, sensations, and imagery. *Also: hyperemperia.*

TAKEAWAY—*noun:* a pickup technique in which a man who has approached a woman and is getting along with her leaves—for as little as a few seconds or as long as a couple hours—in order to demonstrate a lack of neediness and increase her attraction to him. *Also: false takeaway.*

TARGET—*noun:* the woman in a group whom the pickup artist desires and is running game on. Origin: Mystery.

THREE-SECOND RULE—*noun:* a guideline stating that a woman should be approached within three seconds of first seeing her. It is intended to prevent the man from thinking about the approach too much and getting nervous, as well as to keep him from creeping the woman out by staring at her for too long. Origin: Mystery.

TIME CONSTRAINT—*noun:* to tell a woman or a group of people that it is necessary to leave them soon. The purpose of a time constraint is to lessen a woman's anxiety that a man she has just met will hang around her all night, or that she is expected to have sex with a man upon entering his house. *Also: false time constraint*. Origin: Style.

TIME DISTORTION—*noun:* originally a hypnosis term referring to a subject's loss of awareness of how much time is passing, it also refers to the pickup technique of making a woman feel she has known a pickup artist longer than she really has. Examples of time distortion include taking a woman to several different places over the course of a night or having a woman imagine future events and adventures together. *Also: future pacing* or *future events projection*.

TRANCE WORDS—*noun:* the words a person emphasizes or repeats when speaking, indicating that they have a special meaning to the speaker. Once a pickup artist knows a woman's trance words, he may use those words in conversation to make her feel a sense of understanding and connection with him. Origin: Richard Bandler and John Grinder.

TRIANGULAR GAZING—*verb:* a technique used directly before attempting to kiss a woman, in which, while making eye contact, a man takes several short, suggestive glances at her lips.

WBAFC—*noun* [way-below average frustrated chump]: a man who is extremely unsuccessful with women, usually due to awkwardness, nervousness, and lack of experience.

WING—*noun:* a male friend, generally with some pickup knowledge, who assists one in meeting, attracting, or taking home a woman. A wing can help by keeping a woman's friends occupied while the pickup artist talks to her, or by talking to the woman directly about the pickup artist's positive traits. *Also: wingman*.

WINGWOMAN—*noun:* see pivot.

WOOD—*noun:* useless; a waste of paper; generally used to describe a woman's phone number when she gives it to a pickup artist freely but is unlikely to call him back when he phones.

YES-LADDER—*noun:* a persuasion technique in which a person is asked a series of basic questions designed to elicit positive answers, increasing the likelihood that the person will also respond in the affirmative to a final, open-ended question. For example: "Are you spontaneous? Are you adventurous? Would you like to play a game called the cube?"

ACKNOWLEDGMENTS

Where are they now?

In the time since this book was written, enough has occurred in Project Hollywood and in the lives of the characters in this book to warrant a sequel. However, a synopsis will have to suffice. My story is done. Let the credits roll . . .

Thanks to Mystery, who followed through on his plan to move to Las Vegas with his girlfriend, Ania. They live together in an apartment on Las Vegas Boulevard. He finally found a worthy business partner, Savoy, who has turned his financial life around. He now runs workshops nearly every weekend. The price is a staggering $2,250, but from what I've seen, everyone leaves happy. His first friend in Las Vegas: David Copperfield, who saw the article on the community in the *New York Times,* contacted Mystery and now talks to him almost daily. However, Mystery has yet to succeed in talking Ania into a threesome.

Thanks to Tyler Durden and Papa, who soon fled Project Hollywood themselves. After several more PUAs came and went ignominiously from the house, they moved a new age couple into Mystery's room in exchange for the right to use the couple's New York apartment as a base for workshops. Hare Krishna devotees of the new residents dropped by to pay tribute almost daily—offering song, dance, and psychic battles in the Project Hollywood living room. But when Tyler Durden went to Manhattan to run a weekend workshop, the person living in the couple's apartment wouldn't allow him to teach there. In the meantime, according to house residents, a struggle for control of Project Hollywood began.

The truth about what happened next may never be known. The new age couple contend that Tyler Durden and Papa skipped out after local authorities tried to deliver a summons charging them with running a commercial business in a residential zone. Tyler Durden and Papa maintain that the Project Hollywood rent was simply draining too much company income. Either way, a month and a half before the eighteen-month lease was up, Papa, Tyler Durden, and the rest of the pickup artists living in the house suddenly packed a U-Haul van and left. They moved into an apartment complex a block away from Lisa and the mental care facility where I took Mystery. Tyler Durden lives there with his new girlfriend, and Papa continues in his quest for Paris Hilton. He feels he is getting close. The pair continues to run Real Social Dynamics and receive extraordinary testimonials from students.

Thanks to Project Hollywood, which is now inhabited by an eccentric new age couple and a wonderful cleaning lady. She calls herself the Cleaning Buddha, and she lives in my old bedroom.

Thanks to Herbal and Katya, who remained together for six months in Austin. Herbal lives with his wallaby, Shaniqua, in the house he owns there, where he is training to beat the 100-meter dash record for a bet and offering a reward to anyone who can successfully master the sleep diet. Katya returned to New Orleans, where she is working as a model and makeup artist. Her brother became a born-again Christian and has not had a symptom of Tourette's in over a year.

Thanks to Sickboy and Playboy, who were not able to leave the seduction world behind when they returned to New York. They now run a company together, Cutting Edge Image Consulting, which offers audio programs, workshops, and e-books in image enhancement and dating.

Thanks to Dustin, the king of the naturals, who is still living in Jerusalem, where I was unable to attend his wedding to a Rabbi's daughter.

Thanks to Marko, who is now engaged in Belgrade. He tells me that he rejected the advice of the PUAs and wooed his fiancée over a period of several months with poetry, flowers, and proper dates. They plan to move to Chicago and start a family together.

Thanks to Ross Jeffries, who eventually ended his rivalry with Mystery. He dated a nurse briefly and is now back in the field sarging, making, he says, major breakthroughs in helping guys overcome their fear, shyness, and old habits of thinking. He has been branching out from NLP, and exploring more spiritual ideas for personal transformation with a heart awakening instructor and a yoga teacher.

Thanks to Courtney Love, who has resolved her court cases and managed to stay out of the tabloids so far. She is happily living in her own house in Los Feliz with her daughter and working on a new album with Billy Corgan and Linda Perry. She says that she wants to play Katya in the movie.

Thanks to Formhandle, who has thanklessly and tirelessly kept this community running. His Fast Seduction website remains the clearinghouse for all matters pickup-related, and his research and website were instrumental in putting the glossary together. And to Cliff, the other pillar of the community, who recently brought hundreds of students and several dozen instructors to Montreal for his first annual pickup artist convention.

Thanks to Sin, who married the woman he liked walking on a leash in Atlanta. I recently had the honor of meeting her; you'd never suspect it.

Thanks to Britney Spears, who also got married. Twice. And to Tom Cruise, who recently announced his engagement and wasn't afraid to proclaim his love from the rooftops. Every time I have to make a tough decision, I ask myself: "What would Tom Cruise do?" Then I jump up and down on the couch.

Thanks to Dreamweaver, who is now writing screenplays. Shortly before publication of this book, he was diagnosed with brain cancer and brought to the hospital by Maverick. The father of Versity, one of the members of Mystery's Lounge, is a top cancer surgeon, and has offered to help. Dreamweaver, you are one talented, creative person, and our prayers are with you.

Thanks to Grimble, who devoted himself full-time to marketing his seduction e-books and audio courses; to Twotimer, who left Los Angeles to attend graduate school; to Vision, who recently became the godfather of Versity's child; and to Sweater, who is in the process of separating from his wife.

Thanks to the community itself and to the hundreds of friends I've made over the last two years. May you all find what you're looking for—in love and in life. Some of you may fret that I've given the game away. But don't worry: There will always be a way for a man and a woman to meet and have sex. And whatever that way happens to be, all of you will find it.

Thanks to Caroline, Nadia, Maya, Mika, Hea, Carrie, Hillary, Susanna, Jessicas I and II, and all the other amazing, unique women who became part of my life. Call me, and I'll explain everything.

Thanks to all the rest of the gurus: David DeAngelo, whose mailing list has grown to an estimated 1.1 million names and who is now offering women advice on how to catch and keep men; Rick H., who moved to Romania to pursue his latest business and romantic adventures; Steve P. and Rasputin, who are sharing their techniques in a video series. Thanks also to Swinggcat and David Shade.

Thanks to everyone who allowed me to reprint their posts and field reports. Juggler, who has put his comedy career on hold to expand his seduction business and complete his e-book, is living with his new girlfriend, a fitness trainer and marathon runner; he still likes Barry Manilow. Extramask, who separated entirely from the community to focus full-time on starting a comedy career and a weekly live show. Jlaix, who found the bisexual girlfriend that

Mystery has always dreamed about and has detailed their adventures in a series of careening field reports that are worthy of their own book.

Thanks to Judith Regan, who accused me of attracting her thirteen-year-old daughter on page six of the *New York Post*. She was joking, I think. And even if she wasn't, I'd forgive her. She supported me in this whole crazy adventure from day one, and has been not only a publisher but also a patron saint.

Thanks to the rest of the staff at ReganBooks, particularly my [insert hyperbolic adjective here] editor Cal Morgan, who was so excited to meet Lisa after editing the book that when he saw her he was too tongue-tied to speak a word. Thanks also to the long-suffering Bernard Chang, Michelle Ishay, Richard Ljoenes, Paul Crichton, Cassie Jones, Kyran Cassidy, and Aliza Fogelson.

Thanks to Ira Silverberg, my agent, who keeps trying to get me to write about a highbrow topic. And thanks to Anna Stein and the rest of the staff at Donadio and Olson.

Thanks to David Lubliner, Andrew Miano, Craig Emanuel, Paul Weitz, Chris Weitz, Andrea Giannetti, Matt Tolmach, and Amy Pascal for support with the other Project Hollywood.

Thanks to Fedward Hyde, my humble correspondent, for research assistance, and for sesquipedalian e-mails worthy of a Joyce. Maybe not James Joyce, but at least Dr. Joyce Brothers. (You've been Stylemogged.) Thanks to Lovedrop, who created the original Mystery Method course handout. And thanks to Sue Wood, who patiently transcribed tape after tape, which was no easy feat considering the many hours of hypnosis and house meetings contained therein. Thanks also to Laura Dawn and Daron Murphy for laboring through additional tapes.

Thanks to my many self-improvement instructors, among them Joseph Arthur (for voice lessons, infinite wisdom, and an eye-opening Esalen retreat) and Julia Caulder (for teaching me Alexander Technique and letting me watch her sing Wagner at the Los Angeles Opera).

Thanks to everyone who read early manuscripts, among them Anya Marina, Maya Kroth, M the G, Paula and Hazel Grace, Marg the mean babysitter, and my brother, Todd, who now has images in his head that he'd rather forget.

Finally, yes, Lisa and I are still together. And though I've learned everything there is about attraction, seduction, and courtship in the past two years, I learned nothing about maintaining a healthy relationship. Being together has required a lot more time and work than learning to pick up women ever did, but it has brought me far greater satisfaction and joy. Perhaps that's because it is not a game.